Developing Library and Information Center Collections

LIBRARY SCIENCE TEXT SERIES

Developing Library and Information Center Collections

Second Edition

G. EDWARD EVANS
Librarian of the Tozzer Library
Harvard University

1987
LIBRARIES UNLIMITED, INC.
Littleton, Colorado

LIBRARIES UNLIMITED, INC.
P.O. Box 263
Littleton, Colorado 80160-0263

Library of Congress Cataloging-in-Publication Data

Evans, G. Edward, 1937-
    Developing library and information center collections.

    (Library science text series)
    Includes index.
    1. Collection development (Libraries) 2. Information services--Collection development. I. Title. II. Series.
Z687.E92 1987   025.2   87-3224
ISBN 0-87287-463-X
ISBN 0-87287-546-6 (pbk)

Libraries Unlimited books are bound with Type II nonwoven material that meets and exceeds National Association of State Textbook Administrators' Type II nonwoven material specifications Class A through E.

For

Tombeau and Mary Ann

with love

"No Library of One Million Volumes
can be all
BAD!"

(from a cover, *Antiquarian Bookman*)

Contents

Preface to the First Edition

Collection development is an exciting and challenging area in which to work, and selecting the right materials for the library's community is as intellectually demanding an activity as a librarian will encounter. The selection of library materials is a highly personal process — something that takes a lifetime to learn — and the rewards are great. This book can serve as the starting point in that learning process. Any textbook that attempts to cover all aspects of collection development must give coverage to many topics. This text provides practical information on materials producers and distributors, community survey techniques, policies, materials selection, acquisition, weeding, and evaluation in order to minimize the variables involved in the selection process. Beyond the physical processes of collection development, though, are issues with which a selector should be concerned, as they influence how the collection will and can be developed. Thus, *Developing Library Collections* also delves into library cooperation, copyright (reflecting the changed statutes), and censorship as they affect the process in its entirety.

An author of a collection development textbook should acknowledge that, to a very great degree, the emphasis given each topic is based on a subjective assessment of its importance, reflecting the values and judgments of that author. Certainly, anyone with practical experience in this area knows that selection and collection development are arts, not sciences; and, as with any artistic endeavor, a person wishing to practice the art must devote years to developing the necessary skills. The basic elements of the collection development process — determining what information resources are needed, identifying the appropriate items, acquiring the items, and evaluating the collection — are rather well agreed upon. What is open to debate is how much emphasis to place upon individual steps in the process, and the interrelationship of all the elements.

A person cannot learn selection and collection development only in the classroom. A student will be able to learn the basic elements from this book; whether the student accepts the emphasis placed upon the elements is another matter. With the concepts presented in this book as a base, and using the recommended further readings, however, the student should begin to develop a solidly based, personal approach to selection and collection development.

The purpose of this book is to help library students gain an overall understanding of what is involved in building a collection for a library. Within rather broad limits, one may say that all libraries share certain general characteristics, including the need to assemble a collection of books and other library materials needed by their patrons. This book was written with the intent of emphasizing the similarities between types of libraries in the process of developing a collection.

Unlike any other book on collection development or book selection, *Developing Library Collections* provides an integrated approach to the process of building a library collection for a specific community of users — integrated in the sense that each element in the process is treated as flowing from one to another, and when something occurs in one element, it will have an impact on the others. Thus, as each element is discussed in detail, its relationship with the others will be examined as well, the underlying emphasis always being on the ultimate goal of the process — serving the library's community. To some degree, every chapter in this book has some application to any library. However, some aspects of collection development have more application, or at least are more widely used, in one type of library than another. For example, community analysis has been most widely used in public libraries, and as a result, chapter 4 tends to emphasize community analysis in the public library. Chapters 14 and 15, on weeding and evaluating the collection, deal with issues most pertinent to academic libraries, and this emphasis is reflected in the citations. Nevertheless, every chapter provides information relevant to all types of libraries.

In one sense, this is a jointly authored work. Any librarian who has written or talked about this subject has probably influenced my thinking to some degree. The further readings at the ends of the chapters reflect some of the works that have directly affected my point of view; they are but a fraction of the total waiting to be read. These writings will serve as an excellent starting point for further reading, which will need to continue as long as a librarian is involved in collection development work.

Preface to the Second Edition

The slight change in the title of this book is a reflection of a shift in emphasis from the book and other "information packages" to the information contained in the package. Selection work has always been concerned with the contents of items being considered for a collection. What has happened over the past 15 years is that society has become aware of and concerned about the "value" of information. New systems, often computer based, offer alternative means of providing information for patrons or clients. It appears likely this trend will continue for some time.

In the first edition the first chapter was concerned with definitions and concepts, and so is the first chapter in this edition. However, more emphasis is placed on concepts of information and information transfer. It is virtually a new chapter. Most of the chapters from the first edition have been extensively revised and updated, and additions have been made. The former chapter on selection is now divided into two chapters, on theory and practice. New chapters dealing with serials, government documents, fiscal management, automation, and preservation have been added.

Suggestions for further reading are included in each chapter. Items listed were selected on the basis of ease of availability and currency. (Also, all the items mentioned in a chapter are included regardless of date of publication.) An effort has been made to provide a few references for academic, public, school, and special libraries and information centers in each chapter.

I wish to thank all the individuals who read one or more chapters of this edition and provided many helpful suggestions: Herbert Achlietner, Peter Briscoe, Alan Ericson, William Fisher, Dale Flecker, Doris Frietag, Irene Godden,

William McGrath, Assunta Pisanti, Benedict Rugaas, Joel Rutstein, and Sally Williams. Naturally they are not responsible for any of the book's shortcomings. Finally, I want to thank Morris Fry for his copyediting work, Julie Wetherill for the many hours of typing, and Nancy Lambert-Brown for the figures and charts she prepared.

1

Information Age — Information Society

Introduction

"Information business" and "information explosion" are phrases we frequently see and hear. The frequency of use has dulled their meaning, sometimes they are misused, and many times they are misunderstood. On the one hand, some individuals talk as if "information" were a newly discovered, mysterious, natural phenomenon. On the other hand, for librarians and others working in information centers, information is neither new nor mysterious; it is the "product" they have always worked with, an old friend. Both perspectives contain an element of truth.

Libraries and their collections (information) have existed for thousands of years. (For example, the Red Temple at Uruk, dating from about 3000 B.C., contained a library.) Even the value of information was recognized, in a rather unusual way, in medieval libraries, where books were chained to reading stalls. (The books were chained for a number of reasons, the value of the information in them being one.) Collecting and organizing information and making it available to individuals have had a long history. However, over the last 15 to 20 years there has been a major shift in the attitudes of Western societies toward information. More and more it is being treated as an economic product, like petroleum, cardboard boxes, or automobiles. For example, there are a number of newsletter/looseleaf notebook information services that charge tens of thousands of dollars for one year's service. A less dramatic, but still impressive, example was reported in 1985 by *Library Journal*: the Book Industry Study Group offered a study of the American book trade and reading patterns in 1983 for a mere $5,000 per

1

copy.[1] Combined with this different attitude toward information is a variety of technological developments that affect the generation, storage, and retrieval of information. The net effect of this combination is a new phenomenon which creates problems for libraries and society. Many problems relate to handling the economic aspects of "information" and access to information. Although a detailed discussion of these problems is beyond the scope of this book, they will be mentioned where they have an influence on collection development/resource management.

What are some of the problems and changes that have taken place? If information is an economic resource, as many people now contend, it has a number of characteristics that are special, so special as to make information almost unique. Unlike other economic commodities, it is shared even when it is sold. Sellers always retain the information in some forms, if only in a person's memory. There are two economic aspects to the sale of information: the cost of "packaging" the information, and the cost/value of information contained in the package. When the package is a book, newspaper, magazine, or video- or audiotape, for example, people tend to think of the package *as* the information. When an individual is confronted with an online system where he or she must pay for information by the "screen" and yet cannot retain a hard copy, or is faced with a $5,000 per copy report on the book trade, one begins to appreciate information value as opposed to information package value.

Another special characteristic of information is that it is neither scarce nor depleting. In fact, the more it is used and manipulated, the more information there is; many information problems are the result of too much information rather than too little. The problem is to locate the required information at the right time. To some extent the changes discussed above are contributing to copyright problems (see chapter 18 for a discussion of copyright). *Ownership* of ideas, facts, or information is more of an issue today, in contrast to the past, when the primary issue was the *expression* of ideas, facts, and information.

Other characteristics of information that make it a special "commodity" are transportability, intangibility, compressability and expandability, storability (in a variety of forms and formats), and manipulability. A recent topic of discussion and matter of concern to many people is the "transborder flow" of information. Most concern has been about electronic data flows from one country to another. Hugh Donaghue, a vice-president at Control Data Corporation, addressed this topic at the 1982 International Federation of Library Associations Conference in Montreal. In his concluding remarks about international library networks, he noted, "Two economic threats could make such networks too costly for libraries to afford unless government exemptions can be obtained. These are: tariffs which may be applied to incoming information and data; and transmission rates based on volume rather than time."[2] For libraries in countries that are either less well developed or having severe economic problems, there is a third concern — the lack of the technology needed to participate in such a network.

As more governments ponder the idea that information is an economic commodity worth placing tariffs and controls on, and as more and more of the world's information is being generated and stored in electronic equipment, librarians and information specialists must begin to think in terms of information itself and less about information packages.

Almost every issue of a newsletter from a professional (library) or information association contains one or two items about a new information service or product that uses one of the electronic technologies, or some nonprint service;

fewer and fewer of the "news" items are about traditional print formats. A few examples will illustrate the trend; most were reported in *Library Hotline* between September 1984 and September 1985.

- The British Library now provides access to "grey literature" (material that is often a major part of the acquisitions of a special library) through its SIGLE (System for Grey Literature in Europe) as part of its online services. Grey literature is normally noncommercial publications (local government documents) and a variety of less formal publications— working papers, "private" communications, preprints of conference papers, and various scientific research reports.[3]

- Pacific Northwest Bell Telephone Company tests a service called "Telequest" providing answers to questions for $1.55 per question. Although the report indicated that most of the service appeared to be a more sophisticated directory assistance program based on the classified section of the telephone directory, the concept does raise several possibilities. Wes Doak, the Oregon State Librarian, was cited as raising two possibilities: either the telephone company might expand its service by using some of the online databases to answer more traditional library reference questions, or the public and government officials will begin to pressure libraries to charge for services.[4] The fact that a telephone company sets the price for information found in its directory at $1.55 per question answered reinforces the earlier point that people and organizations now view information as an economic commodity to a degree never seen before.

- Videotapes circulate at a rate of 8,000 per month from the Thousand Oaks Public Library, California.[5]

- Public libraries (150) in California are being tied together with an online catalog based on OCLC membership. Seven years of MARC records will be contained in the system and libraries will access the system either through a dedicated line or by dial access.[6]

- Japanese MARC records for post-1969 publications are available to North American libraries through the UTLAS system. Eleven Japanese academic libraries have been using UTLAS by means of a satellite link.[7]

- A public library in Bloomington, Illinois installed a satellite "downlink" for teleconferencing. The news report indicated that for the time being the system was to be used for live programming and noncommercial services; the example given was of a national program for fire departments (3,500 receiving sites were linked together) on handling hazardous wastes and spills. Director Saul Andrusky hoped that in the future the library could tape incoming programs for replay for persons unable to attend the live sessions.[8]

What are some possibilities for the future? A California report on telecommunications in 1990 made eight predictions regarding libraries in the state; most of the predictions could apply to all American libraries and to those in other countries in which telecommunications are undergoing rapid development.

- Over three-quarters of public library "records" will be machine-readable and available through a statewide online network (see above).

- Academic and public libraries using online systems will be linked together regardless of their bibliographic utilities memberships.

- Over 75 percent of all interlibrary "correspondence" will be handled using "electronic mail" systems rather than the U.S. Postal Service.

- Use of videotext will be widespread among California residents (60 percent) and many (40 percent) will gain access to library information by means of videotext services.

- Libraries will be making fairly heavy use of satellite systems. Thirty percent will have receiving equipment installed for use in teleconferencing.

- Cable television service from libraries will expand in both the number of libraries offering service and in the variety of services available.

- Use of microcomputers continues to grow in libraries, and collections of software will become more and more common.

- Government information will be less available in print form and will increasingly be distributed online—libraries will be the primary public access point.[9]

Some of these predictions are already materializing, while others are being debated. Much of the debate centers on whether a "library" or a profit-oriented organization will deliver the service; it is not a question of service but the means of delivery that is at issue.

Another interesting set of predictions appeared in the March 1985 issue of *Online*. Jack W. Simpson, president of Mead Data Corporation, listed 10 megatrends for information, many of which were touched upon earlier in this chapter.

1. Information is becoming a strategic weapon.

2. Ownership of information is at the root of a growing world conflict between government and private enterprise.

3. Information is no longer free.

4. All high-value information will be available in digital form.

5. A worldwide "megalibrary" of electronic information is emerging.

6. Intelligent electronic books will evolve to access the "megalibrary."

7. New technology will reshape our concepts of privacy, security, and property.

8. Exchange of information through shared networks will break down barriers of geography and culture.

9. A conflict over control will occur between end users and the MIS (management information systems) function.

10. Librarians and information specialists are becoming a major force in helping end users interact with the megalibrary.[10]

Whatever form the future "megalibrary" may take, it is certain that it will be based on a collection of information resources. Unless there is a plan for what is contained in the collection, the megalibrary will have limited, if any, value. The purpose of this book is to assist in gaining an understanding of how one goes about developing an intelligent and useful collection for individuals using the materials in the collection.

Concepts and Terms

A number of concepts and terms need to be defined as they will be used throughout the text. Starting with some basic general terms, such as *information*, and ending with a specific concept, *collection management*, this section provides a foundation for the remainder of the book. One change I have tried to make in this edition is to present a more generic picture of collection development — generic in the sense that it is not tied to a specific institutional or organizational form (i.e., library).

Information is the recognition of patterns in the flow of matter and energy reaching an individual or organization. All flows of matter and energy have the capability of carrying patterned signals. Only when the pattern is recognized is there information. Each person develops a set of recognized patterns, and not everyone recognizes the same patterns or necessarily interprets a given pattern in the same way. For example, a strange noise in an automobile may mean nothing to a driver, but to a trained auto mechanic the sound indicates that the universal joint needs servicing (information). Two other examples of recognition of a pattern are well logs (records of drilling operations) and spectrum analysis. To the untrained person a well log is meaningless and of no value. To a geologist or other trained professional, these long strips of paper are an invaluable source of information about subsurface conditions and formations, and depending upon how the information is interpreted, may save, cost, or make a company thousands or even millions of dollars. For astronomers, colors in a spectrum analysis convey information about the distance, movement, and composition of stars, while to the layperson it is an interesting or pretty display of color.

Each person is constantly involved in an information cycle (figure 1.1) as matter and energy flow by. "Objects" emit patterned signals that flow past individuals (subjects). People identify the signals and evaluate the patterns based on past experience. They ignore most of the signals and take action only when the pattern provides information. When a person receives an information (action) signal, he or she implements the action that will provide satisfaction. An example of how the same "signal" can carry different meanings took place for me several years ago when I taught a summer class in an old building with no air conditioning. Each summer the building fire alarm would sound when the

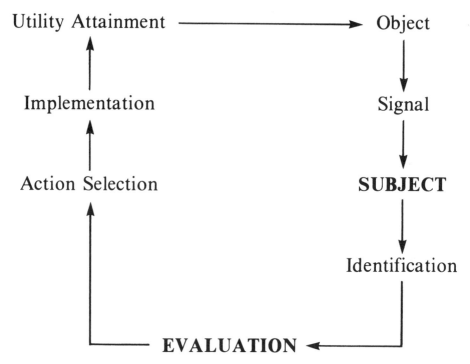

Fig. 1.1. The information cycle.

temperature on the top floor reached a certain point. Until I "learned" what the problem was, I reacted much as the students in the class, concerned and eager to leave the building. We recognized the "signal," evaluated it in the same way, and selected the same course of action. After I learned that the signal was 99 percent likely to be a false alarm, my evaluation and course of desired action were very different from those of the students. Not knowing it was almost certainly a false alarm, the students' "utility attainment" was the safety of evacuating the building; in my case the goal was to finish the class and not waste time.

The information cycle is very similar to the human communication model taught in many undergraduate courses. For human communication to take the "information patterns," it must be expressed in a symbolic form that is widely known and understood. For communication to occur there must be a shared symbol-referent system. Figure 1.2 illustrates the components of the communication model. The sender, wishing to communicate with the receiver, has an idea or feeling (a "meaning") in mind; the meaning is encoded using the appropriate symbols representing the desired meaning, thus creating the message. A means of delivering the message (channel) must be selected—written, oral, pictorial. On the receiver's side, the message arrives and is decoded, and a meaning is assigned to the message. When the process is completed, communication has taken place; however, this does not necessarily imply that the meaning intended by the sender is identical to the meaning the receiver assigned to the message. Just as in the case of the information cycle, a single symbol may have multiple meanings. The more abstract the idea being communicated, the more likely it is that "noise"

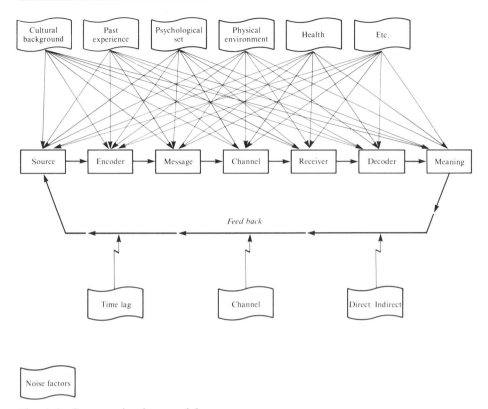

Fig. 1.2. Communication model.

somewhere in the system will distort the meaning. Some common noise factors for people are differences in education, experience, and mental state. Normally, the "general" meaning will be the same, but often the general meaning is not adequate and an identical meaning is required. The "feedback" loop allows for clarifying meanings, so closer if not identical meaning and understanding can be achieved. Since an information center or library may work with all forms of human communication, some knowledge is helpful in a variety of ways. Later in this volume conducting needs assessments, developing collection policies, evaluating collections, and handling complaints are discussed. All of these activities involve the communication process (model), and remembering to use the feedback loop to verify meaning and to control the "noise" in the system will make the library or information center a more effective service organization.

The term *organization* is used in this volume in two ways. One meaning, and the least often used, refers to the process of arranging information, knowledge, and materials so they can be easily retrieved (i.e., the organization of knowledge/ the organizing of a collection). The second and most frequent meaning relates to people and is based on work done by a well-known management writer, Chester Barnard. Barnard's work on human organization is extensive, and what follows is a very simplified explanation of his concept; however, the basic elements are all described. Human organization, according to Barnard, consists of five basic elements—size, interdependence, input, throughput, and output.[11] An organization can vary in size from something as large as the U.S. federal government to something as small as two people. The size factor is important for information service work because there is often a tendency not to consider two or three people working together as an organization. Barnard's model does not include any time factor—if all five elements are present, an organization could exist for just a few hours or for centuries. What differentiates a group of two or more people from an organization of two or more people arises from the other elements. Interdependence means that there is a recognition that one or more goals are shared and that by working together (cooperating), the achievement of the shared goals will be easier, faster, or in some manner beneficial to all members of the organization. Disagreement and tension can be and usually are present, but the value of mutually shared benefits holds the organization together. Once the goals are identified, the organization must acquire the material, energy, money, and information ("input") needed to accomplish the goals. After the resources have been acquired, the resources must be employed (throughput) effectively to achieve the desired results. The end "product" of the processing activities is the output, which is disseminated to the organization's environment. Output can be as tangible as an automobile or as intangible as ideas that may help people create a safer environment.

Information is one of the resources organizations acquire to accomplish desired goals. The information will be in one of four forms: data, text, image, or sound. Most organizations use all four forms and a library or information center serving the organization should be ready and able to handle all forms of information. More and more new technologies are drawing these four forms closer together, and sometime in the not-too-distant future there may be an "integrated information resource" (figure 1.3). The computer is rather like the steam engine at the start of the Industrial Revolution—it is the "power source" for the integration process. There are now "reading machines" that are capable of recognizing printed words and converting the recognized patterns into oral presentations (speech synthesizers). Videotext and teletext are other examples of the blending of forms that is taking place. (These technologies are further discussed in chapter 9.)

Several years ago, S. D. Neill questioned the information role for the library. Neill suggested that the appropriate role is the knowledge center.[12] Which role one selects depends in large measure on how the concepts are defined. In addition to information, *knowledge* and *wisdom* need to be defined. *Knowledge* is the result of linking together a number of pieces of information into patterns of meaning. *Wisdom* is the ability to draw accurate conclusions from the available information and knowledge. Knowledge and wisdom are individual (personal) processes, and what may be knowledge for one person may be someone else's information. In my opinion, libraries and information centers can supply information, including recorded knowledge and wisdom. We can inform, but it is up to users to gain knowledge and wisdom.

A somewhat different sequence has been proposed by Robert S. Taylor. Taylor's "value-added hierarchy" consists of five levels: the lowest level is data, followed by information, informing knowledge, productive knowledge, and finally, action. Although his primary concern is with the means by which "value" is associated with information, a topic beyond the scope of this book, anyone interested in developing collections should read this article. *Informing knowledge* is similar to the definition of knowledge given above. *Productive knowledge* is "a

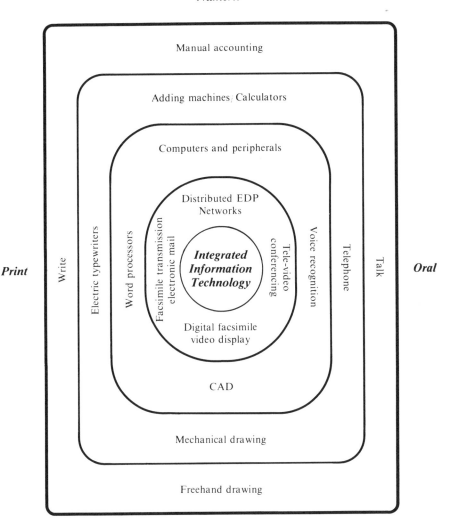

Fig. 1.3. Convergence of information technology and organizational information processing.

judgmental process, where options are presented and advantages and disadvantages weighed."[13]

Certainly one's definitions of the various terms (data, information, knowledge, wisdom, and so forth) as well as one's opinion concerning the role the library or information center is to play affects the type of collection an information specialist will build. Another important factor is the "organizational environment" of the library. Several years ago, F. Emery and E. L. Trist identified four basic types of organizational environments: placid-randomized, placid-clustered, disturbed-reactive, and turbulent.[14] Although not directly concerned with information, their descriptions of the environments do indicate how the environment would affect information work. A *placid-randomized* environment is one in which both goals and dangers are assumed to be basically unchanging. The goals are long term and are seldom adjusted. The dangers are randomly distributed, and there is little or no predictability as to when a danger will be encountered. A danger is something that would adversely affect the viability of the organization. In such an environment, information would be collected to meet long-term goals. It would be, or would be thought to be, very predictable, making collection development relatively easy. Large research libraries, museum collections, and archives are examples of organizations operating in a placid-randomized environment; at least this was the case in the past. Today and in the future it seems likely that many organizations will be operating in such an environment.

Many libraries and information centers operate in a *placid-clustered* environment. Emery and Trist defined this environment as one in which goals are primarily long-term but are adjusted quickly if there is a significant change in the external factors. Dangers and, to some extent, opportunities are assumed to be clustered, and some effort can and should be expended in identifying and collecting information about the clusters. From a collection development point of view, this would mean there would be a basic body of relatively unchanging organizational goals, but some time, energy, and money would go toward identifying and collecting information that might affect the goals. Most educational institutions and public libraries are operating in this type of environment. Generally, the long-term goals are set and do not often change. However, dangers such as changing attitudes of the public about the value of social services in general, and library services specifically, are recognized. The pattern seems to be that once the questioning starts, it generally expands in scope (it is clustered) and does not disappear quickly. Also, new service opportunities arise as new technologies become available that may be appropriate for the institution to use, and which in turn may counteract some or all of the dangers (e.g., competition) arising from the new technologies.

Disturbed-reactive environments are those in which the organizations are faced with acknowledged competitors. In this environment, having prompt, accurate information about what the competitors are doing, and when possible, what they are planning to do, is very important. Although there are long-term goals, they are revised in light of information received about the competitors' activities. Business/industrial "special" libraries operate in such an environment. Here four or five years may represent a significant amount of time for long-term collection goals. Also, significant resources are devoted to determining what the competition is doing.

Finally, there is the *turbulent* environment. Not only do competitiors exist, but the level of competition is at the level of survival. As a result of knowing what others are doing or planning to do, an organization may make a radical change in its basic purposes. Anyone reading business sections of newspapers encounters examples of organizations that made successful basic goal changes and those that failed because they did not change. On a less extreme level, an information center or library serving a research and development team experiences occasional abrupt shifts in collecting emphasis, partly due to the knowledge gained from the information collected about the competitions' work and progress. Thus the organization environment is also an information environment, and the nature of the environment affects the nature of the collection development activities.

With this background we can now look at how organizations and individuals process information. Figure 1.4 represents how this process works. Space 1 indicates the totality of matter and energy surrounding an organization or individual. The line separating spaces 1 and 2 represents the boundary between noise and patterned signals (information) as identified by a person or organization. Only a small portion of the total flow is so identified by a person or organization, and as the information environment changes so does the boundary between spaces 1 and 2. Some of what is identified as information is deemed to be of sufficient importance for it to be stored for a short time; space 3 represents the information that is placed in short-term storage. Of that total, a smaller amount of information is selected for long-term/indefinite retention (space 4). The dotted line within space 4 creates an area labeled 5, which represents the information that is used from long storage and disseminated to the external environment.

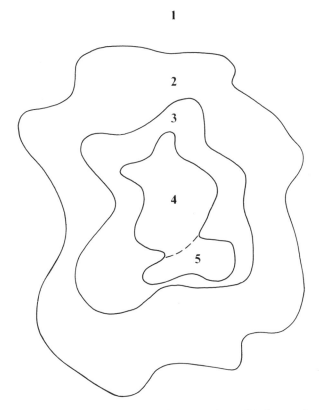

Fig. 1.4. Organizational processing of information.

On a personal level, in the United States anyone who receives mail for any length of time uses the above process. Almost every time a person picks up the mail (the total flow), there is an assortment of material in the delivery. Each piece is recognized as an attempt at communication. Some of the material is not within the boundary of information, as defined by the person in question, and is thus noise (space 1). Items in this category go straight into the trash. Other pieces may be about something of interest but not high interest at the present time (space 2); items in this category go into the trash as well, but there is a slight pause as the information cycle is completed and one selects the desired action. A few pieces may relate to something of some interest, and this material is set aside for consideration later when there is time. Depending on the person, days, weeks, or even months go by before the material is looked at, and more often than not, as a result of a changed "environment," this material also ends up in the wastebasket. Just a few of the items received and identified as information are given long-term retention. Some things, such as insurance policies, legal documents, and letters from friends and family, are filed away for safekeeping (space 4). Of the total retained in this manner, only a few (bills) will require or motivate a person to process the information and respond at once (space 5).

Libraries and information centers engage in exactly the same process. No organization can take in and process all the patterned signals; some dividing line is drawn between information and noise. Where the line is drawn will depend upon the nature of the organization being served and its information environment. The line might be drawn in terms of language, subject matter, depth of treatment, format, or combinations of factors. Even within the limits of what is defined as information, only a portion of the total will be retained for storage. Some items are acquired and stored for short periods of time because their value to the organization is short-term due to changing interests, or because they are superseded. Libraries and information centers normally acquire and store for long periods of time more information than the organization will use and in some manner disseminate into the external environment. The percentage allocated to long-term retention varies among organizations. Organizations operating in a placid-randomized environment tend to have a very large percentage of retained but not disseminated or used information (50 percent or more). At the other end of the spectrum (turbulent) there should be and usually is very little difference between the two categories. Archives and research libraries tend to be at the high retention/low dissemination end, while information centers and libraries in profit organizations tend to be at the opposite, low retention/high dissemination end.

Libraries' and information centers' primary purpose is to assist in the transfer of information and the development of knowledge. What is involved in information transfer work is illustrated in figure 1.5. The transfer process is represented by the nine circles. Information transfer is an elaboration of the basic information cycle described earlier. There is the identification stage, in which appropriate information is segregated from the nonappropriate. In most instances, there is more appropriate information available than the system is able to handle, so there is a need to select the most appropriate information. Once selection is completed, the information must be acquired. After acquisition, the information is organized in some manner; this is followed by the preparation of information for storage, which takes into account some means of retrieving the information efficiently. The information is stored and users are assisted in describing their needs in ways that lead to locating and retrieving the desired information (interpretation). Users draw upon the information to aid them in their activities/work (utilization) and the outcome of the work is disseminated into the external and internal environment. In order for the transfer process to function properly, there must be procedures, policies, and people in place to carry out the necessary operational steps. Finally, there must be coordination and money for the operations to do what they were set up to do; this is the administrative and management aspect of information work.

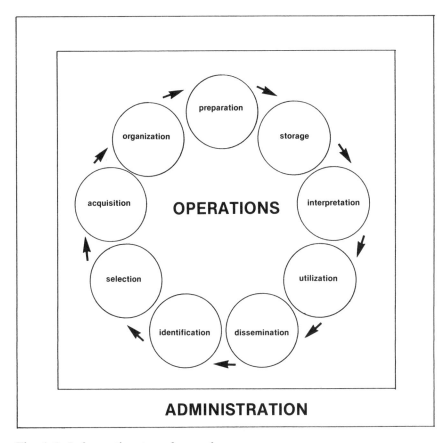

Fig. 1.5. Information transfer work.

The foregoing discussion helps set the background for this book, which is concerned with the process of building the information collection for long- and short-term storage. *Collection development* or information acquisition is one of the common areas between librarianship and information resource management. In the first edition, I defined collection development as "the process of identifying the strengths and weaknesses of a library's materials collection in terms of patron needs and community resources and attempting to correct existing weaknesses, if any." With only minor modifications, the definition can apply to both libraries and information collections in any organization. Collection development is the process of making certain the information needs of the people using the collection are met in a timely and economical manner, using information resources produced both inside and outside of the organization. This new definition is broader in scope and places emphasis on thoughtful (timely and economical) collection building and on seeking out both internal and external information resources.

Collection development is a universal process for libraries and information centers. Figure 1.6 illustrates the six major components of the process. There is a relationship between figures 1.5 and 1.6 in that collection development involves three of the nine information transfer elements (identification, selection, and acquisition). As implied by the circle, collection development is a constant cycle that continues as long as the library or information center exists. All of the elements in the cycle will be discussed in subsequent chapters.

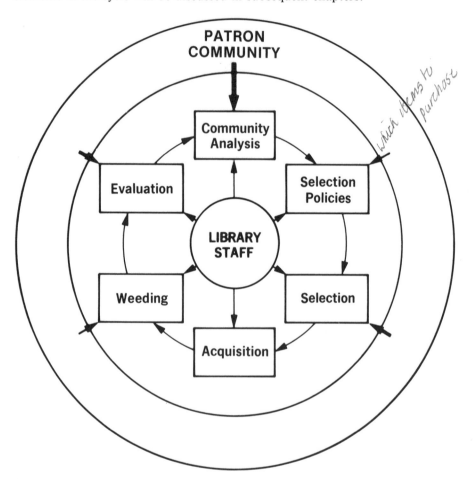

Fig. 1.6. Collection development process.

Because of my philosophy of collection development, that is, building to meet some likely patron demand, I begin the discussion of the process with the needs assessment (community analysis) element. *Needs assessment, community analysis,* and *patron community* are used throughout this book to refer to the group of persons that the library *has been established to serve.* They do *not* refer only to the active users; they include everyone within the community's defined service limits. Thus, a community might be an entire political unit (i.e., nation, region, state, province, county, city, town, etc.) or a more specialized grouping or association (i.e., university, college, school, government agency, or private organization). Also, the number of patrons that the library is to serve may range from the tens to the millions. As discussed in chapter 2, data for analysis can be assembled from a variety of sources, not just staff-generated material. For collection development personnel, the assessment process provides data on what information the clientele needs; it also establishes a valuable mechanism for patron input into the process of collection development. (Note the size of the arrow in figure 1.6 from the community to collection development, the size indicating my view as to the level of patron input that is appropriate for each element.)

One use for the data collected for a needs assessment is as part of the preparation of a collection development policy. Clearly delineated policies on both collection development and selection (covered in chapter 3) provide collection development staff with guidelines for choosing items for inclusion in the collection. (Collection policies, it should be noted, cover a wider range of topics than selection policies. For example, *selection* policies normally provide only information useful in deciding which items to purchase, while *collection* policies will cover that topic and such related issues as gifts, weeding, and cooperation.) Most libraries have some of the required information available for their collection development personnel, although it is not always labeled "policy." Some libraries call it an acquisition policy; some, a selection policy; some, a collection development policy; and others, simply a "statement." Whatever the local label, the intent is the same: to define the library's goals for its collection(s) and to help staff members select and acquire the most appropriate materials.

Using whatever written policies or statements their libraries have prepared, at this point the staff members begin the procedures for selecting materials (covered in chapters 4, 5, 8, and 9). For many people, this is the most interesting element in the collection development process. One constant factor in collection development is that there is never enough money available to buy everything that might be of value to the service community. Naturally, this means that someone, usually one or more professional staff members, must decide which items will or will not be purchased. *Selection* is the process of deciding which materials to acquire for a library collection. It may involve deciding between items that provide information about the same subject; deciding whether the information contained in an item is worth the price; or deciding whether an item could stand up to the use it would receive. In essence, it is a matter of systematically determining quality and value. Selection is a form of decision making. All too often it is not just a matter of identifying appropriate materials, but of deciding between items that are essential, important, needed, marginal, nice, or luxurious. Where to place any item in the sequence from essential to luxurious depends, of course, on the individual selector's point of view; and as someone said, "it's just a matter of perception." So it is with library materials.

An item purchased by an individual is paid for with that person's money. When it is a question of spending the library community's money, whether derived from taxes or a company's budget, the problem is more complex. The question of whose perception of value is to be used is one of the challenges in collection development. Needs assessments and policies help determine the answer, but a long-standing question in the field is how much emphasis should be placed on clientele demand and how much on quality of materials. Often the question of perception arises when someone objects to the presence of an item in the collection. (Chapter 19 discusses this topic in more depth.)

Once an item has been selected, the acquisition work begins (see chapters 10-13). *Acquisition work* is the process of securing materials for the library's collection, whether by purchase, as gifts, or through exchange programs. This is the only point in the collection development process involving little or no community input; it is a fairly straightforward business operation. Once the decision has been made to purchase an item, the staff proceeds with the preparation of an order form, the selection of a vendor, the recording of the receipt of the item, and finally, payment. While details may vary, the basic routines remain the same around the world. Remember that acquisition does not always mean buying an item; it can be acquired as a gift or through an exchange program.

After an item has been acquired, it is processed through a series of internal library operations (beyond the scope of this book) such as cataloging, and is eventually available to the patron community. But in time, nearly every item outlives its original usefulness to the library; in most cases, these items must be removed from the main collection. The activity of examining items in the library and determining their current value to that library's collection (and hence, to the service community) is normally called *weeding* (covered in chapter 14). When a library decides that a given item is no longer of value, it will dispose of the item — sell, give, or even throw it away. If the item still has some value for the library, it will probably be transferred to a less accessible and usually less expensive storage location. A few librarians have commented that weeding is nothing more than selection in reverse, and use the term *deselection*.

Evaluation (examined in chapter 15) is the last element in the collection development process. To some extent, weeding is an evaluative activity, but weeding is also more of an internal library operation. Evaluation of a collection may serve many different purposes, both within and outside the library. For example, it may help to increase funding for the library; it may aid in the library's gaining some form of recognition, such as high standing in a comparative survey; or it may help to determine the quality of work being performed by the library. In order for effective evaluation to occur, the service community's needs must be considered, which brings us back to community analysis.

There is little reason to define library materials other than to emphasize that we will be concerned with various formats, not just books. Different authors writing about library collections have used a number of related terms — *print, nonprint, visual materials, audiovisuals, a-v, other media*, etc. — there is no single term encompassing all forms that has gained universal acceptance among librarians. *Library materials* (or simply, materials) is a nonspecific term with respect to format, while being otherwise inclusive; it will, therefore, be used throughout the text. Library materials (materials) may be books, periodicals, pamphlets, reports, manuscripts, microformats, motion pictures, video- or audiotapes, sound recordings, realia, and so forth. In effect, almost any physical object that conveys information, thoughts, or feeling potentially could be included in a library collection.

Two last terms need to be defined: *collection management* and *information resource management*. The terms are closely related and differ primarily in organizational context. Collection management, as used today, relates to a library environment (in the traditional sense), where the emphasis is on collecting materials produced by other organizations. Information resource management, as used today, relates to any organizational context, often without any centralized collection of materials, in which both internal and external sources of information are acquired and organized. Both terms incorporate all the aspects of collection development discussed earlier plus managerial aspects such as budget planning and control, staffing patterns, and physical facilities.

Collection Development
and the Community

Collection development is influenced in a number of ways by factors both within and outside the library. Among these factors are the library's structure and organization, the production and distribution of the information materials, and the presence of other libraries in the area. Figure 1.7 illustrates some of the interrelationships among the library organization, the producers and distributors of materials, and other libraries.

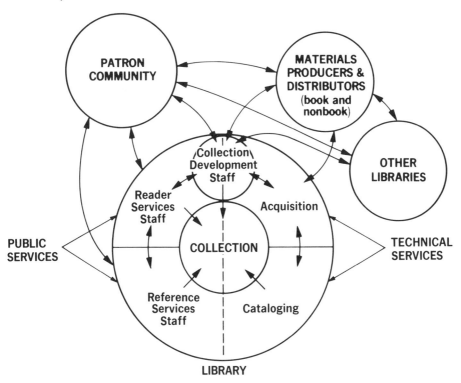

Fig. 1.7. Collection development, the library, and the community.

The internal activities of libraries are usually organized into public and technical services. Those activities in which the staff has daily contact with patrons are usually considered public services; almost all other activities are technical services. Library staff members responsible for collection development provide information to the acquisitions department (usually classed as a technical service), which in turn orders the desired items from the materials producer, or a distributor. After receiving the materials and clearing the records, the acquisitions department sends the items on to the cataloging department for processing; processed items are subsequently placed in the collection. Both the public service staff and the patrons using the collection provide input concerning the value of individual items, information that is then considered by collection development staff during the processes of weeding and evaluating. The information generated from these sources may eventually influence the library's written policies for collection development.

Materials producers exert several significant influences. They control what is available for library purchase by their choice of whether or not to produce any given item. (Chapter 6 describes some of the factors considered in making such a decision.) Furthermore, their business requirements occasionally cause libraries to modify their acquisition procedures; however, most producers and vendors are very good about accommodating rather unusual library requirements. Finally, producers market their products directly to the patron community, thus generating demand that is frequently transmitted to the library by the patron and causing an indirect response to the marketing activities of the materials producers.

Materials and services in other libraries and information centers used by the service population also influence collection development. Cooperative collection development programs can enable libraries to provide more service or a wider range of materials, and they can reduce duplication of materials that results from overlapping service communities and patron influence on collection development. For example, a person might engage in business research during the day in the company's library. The person may take evening classes at an academic institution, using that library for class-related and business-related materials alike. That same individual also may rely on a local public library, because of its convenience, to supply information on both job-related and recreational concerns. Thus, one person's requests for job-related materials in both the academic and public libraries could influence three different types of libraries in the same area to collect the same material. Despite numerous advantages, working out effective cooperative programs can be very difficult, as is discussed in chapter 16.

Collection Development and Institutional Environments

Information services are offered in most institutional settings, and the range of possibilities is large. However, it is possible to discuss a few broad general categories: educational, business, governmental, and research. These categories share some very basic characteristics. They have a specific service population; materials must be collected and preserved in a form suitable for use by that population; and materials must be organized in a manner designed to aid in the rapid identification and retrieval of the desired material(s). The definitions given earlier also apply to all of the categories. Differences emerge as a result of both the specific service population and the limits set by the governing body of the institution being served.

Collection development is a universal process for all types of libraries. But as one moves from one environmental setting to another, differences in emphasis on the various elements of the collection development process become apparent. For example, some educational (school) and governmental (public) libraries tend to place more emphasis on selection activities than do business and research libraries. Also, differences in emphasis occur within a type, so that occasionally, a community college library (educational) might more closely resemble a large public library (governmental) in its collection development activities than it does a university library (educational). The approach taken in this book is to present an overview and, when necessary, note the differences that arise between and within types.

To some extent, the chapters in this book reflect these differences in emphasis. For several reasons, needs analysis is very important in public and school libraries, as well as in information centers (the business world) and is given less emphasis in college and university libraries. In public libraries, selection is usually the responsibility of librarians, whereas in other types of information centers patrons have a stronger direct voice in the selection process. Public libraries need the information derived from an analysis in order to build an effective collection; therefore the chapter on needs analysis has a public library's slant.

The size of a library's service community has definite bearing on collection development. In fact, three "laws" of collection development can be stated as universals:

1. As the size of the service community increases, the degree of divergence in individual information needs increases.

2. As the degree of divergence in individual information needs increases, the need for cooperative programs of information materials sharing increases.

3. It will never be possible to completely satisfy *all* of the information needs of any individual or class of clientele in the service community.

Even special libraries and information centers, serving a limited number of persons, encounter problems in relation to these laws, since no two people are identical, and it is impossible for their materials needs and interests to coincide completely. In the special library environment, the interests of patrons can be and often are similar, but even within a team of research workers exploring a single problem, individual needs will vary. The needs of a small group are not as homogeneous as they may at first appear.

The element of collection development that varies the least is collection development policy. Simply put, as the collection grows in size, the need for more complex and detailed policy statements increases. Generally, the most comprehensive collection policy statements are found in the large academic research libraries.

Selection is the element in which the greatest variations are found between and within the types. Due to the many variations, it is dangerous to attempt sweeping generalizations. However, with that warning in mind, the following are some general statements about the variations:

1. Public libraries emphasize title-by-title selection, and selection is done by one or more librarians.

2. School libraries also emphasize title-by-title selection, and while the media specialist may make the final decision, a committee composed of librarians, teachers, administrators, and parents may have a strong voice in the process.

3. Special/corporate libraries select materials in rather narrow subject fields for specific research/business purposes, and very often, the client is the primary "selector."

4. Academic libraries select materials in subject areas for educational and research purposes, with selection done by several different methods: faculty only, joint faculty library committees, librarians only, or subject specialists.

Size of the collection is also a factor in determining the who and the how of selection. In small public libraries, most of the librarians are involved in selection. (Very often there is only one librarian to do all the professional work.) As the library system grows, adds branches, and expands services, selection is usually delegated to department heads and branch library supervisors. A large metropolitan system frequently assigns selection activities to a committee composed of representatives from all of the service programs, though not from every branch. This committee generates a list of titles that individual services and branches are expected to select from; in essence the committee does the initial screening/identification work.

A similar progression in size exists in academic libraries and some special libraries, but the selectors in these cases, more often than not, are the patrons—academic faculty or staff. Even when librarians are responsible for selection in libraries serving institutions with hundreds of subject specialists, the faculty members or researchers have a significant voice in what is selected. Obviously, the in-depth knowledge of a subject specialist can become the deciding factor in making a selection. A fairly common practice in both types of libraries is to hire librarians with graduate degrees both in librarianship and one other subject area. Even then, most materials in subject fields at the advanced levels of research are so specialized that the library must draw on all of the subject expertise available.

In small academic and special libraries, selection is in the hands of the subject specialist, unless the librarian is also an expert in the particular field. Indeed, small academic institutions usually expect the teaching faculty to build the library collection. As small budgets for materials are increased and as the collection grows proportionally, the librarians become more involved.

Eventually a collection can fill all the available shelf space; before that happens decisions must be made to reduce its size (weeding). In school and public libraries, this does not present too great a problem, as many items are used so extensively they disintegrate. Very often, such libraries buy multiple copies of materials; then, by keeping just one copy after demand drops, they regain some space. Also, only the very large public libraries have major archival responsibilities; thus, weeding is somewhat easier. Academic and research libraries seldom buy multiple copies and have significant archival responsibilities which make weeding an involved process. Special (business) libraries generally have to weed on a regular basis because of space limitations. Very often, this results in "rules" for weeding. (For instance, all monographs five years old are to be discarded.) Rules of this kind help to solve one problem—lack of staff time for weeding—but they may increase the demand for interlibrary loan of items discarded as a result of this less-thoughtful approach to the problem. More research has been done on weeding in academic libraries than for all of the other types of libraries combined, and this is reflected in the emphasis on academic libraries in chapter 14.

Although the final phase of the process, collection evaluation, takes place in all types of libraries, it is especially significant in libraries serving educational organizations. Most schools and academic institutions are evaluated by some outside agency to determine the quality of education being provided. If nothing more, the agency (governmental or private) that funds the institution will require periodic assessments, which will invariably include the library and its collection. For such libraries, the evaluation process may have far-reaching effects. Naturally, librarians in educational institutions have been very interested in improving the evaluation process, and they have written a great deal about the topic. Chapter 15 draws heavily upon this literature as well as the literature on accreditation.

Every organization and person needs and uses information in order to survive. The ways in which information is located, collected, and stored range from totally unstructured chance encounters to a tightly structured, carefully planned process. In the latter case, the information collected and the collection process itself may require considerable resources; furthermore, the ways this information is organized, stored, and retrieved are seen as vital to the success of the operation. The definitions in this chapter and the concepts described in this book form the foundation upon which one actively develops a collection of information materials to meet the specific needs of a person or a nation.

Collection development is a dynamic process that should involve both the information professional and the service community. Few information professionals question the need or value of client input; the question is, how much should there be? The best answer seems to be, as much as the organization can process and still carry out its basic functions and as much as the community is willing to provide. The following statements are the philosophical foundations of this work.

1. Collection development should be geared primarily to identified needs rather than to abstract standards of quality; however, an identified need can be a long-term (more than five years off) need, not just an immediate need.

2. Collection development, to be effective, must be responsive to the *total* community's needs, not just to those of current or most active users.

3. Collection development should be carried out with knowledge of and participation in cooperative programs at the local, regional, national, and international levels.

4. Collection development should consider all information formats for inclusion in the collection.

5. Collection development was, is, and always will be a subjective, biased work. The interventions of a selector's personal values into the process can never be completely avoided.

6. Collection development is not something that one learns entirely in the classroom or from reading. Only through practice and making mistakes will a person become proficient in the process of developing a collection.

One can engage in collection development in libraries and information centers that are formally or informally organized. Although organization labels will vary, the process is the same. Almost all large organizations now view information and its management and control as essential as any other resource they employ. In fact, obtaining the right information at the right time — and being able successfully to analyze and apply it — is crucial not only to an organization's success, but to its survival. As a result, organizations are training or are hiring people who know how to acquire and manage the organization's information resources. While these individuals are not called librarians, and do not work in "libraries," they need and use many of the same skills librarians have traditionally employed. Whatever environment one works in, collection development is an exciting challenge which requires lifelong learning.

Notes

[1]"Book Industry Study Group Reports on Reading in 1983," *Library Journal* 110 (August 1985): 12.

[2]Hugh Donaghue, "Implications of Transborder Data Flows to Library Networks" (Paper delivered at the 48th International Federation of Library Associations General Conference, Montreal, Que., IFLA, 1982), 6.

[3]*Library Hotline* 13, no. 28 (10 September 1984): 4.

[4]*Library Hotline* 13, no. 32 (8 October 1984): 2.

[5]*Library Hotline* 14, no. 17 (29 April 1985): 4.

[6]*Library Hotline* 14, no. 18 (6 May 1985): 1.

[7]*Library Hotline* 14, no. 28 (9 September 1985): 1.

[8]*Library Hotline* 14, no. 30 (25 September 1985): 5.

[9]"Public Sector Telecommunications in California" (San Diego, Calif.: Center for Communications, San Diego State University, 1983), 27-28.

[10]Jack W. Simpson, "Editorial," *Online* 10 (March 1985): 627.

[11]Chester Barnard, *Organization and Management* (Cambridge, Mass.: Harvard University Press, 1956).

[12]S. D. Neill, "Knowledge or Information — A Crisis of Purpose in Libraries," *Canadian Library Journal* 39 (April 1982): 69-73.

[13]Robert S. Taylor, "Value-Added Process in the Information Life Cycle," *Journal of the American Society for Information Science* 33 (September 1982): 342.

[14]F. Emery and E. L. Trist, "The Causal Texture of Organizational Environments," *Human Relations* 18 (1965): 21-32.

Further Reading

General

Adams, R. J. *Information Technology and Libraries*. London: Croom Helm, 1986.

Brownrigg, E. B. "Library Telecommunications and Public Policy." In *Telecommunications Networks: Issues and Trends*, edited by M. E. Jacob. White Plains, N.Y.: Knowledge Industry Publications, 1986.

Buckley, B. J. "Technology's Claim to Reduce General Reading Meets Opposition." *Library Association Record* 83 (November 1981): 525, 527.

Donaghue, H. "Implications of Transborder Data Flows to Library Networks." In *48th IFLA General Conference, Proceedings*. Montreal, 1982, 136/MA/2-E.

Emery, F., and E. L. Trist. "The Causal Texture of Organizational Environments." *Human Relations* 18 (1965): 21-32.

Information Policy: A Select Bibliography. Compiled by Margaret Mann. London: British Library, 1985.

Kohl, David F. *Acquisitions, Collection Development and Collection Use: A Handbook for Library Management*. Santa Barbara, Calif.: ABC-Clio, 1985.

Libraries and the Learning Society: Papers in Response to "A Nation at Risk." Chicago: American Library Association, 1984.

Lopez, M. D. "Guide for Beginning Bibliographers." *Library Resources and Technical Services* 13 (Fall 1969): 462-70.

Martin, J., and A. D. J. Flowerdew. *Economics of Information*. London: British Library, 1983.

Mosher, P. H. "Collection Development to Collection Management." *Collection Management* 4 (Winter 1982): 41-48.

Neill, S. D. "Knowledge or Information—A Crisis of Purpose in Libraries." *Canadian Library Journal* 39 (April 1982): 69-73.

Academic

Gormans, G. E. "Collection Development and Acquisition in a Distance Learning Environment." *Library Acquisitions* 10, no. 9 (1986): 9-66.

Molholt, P. "On Converging Paths: The Computing Center and the Library." *Journal of Academic Librarianship* 11 (November 1985): 284-88.

Moran, B. B. *Academic Libraries: The Changing Knowledge Centers of Colleges and Universities.* Washington, D.C.: Association for the Study of Higher Education, 1984.

Segal, J. A. S., and J. Tyson. "The Library's Changing Role in Higher Education." *Library Journal* 110 (15 September 1985): 44-46.

Veaner, E. J. "1985 to 1995: The Next Decade in Academic Librarianship." *College & Research Libraries* 46 (May 1985): 209-29.

_____. "1985 to 1995: The Next Decade in Academic Librarianship." *College & Research Libraries* 46 (July 1985): 285-319.

Public

Dowlin, K. E. *Electronic Library.* New York: Neal-Schuman, 1984.

Hendry, J. D. "Public Libraries Versus the Electric Soup." *Library Association Record* 85 (July 1983): 267-68.

Kempson, E. "Information for Self-Reliance and Self-Determination: The Role of Community Information Services." *IFLA Journal* 12 (August 1986): 182-91.

McDonald, M. M. "Public Library Service to Young Adults." *IFLA Journal* 12 (May 1986): 104-8.

Penland, P. R. "Client-centered Librarians." *Public Libraries* 21 (Summer 1982): 464-67.

Public Library Association. "The Public Library Association Response to *A Nation at Risk.*" *Public Libraries* 23 (Winter 1984): 122-23.

"Public Sector Telecommunications in California." San Diego, Calif.: Center for Communications, San Diego State University, 1983.

Saunders, A. W. "Big Brother, or Space Odyssey? Public Librarianship—The Next Decade and Beyond." *SLA News* 184 (November/December 1984): 24-27.

School

Callison, D. "Justification for Action in Future School Library Media Programs." *School Library Media Quarterly* 12 (Spring 1984): 205-11.

Craver, K. W. "Future of School Library Media Centers." *School Library Media Quarterly* 12 (Summer 1984): 266-84.

Dede, C. "The Future of School Libraries." *School Library Media Quarterly* 13 (Winter 1985): 18-22.

Liesner, J. W. "Learning at Risk: School Library Media Programs in an Information World." *School Library Media Quarterly* 14 (Fall 1985): 11-20.

Thomas, C. "Building Library Media Collections." *Bookmark* 41 (Fall 1982): 16-19.

Special

Cleveland, H. *The Knowledge Executive: Leadership in an Information Society.* New York: Dutton, 1985.

Framel, J. "Information Strategies." *Journal of Information and Image Management* 17 (September 1984): 24-27.

Heilprin, L. B. *Toward Foundations of Information Science.* White Plains, N.Y.: Knowledge Industry Publications, 1985.

Lynch, C. A., and E. B. Brownrigg. "Electrons, Electronic Publishing and Electronic Display." *Information Technology and Libraries* 4 (September 1985): 201-7.

_____. "Library Applications of Electronic Imaging Technology." *Information Technology and Libraries* 5 (June 1986): 100-105.

Misinoky, J. "The Corporate Library: Gearing for the Late 1980s." In *Festschrift in Honor of Dr. Arnulfo D. Trejo*, 75-82. Tucson, Ariz.: Graduate Library School, University of Arizona, 1984.

Mount, E., and W. B. Newman. "Top Secret/Trade Secret: Restricting and Accessing Information." *Collection Building* 7 (Summer 1985): 3-7.

Simpson, J. W. "Information Megatrends." *Online* 9 (March 1985): 627.

Taylor, R. S. "Value-added Process in the Information Life Cycle." *Journal of the American Society for Information Science* 33 (September 1982): 341-46.

2
Information Needs
Assessment

Knowledge of the service community is the keystone to effective collection development. While it is difficult and unnecessary to collect information about all aspects of the lives of the individuals served, the more the collection development staff knows about the work roles, general interests, education, information/communication behavior, values, and related characteristics of potential patrons, the more likely it is the collection will be able to provide the desired information at the time it is wanted. Another reason for wanting and collecting data about the service population relates to one of the collection development "laws," that is, no collection can meet all the information needs of an individual patron or class of patron. With limited resources to serve a wide range of interests, even in the context of a small research and development unit, there must be a solid base of facts upon which to build an effective collection development plan. The data collected are for planning purposes and are useful for more than collection development

Areas in collection development affected by the service group data are policy formulation, selection and evaluation. Policy formulation and modification should be based on the data collected. Although the data will seldom provide help in the selection of a specific item, they can help establish selection parameters. Any assessment of the collection should include a consideration of how well it has met the expectations and needs of the people served.

A number of terms are used in relation to the concepts in this chapter: *community analysis, information needs analysis, needs analysis, needs assessment, role analysis, user studies,* and even *market analysis.* On a very general level they are identical, but they differ greatly in the specifics of application and purpose.

Community analysis usually refers to a public library's data collecting. Sometimes the term *planning process* more accurately identifies the purpose of the activity. *Needs analysis* and/or *assessment* are terms most often used in the special library, information center, or information broker setting and often refer to an individual or small number of individuals. (Both concepts are discussed in more detail later in this chapter.) *User studies* usually tend to denote research projects designed to gain insight into how, why, when, and where people seek information and use information resources. *Market analyses* are normally studies of communities or people to assess interest in or reactions to a service or product. Although it is far beyond the scope of this chapter to address it, there is a major problem in defining concepts such as *information need, information want, expressed demand, satisfied demand, information behavior* and other related terms. (A good article on this subject is T. D. Wilson's "On User Studies and Information Needs.")[1]

Conceptual Background

People seek information from either a formal or an informal system. Informal systems are of three general types: the flow of matter and energy discussed in chapter 1; friends and colleagues; and organizations not designed as formal information sources. Without question, the informal systems provide the bulk of an individual's everyday or common information. Daily living activities generate dozens, perhaps hundreds of information needs, ranging from what the weather will be to the interest rate on loans for buying a home. Depending upon the urgency, the information will be located with greater or less effort, speed, and accuracy. Most of the daily living and activities information requirements are local in nature, and the information frequently is not found in commercial sources. Mass market sources such as newspapers, radio, and television answer some of the local information needs; however, even these sources often serve an area so large and/or diverse in character that information is not as precise as might be desired for local needs.

As the importance of the information increases, so do the amounts of money, time, and other resources devoted to securing precise, accurate information. For most people a weather forecast (covering 18 to 24 hours) prepared and printed in a newspaper several hours before the paper is read is adequate. Because the weather forecast is only of marginal importance for most people, little time, effort, or money is expended on securing up-to-the-minute, accurate weather information. On the other hand, for airline pilots and those who fly with them, weather information is much more important, and significant resources are devoted to having the latest, most exact data. When there is to be a space shuttle launch an entire meteorological network is created to supply the needed information. Everyone from the individual to the largest organization places value on each type of information used, often without being fully aware of that fact. The value is influenced by role, type of information needed, form of information package, access, and by what has been labeled the "law of least effort."

According to the law of least effort, people and organizations expend as little as possible of their available resources (time, money, or effort) to secure information. It frequently happens that one is preparing a paper, report, or memo, realizes that more accurate or more current information is needed, and first turns to materials immediately at hand, even when he or she knows there is only a slight chance of finding what is needed. Most people try this even when they know where the information can be secured, though in a less convenient location or source. In a work environment, fellow workers are usually asked before formal information resources are consulted. Scholars and researchers make frequent and successful use of what has been termed the "invisible college," the communication network linking people interested in similar topics. One reason for the success rate of this informal system is that the formal information system is slow in distributing the latest data.

Knowing what the informal sources are within a service community is important for a collection development staff. In some cases it may be possible to incorporate some of these sources into the formal system, thereby providing better service to all the clientele and occasionally improving the quality or retrievability of information. Many libraries and information centers have referral services (for example the Colorado Springs Public Library) that supply names of people or organizations who are experts in an area and who are willing to supply information. An equally important piece of knowledge is how people use the informal system, as this may influence both how one structures a formal information system (e.g., a library collection) and what is contained in it.

Research on both formal and informal information systems has been done for some time. Generally, the studies can be placed into one of four categories: key informant, "community" forum, social indicators, and field/user studies. They use and examine terms such as *information user* (who), *information need* (what and why), *information-seeking behavior* (how), *demand on formal and/or informal information systems* (amount, when, why), *information use* (how), *information transfer* (how) and *information success and failure* (why). We know that a number of variables affect the individual when there is a "need" for information. Cultural background is a central factor because it creates the basic values and attitudes of the individual. Knowing about the extent of different cultural backgrounds in a service population and the various attitudes held about formal information systems can be of value in planning the services and content of the collections. Very few formal information systems have a monocultural service population any longer, and it is important that we take the time to study and, to some extent, understand the cultural contexts represented.

Present and past experience with the political system also affects a person's expectations regarding formal information systems. As the degree of control (governmental or organizational) increases, there is a corresponding decrease in the variety and range contained in the formal information. In a less-controlled environment, an individual has every reason to expect the formal information system to contain a full range of opinions on most, if not all, topics of concern for that system. As people move from one context to another, they carry their past experiences and expectations. Past experience "baggage" influences information-seeking behavior. Again, knowledge of backgrounds in the service population can be helpful in the planning and collection building process.

Group membership, reference groups, and the invisible college all influence how an individual responds to formal information systems. In the work situation the organization and work responsibilities also enter into the picture. Organizations establish their special, if not unique, set of values regarding information—what constitutes *information* for the organization, how valuable information is, and how much of its resources will be expended on information activities. Within that context, departments and work units will establish their value systems.

One influential variable is the individual's mental set. We all have days when things go right and those when nothing seems to work. We also have variations in the intensity of our law of least effort. Some days we are satisfied with a close approximation, and on others no effort is too great to obtain the precise information. Mental set may be the most important variable, which may be very unpredictable in terms of our service population, and not subject to control by information professionals.

In the long run, legal, economic, political, and technological variables have the greatest influence on the structure and content of formal information systems. (Chapter 18 discusses some of the specifics concerning current laws.) Economic considerations are more and more a factor in decision making in the information center environment. Twenty years ago in the United States, almost no one would have questioned the idea of a totally free public library or the desirability of having such a library in every community. Previously there was discussion of costs and benefits in terms of library services and materials; now there is more and more frequent discussion of cost recovery. A future may exist only for "profit" or break-even libraries in which no public monies are spent.

Studies of users and the service community can provide us with the information we need for effective planning. As pointed out by T. D. Wilson and C. Mick, studying information behavior is important because:

- our concern is with uncovering the facts of the everyday life of the people being investigated;

- by uncovering those facts we aim to understand the needs that exist which press the individual towards information seeking behavior;

- by better understanding those needs we are better able to understand what meaning information has in the everyday life of people; and

- by all of the foregoing we should have a better understanding of the user and be able to design more effective information systems.[2]

There is now a backlog of nearly 1,000 information needs and use studies, but they provide little information which can be applied to problems involving either the management of information work or the design of information products and services. In short, the reason information innovations are technology and content driven is because information behavior studies have failed to provide information which can be used in the design of systems and services.[3]

In the seven years that have passed since the latter statement was made, there has been a small but steady increase in the pool of useful information available. Douglas Zweizig, who has published several pieces on community analysis, is pessimistic about the real value of such studies:

Community analysis will not result in direct identification of community information needs. False expectation is associated with community analysis. It is raised by rhetoric that urges community analysis so we may be "responsive to the information needs of the community" ... by studying the community, we can diagnose information needs and prescribe appropriate materials and services.... But the metaphor only serves to conceal our ignorance from even ourselves ... "information need" is only our idea, not necessarily something that exists in the minds of our patrons ... findings have advanced our understanding of individual information seeking but, as libraries are presently organized, the findings do not provide guidance on what programs to plan or what materials to buy.[4]

Despite this cautious view of the value of user/community studies, Zweizig does support the importance of conducting and using the results of such studies. Recognizing the limitations and dangers involved is important, and knowing what to do with the results is critical for a successful study. Using a conceptual framework is very important. (One good model for the framework can be found in the Mick, Lindsey, and Callahan article cited in note 3.)

Practical Aspects

There are a number of uses for the data collected in a survey, and while a project may be designed to meet only one objective, the data may be of value in a later project. (Note: Surveys are a starting point and when properly conducted provide a base upon which to build. By employing other techniques of information gathering and by use of quantitative analysis one is able to begin to accurately assess information needs. However, first one needs an accurate picture of the service community, and this is what the survey is designed to do.) During the years I taught at the University of California, Los Angeles (UCLA) library school, many students elected to do their specialization paper on some aspect of collection development, and several did some form of user/community analysis project. As a result of these projects, we identified seven areas in which survey data can assist in planning and managing library or information center activities.

One obvious area is collection development. Studies for this purpose range from broad-based studies identifying basic characteristics of the service population to an in-depth analysis of who makes the heavy use of the collection and why, as well as how the materials are used. One study was done in response to a statement from the Los Angeles city attorney's office that the Los Angeles Public Library (LAPL) system might be violating a number of civil rights laws with regard to equal access and service. The city attorney's office noted that there was a marked difference between branches serving white and nonwhite communities. Differences existed in all areas—staffing, hours, collection size, amount spent on materials, and so forth. There was no intent on the part of LAPL to discriminate; the discrepancies resulted from a complex series of events over a long period of time (primarily a budgeting system based on circulation data). Collections did not change as quickly as the service population, resulting in lower circulation and funding. A lack of consistent monitoring of changes in the community perhaps added to the problem. One student studied the relationship between branch collections, service area demographic data, and commercial materials available in the service area. There was a stronger correlation between branch collections than there was with the service community.

Frequently libraries have a desire to provide innovative, or at least new, services for their clientele. Which services and at what level would be best are difficult questions to address, but with data from a properly constructed survey the decision makers will have the basis for projecting user response. Should we offer computer software, should we have computers for clients to use, should we offer online database searching, can we charge for such searching, and how much? These are but a few of the questions that can arise, and in the absence of sound data from a survey, decision makers are merely guessing. One interesting study compared four groups' ranking of desired services: the library patrons (public), part-time workers in the library (primarily shelvers), clerical/para-professional staff, and professional staff. Professional staff estimates of what would be desirable differed significantly from the patrons' views while the part-time employee rankings were very similar to those of the patrons. Although this study was too small in scope to generalize beyond the one community, it does suggest that a cautious approach to instituting new services would be wise, especially if there are no hard data from the users.

Two related uses of these studies are determining service points and changing physical facilities requirements. With an ever-increasing ability to deliver information electronically, the question of whether there should be service points and where they should be located will become very important. Commitments from funding authorities for capital expenditures for new facilities or long-term leases of space will be harder to secure. Mobile delivery services are being questioned because of high energy and maintenance costs. These factors, along with other economic concerns, often make it appear that electronic delivery will or would be the best solution. However, these solutions also have long-term cost implications, and raise questions regarding to whom and how access to electronic systems will be provided. Data from an assessment project will be helpful in making a more informed decision.

Many facilities are not designed with the needs of the handicapped and elderly in mind. With steadily improving health care and increased longevity, an increasing number of individuals in the service population will be in one or both of these categories. Modifying existing structures is often more expensive per square foot than new construction. When and if such modifications need to be made are costly decisions and again, data about how many and what handicaps are present in the service population will assist in making the decisions.

All libraries and information centers are dependent on the good will of their clientele. Complaints to funding authorities, be they profit or nonprofit in outlook, will cause the authorities to question whether funds provided are being spent appropriately. An ongoing assessment program can be helpful in gauging attitudes of the service population about services and activities. Having current information readily available may make the difference between receiving quick approval of a project or budget or undergoing a long, possibly painful, review and justification process.

As community demographics change and interact, it may be necessary to adjust the staffing pattern of the library or information center. Changes in subject expertise, bilingual skills, attention to special population groups (children, institutionalized, or the elderly, for example), more technical skills in various electronic fields, indexing, abstracting or information consolidation skills may be required. The process of hiring people is fairly involved by itself, and when one adds to this securing additional staff or restructuring and redefining duties of existing positions, the process takes a long time. Survey data about the shifts in the service community can assist in projecting when one should start the planning for staff changes that will allow the library or information center to respond in the most timely manner.

All of the areas discussed have some cost and budget implications. Funding authorities tend to look with favor on budget requests that are supported by objective data and come from individuals whose past requests have generally been accurate. The above list is not exhaustive, but illustrates the range of activities that can benefit from such studies and points out that they serve a much greater purpose than just collection development.

Needs assessment projects for libraries and information centers and market research for profit organizations have a number of things in common. Both types of studies are often concerned with who does or does not use the "product"—for example, why a particular product or service is or is not used; how the product or service is used; where it is acquired and used; what is good and bad about the product or service; what new products or services would be of interest; and occasionally, how much the user would be willing to "pay" for a product or service.

When considering an assessment project, some basic concerns about the outcome will arise. Careful planning using sound research methods will take care of such technical data issues as sample size, pretesting requirements, question bias, interviewer influence, and so forth. Questions which can be difficult to answer include: (1) Is the population to be studied knowledgeable or interested enough to respond to complex questions, or would many simple questions covering a complex question be better? (2) Is the cost, in time and energy, of providing adequate background information to individuals lacking the necessary knowledge balanced by more or better research data? (3) To what extent will the data accurately reflect attitudes, opinions, needs, etc., rather than responses that are thought to be wanted? and (4) Will the survey process result in unrealistic expectations in both respondents and staff? Answers to these questions are never fully known until the process is completed; however, by thinking them through in advance, some of the negative elements can be avoided.

Occasionally there is an opportunity to "piggy back" a study with another study; sometimes it is possible to locate a recent previous study conducted for another purpose that contains data useful for the present study. In such cases, it is possible to reduce the risk of the negative elements related to unrealistic expectations and the possibility of responding in terms of what is thought to be desired. An example of finding information useful to libraries in an existing nonlibrary study appears in a report on the results of reanalyzing data from a survey on lifestyles done by a large advertising agency.[5] One of the more than 200 questions asked by the marketing firm was, "How frequently did you use the library in the last year?" Because the survey was from an advertising agency, fewer people responded with inaccurate data about library use than would have done had the survey been sent out by a library. (Too often people answer questions the way they think the sponsoring body would like the question answered rather than giving a truthful but less positive response.) Some bias undoubtedly exists in the data, as there is still a tendency for people to think of library use as "good" and to respond in a manner that makes them look good. While some librarians did not agree with Madden's conclusions based on the reanalyzed data, the data were not questioned. Being aware of studies like this one can save time and effort.

More often than not the library will have to develop, or have developed, a customized study. A number of sources will assist in formulating a project.

Almost any basic research methods textbook will outline the fundamentals and many marketing books will also be of assistance. Beyond the fundamental level there are more specific aids, including the following:

Association of Research Libraries. *User Studies—Spec Kit 101* (Washington, D.C.: Association of Research Libraries, February 1984).
The Association of Research Libraries publishes a number of items that can be useful in the academic environment; this is one of most interest.

Martha Hale. "Administrators and Information: A Review of Methodologies Used for Diagnosing Information Use." In *Advances in Librarianship* (New York: Academic Press, 1986).
This is an excellent survey article.

Forest W. Horton. *How to Harness Information Resources* (Cleveland, Ohio: Association for Systems Management, 1974); *Information Management Workbook* (Washington, D.C.: Information Management Press, 1983).
Of greatest interest to special libraries, information brokers, and those in less traditional information center environments.

Roger Kaufman and Fenwick English. *Needs Assessment* (Englewood Cliffs, N.J.: Educational Technology Publications, 1979).
This is another useful publication.

James Liesner. *A Systematic Process for Planning Media Programs* (Chicago: American Library Association, 1976).
Although intended for the elementary and secondary educational environment, the method could be modified to serve the needs of any educational system.

Vernon E. Palmour, Marcia C. Bellassai, and Nancy DeWath. *A Planning Process for Public Libraries* (Chicago: American Library Association, 1980).
This contains many useful ideas for developing a survey. However, many practicing librarians have not found it to be all they had expected as a complete planning tool.

R. L. Warren. *Studying Your Community* (New York: Russell Sage Foundation, 1955).
This is old, but still very useful for public libraries.

Full-scale studies are very expensive and time-consuming, but they have to be done occasionally. Studies of modest scope can be conducted between large projects, cost less and can produce reliable data. Following are some suggestions for the content of both large- and small-scale projects, with a focus on how collection development activities may be improved as a result.

Elements of the Survey

As soon as it is determined that a study should be conducted, several questions must be answered: (1) Who is to collect the information? (2) What information is needed? (What will be studied?) (3) What methods will be employed to collect the data? (4) Where can the data be found? (5) How will the data be interpreted?

Who Will Do the Study?

Who or how many people will be responsible for supervising and running the study depends on several factors: the financial support (library budget or supplemental funds), the number and qualifications of personnel available (staff members or outside consultants), and the depth and breadth of the study.

Any survey of major proportions must have the financial backing to hire a consultant to assist in planning the study, unless there is staff expertise available in the area of designing assessment projects. Occasionally, limited funding results in a committee made up of paid and volunteer workers. Collection development personnel and the rest of the staff must be involved if the project is to succeed. The use of a staff project team, while a financial saving, needs to be considered carefully. An inexperienced team can waste inordinate amounts of time and energy. Furthermore, team members would normally work on the survey during their regular working hours, which may cause staffing problems. A staff team may also draw conclusions based upon individual members' personal biases concerning a particular area or aspect of the service community, rather than upon the research data.

A compromise solution is to hire an outside consultant to formulate the plan that is then implemented by the staff. A problem with this approach is that the consultant must divide the tasks into units small enough to be handled by personnel who are not fully trained in survey methods. The staffing problem, which is a significant one, must be weighed against the consequences of failing to conduct any survey at all. One way to overcome the problem of a lack of staff time and experience in assessment work is to build the project into the regular collection development activities. Many of the larger academic libraries have started moving in this direction already with subject specialists. To some degree this movement is accidental, because the literature on the reasons for and functions of the subject specialist gives little indication that formalized survey work is ever a primary concern. Contact with faculty, work in conjunction with faculty and specialized users, development of subject areas in the light of institutional and patron needs, syllabus analysis, and citation analysis are some of the cited activities. In essence, the basis is present in such libraries for subject specialists to conduct ongoing assessments. A meeting once a year with each faculty member whose subject interest touches on the area of responsibility will maintain close contact with community needs.

If the job description for collection development staff includes survey work, the problem is solved. By including assessment as one of several tasks making up the full-time position, adequate time and staffing are built into the system, and assure an ongoing program. Naturally, there is the problem of convincing funding authorities. Adding survey work to job descriptions may, in effect, increase the staff size by one (or more) full-time position(s). Apparently, needs assessment work has not been thought to be that important, because very few libraries and information centers employ this technique.

Using the library staff as the data collecting group does offer several advantages. First, data will be collected with a thorough understanding of how they are to be used. A staff team should have already gained useful information through day-to-day work; for example, they will have taken requests for and/or attempted to locate information that is not available in-house.

Another useful outcome of using a staff team is the personal commitment that can be gained through the process of the team's members learning about their service community. Also, there is greater willingness of those involved in a project to accept and implement the results and to use those results on a day-to-day basis. Less time is required to inform the rest of the staff about the results because normal social interaction cuts across many barriers; often more time is needed when the study is handled by an outside consultant, since resistance may be higher and communication of results more difficult. Once the decision as to "who" will run the project has been made, a clear statement of the study's objectives and a detailed listing of the steps to be taken and the questions to be asked must be developed. Unclear goals lead to disastrous results and open the way for self-serving interpretations of the data collected.

What Will Be Studied?

Each type of library or information center will have a slightly different definition of the word *community.* In the context of the public library, it will mean the political jurisdiction that such a library serves; for the academic library it will be the institution to be served; and for the special library it will be the company, business, institution, or foundation that established it. With these basic distinctions in mind it is possible to identify 11 broad categories for which data can be collected and that apply to all types of libraries.

Historical data are useful in several ways. Understanding a community's historical development may lead to a better, and sometimes quicker, understanding of where that community stands today. Historical background information may also provide clues as to which areas of the collection might be weeded or in which areas it is no longer necessary to acquire material.

Geographic information may involve such questions as: In which physical direction is the community growing? What is the distribution of population over the geographic area? This type of information helps in the determination of service points, which in turn influences the number of duplicates that the library needs to acquire. (Duplicate copies cut into the number of *titles* the library can buy.) Geographic data and transportation data, which will be considered next, are intertwined and should be considered together.

Transportation availability data, combined with geographic factors, are important in deciding how many service points are needed and where they are to be located. Merely noting the existence of a bus service does not provide enough information for a meaningful survey. How often is there service? What does it cost? What are the hours of service? What is the level of use? Answers to these questions become vital to determining service points and service hours. As noted above, service points and hours have an impact on plans for developing the collection. Often, large academic and industrial organizations provide their own internal transportation systems, especially in urban areas. The existence of its own good internal transportation system may help a library to build a more varied collection. A courier system may help alleviate the need for as many (or as large) branch operations. Reduction in the number of branches, while still maintaining the same level of service, can reduce the need for duplicate materials.

Legal research will not be too difficult, nor will the amount of data be large. Nevertheless, it may determine how the collection is to be developed. In some academic institutions, the teaching faculty has the legal right to expend all book funds. Although there is no longer any American university where this legal authority is exercised to its fullest extent, cases of limited implementation do exist. Also, this right may exist, but most persons—including librarians—will have forgotten about it until a problem arises. Preparing for a possible problem is usually less difficult than dealing with an existing one, or with a surprise. Clear-cut policies about the delegation of selection authority and responsibility may help to avoid a problem.

Knowledge of how a community's legal system functions can also be important. Where does authority lie? To which bodes is the library accountable, especially for collection development? Are there any legal restrictions on what the library may buy with monies allocated for collection development? Some jurisdictions, until a few years ago, had regulations making it illegal to buy anything except books, periodicals, and newspapers—other media could not be purchased. How does one go about changing the regulations? Knowledge of the library's legal position will help answer the questions.

Political information is related to legal data on both the formal and informal levels. Formally, such questions arise as: To what extent is the library a political issue? If political parties exist, are there differences in their attitudes toward library and information services? What is the distribution of party affiliations in the community? Are some areas more politically conservative or liberal than others? Should library service point collections reflect these philosophical differences? Informally, such questions arise as How do the politics of the community work? Who are the individuals who influence fiscal decisions? In an academic or special library environment, what are the politics of the allocation of collection development funds? Answers to most of these questions will not have a direct bearing on which actual titles go into the collection. They will, however, influence the way in which funds are secured and allocated.

Demographic data are fundamental in formulating a knowledgeable collection development program. Basic changes in the composition of the population are inevitable, but only by monitoring the community can such changes be anticipated. Waiting until change has occurred creates at best an image of a slow-to-change "establishment" institution. Libraries have enough problems with their images without adding to them unnecessarily. For example, American academic institutions and libraries operated for years on the premise that their student bodies would continue to grow in size.

Census data in the 1960s indicated a sharp drop in the birthrate. This fact, combined with widespread discontent with the higher education system, should have been a clear indication that the growth would not continue. However, only after several years of declining or stable enrollment did academic institutions react to the "news," which had been available for more than 18 years. Public libraries had a somewhat similar problem with shifts of population out of the inner cities. Occasionally, such shifts can change the city's tax base, which in turn affects the library. Other changes in the population (age, education, nationality, health, etc.) should be considered in developing a collection.

Los Angeles offers a dramatic example of shifting composition and location of population groups and the effect on the library caused by responding to these shifts as they occurred. In 1950, 86.3 percent of the population of Los Angeles was Anglo; by 1980 the Anglo percentage was 48.7, while the Hispanic percentage went from 6.9 to 29.2. Other "minority" groups also grew in size. Figures 2.1 to 2.4 illustrate what happened in just one area of Los Angeles. The maps are based on census tracts in the Santa Monica, Westwood, Venice, Marina del Rey region. Unshaded tracts on the map indicate a 51 percent or more Anglo population:

　shading is for Asian

　for Black

　for Hispanic

　represents tracks that had no "ethnic" category over 51 percent ("transitional").

In 1950 only a few tracts were "transitional," that is, no majority ethnic grouping dominated. By 1960 the 1950 transitional tracts were predominantely Asian and a number of new transitional tracts had appeared. Ten years later additional transitional areas were added along with three Black, one Hispanic and another large block of Asian dominated tracts. Most dramatic is the change between 1970 and 1980, when non-Anglo groups became the majority in Los Angeles.

Not shown on the maps is where the Anglo population moved, which was to new housing developments in what had been agricultural land. As the city grew out from the "core," new branch libraries were built to service the new residential areas. Old branches naturally remained in place; unfortunately, so did the original collections. I mentioned earlier that the Los Angeles City Attorney's Office suggested that the Los Angeles City Public Library (LAPL) discriminated against minority groups and produced a series of charts showing the great differences in almost all aspects of library service between Anglo and minority areas. To a large extent the problem arose from a failure to monitor changes in the service community and to adjust the collection to the changing interests and needs. Like many public library systems, LAPL used use/circulation data as a major factor in allocating money to branch libraries. That is, as use/circulation went up or down, so did each branch's budget. If there is a major shift in the service

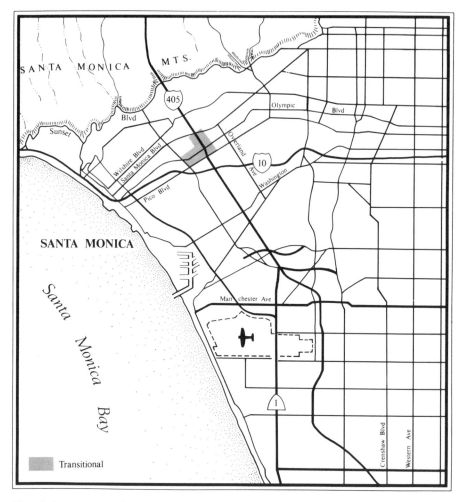

Fig. 2.1. Los Angeles/Santa Monica distribution of ethnic populations, 1950. Map drawn using data from the U.S. Census, 1950.

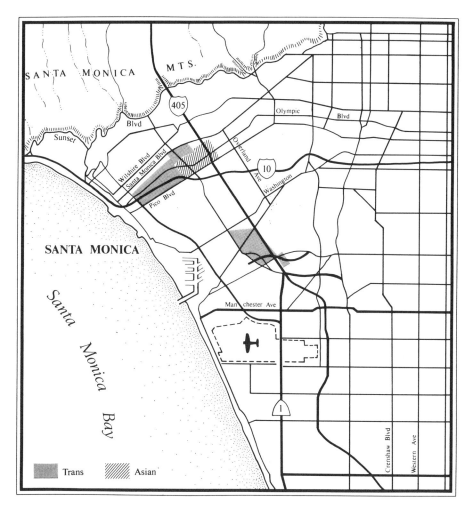

Fig. 2.2. Los Angeles/Santa Monica distribution of ethnic populations, 1960. Map drawn using data from the U.S. Census, 1960.

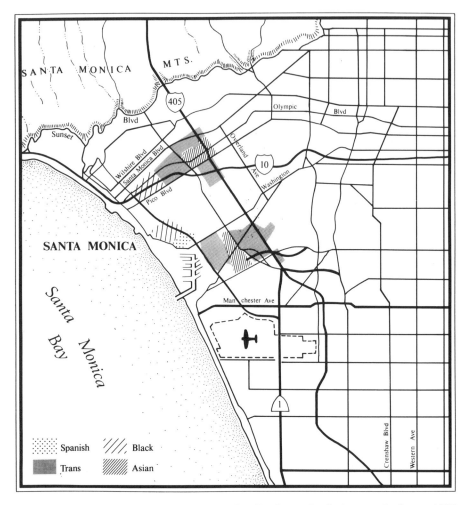

Fig. 2.3. Los Angeles/Santa Monica distribution of ethnic populations, 1970. Map drawn using data from the U.S. Census, 1970.

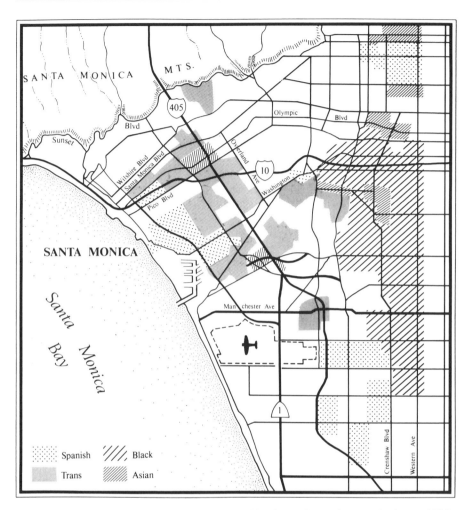

Fig. 2.4. Los Angeles/Santa Monica distribution of ethnic populations, 1980. Map drawn using data from the U.S. Census, 1980.

population and there is no corresponding shift in the collection, there can be a drop in use/circulation and a drop in funding. When this happens, a library can be caught in a cycle that is difficult if not impossible to break. Even if the problem is known, there may not be enough money to effect a change which would adequately reverse the down trend. Flexibility in funding is necessary to help break the cycle when the situation has gone on for any length of time.

Two things are reasonably clear from this example. First, monitoring the service community and adjusting to the changes discerned is important. Second, major shifts can take place almost overnight, even in a very large community. (Ten years in the history of a city of millions of people is almost overnight.) In the case of Los Angeles there was an official agency that alerted city agencies to the trends and in 1976 predicted quite accurately the 1980 census results. (Predicted Anglo population, 49.4 percent—actual 48.7 percent; predicted Black population, 16.2 percent—actual 16.8 percent; and predicted Hispanic population, 28.8 percent—actual 29.27 percent.) Making use of data from such agencies saves time, money, and work.

Economic data are useful from the standpoints of general planning and collection development. Knowledge of the existing economic base of the community and possible changes can be used to plan overall collection development activities. Anticipating increases or decreases in funding can lead to a more even collection, especially for serial publications. When we view the collection as a whole, we realize that an economy based upon semiskilled or unskilled workers will call for one type of collection; a skill-based economy, another; while the group labeled "knowledge workers" would require still another. Communities with a seasonal economy or a predominantly migrant worker population will be faced with several problems. If the seasonal population is to be given service, what type of service and which formats would be best? The answers to these and similar questions can help in building a useful collection.

Communication systems available to the community can be of some importance to the library's mission. Closed circuit and cable television may become very valuable resources. Already important in the primary and secondary schools, television is becoming a factor in higher education and in the education of the whole community. Public access to cable television— one channel exclusively reserved for community use—has already had some impact on libraries. Community reference service by cable television and telephone are becoming common, and some have story hours on cable. Cable television as well as video and teletext will open up new areas of service, patron access, and collection development needs.

Social and educational organizations reflect community values. While social patterns are slower to change than individual attitudes, such patterns must be considered in planning an integrated collection building program. Social clubs, unions, and service organizations all have an impact and reflect community interests. The most important organizations are educational. An academic institution no longer just offers two-year, four-year, and postgraduate programs. Evening adult education classes, day and night degree programs, off-campus classes, and even some "remedial" high school level courses create complex instructional programs, each facet having rather different information needs. Public libraries need to be concerned not only with public and private primary and secondary schools, but also with adult vocational programs and higher education. Special libraries in business are usually set up to serve specialized research and development needs; however, in-house training and development programs may also require library support.

Cultural and recreational organizations also reflect community interests. As is the case with social organizations, these formal groups provide useful clues to highly specialized interest areas with enough community interest to maintain a formal group. Such groups, when given library service, often become some of the library's most solid and influential supporters. (This category does not really apply to the special library, because its collection and service areas are clearly defined by the organization it serves.)

Other community information services are, in some respects, the most important elements in the collection development program. If a number of community information sources are identified, and if a working cooperative agreement is reached, everyone will benefit. All too often the public, school, and academic libraries in the same political jurisdiction will operate as if they existed in total isolation. When all the libraries are publicly supported, considerable resources and service are wasted if there are no cooperative programs. The first step in achieving a cooperative arrangement is to know who has what. In addition to knowing what library resources exist in the community, the librarian should know about other information resources such as bookstores, record shops, newspapers, radio and television stations, and motion picture theaters. Some writers on selection have suggested that fewer recreational materials are required in the library if other recreational outlets are available to the community.

How and Where Are Data Collected?

Knowing what one needs to know is only one-third of the battle; knowing how to get the information is the remaining two-thirds. The fields of social welfare and sociology have developed a number of methods for systematically studying the community. Community studies may be divided into four primary types: (1) key informant, (2) community forum, (3) social indicators, and (4) field survey. All of these methods can be employed in various combinations—they are not mutually exclusive. A combination of approaches is a good technique to employ since it helps to ensure obtaining valid unbiased data.

Key Informant

Key informants are individuals in a position to be aware of the needs of the people of the community. Included are public officials, officers of the community organizations, business leaders, the clergy, and certain unofficial (non-office holding) leaders in the community who are nonetheless influential and are viewed as knowledgeable about community affairs. These individuals are contacted and interviewed to ascertain their opinions and ideas concerning the community's information needs. In order to be effective, a tested interview schedule needs to be drawn up. A tested interview schedule is one that has been pre-used (tested) to determine the types of answers the questions will generate. Individuals will always differ as to what a question "really means." Pretesting questions allows a team to reduce the range of interpretation by rewording ambiguous or confusing questions. There should not be too many interviewers, and unless they have had extensive experience in interviewing, they *must* have thorough training before they begin.

Potential shortcomings of the key informant approach include the problem that the informants do not totally represent the community, and since they are not randomly selected, the data cannot be treated as if they did represent the community population and what it requires in the way of library services. Their opinions have a personal bias; they may perceive the community's information needs differently than do the individuals who make up the community. In essence, this kind of interview supplies a great deal of subjective but useful information about the perceptions of the community.

The key informant approach is relatively easy to prepare and implement; it requires the least amount of data collecting time, and it is very helpful in making the key community figures aware of the information problems of a diverse community. These data must be supplemented with published (objective) data and, when possible, with a representative cross-section of community opinion.

Community Forum

The community forum can be compared to a town meeting. This approach avoids selection bias by the researcher, as all members of the community are invited to participate in a number of public meetings, and to express their opinions about what can or should be done to improve library services or other library issues. The key to success for this approach lies in extensive publicity. Several methods can be used to encourage people to attend. Letters can be mailed to individuals and selected organizations to publicize the meeting and its purpose. Use of the mass media, newspapers, radio, and television is also a standard means for advertising public meetings. In a large community, a number of meetings may have to be planned in order to keep the groups small enough so that people will feel comfortable in expressing their opinions and there is time for hearing all points of view. In order to make these meetings useful, some structure must be provided by the survey team. A set of questions must be discussed at all the meetings as well as the questions which will arise from the audience. It is usually desirable to have the entire survey team present at all meetings or to arrange for the meetings to be taped.

Two advantages of the community forum are that it is easy to arrange and inexpensive. Forums also help identify individuals who are interested in improving the quality of library service in their community. These people may later be persuaded to help implement the programs that are necessary to correct any deficiencies in library service. One glaring disadvantage of the community forum is that people who are nonusers of the library will not, in all probability, attend the meetings. If they feel they have no need for the library, why should they be interested in spending their time to improve services they never use? Another major disadvantage is that the data obtained are impressionistic and subjective. These data are extremely difficult to categorize, and are not readily amenable to systematic analysis. Although these disadvantages are serious, the community forum still is useful as a major grassroots democratic process for soliciting opinions, ideas, and criticism from the general population.

Social Indicators

Recently, social scientists have developed a method for determining the needs of various segments of a community. *Social indicators* is the term that describes this method. "The notion of the city as a constellation of 'natural areas' has ... proven useful as a method of describing social subdivisions within communities."[6] A *natural area* is a unit within the community that can be set apart from other units or areas by certain characteristics. Those characteristics, or social indicators, may be geographical features such as rivers or transportation patterns; sociodemographic characteristics, such as age, sex, income, education, and ethnicity; population factors, including distribution, density, mobility, and migration; the spatial arrangements of institutions; and health and social well-being characteristics, such as condition of housing or suicide rates.[7]

The social indicators approach to needs assessment can determine certain needs of a community by studying the relevant indicators. By using descriptive statistics found in public records and reports, the library involved in community analysis can deduce certain of the information needs of the community's population. By selecting factors that have been determined to be highly correlated with those groups in need of information, surveyors are able to extrapolate the information needs of the whole community. What these social indicators (also called *factors, variables,* or *characteristics*) may be is a point of much disagreement among researchers in the field of library and information science. Following are some examples of social indicators found in the literature that illustrate the great diversity of opinion:

age	health
sex	employment
education	marital status
income	domicile/work location

What are the implications of those indicators for library users? Following are some broad generalizations based on research that has accumulated over several years. Use of libraries and information centers tends to decrease with age. Older adults (over 55) tend to use the public library less as their age increases. Senior faculty, researchers, and organization officials tend to use libraries and information centers less as they increase in status and age; although they still gather information, the actual gathering is done by junior/support staff, who tend to be younger. Women make greater use of libraries and information centers than men—this is true regardless of institutional environment. As the number of years of education increases for an individual, there is a corresponding tendency to use libraries more, up to about 16 years of formal education. After the bachelor's degree is received the curve is downward. Graduate and postgraduate education apparently moves the person into the "invisible college" network, so there is less need to use formal information systems. Income level and use of formal information systems also reflect a "J" shape curve, in which low income usually means low use, use rises through middle and upper middle income levels, and use turns rather sharply downward at high income levels. Apparently, high income groups acquire a high percentage of the information they require by purchasing the needed material. Generally, as the state of health declines, there is a decrease in the use of formal information systems. However, with proper equipment and special services this tendency is often reversed. Persons employed in manual (unskilled) labor tend not to use formal information systems. Use tends to increase in direct relationship to increased levels of skills required to perform the work. The law of least effort is apparent in the finding that as the distance of the residence or work station from the information center increases, there is a corresponding drop in use. Single persons and married couples with no children tend to use formal information systems less than couples with children, and as the number of children rises so does use.

Once the indicators have been determined, the needed data can then be collected from several existing sources. The most detailed and accurate source for such data is the U.S. Census. Census tracts (the breakdown into neighborhoods or communities of a few thousand people) are excellent sources and are available from the Bureau of the Census. The major drawback with census data is that a complete study is done only once every 10 years. (A population estimation is done annually, but statistics are not compiled for areas smaller than counties.) In rapidly changing communities, this can be a problem because the statistics may be misleading once several years have elapsed since the last census. But other sources are available for up-to-date local data. Regional, county, or city planning agencies gather statistics and make projections that can be useful. In addition, school boards, chambers of commerce, and police departments compile useful data.

For actual investigation, a unit of analysis such as census tracts or block groupings must be selected. Census tracts appear to be the most widely used unit of analysis for community studies, and the data from the tracts are readily available. Often, the ease with which the data can be collected serves as the basis for selecting the study unit. However, the ease of data collecting should never jeopardize the integrity of the study.

The Field Survey

The field survey approach to community analysis is based on the collection of data from a sample or entire population of people living within a given area. The most common means of collecting data is through interview schedules or questionnaires. The methods most frequently used are the telephone interview, the person-to-person interview, and the mailed questionnaire, each of which employs a series of questions. In the community survey for public libraries, questions may be designed to elicit from an individual or household information regarding frequency of use of the library, reading habits, economic and/or educational background, or any other information that the library believes will provide insight into need, use, and especially nonuse, of the library.

Care must be taken when designing questions so that the individual's right to privacy is not violated. If the person or group designing the questionnaire is not certain of the legality of the questions, reliable legal counsel should be consulted. Questions that are asked of the community should have a direct relationship to the objectives of the survey. Those questions that are designed to elicit peripheral information lengthen the questionnaire, raise the cost of the survey, overburden the respondent and often tend to create unrealistic expectations. This, in turn, may decrease the response rate and reduce the validity of the findings.

A choice should be made between a structured or unstructured format for the questionnaire. Open-ended questions (unstructured format) take more time to answer than the fixed-alternative type of questions (structured format), a choice which can in turn affect the response rate. Open-ended questions are also much more difficult to code and analyze and are limited to only a few methods of statistical analysis. When using volunteers to conduct interviews or to code and analyze the data, the structured format is much easier to administer and, because of the homogeneity of the responses obtained, it is more readily coded and analyzed. Use of volunteers also requires that careful instructions be prepared to assure accurate results.

The next step in the field survey is to select a sample. "The selection of the sample depends largely upon the information needed: the unit for analysis, i.e., individuals, households, etc.; the type of data gathering techniques used; and the size it must be to adequately represent the population from which it is drawn."[8] Also, cost must be taken into account when selecting a sample. A large sample may call for complex selection methods and will require more time to complete. Of course, the use of volunteers can keep the cost down, but the survey method, including sampling, is not a simple procedure. This is an area in which the service of a paid consultant may be required.

A popular method of obtaining information from respondents is through the personal interview. This permits face-to-face contact, stimulates a free exchange of ideas, and has a high response rate. The telephone interview can also be used, but there is a limit to the amount of time that the interviewer can hold the interest of the respondent. Twenty minutes appears to be the maximum length for an efficient telephone interview. If the interview schedule is highly structured and the interviewer well trained, this can be an adequate amount of time to gather the necessary data.

Mail surveys also have certain inherent advantages and disadvantages. They require less staffing and training than surveys that depend on in-person interviews. These two advantages can greatly reduce the cost in time and money in conducting a survey. However, there are two significant disadvantages to the mailed survey.

One disadvantage is that generally there is a low response rate. Organizations conducting mail surveys have reported a response rate as low as 35 percent, and such rates can seriously affect the validity and reliability of the collected data. Even with repeated mailings the response is low, and the cost of keeping track of who has or has not responded is high. Second, some persons in the community are unable to respond to anything but the simplest of questions. This may be especially true in bi- cr multilingual communities. Of course, the problem of language can be overcome by printing the questionnaire in all the appropriate languages, but there will still be the problem of the literacy level, no matter what language is used. Because of these disadvantages, then, libraries using the mail survey must carefully design the questionnaire, and use the simplest and most succinct language possible while still meeting their established objectives for gathering the needed information. They should also attempt to determine what the response rate will be before expending the time and money for a survey that could be of questionable value.

The survey approach, like the other needs assessment approaches, has certain advantages and disadvantages. The primary disadvantage is its cost. Designing large-sample methods, extensive interviewing, and advanced statistical analysis, for example, tend to cost more than other approaches. Another disadvantage is that many individuals refuse to supply information about themselves or other family members. In many communities, the refusal or nonreturn rate may be so high as to make the data of questionable value.

However, one important advantage to the survey approach is that, if carefully designed and administered, it will produce the most accurate and reliable data for use in determining the information needs of the service community. The other community needs assessment approaches are useful, but they have basic drawbacks: the key informant approach is not fully representative of the community; the community forum will probably not draw nonusers; and variables indicating library use and what benefits are derived from that use have not been established yet for the social indicators approach. But when the field survey approach is combined with one or more of the other methods, it greatly enhances the findings. Results from the different methods can be compared and contrasted; especially valuable is the comparison of data from a user study with the data gathered by a field survey approach.

How Are Data to Be Interpreted?

Once collected, information must be prepared for analysis. The method chosen will depend upon the approaches used to collect the data and the capabilities of the agency or group performing the analysis. Tally sheets should be developed so that each aspect or question of the study is listed along with its value and range of responses. Each element is then tallied and the totals are calculated. Elementary statistical analysis, such as averages and standard deviations, can be performed at this time.

One simple and inexpensive method of analysis is to prepare maps indicating the units of analysis (e.g., census tracts) and the variable or responses analyzed. This method can be improved upon by using overlays, which can illustrate distribution of and relationships between the selected variables. This produces the best results when there are a small number of variables; analysis involving a large number of variables should be carried out by use of a more sophisticated technique. If a computer is available, more sophisticated analysis may be performed, but one must be certain to have sound reasons for each type of analysis. A mass of statistical test results can be just as hard to draw conclusions from as raw data, if one has not planned for each test.

In order to present the findings of the study, a suitable format needs to be selected. The format will depend upon the community being studied, the type of survey, and the audience being addressed. Advanced statistical analysis may be a suitable format for those audiences that can understand the assumptions and implications of such tests. But assuming that community study is to improve library services in the community, the findings should always be presented in such a way that individuals in the community, in public office, and in the library can easily understand their implications. This is best accomplished by descriptive summaries, charts, diagrams, and other visual aids.

Of course, the group which is primarily responsible for the analysis and presentation of the data is the project team. But just as they solicited the help of individuals and groups within the community to conduct the study, they should also ask these individuals to help with the analysis and presentation of the findings. The team should first present their findings in a preliminary report, which could be distributed to all those groups involved for their comments and suggestions.

The examination of the data by several individuals and groups allows for the identification of areas requiring action. This can be done by providing the opportunity for group discussions of the preliminary results; for instance, meetings such as those discussed in the section on the community forum approach can be used to obtain citizen feedback. If the preliminary conclusions are weak or unsubstantiated, group discussion will reveal it. These discussions will also indicate to the community the areas where action must be taken to improve library services. This type of public discussion can help create a strong commitment among all interested parties in seeing that action is taken to improve services. Another advantage of involving several groups in the analysis is the identifying of certain unmet needs and interests of the community that are not the responsibility of the library. Public disclosure of such community problems will bring them to the forefront, and possibly force some agency or group to assume responsibility for their correction. In this matter, not only will the study help to improve community access to information, but it can also benefit all aspects of community life.

Once the project staff has gathered all of the comments, suggestions, and citizen feedback, they should analyze their conclusions once more in preparation for the final report. The final report should include the objectives of the study, the methodology used to collect the data, a list of the identified problem areas, and a list of recommendations with priorities indicated for their implementation. The recommendations should include those that can be easily and economically implemented as well as those that call for extensive programming changes, but *all* recommendations should be realistic and feasible. "Blue sky" reports, where recommendations are uneconomical or unfeasible, are usually considered pipe dreams by those who are responsible for the allocation of funding. The present and future resources of the library must be considered when making recommendations that will improve its services.

Each unit of the library should then examine the report for implications for its work. Only after all units have completed their work can the selection staff start to assess the impact of the report. Only after all of the needs and desired changes in programs and services are determined can a realistic collection development program be formulated.

The study may reveal segments in the community that are not being served by the library. The findings should indicate what areas of library factors have contributed to this failure. Hours of service, location or lack of service points, attitude of staff, citizens' lack of knowledge about library programs, etc., are problems that could be identified and then corrected through recommended programs. For example, an extensive publicity campaign can be implemented using newspapers, radio, posters, and bulletins to inform the community of new and existing programs.

Since the information needs and interests of the community have been researched and identified, the collection development policy can be adjusted accordingly. For example, more older people may have moved into the community, requiring large print books and materials dealing with the problems of living on a limited income. But the most important element is: *Do the present objectives of the library coincide with its new knowledge of the community?* Are the objectives in line with the current needs of the community, do they reflect a past need, or are they only self-serving? The findings of the study should make the answers to these questions apparent, and if the objectives of the library do not reflect the needs and interests of its community, recommendations should be made for specific changes to assure that they do.

Following the completion of the study and the implementation of the recommendations, a program of continuous community analysis should be initiated. Statistical information can be easily kept current and additional information can be gathered by a smaller sample than that of the original survey. The amount of time and manpower needed for continuing analysis will be a fraction of that devoted to the original study. Once the initial study has been completed, the library's objectives, programs, and collection can be continuously adjusted to meet the changing information needs and interests of the people in the community, as reflected in the ongoing analysis.

Citizen Participation

The idea of citizen participation in community analysis is drawn both from the literature of library science and from that aspect of social work called community organization. "Community organization refers to various methods ... whereby a professional ... helps a community ... composed of individuals, groups or organizations to engage in planned collective action in order to deal with social problems within a democratic system of values."[9] Practitioners in community organization see "the participation of service users in institutional decision-making [as] one means of promoting consumer needs and protecting consumer interests."[10] In other words, in community organization the people of a community are seen as having a definite role in determining the type and quality of services that their institutions can provide to fulfill their needs.

Participation of citizens in the operation of public institutions is part of the democratic heritage: citizens must share in the decision-making process of the institutions that exist to serve them. To do otherwise is to undermine the very foundations upon which a free society is built. However, a select few have always tended to dictate to others what they think is best for the general welfare. Most citizens are aware that if public officials are allowed to make all decisions concerning public welfare, the people may suffer. Consequently, if legislation has not mandated citizen participation, then the people themselves have demanded it. Libraries are not exempt from this phenomenon. They are beginning to see the writing on the wall regarding community participation in policy making. Lowell Martin has expressed this concern this way:

> Policy-making for libraries has been mainly in the hands of the professionals; the administrator and staff determine aims and programs for the most part, with trustees furnishing the stamp of approval. This may not be the structure of the future. Our institutions are being questioned, as is the role of professionals within them. If and as libraries become more essential, people will seek a more direct and active voice in what they do.[11]

Ensuring citizen participation in library affairs, especially in community analysis, is not an easy task, and several problems will be encountered when initiating a program of community participation. For example, it is difficult to find citizens who are both representative of the community and willing to participate. Recruitment and training of volunteers is also a difficult and time-consuming task. However, the greatest problem lies with librarians them-selves. Most library administrators are trained professionals who feel that they have the expertise to run the library without the help of citizens in the community. They contend that citizen participation will be extremely time-consuming and actually may hinder the library's overall operation. They also believe that the general population does not have enough knowledge about libraries and librarianship to participate in decision-making functions concerning them.

These objections have some validity, but they can be overcome if the library administration believes that community service is the library's primary function, and that this service can be immensely improved by community analysis with the help of participating citizens. Of course, citizen participation is going to be a time-consuming affair, but there are few new programs in a library that will not require large amounts of time to initiate. In response to the criticism of the public's lack of knowledge in library affairs, this book is written in the belief that people in the community cannot learn about their library and its operation unless they are invited to participate. Participation becomes an educational experience for those citizens who volunteer or are asked to volunteer their services.

The traditional routes of citizen participation, such as library boards, Friends of the Library groups, and volunteers, often overlook the disadvantaged and the nonusers. These traditional methods do not encourage participation from all segments of the community. However, by relying mainly on citizens from all segments of the community (as opposed to one or more experts) to conduct the community study, the library is soliciting a diverse number of opinions and ideas, some of which may never have been considered or explored by the experts. Also, who could be more knowledgeable about a community than its own residents?

Libraries have a democratic responsibility to make use of citizen participa-tion to provide improved library services. By combining citizen participation and community analysis, the library is reaching out to the community and fulfilling its democratic obligations, while at the same time, it is determining what information the community both needs and desires. Community study is an essential element in providing sound data which, with other data, can lead to library services that fulfill the information needs of the community. However, by using citizen participation to conduct community analysis, the library can also fulfill the four-fold purpose of gaining publicity, acquiring voluntary help, encouraging the direct expression of needs, and securing the involvement of the people in library affairs. This democratic process will benefit both the library and the community.

Sample Forms

The following forms can be used in either a small community or a large city. With some rewording the forms could be used in a variety of information environments, not just public libraries. The "Citizen survey" (figure 2.5) could be distributed in a variety of ways. "Highlights from a community survey" (figure 2.6) is a fictitious result used in a workshop on community analysis in a rural community (Plainsville, Colorado). The "Community profile" (figure 2.7) is also a fictitious example of the type of statistical data that can be easily collected. "Current collection analysis" (figure 2.8) illustrates a simple method for record-ing data about the existing library collection in the Plainsville Library. And the

"Analysis" (figure 2.9) form shows how the community analysis data and collection data can be combined to improve the library's collection and service.

The staff and directors of the Our Town Public Library are conducting this survey to evaluate library service and plan for the future. Your input would be greatly appreciated. Thank you.

1. Do you know the location of the Our Town Public Library?   yes   no

2. Have you ever used it?   yes   no

   If no, why not?

3. Is there another library you use regularly?   yes   no

   Which library?

   Why?

4. When is the last time you used the Our Town Public Library?

   _____ In the last week   _____ In the last six months
   _____ In the last month   _____ In the last year
   _____ In the last three months

5. Why do you usually come to the library?

   _____ Keeping up on a topic or   _____ Sports or recreation
         subject   _____ Personal or family health
   _____ Making or fixing something   _____ Government information (Social
   _____ My work or job   Security, council minutes, etc.)
   _____ A hobby   _____ To attend a program
   _____ Personal interests   _____ To bring my children
   _____ Class or course reading   _____ Other (Please specify)_____
   _____ A course paper or report   _____

6. How often do you find what you are looking for?

   _____ Less than 50% of the time
   _____ 50-75% of the time
   _____ More than 75% of the time

7. Which of these items have you used or checked out from the library?

   _____ paperback books   _____ magazines
   _____ records   _____ newspapers
   _____ cassettes   _____ children's toys
   _____ films   _____ cameras
   _____ videocassettes   _____ art prints
   _____ equipment loan   _____ maps

8. Which of these services have you used?

   _____ children's story time   _____ bookmobile
   _____ films or lectures   _____ referral to other places
   _____ books from other libraries   _____ adult tutoring
   _____ books by mail   _____ library books available at another
   _____ phoning the library to answer   place
         a reference question

9. What two things would increase your use of or satisfaction with the library?

____ open more hours   ____ more newspapers
____ more help with looking for   ____ more copies of popular books
     books and materials   ____ more children's books
____ more help answering questions   ____ more teen-agers' books
____ more programs   ____ more adult books
____ more magazines

Please specify any subject areas in which you would like more books (i.e., health, hobbies, science fiction, etc.).

_____

_____

10. What age group are you in?

____ Under 12   ____ 40-64
____ 13-18   ____ 65 +
____ 19-39

11. Sex   ____Male   ____Female

12. Occupation

____ Agricultural   ____ Military
____ Business/Professional   ____ Retail
____ Government   ____ Retired
____ Homemaker   ____ Student
____ Industry/Manufacturing   ____ Unemployed

13. What was your approximate household income last year?

____ $0-$9,999   ____ $35,000-$44,999
____ $10,000-$14,999   ____ $45,000 or more
____ $15,000-$24,999   ____ Don't know
____ $25,000-$34,999

14. Highest education level you have reached

____ Less than high school   ____ Some college
____ High school graduate   ____ College graduate

15. Number of people in your household ____

16. Number of library cardholders in your household ____

17. How long have you lived in Our Town?

____ All my life   ____ 5-10 years
____ 20 years or more   ____ less than 5 years
____ 10-20 years   ____ I don't live in Our Town

18. Part of town you live in *(In a large town, this could be the zip code. In a smaller town, it could be a small map, and people could indicate which section.)*

Thank you for taking time to answer this survey. Do you have any other comments or suggestions for us?

Fig. 2.5. Citizen survey. Used by permission of Barbara Doyle and Veronica Storey-Ewoldt.

Reasons for usually coming to the library:

    Leisure reading, fiction—39%
    Making/fixing something—11%
    My work or job—11%
    Hobbies/personal interests—9%
    School related—8%
    Sports and recreation—7%
    Personal or family health—7%
    Other—8%

Requested materials and/or services:

    More romance, mystery, westerns
    Open evenings and all day Saturday
    More magazines
    New children's books

Subject areas of greatest interest:

    Medicine
    Agriculture (general and animal husbandry)
    Home economics (cooking and nutrition, sewing, grooming, childrearing)
    Children's 300/500/600/fiction
    Sociology and anthropology

Fig. 2.6. Highlights from a community survey. Used by permission of Barbara Doyle and Veronica Storey-Ewoldt.

I. POPULATION DESCRIPTION
    1. Population

	10 years ago	Present	Anticipated in 10 years
City	7,500	8,000	9,000
County	11,000	12,000	11,500

Is your population growing? Decreasing? Transient? Stable?
decreasing slightly; pretty stable

    2. Demographics
        A. Age Levels

Under 5 13 %   19-39 35 %
5-12 6 %   40-64 27 %
13-18 8 %   65 + 11 %

        B. Family Structure
            Two adults, both work 18 %
            Two adults, one works 33 %
            Single adult, no children 12 %
            Single parent, children 3 %
            Retired 10 %
            Other 24 %

        C. Sex
            Male 40 %
            Female 60 %

        D. Racial Composition
            Black 1 %   White 93 %
            Hispanic 5 %   Other 1 %

            Are there notable changes over the past five to ten years?
            no
            Are there anticipated changes in the near future?
            no

    3. Education — years completed
        Fewer than high school 27 %   Some college 8 %
        High school graduate 60 %   College graduate 5 %

    4. Income
        Average family income $ 22,000
        Average income per person $11,000
        How does this compare with other communities the size of yours?
        slightly below

    5. Occupations

Agricultural	22 %	Military	0 %
Business/Professional	11 %	Retail	17 %
Government	7 %	Retired	3 %
Homemaker	15 %	Student	5 %
Industry/Manufacturing	18 %	Unemployed	2 %

Who are the major employers in your community?
junior college, container factory, hospital

Are there new businesses or industries coming into your community?
new shopping mall is in planning stages

II. ENVIRONMENTAL DESCRIPTION

6. Level of Library Support
    allotted annually from city budget
    Assessed valuation—city _____
    Assessed valuation—county _____
    Current mill levy _____ OR
    Mill rate equivalency _____
    Is property value increasing or decreasing?
    increasing a little

	Present	Five years ago
Annual library budget	$25,000	$20,000
Percentage allotted to staff	40% $10,000	$ 9,000 45%
Percentage allotted to materials	$ 2,000	8% $ 1,600 12.5%
Per capita materials allotment	$ 16¢	$ 14¢

    Is annual budget increasing or decreasing? increasing
    Is annual budget keeping pace with inflation? no

7. Educational Opportunities (Continuing or adult education programs, community schools, nonprofit institutes, colleges, etc.)
    continuing education classes and non-degree course-
    work at the junior college--they are beginning a mar-
    keting program directed at attracting more part time
    students

8. Social and Recreational Opportunities (Sports, clubs, associations)
    Lions, Elks, 4-H, Grangers, municipal softball
    leagues, rifle club, annual rodeo

9. Information Sources (Newspapers, other libraries, radio stations)
    local radio station, weekly newspaper, junior
    college library

10. Cultural Facilities (Art galleries, music)
    Historical Society Museum, art guild, town march-
    ing band

11. Churches (Number, denominations)
    about 25 churches, including Catholic, several
    Protestant denominations, Jehovah's Witnesses and
    Pentecostal

12. Institutions (Nursing homes, hospitals, prisons)
    hospitals, nursing homes, county jail

13. People:

    Governing officials

    Superintendent of schools

    Other visible leaders

    Other librarians in the community

14. Physical characteristics (Library accessibility via autos, public transportation; proximity to banks, grocery stores, etc.; transportation patterns)
    large county in terms of square miles; population is
    widely spread; library is located in center of small
    downtown area, next to the museum, one block from
    Safeway; library hours are 10-4, M-Th and 9-12 Sat.

Fig. 2.7. Community profile. Used by permission of Barbara Doyle and Veronica Storey-Ewoldt.

SUBJECT AREA	DEWEY NO.	ADULT						JUVENILE						YOUNG ADULT					
		% holdings	Median age	Availability	% of use	Age of circ	% of ILL	% holdings	Median age	Availability	% of use	Age of circ	% of ILL	% holdings	Median age	Availability	% of use	Age of circ	% of ILL
1. Fiction		40	'76	69	50	'84	.5	70	'78	40	65	'82	0	95	'80	100	9.8	'80	0
2. Agriculture (general)	630-639,710,712-716,718,719	.5	'68	99	.2	'71	1	.1	'67	100	0	–	0	0	–	–	–	–	0
--Animal Husbandry	636-638	.2	'70	50	4	'80	7	.2	'66	40	9	'69	0	0	–	–	–	–	0
3. Arts	700-709,717,720-	3	'80	85	3	'83	1	1	'80	50	2.1	'80	0	0	–	–	0	–	0
4. Biography	920-928	3	'72	50	5	'81	2	5	'69	70	2	'75	0	1	'81	100	–	–	0
5. Economics & Business	330-339,380-389	2	'81	69	2	'83	3	0	0	–	–	–	0	0	–	–	–	–	0
6. Education	370-379	2	'68	95	.5	'75	0	0	–	–	–	–	0	0	–	–	–	–	0
7. Engineering & Technology	600-699	2	'70	85	3	'83	6	.3	'78	70	2	'81	.5	0	–	–	–	–	0
8. Generalities	001-099	10	'72	98	.3	'65	0	10	'78	98	3	'80	0	0	–	–	–	–	0
9. History & Travel (N. America)		3	'78	91	.5	'79	.5	3	'78	72	3	'81	2	0	–	–	–	–	0
--Colorado History		.1	'69	89	.5	'72	1	0	–	–	–	–	0	0	–	–	–	–	0
10. History & Travel (Non-N. America)	900-916,918-919 929-969,980-999	4	'77	75	2	'80	.5	1	'79	70	2	'80	.1	0	–	–	–	–	0
11. Home Economics	640,643-645,648	2.5	'80	69	2	'82	0	0	–	–	–	–	0	0	–	–	–	–	0
--Cookery	641-642	3	'79	68	5	'81	.5	2	'53	98	.3	'80	0	1	'65	100	0	0	0
--Sewing & Grooming	646	.5	'75	90	.3	'79	0	2	'55	100	0	0	0	0	–	–	–	–	0
--Child Rearing & Home Care of Sick & Infirm	649	2	'82	80	2	'80	1	0	–	–	–	–	0	0	–	–	–	–	0

(Fig. 2.8 continues on page 58)

Subject Area	Dewey No.	ADULT % holdings	ADULT Median age	ADULT Availability	ADULT % of use	ADULT Age of circ	ADULT % of ILL	JUVENILE % holdings	JUVENILE Median age	JUVENILE Availability	JUVENILE % of use	JUVENILE Age of circ	JUVENILE % of ILL	YOUNG ADULT % holdings	YOUNG ADULT Median age	YOUNG ADULT Availability	YOUNG ADULT % of use	YOUNG ADULT Age of circ	YOUNG ADULT % of ILL
12. Language & Literature (English & General)	420-429,070-070.9	1	'70	95	.5	'82	0	1	'78	98	.5	'81	0	0	–	–	–	–	0
	800-829																		
13. Linguistics, Language	400-419,430-498	.5	'70	95	.2	'70	0	.1	'72	100	0	–	0	0	–	–	–	–	0
14. Literature (Non-English)	830-899	.5	'79	85	1	'83	2	.1	'78	95	1	'81	2	0	–	–	–	–	0
15. Medical Sciences	610,614,615-618	.5	'69	98	1.5	'80	1	.1	'78	100	1	'82	1	0	–	–	–	–	0
--Human Anatomy & Physiology	611-612	.6	'79	69	3	'81	1	.1	–	–	–	–	0	0	–	–	–	–	0
--Personal Health & Hygiene	613	.2	'77	95	.5	'80	.5	0	–	–	–	–	0	1	'81	60	.2	'81	0
16. Music	780-789	1.5	'75	82	.5	'75	1	.1	'75	100	.1	'79	1	0	–	–	–	–	0
17. Philosophy & Religion	100-299	4	'78	80	2	'81	.5	2	'76	87	1	'75	0	0	–	–	–	–	0
18. Politics & Government	320-351,353-359	.1	'80	100	1	'80	.1	.1	'73	81	2	'80	1	0	–	–	–	–	0
--Local Government	352	4	'78	69	3	'82	1	0	–	–	–	–	0	0	–	–	–	–	0
19. Psychology	130-139,150-159	4	'79	62	4	'81	1	.1	'79	89	1	'82	0	0	–	–	–	–	0
20. Recreation & Sports	790-799	2	'77	90	.5	'82	1	1.6	'79	60	4	'81	0	2	'82	60	90	'82	.1
21. Science	500-599	3.2	'82	80	2	'83	1	.2	'75	95	1	'78	1	0	–	–	–	–	0
22. Sociology & Anthropology	300-309,310-319							.1	'70	98	1	'72	1	0	–	–	–	–	0
	360-369,711,390-																		
	398																		

Fig. 2.8. Current collection analysis. Used by permission of Barbara Doyle and Veronica Storey-Ewoldt.

Plainsville, CO

Total volumes — 10,000

7,600	Adult	76%
2,300	Juvenile	23%
100	YA	1%

Each collection is analyzed separately not including reference or noncirculating items. Based on the community profile information, the following areas are questioned:

Adult:

Agriculture Questions:

— Collection is quite old — should be weeded and updated?
— Users are using old materials — but also requesting items on ILL. Because this is important area to community — should we increase acquisitions and attempt to meet more of their needs on site?

Sociology and Anthropology Questions:

— Should we decrease acquisitions in this area? Community college is open to public and strong in this area.
— Better to spend some of the $ on weaker areas of adult collection.

Fiction Questions:

— Major use of collection although readers prefer newer titles — need to allocate $ to keep new titles available?
— Low ILL — perhaps libraries will not lend or users do not want to wait?
— May need to weed old titles that have not circulated (69% available on shelf despite high circulation)?

Juvenile and YA:

23% of the collection for juveniles for 10% of population
1% for YA for 7% of population.

Questions:

— Does school take care of YA needs or are they not interested in library?
— Is too much going into juvenile fiction; and more attention to nonfiction areas?
— Do YAs use adult materials — should nonfiction collections be integrated?
— Median age of juvenile nonfiction is old — should be updated and weeded?
— YA use the sports books more than any other area — more attention to this area.
— perhaps fiction titles are not appropriate.

Fig. 2.9. Analysis. Used by permission of Barbara Doyle and Veronica Storey-Ewoldt.

Information Center Studies

Normally, the focus in the special library or information center environment is on small groups and individuals. Thus, the techniques described above, dealing with large groups, are not always appropriate for the library setting. Five basic methods are currently used to assess individual and small group information needs: activities, data analysis, decision making, problem solving, and empirical analysis. The *activities approach* uses an in-depth interview with the individual or group and has as its objective the outlining of all the activities of a typical day or project. What decisions are made, actions taken, topics discussed, letters or memos written and received, and forms processed are typical issues covered in the interview. The assumption is that the activities fall into a regular pattern, and once they are identified they can be translated into specific information requirements. One problem with this method is that people often forget important but infrequently performed tasks. Another drawback is people's tendency to overemphasize the most recent problems.

Data analysis is a "survey" method in that the investigator examines sources used and materials produced by the person or group being studied. This approach circumvents the problems of forgetfulness and the overemphasis on recent work. Reports, files, letters, and forms are studied to identify what information was used in their production. After finishing the examination, each item is discussed in some depth with the person(s) concerned in order to determine what uses were made of the consulted material in creating the new documents. Through this process it is possible both to identify unnecessary information sources in the system and to determine what needs are not being met.

Decision making is an approach similar to data analysis, but it focuses on the decision-making process. Again, the origin of information that was used to formulate the decision is examined; information that was received but not used is looked at as well. During the interview the cost of not having the right information or not having it as soon as required can also be explored. In the profit sector, either or both factors can have serious financial implications for the organization. *Problem solving* is similar, except that the focus is shifted to a different activity. A problem-solving activity frequently cuts across several departments or units and thus takes more time to complete. It can provide a better organizational picture more quickly than will the decision-making approach.

All of these methods are dependent upon the user providing accurate information about what was or was not used. *Empirical studies* are based upon observation of what is done, the user's behavior, and what is used. If a formal information center exists, experiments might be conducted by varying the location or removing the information sources to determine if the users' perceptions of value of an item (perhaps high or low use) are reflected in their behavior in using the item. (All of these techniques are covered in detail in the books listed on pp. 63-64, particularly those by F. W. Horton.)

Summary

Effective collection development is only possible when based upon a sound knowledge of service community. All types of libraries should engage in needs assessment. The suggestions for further reading provide items for each type of library.

Notes

[1]For a discussion of this problem see T. D. Wilson, "On User Studies and Information Needs," *Journal of Documentation* 37 (March 1981): 3-15.

[2]Ibid.

[3]Colin Mick, et al. "Toward Usable User Studies," *Journal of the American Society for Information Science* 31 (September 1980): 347-56.

[4]Douglas Zweizig, "Community Analysis," in *Local Public Library Administration*, 2d ed., ed. E. Altman (Chicago: American Library Association, 1980), 38-46.

[5]Michael Madden, "Marketing Survey Spinoff Library User/Nonuser Lifestyles," *American Libraries* 10 (February 1979): 78-81.

[6]G. J. Wahrheit, et al., *Planning for Change: Needs Assessment Approaches* (Rockville, Md.: Alcohol, Drug Abuse and Mental Health Administration, n.d.), 48.

[7]Ibid.

[8]Ibid.

[9]R. M. Kramer and H. Specht, *Readings in Community Organization Practice*, 2d ed. (Englewood Cliffs, N.J.: Prentice-Hall, 1975), 6.

[10]G. Brager and H. Specht, *Community Organizing* (New York: Columbia University Press, 1969), 34.

[11]Lowell Martin, "User Studies and Library Planning," *User Trends* 24 (January 1976): 483-96.

Further Reading

General

Brager, G., and H. Specht. *Community Organizing.* New York: Columbia University Press, 1969.

Chen, C., and P. Hernon. *Information Seeking: Assessing and Anticipating User Needs.* New York: Neal-Schuman, 1982.

"Community Analysis and Libraries," edited by L. Bone. *Library Trends* 24 (January 1976): 429-643.

Kramer, R. M., and H. Specht. *Readings in Community Organization Practice,* 2d ed. Englewood Cliffs, N.J.: Prentice-Hall, 1975.

Krikeles, J. "Information-seeking Behavior: Patterns and Concepts." *Drexel Library Quarterly* 19 (Spring 1985): 5-20.

Rouse, W. B., and S. H. Rouse. "Human Information Seeking and Design of Information Systems." *Information Processing and Management* 20 (1984): 129-38.

Wilson, T. D. "On User Studies and Information Needs." *Journal of Documentation* 37 (March 1981): 3-15.

Academic

Association of Research Libraries. Office of Management Studies. *User Studies.* Washington, D.C.: Association of Research Libraries, 1984.

Govan, J. F. "Community Analysis in an Academic Environment." *Library Trends* 24 (January 1976): 541-56.

"Information for the Management of Higher and Further Education." *Aslib Proceedings* 36 (November/December 1984): 411-35.

Okazawa, K. "Information Needs and Uses of Scholars in the Humanities." *Library and Information Science* 21 (1983): 29-48.

Roberts, S. A. "Management and Development of Information and Library Provision in the Social Sciences." *Journal of Documentation* 40 (June 1984): 94-119.

Public

Engel, D. "Putting the Public First: The Baltimore County Approach to Collection Development." *Catholic Library World* 54 (October 1982): 122-26.

Jordan, P., and E. Walley. *Learning about the Community: A Guide for Public Librarians*. Leeds, England: Leeds Polytechnic, School of Librarianship, 1977.

Madden, M. "Lifestyles of Library Users and Nonusers." *University of Illinois Graduate School of Library Science Occasional Papers*, no. 137. Urbana, Ill.: Graduate School of Library Science, 1979.

Martin, L. "User Studies and Library Planning." *Library Trends* 24 (January 1976): 483-96.

Palmour, V. E., M. C. Bellassai, and N. DeWath. *A Planning Process for Public Libraries*. Chicago: American Library Association, 1980.

Warncke, R. "Analyzing Your Community." *Illinois Libraries* 57 (February 1975): 64-76.

Warren, R. L. *Studying Your Community*. New York: Russell Sage Foundation, 1955.

Webb, T. D. "Hierarchy of Public Library User Types." *Library Journal* 111 (15 September 1986): 47-50.

Zweizig, D. "Community Analysis." In *Local Public Library Administration*, 2d ed., edited by E. Altman, 38-46. Chicago: American Library Association, 1980.

School

Kaufman, R., and F. English. *Needs Assessment*. Englewood Cliffs, N.J.: Educational Technology Publications, 1979.

Liesner, J. *A Systematic Process for Planning Media Programs*. Chicago: American Library Association, 1976.

Stroud, J. G., and D. V. Loertscher. "User Needs and School Library Service." *Catholic Library World* 49 (November 1977): 162-65.

Special

Horton, F. W. *How to Harness Information Resources*. Cleveland, Ohio: Association for Systems Management, 1974.

_____. *Information Management Workbook*. Washington, D.C.: Information Management Press, 1983.

Mick, C., G. N. Lindsey, and D. Callahan. "Toward Usable User Studies." *Journal of the American Society for Information Science* 31 (September 1980): 347-56.

Mullings, C., et al. *Manual of the Investigation of Local Government Information Needs*. London: British Library, 1981.

Rowland, J. F. B. "Scientist's View of His Information System." *Journal of Documentation* 38 (March 1982): 38-42.

Pruett, N. J. *Scientific and Technical Libraries*, vol. 1, 50-62. Orlando, Fla.: Academic Press, 1986.

Warheit, G. J., R. A. Bell, and J. Schwab. *Planning for Change: Needs Assessment Approaches*. Rockville, Md.: Alcohol, Drug Abuse and Mental Health Administration, n.d.

3
Collection Development Policies

Collection development policies, selection policies, acquisition policies — are they all one and the same? Given the definitions in chapter 1, it is obvious they are not. However, many librarians use the terms interchangeably. Some of the same information in policies is variously identified as a collection development, a selection, or an acquisition policy, assuming that the library has a written policy. One library school professor who teaches collection development tells her classes, "On the first day you go to work in collection development ask to see the written policy so you can study it. When they tell you they don't have one, faint. By the way, you need to practice fainting and falling so you don't hurt yourselves — not many libraries have written collection development policies." In the mid-1980s this may be somewhat less true than it was 10 years ago; however, a great many libraries still do not have any written guidelines, much less a formal policy.

What Are Collection Development Policies?

Although selection and acquisition policy statements may contain most of the information to be found in a good collection development policy, they tend not to include some important items. As stated previously, the definition of collection development is the process of making certain that the information needs of the people are met in a timely and economical manner, using information resources produced both inside and outside of the organization. Effective collection development requires creating a plan to correct any weaknesses in and maintain the strengths of the collection. A collection development policy is the written statement of that plan, providing details for the guidance of the library staff. Thus a policy statement is a document representing a plan of action and information that is used to guide the staff's thinking and decision making; specifically, the policy is consulted when considering in which subject areas to acquire material and deciding how much emphasis each area should receive.

Why is it that libraries frequently do not update their collection development policy or do not have one at all? One of the major reasons is that a good policy statement must be based on a great deal of data. It is necessary to know (1) the strengths and weaknesses of the collection; (2) the community being served and where that community is going; and (3) other resources available locally (to patrons) and those accessible through interlibrary loan. Only when all of this knowledge is in hand is it possible to start developing a policy.

People can and do point out that there are thousands of libraries and information centers with excellent, even outstanding, collections, that have no written policy. Some element of good fortune is required to have developed an excellent collection without one—good fortune in the sense that the individuals charged with the responsibility of building the collection are highly intelligent and motivated by a deep commitment to both the library and its collections. As a result, they stay at that library for most if not all of their careers and have an extensive knowledge of what is in the collection and of the needs of their service community. In talking to these people one finds that they *do* have a plan and a policy, even though it is not on paper.

While it is still possible for the situation above to occur today, it is not very probable. In the United States, career development in librarianship generally involves moving from one library to another, and occasionally changing the type of library. Another factor is the growth in the number of libraries, even of "instant libraries," as a 1986 advertisement in an American library publication illustrates—a 15,000-title "opening day collection" was sought. Rapid development without a policy and a plan is not likely to lead to an excellent collection. The problem is often a lack of continuity in both staff and funding. A written policy helps assure some continuity and consistency in the collecting program even though there are changes in staff and funding.

Another reason policies are lacking is that they require a great deal of thought. A policy needs to change to reflect a changing community and, therefore, the librarian's thinking and data collecting are never finished. Some librarians say it is not worth the trouble: as soon as the plan is on paper, the situation has changed so much that the plan is out-of-date—so why bother?

Why bother? A policy statement can provide a framework within which individuals can exercise their own judgment. Unless the library has a dictatorial style of management, its collection development work will involve a number of persons at any one time and a great many throughout the history of the library. Whenever a number of persons set policy without written guidelines, slightly different views of the library's purpose will probably emerge. *Without* written statements the divergence of opinion can be confusing; *with* a policy statement everyone has a central reference point. Differences in opinion can be discussed with some hope that a basic understanding, if not agreement, can be reached. In a school media center setting, differences of opinion about what should or should not be in the collection can and do lead to the courtroom rather than the classroom.

In an academic situation with faculty in charge of selection, numerous points of view come into play. For example, four different anthropology professors might be selectors over four successive years. Lacking a policy statement, each professor would be free to, and sometimes would, buy heavily in a particular area of personal interest. The result might be one year of almost exclusive purchasing of North American ethnology, one of Bantu studies, one of physical anthropology, and one of Oceanic material. In this way the entire field is covered, given enough changes in selectors. The problem is that many fields are completely ignored and are likely to remain so for many years. A professor may not stay long enough to fully develop an area, with the result that the library cannot claim strength in any area. If the professors have full authorization for the selection process, the library can do little to keep a bad situation under control.

Admittedly, a written policy statement will not completely solve this problem, because selectors normally have the authority to make the final decisions. However, if the library has a document outlining the fields in which coverage is required, the policy can serve as a reminder that areas other than the selector's favorites must also be considered. Even the small public library will find that having a written policy is useful, especially if there is community involvement in its approval, if not in its preparation.

A policy statement thus performs the following functions:

1. It informs everyone about the nature and scope of the collection.

2. It informs everyone of collecting priorities.

3. It forces thinking about organizational goals to be met by the collection.

4. It generates some degree of commitment to meeting organizational goals.

5. It sets standards for inclusion and exclusion.

6. It reduces the influence of a single selector and personal biases.

7. It provides a training/orientation tool for new staff.

8. It helps ensure a degree of consistency over time and despite staff turnover.

9. It guides staff in handling complaints.

10. It aids in weeding and evaluating the collection.

11. It aids in rationalizing budget allocations.

12. It provides a public relations document.

13. It provides a means of assessing overall performance of the collection development program.

14. It provides outsiders with information about the purpose of collection development (an accountability tool).

A final point is that a policy statement can be a useful means of communication with the patron. While a complete policy statement runs to many pages, something that few patrons would care to read, a summary of its major points can be a valuable information tool. This is especially true if the patrons have had some say in the formation of the policy.

Elements of a Collection Development Policy

What are the elements that ought to go into a good collection development statement? The following list of elements illustrates why policy formulation is so time consuming, but also why it is so critical to success. (Once the basic work has been done and the policy has been written, keeping the policy up-to-date is not a monumental problem; updating does take time, but if it is done annually, it is almost painless.) The elements can be divided into three parts: overview, details, and miscellaneous. Certainly all American libraries should consult *Guidelines for Collection Development* (American Library Association, 1979). Anyone reading that document will see a strong parallel with what follows; however, some additional considerations are identified.

Element One — Overview

The first element should be a very clear statement of overall institutional objectives in regard to the library. Statements such as "geared to serve the information needs of the community" have little value or concrete meaning. In order to ensure that the statement is of help to the selectors and has specific meaning, all of the following factors should be present in the first section of the statement:

1. A brief general description of the community to be served (town, country, school, business, etc.). What is the general make-up of the community and where is it going? If a thorough community analysis has been made (see chapter 2), this part of the policy and many of the following sections will be very easy to prepare.

2. Specific identification of the clientele to be served. Anyone who walks in the door? Probably not, or at least they probably will not be served at the same level as the primary clientele. Who are the primary clientele? Is it all citizens of the local area, all staff and students of the educational institution, all employees of the business? Will the library serve others? If so, to what degree? Will the service to others be free or will there be a fee? Are there to be differences in service for different groups, for example adults, children, faculty, or students? Must the patron come to the library? Will there be service for the handicapped, the institutionalized, users with less-than-average reading ability or other communication problems? There are no universal answers for these questions and many others that might be listed regarding the clientele to be served. There is only a right answer for a particular library at a particular time, and this "right" answer will change over time.

3. A general statement regarding the parameters of the collection. What subject fields will be represented? Are there any limitations set on the types of format that the library will acquire — just printed materials, such as books, periodicals, and newspapers? What are the limits in audiovisual areas? This section should provide an overview of the details that are specified in the second major element of the policy.

4. A detailed description of the types of programs or patron needs that are to be met by the collection. In a public library, to what degree is the total collection to be oriented toward educational purposes — that is, toward the support of formal educational programs and self-education? Will recreational needs be met and to what degree? Is the collection to be a circulation (loan) collection, or is it for reference purposes only? Academic libraries also need to be concerned with the degree of emphasis to be placed on research material. In the special library, all of these questions may have to be considered.

5. A section on the general limitations and priorities that will determine how the collection will be developed. To what degree will the library collect retrospective materials? One very important issue to cover in this section of the policy is whether the library will buy duplicate copies of an item; if so, what factors will be used to determine the number of copies and how long will the duplicates be retained? The question of duplicates is complicated and difficult. One excellent book that can be of great value in deciding the duplicate question is Michael Buckland's *Book Availability and the Library Users* (Pergamon Press, 1975). This is one of the essential books for members and potential members of a collection development staff to read.

6. A detailed discussion of the library's role in cooperative collection development programs. To be effective, this section must leave no doubt in a reader's mind as to whether the basic philosophy is one of self-sufficiency or cooperation. If the reader is in doubt, it means either that the writer(s) did not want to make a decision on this very critical issue or that they wanted to avoid taking a public stand. Furthermore, if the library is involved in cooperative programs, this section should identify those programs in which participation is to be active and those areas for which the library has a major responsibility. For subject areas not of major concern, the reader should be told where to find those who do have responsibility for their collection.

Element Two — Details of Subject Areas and Formats Collected

It is necessary to break down the collection into its constituent subject areas, identify each type of material to be collected, and specify the class of patron for which this area is primarily intended. This may sound like a lot of work — it is. The information specialist must spend hours talking to patrons about the problem and then spend many more hours thinking about the information.

Priorities must then be assigned to each area (perhaps even by format within each area)—all of this with an eye toward achieving a proper balance of subjects, and taking into account the particular community of users and their needs. The following is a reasonably comprehensive listing of patrons and formats to consider; there is no point in trying to list subjects.

Patrons

Adults
Young adults
School-aged children
Preschool children
Physically handicapped (blind, partially sighted, wheelchair patients, etc.)
Shut-ins and institutionalized persons (in hospitals, homes, prisons, etc.)
Teaching faculty
Researchers
Staff
Undergraduate students
Postgraduate students
Alumni

Formats

Books (hard- or paperbound, monographs, textbooks)
Newspapers
Periodicals
Microforms
Slides
Films and filmstrips
Pictures
Audio recordings (tapes and records)
Video recordings (tapes and discs)
Printed music
Pamphlets
Manuscripts and archival material
Maps
Government documents
Laser formats
Realia
Games
Specimens
Databases

Although these lists are fairly extensive, they are by no means complete; formats constantly change. The lists do provide, though, a rather clear picture of the magnitude of the project, especially when each subject consideration is further subdivided. Although this may indeed seem too time consuming, not all of the categories, formats, or subjects will be considered for any one library.

The setting of priorities, or levels of collecting intensity, can be handled in a number of ways. The ALA guidelines suggest a five-level system—comprehensive, research, study, basic, and minimal. The Research Library Group (RLG), made up of a number of large research libraries in the United States, developed a "conspectus" which is intended to serve several purposes. The Association of Research Libraries (ARL) has adopted the conspectus as well. It helps in formulating a collection policy because it forces a detailed subject analysis (through the use of the Library of Congress Classification System) and is the "subject" guide which indicates both current collecting levels and existing collection strength. RLG uses a numeric coding system for identifying collection strength: 0 (out of scope, not collected), 1 (minimal), 2 (basic information), 3 (instructional support), 4 (research), and 5 (comprehensive). (Chapters 15 and 16 contain additional information about the conspectus.) At the Library of Congress a four-level system is employed: minimal, reference, research, and comprehensive.

One complaint about these systems has been that they seem designed for academic libraries. That was certainly not the intent of the ALA committee that prepared the guidelines, but it is true that most of the systems are geared to the needs of the large collection, which in turn tends to mean academic libraries. In Colorado, an effort was made to tie together all the libraries in the state through the State Library, the Colorado Academic Library Committee, and the Colorado Alliance of Research Libraries. A subcommittee designed a standardized set of collection intensity codes. One version, reproduced in figure 3.1, attempted to define levels for both educational and public libraries. Although no longer used, it does provide an example of how libraries of differing types might use the same levels and definitions.

Once the detailed subject information is available (a complete conspectus), a selector can focus attention on the items appropriate for the collection. Policy statements are only guidelines, with ample room for individual interpretation, but they do narrow the scope of a person's work. Combine the subject intensity section with the patron list and format listing—the result is a solid framework on which to build a sound collection.

Most subject areas will fall into the middle intensity ranges. Most libraries will have only one or two topics in the upper levels; such categories will be highly restricted in most instances to one person (e.g., Goethe) or narrow topic (e.g., pre-Colombian writing systems).

The second part of this element will probably be short but it is very important: it identifies where responsibility for collection development lies. Ultimate responsibility, of course, lies with the head of the library, as it does for all library activities; however, no one expects the head librarian actually to do all of the tasks for which he or she is responsible. Since the collections are important to the success of the library's programs, the question of who will actually develop them is a vital one. This must be decided upon after careful examination of the needs of the library. This section of the policy, then, should contain a clear statement of who will be responsible for selection, what guidelines are to be used, and how the selector's performance is to be evaluated. Media center selection responsibility must be clearly identified because of possible conflicts over control of the collection. The most recent U.S. Supreme Court ruling regarding the content of media center collections (the *Island Trees* case, which is discussed in chapter 19) limited the power of school boards to add, remove, or limit access to materials.

Level	Description		Collecting Scope
	Academic	Public	
0 Out of Scope	--	--	--
1 Basic Information	General "community" support; no courses, except basic introductory study.	Basic introductory level limited in depth; material provides general overview.	a. Dictionaries, encyclopedias, general reference materials, basic bibliographies. b. Selected editions of important works. c. Selected major periodicals.
2 General Support	Undergraduate curriculum through first degree; some honors work, no sustained independent study.	Working collection— moderately advanced. Prior familiarity with subject—beyond introductory level. Meets general community needs.	a.-c. d. Wide range of basic monographs, complete collections of more important authors, selections from secondary writers. e. Selection of representative journals. f. Fundamental bibliographic apparatus in subject fields, broad reference collections, including major abstracts and indexing tools.
3 Introductory Research	Through Master's level, including senior seminars and independent study.	Comprehensive in-depth treatment of a subject. Analytical or technical, theoretical or scholarly orientated. Support special user group in community, but covers wide spectrum of users.	a.-f. g. Extensive monographic collections, including published primary source material, reprints, complete critical works of important authors, broad collections of secondary writers. h. Wide range of professional journals, congresses and proceedings. i. Specialized bibliographies, indexes, and abstracts.

Level	Description		Collecting Scope
	Academic	Public	
4 Advanced Research	Through Ph.D. level.	Extensive coverage of subject. Meet needs of highly specific and specialized portion of community. Highly specialized collections.	a.-i. j. Major retrospective collections, research reporting, experimental results, comprehensive current monograph collecting. k. Extensive collections of specialized serials and technical reports. l. Representative foreign language holdings. m. Selective manuscript collections, complete bibliographic support tools.
5. Comprehensive	Programs of national recognition.	Programs of national recognition.	a.-m. n. Large foreign language collections. o. Complete retrospective serial holdings. p. Recognized special collections and manuscript collections of important authors.
6. Exhaustive	Programs of international recognition.	Programs of international recognition.	a.-p. q. Collects as far as possible, all significant works of recorded knowledge.

(Language Coverage Codes for figure 3.1 appear on page 74.)

Fig. 3.1. Colorado collecting intensities codes.

Fig. 3.1. — *Continued*

Language Coverage Codes

E - English language material predominates; little or no foreign language material in the collection.

F - Selected foreign language material included, primarily Western European, in addition to the English language material.

W- Wide selection of foreign language material in addition to the English language material.

Y - Material is primarily in one foreign language.

Intensity Codes:

Are descriptive values assigned to a collection to determine its relationship to other collections in the state and nation. They are used to identify both the extent of existing codes in a subject field (collection density) and extent of current collecting activity in the field (collecting intensity).

Assumptions:

Definitions of collecting levels are not to be applied in a relative or ad hoc manner (that is, relative to a given library or group of libraries), but in a very objective manner. Consequently, it is quite likely that a large number of libraries will not hold comprehensive collections in any area. Similarly, academic libraries that do not support doctoral programs, or other types of libraries that are not oriented toward special research, may not have any collections that would fall within the research level as defined herein. The definitions are proposed to describe a range and diversity of titles and forms of materials; they do not address the question of availability of multiple copies of the same title.

Who Shall Select?

1. Patrons/users

2. Librarians from public service areas, with no special background or training beyond basic library education

3. Librarians from technical service areas — no special background or training beyond basic library education

4. Subject or service specialists, with special advance training in subject or service areas

5. Department heads

6. Head librarian

How Shall They Select?

1. Independent selectors, with or without a systematic alerting program from the library

2. Committees

3. Centrally prepared list from which selections are made

A few generalizations may be made about differences between types of libraries. Many exceptions to these generalizations exist, but a pattern is apparent in most areas. Educational institution libraries tend to have a higher patron (teachers and students) involvement and greater use of subject specialists than is found in public libraries. Special or technical libraries are often staffed with librarians who have advanced training in the field in which the library specializes, and they, with the frequent assistance of patrons, are responsible for selection. Public libraries normally use librarians (often department heads) from public service areas as selectors, working through selection committees or from lists prepared by a central agency.

When nonlibrarians have an active voice in selection matters, it is usually limited to the working or circulating collection. The library staff normally has the sole responsibility for the reference collection. Patrons tend to be more concerned with current items, books, and monographs, while librarians will also be heavily involved in retrospective buying and in serial and "other media" selection. Allocation of selection responsibility in any given library will depend upon the type of library and the local conditions. Whatever is decided, it should be put in writing so that there will be no question where the responsibility and accountability lie.

Finally, this section should provide some general guidelines concerning what, or what not, to select. Normally, such written guidelines are more important in public library and school media center situations, because usually a wider range of interests is involved, and there is a great deal of concern about the impact of the collection upon the children and young adults using it. Some examples of guideline criteria statements follow:

1. Select and replace items found in standard lists and catalogs.

2. Select only those items that have been favorably reviewed in at least two review sources.

3. Do not select anything that has received a negative review.

4. Try to provide both, or all, points of view on a controversial subject.

5. Do not select textbooks.

6. Do not select items of a sensational, violent, or inflammatory nature.

7. Select only items of lasting literary or social value.

The list could go on and on; however, most of the statements are in fact only variations of the selection criteria discussed in chapters 6, 7, and 8, and do not need to be repeated here. Whatever criteria are used, they should be clearly delineated in this section of the statement.

Element Three — Miscellaneous Issues

The term miscellaneous may cause this section to appear to be of less importance; this is not the case. Each of the subtopics in this section is important, but none of them needs to be very long; nor are they interrelated in the same manner as are the first two elements. Five topics are encompassed by this element: gifts, weeding and discards (deselection), replacements, evaluation and complaints, and censorship.

Gifts

Gifts should not be added to the collection on any other basis than that which is used for items that are purchased. The librarian should resist the temptation to add an item because it is free. No donated item is free — processing costs are the same whether the item is donated or purchased. Expending library resources to add something to the collection just because it is free, when it is not essential to the library's purpose, is a very poor practice. Applying the same standards to gifts as to purchased items will greatly reduce weeding problems.

The policy on handling gifts should be put in writing. The statement must make it clear whether only those items that should be added to the collection will be accepted or if anything will be taken with the proviso that unwanted items may be disposed of in any manner the library sees fit. Equally important is a statement regarding gifts with "strings." Will the library accept a private collection and house it separately if the donor provides the funds? Will it accept funds earmarked for certain classes of materials and use them to acquire new materials? If the collection is to be expanded through gifts and endowment monies, who will be responsible for this activity? Will it be coordinated? These are some of the major questions that should be addressed in a section on gifts.

Gifts and endowment monies are excellent means of developing a collection when and if the library has maximum freedom in their use. A very important public relations question must be answered: Is it better to accept all gifts, regardless of the conditions attached to them, or should the library avoid conditional gifts? If there is a clearly reasoned statement as to why gifts with conditions are not accepted, there should be no public relations problem.

Weeding and Discards

Weeding and discarding materials need to be discussed separately. The level and type of weeding program will vary from library to library, but all libraries will have to face this issue eventually. (Even the largest libraries must decide on what materials will be stored in less accessible facilities.) Chapter 14 provides a fairly detailed discussion of this issue. Once such issues as the criteria, scope, frequency, and purpose of weeding have been decided upon, these decisions should be incorporated into the policy statement. At the present time the question seldom arises for anything but books, except in media centers and public libraries where other media are in high demand (for example, audio and video recordings). Multiple copies of bestseller and high-demand books are an issue in most public and educational libraries. To some extent the McNaughton Plan (short-term rental) can alleviate some of the problem for popular (mass market) titles. Such plans help reduce the cost of popular titles and long-term storage problems of books in high demand for only a short period of time; however, they do not resolve the question of how many extra copies to acquire. There are no easy solutions to the problem of extra textbooks unless a library has a low-cost rental system. Some possible guideline statements would be: "Buy one copy for every ten potential readers during a six-month period"; "Buy one copy for the general collection and acquire one copy for every five readers during x months for the high use or rental collection." Of course, the length of time, number of readers, etc., will be determined by local conditions.

Evaluation

Evaluation is an essential element in collection development. Chapter 15 outlines the major issues and needs to be mentioned in the policy. Indication should be made of whether evaluation will be only for internal purposes (i.e., identifying collection strengths and weaknesses) or for comparative purposes—or perhaps as a review of how well the selectors have been doing their job. Each purpose is different and requires different evaluation techniques or emphases. Making decisions about the how and who of evaluation ahead of time, putting them in writing, and getting them approved will save time and trouble for staff, patrons, funding agencies, and governing bodies.

Complaints and Censorship

The final section of the collection development policy statement can save time and trouble by outlining the steps to be taken in handling complaints about the collection. Eventually, every library will receive complaints about what is or is not in the collection. Naturally it is easier to handle questions about what is not there. (A library can always try to buy a missing item.) The major problem will be complaints about what is in the collection or questions as to why the policy says what it does.

An irate patron on the other side of the desk, who is livid because this "terrible" item has been purchased, can cause many problems. How does one reduce the person's anger? One solution is a "cop-out" — pass the buck to the supervisor. Such buck-passing does nothing to calm an upset patron; if anything it tends to increase that person's level of frustration. Lacking guidelines, however, it is dangerous to try to solve the problem alone. Normally the patron wants the offending item taken out of the collection, which is patron censorship.

A librarian should not promise to remove the item. He or she can and should agree to review it if the library has an established review procedure. It is necessary to identify who, how, and when the review will be handled. One method of doing this is to have a form for the patron to fill out concerning the offending item. While this tends to be a "bureaucratic" approach, it does help everyone to identify the specific problem. Such forms normally consist of two parts, one explaining the library's review procedure, the other asking the patron to identify specifically the offending sections or qualities of the questioned item (see chapter 19 for further discussion). At times this approach only increases anger; but since the librarian is offering to do something, more often than not the patron becomes less angry.

There are other alternatives, but whatever the library is going to do about complaints should be decided upon before the first complaint. Ad hoc decisions in this area can cause a library to have a great deal of trouble with its community. Consistency is not always a good thing, but in this area the merits far outweigh the drawbacks. As with weeding, whatever decisions are reached after due consideration of the basic issues should be incorporated into the written collection development policy.

Getting the Policy Approved

It should now be clear why the process of preparing a comprehensive collection development policy statement is thought to be very time consuming. If the staff — and it should be the library staff — has spent the time preparing a comprehensive policy, it is important that it be approved by the library's governing board. With board approval everyone has a set of agreed-upon ground rules for building a collection serving the local community.

An ideal policy development process would consist of the following:

1. The head librarian appoints a staff committee to draft a basic policy statement, which is to be submitted to the head librarian.

2. The head librarian reviews and comments on the draft and distributes it to the library staff for their comments and suggestions.

3. The original committee then incorporates the comments and suggestions into a revised, final statement. Perhaps a general meeting will be needed to discuss the interim draft before the final version is prepared.

4. The final draft statement is presented to the governing board for review, possible revision, and eventually, approval.

5. Another valuable step can be taken between board review and final approval. That step is to hold an open meeting for patrons to hear about and comment upon the proposed policy. Members of the drafting committee, the head librarian, and representatives of the governing board should be present to explain, describe, and if necessary, defend and modify the statement.

6. The final step is to prepare multiple copies of the final statement for the library staff and those patrons desiring a copy. A good public relations device is to prepare a brief condensed version for distribution to each new user of the library.

These steps can ensure community, staff, and administrative consensus about issues before a problem arises. It is much easier to agree theoretically on evaluation procedures, review procedures, levels and areas of collecting, and so on, in advance than to try to handle them in the heat of a specific disagreement. It also means that later disagreements can be more easily resolved as there is a body of previously established and agreed-upon rules.

Summary

Is all the work that must go into a policy statement really worth it? It is! Collection development is a complex process, highly subjective, and filled with problems and traps for the unwary. A comprehensive written policy, developed with the advice and involvement of all parties concerned, helps to make the process much less ad hoc and, therefore, less problem filled.

Further Reading

General

Collins, J., and R. Finer. *National Acquisition Policies and Systems*. London: British Library, 1982.

Dowd, S. T. "Formulation of a Collection Development Policy Statement." In *Collection Development in Libraries: A Treatise*, pt. A, edited by R. D. Stueart and G. B. Miller, 67-87. Greenwich, Conn.: JAI Press, 1980.

Evans, R. W. "Collection Development Policy Statements." *Collection Management* 7 (Spring 1985): 63-73.

Futas, E. "Issues in Collection Building: Why Collection Development Policies." *Collection Building* 3, no. 1 (1981): 58-60.

_____. *Library Acquisition Policies and Procedures*. 2d ed. Phoenix, Ariz.: Oryx Press, 1984.

Guidelines for Collection Development. Edited by D. L. Perkins. Chicago: American Library Association, 1979.

Perkins, D. L. "Writing the Collection Development Manual." *Collection Management* 4 (Fall 1982): 37-47.

Academic

Bryant, B. "Collection Development Policies in Medium-sized Academic Libraries." *Collection Building* 2, no. 3 (1980): 6-26.

Cargill, J. S. "Bridging the Gap between Acquisitions and Public Services." *Library Acquisitions: Practice and Theory* 3, no. 1 (1979): 29-31.

Donahue, M. K., et al. "Collection Development Policy Making." *Collection Building* 6 (Fall 1984): 18-21.

Farrell, D. "North American Collections Inventory Project (NCIP)." In *Coordinating Cooperative Collection Development*, edited by W. Luquire, 37-48. New York: Haworth Press, 1986.

Gwinn, N. E., and P. H. Mosher. "Coordinating Collection Development, the RLG Conspectus." *College & Research Libraries* 44 (March 1980): 128-40.

Hellenga, R. R. "Departmental Acquisitions Policies for Small College Libraries." *Library Acquisitions: Practice and Theory* 3, no. 2 (1979): 81-84.

Public

Bartle, F. R., and W. L. Brown. "Book Selection Policies for Public Libraries." *Australian Library Journal* 32 (August 1983): 5-13.

Fergusson, D. G. "You Can't Tell the Players without a Program (Policy)." *North Carolina Libraries* 41 (Summer 1983): 80-83.

Giblon, D. L. "Materials Selection Policies and Changing Adult Needs." *Catholic Library World* 53 (Fall 1982): 288-89.

Root, N. J. "Decision Making for Collection Management." *Collection Management* 7 (Spring 1985): 93-101.

School

Adams, H. R. "Media Policy Formulation and Adoption in a Small School District." *Wisconsin Library Bulletin* 77 (Spring 1981): 11-13.

_____. *School Media Policy Development*. Littleton, Colo.: Libraries Unlimited, 1986.

Hardesty, V. H. "Selection Protection." *Indiana Media Journal* 7 (Summer 1985): 5-9.

Hunter, D. "Accessibility to Media in the School Library." *Catholic Library World* 53 (Fall 1982): 378-79.

School Library and Media Center Acquisition Policies and Procedures. Edited by Mary M. Taylor. Phoenix, Ariz.: Oryx Press, 1981.

Special

Collins, J., and R. Finer. "National Acquisition Policies and Systems." *Interlending Review* 10 (October 1982): 111-18.

Mulliner, B. K. "Library of Congress Acquisitions Policies." *Library Acquisitions: Practice and Theory* 6, no. 2 (1982): 103-6.

Tees, M. H. "Special Libraries in the 1980s." *Show-Me Libraries* 33 (October 1981): 33-36.

4

Selection Process: Theory

A central issue in the selection process is whether selection should be made primarily for quality or for use. Is it an either/or situation? If not, what is the best blend, or how can the two concepts be blended? At one extreme, some librarians say that a library is the primary means of raising the literary awareness of the community and therefore should contain only the "best" literature. At the opposite end of the spectrum, other librarians claim that a library is a public institution supported by tax monies and therefore the public should be able to find whatever materials it needs and wants. Of course, another factor is the organizational environment in which the information service occurs. Different environments call for more or less "selection." In many situations it is merely acquiring those items identified as needed by the users.

Quality versus Demand

Community demand as the basis for library collection development was most thoroughly outlined in Lionel McColvin's *The Theory of Book Selection for Public Libraries.* His premises, and those of most librarians who support this concept, are that:

1. public libraries are established in response to, and in anticipation of, demand;

2. the process of book selection involves both supply and demand: the library's function is to discover and assess community demand, then to satisfy those demands.[1]

To some extent, McColvin's premises can be applied to any type of library, not just to public libraries.

Advocates of quality selection find excellent support in Helen Haines's work, *Living with Books.* Haines was concerned with all types of libraries, although many people tend to think of her book as oriented toward the public library. Her basic premise is that a librarian selects books that will develop and enrich the lives of the persons being served by the library. Obviously, this requires an extensive literary background, including a comprehensive knowledge of the "foundation" or "classic" works. Demand is to be met by selecting the highest quality books. She assumes that people exhibit demands (needs) both for ephemeral materials (which can be supplied in other ways) and for materials from "deeper life channels."[2]

No one takes an extreme position on this fundamental issue, so an either/or situation does not really exist. Many individuals, however, are closer to one end or the other of the continuum than they are to the middle. Where a librarian will fall on that continuum will depend upon his or her beliefs about library service and the community the library is serving. Thus, at the very outset of the discussion of selection, we are confronted with one essential fact about the process: it is a highly personal, highly subjective activity.

A brief historical review of some of the major monographs on book selection and collection development will provide a good overview of the basic issues, selection criteria, and how these factors have changed through time. Starting with Lionel McColvin (1925) and ending with Richard Gardner (1981), we will examine sixty years of writing on book selection. Although monographs (at least in librarianship) seldom represent the first appearance of a concept, textbooks generally attempt to summarize developments and reflect thinking on the subject that is current at the time of publication. The works covered are the major ones and are international in scope.

Lionel R. McColvin— *The Theory of Book Selection for Public Libraries* (1925)[3]

As already noted, McColvin was one of the first persons to write a major text on book selection and to advocate the principle that libraries respond to the demands of their communities. McColvin made two assumptions about collection development. First, public libraries (unlike private, national, or general research libraries) are established in response to and in anticipation of demand; their "service" is derived from demand. He further assumed that the process of book selection involves both supply and demand. Therefore, the library's function is a double one—to discover and assess demands and then to try to satisfy them.

His basic principle was that book representation must be comprehensive of and in proportion to demand, not to subject content. In using the term *comprehensive,* he was concerned that the demands be judged not only on their own merits but also in relation to the entire body of demands. Thus, representation becomes a matter of proportions, not of actual volume counts. A large demand may be met by a relatively small number of books on the subject, a situation illustrated by the fact that a very small proportion of the total collection (25-30 percent) usually satisfies anywhere from 60 to 70 percent of the total demand. The proportion is also influenced by such factors as library budget, space, and availability of titles. Intentional duplication is also very important in the representation picture—multiple copies of a title, as opposed to unintentional duplication. In McColvin's terms there is a surprising amount of "unintentional duplication"—a number of titles on a subject that all provide basically the same information with only slight variations. The question is—would it be better to have only one or two titles in multiple copies rather than numerous similar titles? At this point, some of the basic criteria for selecting materials come into play, and according to McColvin, there are seven basic criteria for selection:

1. The information should be as accurate as possible.

2. The book should be complete and properly balanced, with due regard being given to its subject and intended scope.

3. The author should have distinguished between fact and opinion.

4. The currency of the information is frequently the determining factor.

5. The writing style and treatment of the subject should be appropriate to the type of demand to be met.

6. The title reflecting the cultural values of its country of origin is to be preferred; that is, when the subject matter is treated differently in various countries the treatment from the country of origin is to be preferred.

7. The physical characteristics of the book are generally of minor importance unless there are two books similar in terms of content; when this occurs, such factors as typeface, illustrations, binding, paper, indexes, bibliographies, and so forth may help make the final decision.

In essence, McColvin suggested that the size of the collection in a particular subject ought to be proportional to the demand for that subject, regardless of a librarian's subjective assessment of the importance of that topic. He recognized that patrons tend to be inconsistent, responsive to fads, and highly changeable in their demands. He also recognized that librarians and the general public assign relative values to various subject areas. In order to determine the size of the collection for given subjects, two values were to be used—some numerical values. The second number was to be assigned on the basis of the number of requests received for books on that subject. These two numbers would be multiplied to obtain a "representative number." Another possible manner of numerically determining the relative value of a subject would be to rank a subject from one to ten according to the column inches devoted to that subject in general encyclopedias for the particular country in which the library is located. (A very articulate critic of this approach is Rinaldo Lunati.)[4]

A number of flaws exist in McColvin's concept, but at least it represents an attempt to meet demand and, to some degree, to take quality into account. In essence, McColvin's approach (and that of others who follow the demand concept) places a very heavy emphasis on community analysis in order to determine changing demands. Some persons have suggested that this approach creates a situation in which the librarian is converted into a sociologist and is not performing "real" library work. True, community analysis does take time and draws heavily on sociology. However, it is difficult to understand how one can develop an actively used library collection without knowing the community. (See chapter 2.)

The suggestion that librarians leave this work to sociologists and only use sociological data as the library needs them is faulty. Librarians planning a new library building should not expect a functional building if the project is left solely in the hands of an architect. Day-to-day library involvement in the design process, as well as with the supervision of the construction work, is the only way to help ensure a satisfactory physical facility. The same is true of a community analysis project. Without direct, continual involvement by librarians, the data collected may be of limited value. Furthermore, though a building project lasts for only a short period of time, community analysis is an ongoing project. Unless the library has enough funding to hire a resident sociologist, librarians need to learn how to combine this activity with other library functions.

The socioeconomic emphasis in American and British public librarianship was very strong during the 1920s, 1930s, and late 1940s. Considerable emphasis was placed on community studies and on developing programs and services, and in particular, book collections, which were designed to meet local community needs. During the 1950s and 1960s this emphasis faded somewhat: the economic picture was bright and there was an increasing flow of funds to libraries. For many American academic libraries and a few large public library systems there seemed to be no concern with selecting, just with collecting — everything in sight. We have now come full circle. Selection is again the keyword.

Arthur Bostwick —
American Public Library (1929)[5]

A number of subsequent writers followed McColvin's lead and emphasized the demand concept. Arthur Bostwick discussed the problem from the point of view of American public libraries. As he described the dilemma: let the public have what they want and run the risk of having the collections fall to an "unacceptably low level," or collect only the best and risk having a library without readers.

Most of the emphasis in McColvin's seven criteria was on nonfiction. Bostwick explored the issue of fiction as well and made a strong case for its inclusion in the public library, since recreation is a general need and there is a high demand for recreational reading. Perhaps the emphasis on fiction — usually more difficult to judge than nonfiction, especially when there are questions of style and treatment — caused him to take one of the more questionable stands on who should be responsible for selection. He indicated that the board of trustees should have the responsibility unless the librarian knows his job. Unfortunately, Bostwick did not indicate who will determine the extent of the librarian's subject knowledge. Library literature is filled with cases of disagreements between library boards and librarians about who knows what. (It must be remembered, however, that his book covered all aspects of American public library operation, and that the chapter on book selection was only 16 pages in length.)

Bostwick also listed characteristics that he would require of selection librarians. Although his list is not as formidable as some later listings (especially those of Drury and Haines), it is still impressive. Most of the characteristics—forceful, self-confident, sociable, and influential—seem to be required for any librarian, not just a book selector in a public library. He did indicate that book selectors must be dependent in part upon the judgments of other persons because the range of knowledge and output of material is too large for any one person to manage. Certainly this was true in 1929, and is even more applicable today when a library subject expert in a field such as chemistry or history cannot be equally knowledgeable in all the subfields.

As so many others have done, Bostwick suggested a middle ground for book selection: "average taste of users." In many respects this solution is no better in terms of workload than the demand approach—both require extensive socio-cultural investigation to determine the community's level of need or "average taste." Furthermore, the average taste of users would preclude consideration of the nonuser population as a potential service need. In fact, the focus of attention still would be on the users and their tastes rather than on the entire community. A communitywide focus would at least identify nonuser groups and perhaps even provide a mechanism for assessing their interests and needs. That information in turn might suggest new programs or collection development areas for the library.

Francis Drury — *Book Selection* (1930)[6]

Francis Drury's textbook appeared a year after Bostwick's book was published. Drury took the position that the value of a book is the basic reason to include it in a collection. He further indicated that selection should operate on the basis of three factors—the books or titles as individual entities, the patrons using the collection, and the library's resources. A one-phrase summary of his philosophy would be: the best quality reading material for the greatest number of patrons at the lowest possible price. Certainly this is a highly desirable goal for any library.

Drury's concept of "best" is qualified in several ways. That is, it could be the best in the field in which the book will be used, that the use will be "good use," and that it meet certain demands. The best of any type of reading, according to Drury, is characterized by four qualities: truth, clarity, good taste, and literary merit. Of the four, truth is perhaps the easiest to determine, but even this factor is often a question of perspective—"the truth as I see it" is not an uncommon statement. As for the remaining three factors, clarity can often be a function of educational level, while individual preference and experience almost completely dominate judgments as to levels of taste and literary merit. If this were not so, judicial systems would not have so much trouble deciding such issues as pornography and libel.

Drury set up a number of guidelines for selectors, and the following were suggested in order to choose the best books:

1. Establish suitable standards for judging all books.

2. Apply criteria intelligently and evaluate the book's contents for inherent worth.

3. Strive to get the best on any subject, but do not hesitate to add a mediocre title that will be read rather than a superior title that will be unread.

4. Duplicate the best rather than acquire the many.

5. Stock the classics and "standards" in attractive editions.

6. Select for positive use — not just good books but ones that serve usefully.

7. Develop the local history collection — these items will be sought in the library if anywhere.

8. Be broad-minded and unprejudicial in selection; represent all sides fairly — although propagandistic and sectarian titles should only be added as far as use demands it.

9. Do select fiction — it has both educational and recreational value.

10. Buy editions in bindings suitable for library use — circulation and borrowing.

11. Know publishers, costs, and values.

12. Know authors and their works — if possible, develop a ranking system.

These factors are an interesting mixture of achievable and unachievable goals. "Suitable standards" and "apply intelligently" sound good, but what do the phrases really mean? Each person who reads those words will give them slightly different meanings, and if that is the case, how can there be any consistency from library to library, or within a library if more than one person does the selecting?

The second aspect of Drury's basic philosophy — greatest number — resulted in another list of guidelines:

1. Study the library's constituency with an open mind to determine and assess its needs and demands.

2. Develop a selection program that will satisfy community needs and demands and that will develop the community's intellectual level — thereby increasing the sum of its systematic knowledge.

3. Apply the Golden Rule in selecting books for readers.

4. Provide for both actual and potential users: satisfy the former's general and specific demands as far as possible; anticipate somewhat demands that might or should come from the latter.

5. Discard or do not add titles for which there is no actual or anticipated demand — except for classics and standards.

6. Use restraint in responding to demands of aggressive patrons and recognize the inarticulate patron's demands.

7. Buy many works for specialists' and community leaders' needs insofar as this does not draw off too much of the book funds required to obtain material for the primary constituency.

8. Do not attempt to complete sets, series, or subject areas unless there is actual demand for completeness.

These guidelines are general in scope and are to some degree subjective. However, a group of persons responsible for collection development could use them as a basis for establishing their own agreed-upon meanings.

The cost aspect is self-explanatory except for one statement: Drury suggests that one not buy any book without first asking whether its purchase is depriving the library of a better book in as great or greater demand. This is a useful question to ask, but again, it places great emphasis on quality and does not take into account subject matter. For example, consider a choice between a mediocre title on a new field of anthropology with only a limited demand and a good title on gardening, which is in high demand. The library has nothing in the new field of anthropology; it has a number of titles on gardening but not the new one. There is only enough money to buy one of the two books—which should the librarian select, using Drury's guidelines; using his or her own judgment? Why?

All of Drury's guidelines are adapted to creating a value system for selecting books. A selector is supposed to operate in a milieu in which this value system has been converted into a permanent and general scale of literary values, a scale used to judge the merits of any particular title. Furthermore, the librarian should be able to review, evaluate, and decide what type of library should buy a particular title. In many ways the journal *Booklist* (an ALA publication) reflects this concept. It is prepared and published by librarians for librarians and only lists books recommended for purchase.

Drury recognized that no one person could possibly know enough about all subjects to be able to evaluate all books effectively—assuming that there would be time to read all the books. American public libraries have taken this concept to heart and a great many hours of professional time are spent in reading new books (normally on the librarian's own time—nights and weekends) and discussing them in book selection meetings. Personal experience with such meetings suggests that perhaps somewhere in the dim, dark past, a permanent general scale of literary values may have existed upon which each book could be weighed; but somewhere in the more recent, chaotic past the scale was misplaced. (This observation is based upon listening for what seemed to be eternities to two normally friendly individuals argue vigorously about the merits of a particular book.)

The basic selection precept of the right book for the right reader at the right time is modified using the quality approach. It becomes the best book for all readers all the time. If assessing community needs is a time-consuming activity—and it is—think how much more complex the quality factor is to assess. Despite the difficulties, there are many important reasons for buying only the best. An important one is not to waste limited collection development funds. Tax money is always difficult to secure and wasteful practices never make sense. The question to answer is, what is "best?" Does this mean physical characteristics or content? Not too many years ago public librarians tended to view paperback books as being of poor quality. Some claimed that the type of material published in paperback was too low in quality for inclusion in a library collection. Others said that it was just a question of how long the book would last—only a few circulations and it would fall apart. Today, paperbacks are a normal part of the collection, and both inexpensive reprints of popular titles and high quality original works are among the titles being selected.

Poor content, rather than poor physical characteristics, is the usual concern. The main consideration is to maintain the highest literary quality. A collection of the great books and great authors has been the goal of some libraries, which means that raising the community's literary taste has been given the highest priority in collection development. When using the "buy only the best books" principle, however, certain fundamental questions must be considered. One is, are there lists of the best books or can one be developed? Do such lists exist? Yes, there are dozens of "Basic Books for ...," "Best Books of ...," and "All Time Classics" lists available. Some, such as *Standard Catalog for Public Libraries* (H. W. Wilson, quinquennial, with annual supplements) carry with them a certain official standing. Some librarians feel that their collection must contain all of the books that they consider basic before any other items are acquired. If a library did not have most, if not all, of the items on the list, then that library would be considered a failure, applying that standard.

Other questions concern the character of a "best book" list. Was it developed by one or more persons to serve a specified objective? If so, it is necessary to know the identities of the individuals who made the selection, the objectives of the selection process, and the criteria that were employed. One also must decide whether the published list of objectives is sufficiently close to the library's objectives to warrant using the list. Just the fact that so many lists exist indicates some of the problems involved in listing the best books. Each person has an individual, unique value system that will result in differences of opinion about which book(s) should be labeled best. Philosophers have debated value concepts for several thousand years, with no resolution in sight. Why should librarians expect to accomplish the task in less than two hundred?

Authors writing about this concept—buying the best—recognize that in order to select the best a librarian must have an extensive literary background. The amount of time a student must spend in library school makes it necessary for most prospective librarians to come to library school with a literature and subject background if they are to be successful in collection development. Library schools can only help sharpen critical skills and teach a few basics about preparing annotations. (Perhaps the best discussion of how to prepare a library annotation is in Helen Haines's *Living with Books*, a standard textbook in many American library schools for many years; it is examined below.)

Lasting worth or value is easy to determine for books 100 or perhaps even 50 years old. Current books are a different problem. In essence, there is a significant difference between current and retrospective selection, if only in terms of the number of items to be considered. Retrospective selection is aided by time itself. Many titles no longer exist or exist in only limited quantities, primarily in libraries. An interesting study would be to examine the proportion of 1870 imprints still available, compared with the proportions of those published in 1925, 1950, and 1970 and still available. As the volume of books published increases each year, and if the number of librarians does not increase proportionately, the amount of time available per book for review decreases. No one is able to examine every new book published in English each year, let alone read them all. Less and less time for more and more books means that the librarian must depend upon others for judgments about the worth of a particular item.

It is important to note that the concept of acquiring "quality" material is normally applied only to selecting books. Media are a completely different matter, as we shall see in chapter 9. However, periodicals, serials, and other printed matter are also generally excluded from the quality evaluation process— excluded in the sense that often one must accept a particular item or nothing at all. Another factor, especially with periodicals, is that the evaluation should be ongoing. Periodicals or serials constantly change in nature: new editors, new contributors, and changing areas of interest all create an environment in which frequent review is necessary. A title once thought to be the best (or worst) may change completely between two issues.

One interesting feature of Drury's work is his recognition that, despite the best efforts, a considerable number of current selections would not have lasting value. Removal of obsolete items must be considered part of the normal work of persons responsible for collection development, but unfortunately, this aspect of collection development has not received the attention it should in most library schools and libraries. In spite of the recognition of the necessity for weeding, the process is usually ignored until the need has reached crisis proportions.

Perhaps the section of Drury's text that most clearly reveals the difficulties in developing selection guidelines using the quality approach is his extended discussion of the personality and skills required of a person who is to become a selector. If Bostwick's list is impressive, Drury's is overwhelming. He identifies over 24 "essential" characteristics, ranging from judgment, intelligence, and imagination to accuracy, speed, industriousness, and health. Many of the characteristics are desirable in any employee in any situation; some seem essential requirements for acquisitions personnel but marginal for selectors. Finding the person with all of Drury's preferred characteristics would be a time-consuming job, as the ideal individual would be a paragon of virtues and skills. Developing a means of assessing the abilities of each person is almost more difficult than actually carrying out the selection process. Everyone possesses the characteristics identified by Drury; the problem lies in determining the amount and quality.

By the time a librarian finishes reading Drury he or she may well conclude: this is all very interesting but how can I apply it to the "real world" of collection development? The answer is that only time, experience, and making mistakes will show the way. A more practical approach is found in Harold Bonny's work.

Harold V. Bonny—*A Manual of Practical Book Selection for Public Libraries* (1939)[7]

Bonny did not claim to add anything new to the theory of book selection, but he did provide excellent practical advice on how to go about building a library collection. Generally, the practical advice is concerned with knowing the community's tastes and needs. According to Bonny, input into the selection process is derived from three sources: the selection librarian(s), the patrons, and a committee of specialists. Patrons are encouraged to suggest titles for the collection and to volunteer to serve on the selection committee. Another practical suggestion is to form a selection committee composed of persons with a variety of subject backgrounds. This committee could suggest appropriate additions to the collection. (Note that the committee in most cases would not be made up of librarians.) Another use of the committee, as conceived by Bonny, would be as a means of assessing the value of titles suggested by patrons. Such a committee accomplishes several things: it allows community participation in collection development; it helps to ensure a workable level of community input—not too much or too little; and it helps to reduce the need for "super" librarians who know everything about all subjects. As far as Bonny was concerned, this committee should be only advisory, as the final responsibility for selection remains in the hands of librarians. Although the book was written in terms of a public library environment, Bonny's basic concepts apply as well to any type of library. Educational institutions usually have an advisory committee for the library. If the rules governing the committee's powers (whether advisory or decision-making) are properly drawn up, such a committee can be very helpful in collection development. Occasionally, special libraries establish a committee of this type because the library staff is too small to handle the total workload.

Helen Haines—*Living with Books* (2d ed., 1950)[8]

Living with Books has attained almost classic status. Haines's general approach to the problem of collection development is a combination of the ideal and the utilitarian. She acknowledged that in some of her principles there are inconsistencies. However, she felt that the matter, when viewed as a whole, is a dynamic situation in which adjustments must constantly be made in order to achieve some degree of equilibrium. Her basic assumption was that people need and demand not only ephemeral materials such as popular novels, but also materials for "deeper life channels," which require education and lasting, high quality materials.

Haines provided two major principles and a number of related ones. The basic principles are:

1. Select books that tend toward the development and enrichment of life. (In order to accomplish this type of selection, one must know the foundation books—usually the older titles and the "valuable" ones in the current output. The purpose of collection development thus seems to be to enlighten—to lessen patterns of mass thinking that may be prevalent but are not conducive to tolerant living—or to help patrons comprehend vital current issues. This seems, though, to place an inappropriate burden on the selector, since that person must make judgments as to what the community should or should not read.)

2. Make the basis for selection positive, not negative. Every book should be of service, not simply harmless.

Her list of related principles is extensive, and may leave a person wondering when or how all of it can be done:

1. Know the community's general and special character and interests.

2. Be familiar with subjects of current interest—general, national, local.

3. Represent in the collection all subjects applicable to these conditions.

4. Make the collection of local history materials useful and extensive.

5. Provide for organized groups whose activities and interests can be related to books.

6. Provide for both actual and potential readers: satisfy existent demands and anticipate those suggested by events, conditions, and increasing use.

7. Avoid selection of nondemand books; remove those past a useful life.

8. Select some books of permanent value regardless of their potential use; great literary works must remain the foundation of the library's structure.

9. Practice impartiality in selection: no favored hobbies or opinions; in controversial or sectarian subjects, accept gifts if purchase is undesirable.

10. Provide as far as possible for the needs of specialist users; those requiring books as tools have a special service claim on the library, so long as the books are not too esoteric in nature.

11. Strive not for a "complete" collection, but for the "best": the best books on a subject, best books of an author, most useful volumes of a series. Ignore the practice of getting full sets without a need for all the parts of each one.

12. Prefer an inferior book that will be read over a superior one that will not. With wide and discriminating knowledge, it is usually possible to choose a book with both value and interest on its own level.

13. Keep abreast of current thought and opinion; represent adequately significant and influential scientific, intellectual, and social forces.

14. Maintain, so far as possible, promptness and regularity in supplying new books—especially in the case of books both good and popular.

In many ways, this list reflects Drury's work, as it should, since Haines's work was in essence an updating of the earlier title. If anything, however, her list makes an even stronger case for the "quality" collection. Most of the guidelines are modified; some are qualitative statements. As does anyone writing on this subject, Haines recognized the impossibility of one person's handling all the titles in any one major field of interest for a library. She also was one of the first to describe a comprehensive method for dealing with this problem, her solution being to make extensive use of bibliographic/selection aids, supplemented with local input. She listed six types of selection aids, and while one may not agree with her ranking of their importance, the types seem to be comprehensive in coverage. The aids are listed in her order of importance:

1. those issued by library organizations (for example, IFLA, LA, ALA);

2. those issued by individual libraries (for example, British Museum, Library of Congress, Bibliothèque Nationale);

3. those issued by societies and educational institutions (such as UNESCO and the Modern Language Association);

4. those issued by publishing organizations (for example, *Publishers Weekly* and *Bookseller*);

5. those issued by individual publishers (such as catalogs, announcements, and flyers);

6. those issued by other groups as part of their service (book reviews in periodicals and newspapers).

Without an extensive knowledge of these aids and without using them constantly, it would be almost impossible to function as an effective book selector. One must spend a considerable amount of time simply getting to know the tools, their assets, and their limitations. Just as experience is the only way to get to know authors and publishers, the same is true for selection aids.

Haines went further than earlier writers in recommending a specific system for selection work. Although the system is general in nature and could be applied, within limits, in any country with any type of library, she assumed the existence of an extensive and effective bibliographic network. She suggested the following procedures:

1. Examine the bibliographic aids on a regular and systematic basis— publishers' flyers and catalogs, lists of new books published or received, and book review sources.

2. Prepare cards for titles that seem to be of potential value; be certain to indicate the source of the information.

3. Solicit and accept recommendations from patrons.

4. Incorporate into one "possible order" file both suggestions from patrons and those from bibliographic tools.

5. Search for published reviews of titles in the file.

6. Sort the file into two groups—one to order immediately and a "hold" group (usually those for which no reviews could be found).

7. Transfer cards for titles ordered to an "on-order" file; this will save time and effort by avoiding unintentional duplication.

This is a workable system, but it does place great emphasis on reviews and reviewers, whose judgments about a title are made without particular reference to the local situation. Naturally, it is necessary for local professional judgments to be involved in the final decision. A particular problem for academic, research, and special libraries is that the titles they require are in many instances highly technical; reviews, if they appear at all, are often delayed—anywhere from one to two years after publication. In most cases, the library cannot wait that long to buy a particular title. Thus there is a need for a local review process.

Published reviews, although of great potential use, must be used with care and understanding, because all the types of reviews identified by Haines will be encountered by librarians engaged in selection. Haines listed four types:

1. "Reviews" that are solely intended to promote the sales of a title. Although often presented so as to appear to be reviews, these are more rightfully termed announcements and are usually prepared by the publisher at the time of publication.

2. Reviews published in library periodicals. Even though they publish more reviews per year than most other sources, they cannot review every title published. Such reviews usually appear shortly after a title's publication.

3. Reviews published in mass market newspapers and periodicals. If the book review editor is knowledgeable, these are useful in identifying potential high-demand items. This type of review appears within two to six months after publication of a title.

4. Reviews published in specialized subject publications. Usually written by specialists in the field the book is about, these are scholarly assessments of nonfiction titles of scholarly interest—no fiction. These will not appear until nine to eighteen months after a book's publication, or even longer in the case of specialized titles.

No matter what type of review medium a librarian is using, he or she must get to know the abilities and biases of the editors and reviewers. Thus it is more beneficial to use reviews that are signed, so that over a period of time one can get to know the reviewers. Human nature being what it is, we tend to respect and accept the opinions of persons who share our personal biases. Nevertheless, use of reviews does provide a back-up, outside opinion that supports a decision concerning a particular title.

One useful aspect of the review process, if the title is widely reviewed, is that a wide range of opinion about its value will be observed. Some persons may find this difference of opinion a problem; they want to buy titles receiving only positive reviews. Mixed reviews require more local judgment, but the differences in viewpoint may provide just the insight needed to make an informed local decision. It is possible that what was viewed in a negative light by a given reviewer could be just the factor that a library may be looking for, and thus supports the decision to buy the title.

A major problem is that no single review medium in a country with an active book trade is able to review more than a fraction of the annual output. Consequently, some titles are never reviewed, while others seem to be reviewed more widely than their subject matter seems to warrant. Because only a small percentage of titles can be reviewed in a year, the role of the book review editor becomes critical. An editor may receive hundreds of titles and be able to review only half of these. Thus, this person's judgment of what will and will not be reviewed is significant. A librarian may never know which titles were rejected for review, but given time and experience, he or she will soon learn those sources that review the highest percentage of the titles to be considered. Generally, it is necessary to use a number of sources in order to achieve any degree of comprehensive coverage.

What constitutes a good review? Haines not only supplied a sound discussion about what to look for, but also explained how to prepare a good review:

1. There should be a brief, accurate description of the book's subject(s) and its contents. This should be factual in presentation and should include information regarding the stated purpose of the book.

2. There should be, when appropriate, a comparison to similar works by the same or different authors. This should be factual; however, it is also an appropriate place for a reviewer to take a personal stand on the quality and utility of the title under review.

3. There should be a straightforward style in the review. This is not the place for the reviewer to indulge in an elaborate style or wit at the expense of conveying useful information about the title under review.

4. There should be a limited range of topics reviewed by a single reviewer. A reviewer who attempts to write reviews on almost any subject must be suspect. As a librarian, one needs opinions based on in-depth subject knowledge.

5. There may or may not be a clearcut statement — "recommended" or "do not bother to read this one." Regardless of whether such statements are made, the review should be free of bias. Be suspicious of the reviewer who never has anything good or bad to say about any book.

No one would ever say always or never depend upon published reviews. They are a useful aid in the selection process, and as a librarian gains experience, he or she will learn how to make the most effective use of them.

In summary, Haines's book provides a detailed statement about the whys, wherefores, and hows of selecting quality books. No matter what stand is taken on the issues of demand versus maintaining literary standards, her book is essential reading for anyone wishing to become a book selector.

S. R. Ranganathan — *Library Book Selection* (1952)[9]

One of the postwar writers who did all he could to create a more scientific approach to collection development was S. R. Ranganathan. (Without question, Ranganathan was one of the leading thinkers about librarianship. He demonstrated that the central issues and problems of librarianship are international in scope. All librarians ought to read one of Ranganathan's works on cataloging/classification, administration, or collection development.)

In *Library Book Selection*, Ranganathan stated five laws of librarianship, laws that underlie all of his concepts of librarianship and his view of how a library collection should be built:

1. Books are for use.

2. Every reader his book.

3. Every book its reader.

4. Save the time of the reader.

5. A library is a growing organism.

The list is a pragmatic one. Clearly, his first concern was in developing a library that would be a valuable asset to the community being served. Utility was the first consideration; after that, one should be concerned with quality.

Ranganathan suggested two important means of having some quality control, even when there is only a limited knowledge of the content of a specific title. If one knows something about previous works by the same author, he or she will have a clue to the general quality of the new work. (Of course, this assumes that the author is writing in the same general field.) By using current reviews, when available, and a knowledge of past efforts by the same author, the selector can almost make a decision about the purchase of the item without examining the title. The danger in this approach is in being certain of having a sufficiently narrow definition of the phrase "in the same general field." An example of this type of difficulty concerns the American novelist, Allen Drury. As a writer of contemporary political novels, Drury is well known and respected; he has also published two novels with an ancient Egyptian setting. Unfortunately, these latter novels do not come up to the same level of his earlier works. He is still a novelist, but the change from contemporary to historical settings has caused a change in style and quality. With an author such as Drury, the librarian might well continue to buy his historical novels, but perhaps in smaller quantities.

Ranganathan's second suggestion is to study publishing houses. (He did not actually discuss media producers, but his basic ideas apply to them just as much as to book publishers.) Many times, just knowing the publisher or producer will provide enough information to make the selection decision. Some firms have such an extensive reputation for producing only "quality" material that 99 percent of the time it is completely safe to select one of their products, sight unseen and unreviewed. Unfortunately, a few firms have just the opposite reputation, and one should never buy anything from them without extensive individual review of each item. As with any changing situation, one can never produce the definitive list of good and bad companies. Experience and input from colleagues in other libraries will provide the necessary ongoing assessment, but the assessment must be continuous.

In addition to the company's overall reputation, one should consider the reputation of any series produced. Frequently a firm establishes one or more series, each series focused on a limited area of concern—subject, format, purpose, etc. (For example, this book is in Libraries Unlimited's Library Science Text series.) Some series are "house series," that is, handled by a firm's resident staff. Other series have editors who are not full-time members of the firm's staff; this is particularly true in the area of educational materials. Knowledge about series editors will affect the volume of selection work in proportion to the degree of confidence that one has in the series editor's judgment.

Ranganathan's book is a complex mixture of practical advice and philosophy. The five laws are straightforward, but their means of application is left to the reader.

Mary D. Carter, Wallace J. Bonk, et al.— *Building Library Collections* (6th ed., 1985)[10]

Building Library Collections is one of the standard American textbooks on book selection. Over the years a number of individuals have contributed to the success of the book. Originally written by Mary D. Carter and Wallace J. Bonk, the book went through several editions; later, Rose Mary Magrill joined the team. With the sixth edition two new authors have taken over sole responsibility, Arthur Curley and Dorothy Broderick. Perhaps one reason for the success of this title is that the authors are never prescriptive; instead, they present general principles and do not attempt to create a consistent body of rules. They observe that each librarian's conception of the library's purpose determines that person's attitude toward and application of the various principles. To some extent, the size and resources of a particular library will further affect the working out of an individual's point of view. Above all, there is no magic formula for effective selection beyond the use of informed professional judgments. The authors place more emphasis upon developing a plan of action and viewing the problem as the building of a collection, rather than on selecting individual titles.

Their list of principles reiterates the same views that have been listed previously. If they have an emphasis it is slightly in favor of demand, although they do make it clear that they feel "basic items" and a "well-rounded collection" are important.

More emphasis is given to the impact of the environment (different types of libraries) on the selection process than in any of the other books discussed in this chapter. The authors' ideas on this subject are worth repeating here:

1. Large public libraries with both a heterogeneous community to serve and a reasonable book budget theoretically can apply most of the principles with very little modification within the total library system.

2. Medium-sized libraries are also in a similar position, except that the level of funding usually forces greater care in selection—mistakes are more costly.

3. Small public libraries are the ones most limited, and generally they can only hope to meet the most significant community demands from their collections. They lack both the professional staff and money to do more than this.

4. College libraries serve a more homogeneous population, or rather, the service goals are more homogeneous. In most cases, demand is the operative principle: materials needed in support of the instructional program are acquired and the quality of the material is not usually

questioned if the request originated from a faculty member or department.

5. University libraries serve a more diverse population than do college libraries, but their populations generally are more homogeneous than those of the public libraries. Again, the priority goes to meeting academic and research demands of the faculty and students; after those needs are met the collection is "rounded out" as funds permit.

6. Community college libraries are often closer to public libraries than to academic libraries in terms of the diversity of needs that must be met, a result of the wide variety of vocational programs that most community colleges offer. Demand and quality are almost equal factors in this case—limited funds and broad coverage usually mean that the library and faculty must work closely to select the "best" items for their institution.

7. Special library collections are extremely homogeneous and "develop" their collections almost solely by demand.

8. School libraries are unique in that school librarians seldom have sole responsibility for developing the collection. The school system makes the decisions as to what to include; certainly the librarians have input, but their voice is not as strong as in other types of libraries.

David Spiller—*Book Selection: An Introduction to Principles and Practice* (4th ed., 1986)[11]

Book Selection is a standard British work on the subject. Spiller presents the problem of selection as the means of resolving the conflict between two goals—education and demand. Although his work reveals a slight bias in favor of public libraries, the concepts can be applied in any type of library.

Spiller feels that as far as the educational goal is concerned, two important factors must be present. First, there should be a minimum coverage of all subject fields, achieved with standard works. (A problem exists in determining what those standard works are, as well as who will make the decision about superseded items.) The second factor is that all but the very smallest libraries initially should attempt to stock the standard works in both literature and subject fields for both adults and children. (In this area, Spiller's public library bias is most clear. He does not suggest that his book applies to special libraries or academic libraries; however, much of his material pertains to college libraries, including some of the references to children's literature.) As far as demand is concerned, he sees the situation as one in which:

1. community needs and interests merit more than minimum coverage— including those of nonusers if possible—so that special groups who would otherwise be without resources may be serviced (one does this only after minimum coverage is achieved, however);

2. even small public libraries should:

    a. change a large proportion of their stock frequently to give an indication of the total resources available;

    b. attempt to serve a wide range of taste in the community, rather than limiting choices entirely to popular material.

Certainly, demand takes a secondary position to the combination of education and quality in Spiller's philosophy. This is further reflected in his identification of three main reading areas: factual, cultural, and recreational. Factual reading is defined as purposeful reading, with emphasis on a need for practical information. Cultural reading expands an individual's world view and illuminates some aspect of life. Recreational reading for amusement is the least specific area; since alternate sources of recreational reading materials are usually available, a smaller range of such material can be made available. Spiller sees persons reading primarily for one of these three reasons, although he does indicate that at times the purposes may be mixed; of greater importance to the book selector, Spiller asserts that a single title may serve all these purposes for one or more readers.

The library's approach to solving the conflict inherent in education versus demand is modified by its relationship to formal or informal educational programs in the community. The library may choose to complement or support these educational programs. In either case, the identified level of service will also modify the selection process. Finally, there is a factor not often discussed by other writers: the level and effectiveness of interlibrary loan systems. An extensive and effective interlibrary loan system can have a major impact on how one develops a collection. No matter what modifications take place, Spiller sees the aim of any educational library service program to be increased involvement — widening the reading interests of present users from occasional, practical use to wider interest in cultural and purposeful reading, and increasing the number and type of clientele using the library.

Robert Broadus—*Selecting Materials for Libraries* (2d ed., 1981)[12]

Robert Broadus's *Selecting Materials for Libraries* is less explicit about "principles" than most of the other books in this chapter. He provides an inventory of factors or attitudes present in the selection process. The inventory is a mixture of the desirable ideal and practical necessity. As to a personal philosophy of collection development, Broadus places first importance on the type of library and then is concerned about quality and demand. He thinks that the responsiveness of the library to its "parent institution" is the critical factor in shaping the collection. Intellectually a distinction can be made between responsiveness and demand; but on a practical day-to-day basis, the two are almost indistinguishable. If the library is established by a parent institution to support this or that function of that parent institution, it is difficult to contend that the purpose of the library is not to satisfy this demand.

Quality and demand are seen as factors that primarily affect public libraries. In regard to libraries of this type, Broadus takes the position that either factor may be stressed as desired, since the issue is usually never fully resolved in the library's policy. An attempt is made to present the case for both sides, but his position is that the library should meet both the "currently expressed" and "ultimate" needs of the community. To do this the library must make available the best in quality because a small number of persons appreciate quality (this is a demand), and this can help meet future demands for high quality items after the community's conceptions of quality have been raised.

Broadus suggests a number of factors to consider in assessing demand:

1. Be aware of the impact of publicity that may stimulate demand (for example, an author interviewed on radio or television, or a highly favorable review in a local newspaper).

2. Be certain to consider the duration as well as the intensity of the demand (consider renting multiple copies of highly popular titles; the demand for certain titles may decrease after a short period of time).

3. Be certain to weigh the amount of possible opposition to a title (controversy tends to stimulate demand).

4. Be certain to have a reasonably high percentage of "standards" and classics (even if not extensively used, they can be employed as public relations devices with groups that may be concerned with the "quality of the collection").

5. Be certain to consider past loans of specific titles and subjects (past use is one of the most reliable predictors of future use).

6. Be certain to make some provision for serving the needs of potential users in the community (having made such a provision, advertise the fact).

7. Be certain to weigh the differences between "true" demand (reflecting individual needs) and "artificial" demand (organized propaganda efforts). This is especially important when assessing differences in, say, reading abilities, ages, living conditions, ethnic backgrounds, or economic conditions.

Broadus also had some general advice about collection development that is somewhat different from that given by other writers:

1. The maxim "the right book for the right reader at the right time" means accounting for individual readership in selection policy, as there are various individual needs, interests, and capacities for reading, learning, and enjoyment.

2. A decision against a particular book should be based on justifiable selection standards concerned with merit and honesty, and it should not infringe on the freedom to read of either a majority or a minority.

3. The present status of the collection influences the selection process.

    a. A gap revealed by an unsatisifed demand should be of concern — fill it for future users.

    b. A "balanced collection" should really be an optimum collection for a given community of users or ought-to-be users.

    c. Insure the presentation of truth by providing materials on all sides of controversial issues and representing all responsible opinions — although quantitative equality in this matter is not always necessary.

    d. On occasion, a small part of any special collection can be strengthened — thereby gaining the library a distinction and serving a few people that other libraries cannot serve as well. Belief in "balance" should not interfere with this aim.

4. Selection should be influenced by other collections in the community and by particular allegiances that the library may owe (membership in cooperatives or networks of various kinds).

5. Written policy statements are desirable, especially for public libraries. They are of use in:

    a. clarifying the dimensions and limits of the collection being built (through reference to forms, subjects, and users of materials collected);

    b. emphasizing patrons' rights, thus legitimately buffering unjust complaints. A written policy can effectively shift the focus of discussion from a certain title to a question of principle.

One of the strengths of Broadus's book is the emphasis on subject field selection (almost one-half of the book). He provides a sound review of the basic issues in various disciplines and how they influence the selection process.

William A. Katz — *Collection Development: The Selection of Materials for Libraries* (1980)[13]

William Katz, more than any other recent writer on selection, emphasizes the inclusion of all formats in the collection. Over one-third of the book is devoted to "nonbook" materials. Each chapter contains a section on the evaluation of the format covered (recordings, films, periodicals, newspapers, realia, video, and so forth), as well as information about selection aids and acquisition requirements. He also takes a strong stance in favor of the demand principle. "Unless it is a highly unusual situation, demand should override the librarian's negative decision."[14] As with most of Katz's writings, there is a strong emphasis on practical aspects.

An interesting section in the chapter on selection philosophy deals with what he labels the three basic selection philosophies — liberal, traditional, and pluralistic. A liberal position is one that contends that there must be service to the total community, not just the active users. All formats should be in the collection in an effort to cater to all the preferences for securing information. Having a liberal philosophy means equal concern with educational, recreational, and information-seeking needs of the service community, as well as reversing the passive role of libraries and information centers. It also means using technology and cooperative programs actively to reach people with information. In my opinion, based on discussions with students, teachers and practitioners in the United States and a number of other countries, most librarians subscribe to the liberal position. However, most of them have trouble translating beliefs into action for a variety of reasons, but all too often the primary factor is lack of support from the funding body.

A traditional philosophy takes a cautious approach to service; stay with what has always worked, be concerned with the active user. Limited funds require maximum effectiveness: nothing is more effective than doing what we do best, is the view of the traditionalist. Often the traditional point of view is associated with selecting only "quality materials," also a spinoff of the best use of funds position. Again, in my opinion, few professionals claim this as their philosophical position but a surprising number actually implement many elements of the philosophy. Few claim or try to select only the best and thus set a community standard, but many small libraries have so little money for material acquisition that only favorably reviewed items can be purchased.

The most widely practiced position is that of the pluralist. When funds are more readily available, a more liberal philosophy dominates; when funding remains static, or worse, decreases, the liberal aspects of programming disappear and traditional services are emphasized. Most librarians will wish for the liberal approach and find themselves practicing the traditional. When we are able to demonstrate to the funding authorities the essential nature of our "product" and services, we shall be able to implement the liberal views.

Richard K. Gardner — *Library Collections: Their Origins, Selection and Development* (1981)[15]

Although the main strength of Gardner's book is its coverage of the American book trade, including review sources and the book distribution system, the author presents a number of useful suggestions for selectors. He reviews the issue of demand and "value," ending the discussion by stating that selectors will have to learn to live with "a state of tension" between the two factors. He reviews the criteria for judging materials — authoritativeness, accuracy, impartiality, recency of data, adequate scope, depth of coverage, appropriateness, relevance, interest, organization, style, aesthetic qualities, technical aspects, physical characteristics, special features, library potential, and cost. As he indicates, these criteria can be applied to any information format. Needless to say, a selector will be able to use all the factors only when the item is in hand or when the review/listing provides all the information. Unfortunately, the selector often has to make a decision based on less-than-complete information.

Gardner's discussion of selection aids is the most comprehensive of the current selection textbooks. A recommended chapter is the one outlining the review process. After reading that chapter, it is clear why one cannot depend solely upon published reviews if a well-rounded collection is to be a goal. Not only does Gardner provide a sense of the number of items reviewed (a very small percentage of the total output), but he discusses how items are selected for review by the review editors. He details the questions one should seek answers to before making extensive use of a review source: What is the scope of coverage? What, if any, is the editorial bias? Who is the sponsoring organization? Why is it publishing the reviews? Who are the reviewers? How are they selected? What is the frequen-cy of publication? What, if any, restrictions are placed on the format of the review? (length is the most common); Is the librarian informed about what was examined but not selected for review and the basis for making those decisions? How fast are review copies received? and, finally, How long do the reviewers have to prepare their reviews? Most of the answers will be easy to secure (included with each issue of the publication); some will take time and effort to answer (reviewer selection and speed of reviews, for example); and seldom will the selector learn which items were considered but rejected.

An interesting example of the problem of review editors' bias in selecting titles for review came to light in 1984. A well-known author, Doris Lessing, undertook a project to illustrate how difficult it is to get reviewed, especially for "first-time authors." Lessing published a book under a pseudonym, Jane Somers. The lead sentence from a *Time* magazine article summed up the project: "the trouble with Jane Somers' first novel was not that it was poorly reviewed but that it was scarcely reviewed at all."[16] Lessing had two purposes in playing her "joke." First, she wanted to highlight the problem of the first-time writer, particularly the novelist. That purpose was amply accomplished and reinforced the results of research studies on the subject. Her second purpose was to be reviewed free of the "Doris Lessing" image and reviewer expectations. Well-known authors are very likely to be repeatedly reviewed because they are known, but they are usually reviewed in the light of certain expectations that may not be appropriate for the item in question. Moving from one type of writing to another is not always easy or possible for many writers, if they do not use a pen name to avoid the expectations of reviewers and readers.

Reviewing is an important element in the selection process, and Gardner does an excellent job of describing its components. Selectors, even in a one-person operation, should never be totally dependent on published reviews. Ultimately, the selector must be responsible for what is and is not in the collection. Telling a patron a desired title or subject is not in the collection because one could not find a favorable, or perhaps any, review is not likely to enhance a librarian's or the field's professional reputation. A librarian should understand the review process, use existing review sources intelligently, and contribute to the review sources if so inclined, but should not use reviews as a substitute for personal professional judgment.

Thoughts on the Selection Process

All of the foregoing books contain a wealth of information for anyone interested in collection development and/or book selection. Because the process of book selection is subjective, the librarian needs to formulate a personal philosophy. In addition to this personal perspective, selection work will be influenced by the type of library one works in, its policies, and the community it serves. The following are suggestions concerning what a person should do if serious about becoming a first-rate book selector:

1. Do not forget that collection development is a dynamic series of inter-related activities, and actual selection is but one of six activities.

2. Take time to learn about the basics of the book trade and audiovisual production.

3. Get to know book editors and producers of audiovisual materials.

4. Study the publishers who produce the best materials for the library—examine their catalogs in detail, look for advertisements, learn the names of their editors.

5. Spend time reading reviews in a wide variety of sources, not just personal favorites—determine what the review editors and reviewers both like and dislike, and compare these findings with what the library requires.

6. Examine the trade and national bibliographies with great care—determine how accurately they report the materials that the library needs.

7. Knowledge of the library's community is the foundation upon which to build its collection. Do not stay in the library and expect to have a useful (and used) collection. Only by going into the community, meeting people, and becoming involved in community organizations can one develop the necessary "feel" for what is needed.

8. Read as much as possible about the philosophies and processes of book selection, reviewing, and acquisition activities.

9. Make independent personal judgments about specific titles, and compare those judgments with those found in national reviews.

10. Be interested in what is going on in the world, and *read, read, read*!

Notes

[1] Lionel McColvin, *The Theory of Book Selection for Public Libraries* (London: Grafton, 1925).

[2] Helen E. Haines, *Living with Books*, 2d ed. (New York: Columbia University Press, 1950).

[3] McColvin, *Theory of Book Selection*.

[4] Rinaldo Lunati, *La scelta del libro per la formazione e lo sviluppo delle biblioteche* (Firenze, Italy: Leo S. Olschki Editore, 1972).

[5]Arthur Bostwick, *American Public Library* (New York: Appleton, 1929).

[6]Francis Drury, *Book Selection* (Chicago: American Library Association, 1930).

[7]Harold V. Bonny, *A Manual of Practical Book Selection for Public Libraries* (London: Grafton, 1939).

[8]Haines, *Living with Books*, 2d ed.

[9]S. R. Ranganathan, *Library Book Selection* (New Delhi: India Library Association, 1952).

[10]Arthur Curley and Dorothy Broderick, *Building Library Collections*, 6th ed. (Metuchen, N.J.: Scarecrow Press, 1985).

[11]David Spiller, *Book Selection: An Introduction to Principles and Practice*, 4th ed. (London: Clive Bingley, 1986).

[12]Robert Broadus, *Selecting Materials for Libraries*, 2d ed. (New York: H. W. Wilson, 1981).

[13]William A. Katz, *Collection Development: The Selection of Materials for Libraries* (New York: Holt, Rinehart and Winston, 1980).

[14]Ibid., 97.

[15]Richard K. Gardner, *Library Collections: Their Origins, Selection and Development* (New York: McGraw-Hill, 1981).

[16]R. Zoglin, "The Golden Hoax Book," *Time* 124 (1 October 1984): 83.

Further Reading

General

Broadus, R. N. *Selecting Materials for Libraries.* 2d ed. New York: H. W. Wilson, 1981.

Drury, F. *Book Selection.* Chicago: American Library Association, 1930.

Building Library Collections. 6th edition by A. Curley and D. Broderick. Metuchen, N.J.: Scarecrow Press, 1985.

Collection Development. Edited by R. D. Stueart. Greenwich, Conn.: JAI Press, 1980.

Gardner, R. K. *Library Collections: Their Origins, Selection and Development.* New York: McGraw-Hill, 1981.

Haines, H. E. *Living with Books.* 2d ed. New York: Columbia University Press, 1950.

Katz, W. A. *Collection Development: The Selection of Materials for Libraries.* New York: Holt, Rinehart and Winston, 1980.

Ranganathan, S. R. *Library Book Selection.* New Delhi: India Library Association, 1952.

Spiller, D. *Book Selection: An Introduction to Principles and Practice.* 4th ed. London: Clive Bingley, 1986.

_____. "Book Selection in Hard Times—A Sadly Neglected Science?" *Library Association Record* 84 (September 1982): 297.

_____. "Discussion." *Library Association Record* 84 (November 1982): 395.

Welsch, E. "A Social Scientific View of Collection Development." *Collection Management* 4 (Fall 1982): 71-84.

Academic

Hodowanec, G. V. "Literature Obsolescence, Dispersion and Collection Development." *College & Research Libraries* 44 (November 1983): 421-43.

Metz, P. *Landscape of Literatures.* Chicago: American Library Association, 1983.

Public

Baker, S. L. "Does the Use of a Demand-oriented Selection Policy Reduce Overall Collection Quality?" *Public Library Quarterly* 5 (Fall 1984): 29-49.

Bob, M. L. "Aspects of Collection Development in Public Library Systems." *Bookmark* 38 (Spring 1980): 374-77.

Bonny, H. V. *A Manual of Practical Book Selection for Public Libraries.* London: Grafton, 1939.

Bostwick, A. O. *American Public Library.* New York: Appleton, 1929.

Collection Management in Public Libraries. Edited by J. Serebnick. Chicago: American Library Association, 1986.

McColvin, L. R. *The Theory of Book Selection for Public Libraries.* London: Grafton, 1925.

School

Broderick, D. M. *Library Work with Children.* New York: H. W. Wilson, 1977.

Issues in Children's Book Selection. New York: R. R. Bowker, 1973.

Thomas, L. "Building School Library Media Collections." *Bookmark* 40 (Fall 1982): 16-19.

Van Orden, Phyllis J. *The Collection Program in Elementary and Middle Schools.* Littleton, Colo.: Libraries Unlimited, 1982.

_____. *Collection Program in High Schools.* Littleton, Colo.: Libraries Unlimited, 1985.

Special

Hoffmann, E. "Defining Information." *Information Processing and Management* 18, no. 3 (1982): 115-23.

Hurt, C. D. "Important Literature Identification in Science." In *Advances in Librarianship*, vol. 13, 239-58. New York: Academic Press, 1984.

5

Selection Process: Practice

The preceding chapter covered what some writers have identified as important factors in the selection process. We now turn to a somewhat more practical side of the process and explore, in general terms, what takes place in "the real world" of libraries and information centers. This chapter examines how different environmental settings influence selection work, and describes general categories of selection/acquisition aids. First, however, a few more basic points about selection need to be covered.

What Happens in Selection

No matter what type of library one works in, there will be several steps to the selection process. First, it is necessary to identify the needs of the collection in terms of subjects and specific types of material. The next steps involve determining how much money is available for collection development and allocating a specific amount for each category or subject; developing a plan for identifying potentially useful items to acquire; and conducting the search for the items. In most situations, the identification of possible items draws heavily from published lists, catalogs, flyers, announcements, and bibliographies. After the list is secured (and this may be more difficult than locating a copy of a current bibliography), a person or group assesses the worth of various titles on the same topic. In some cases only one book will be available. When that occurs the only questions to resolve are: Is the price reasonable for the level of use that the book will receive? and Is the book physically suitable for the projected use? If both questions are answered in the affirmative or the negative, there is no problem. When they are answered differently, more information about the level of need for that item must be secured.

More often than not, the assessment is made using published information rather than a physical examination of the book. An item-by-item physical examination and reading would be ideal; however, for most libraries there simply is not enough time to secure examination copies and review each item they buy. School and public libraries generally devote more time to looking over "approval" copies than do academic libraries, although large university and research libraries do use approval plans. Large public libraries frequently use the Greenaway Plan, discussed in chapter 6, for securing examination material. The Greenaway Plan is a contract between a library and a publisher for a library to buy, at a large discount, one copy of all or most of the publisher's trade books. The purpose is to provide examination copies immediately after publication so that the library can decide which titles should be acquired in multiple copies. If the library does not buy multiple copies, however, publishers will cancel the agreement.

Almost all wholesalers and jobbers will provide libraries with examination copies if there is a reasonable expectation of purchase of each title sent or of multiple-copy orders being placed. For example, if a librarian requested 100 titles on approval and kept 90, the jobber would probably send other titles on approval. However, if the library kept only 65 titles, it would be necessary to convince the firm that there was good reason for this high rejection rate (unless additional copies of most of the retained titles were ordered) before another approval shipment would be sent. The reason is simple: it costs as much to select, pack, and ship an approval order as it does a firm order. (This is true for both the library and vendor.) Thus, the more a library can depend upon published selection aids to reduce the number of examination copies it would otherwise receive, the better off everyone will be. Most academic libraries use a jobber approval program, but the principle remains the same for all types of libraries: the return rate must be low. Vendors will want to reassess a plan if the return rate rises above 10 percent.

This is a good place to note some common terms used in selection and acquisition work. Four related terms are *standing order*, *blanket order*, *approval plan*, and *Till Forbidden*. Although some people use these in an imprecise manner, each one has a specific meaning. Till Forbidden is used by the library in serials work to indicate that the publisher or supplier of a journal should automatically renew a subscription without any further approval from the library. This system saves time and money for both the library and publisher or supplier by reducing the amount of paper work required to maintain subscriptions. (This is discussed further in chapter 7.) Standing and blanket orders are similar; in both cases the library is committed to purchasing everything sent by a publisher or vendor under the agreement. (From a collection management point of view, such orders create a high degree of uncertainty in terms of the total annual cost, although some libraries do set an upper limit on total cost of materials a jobber may send without permission. Using the prior year's cost and an inflation factor is the best one can do to make an estimate, but variations in publishing schedules can cause marked variations in actual costs.) The difference between the two types of orders is that a standing order is normally placed for a series—for example, Studies in Archaeology from Academic Press—while a blanket order is placed in terms of a subject field, grade level, or country's publications—for example, all books about politics in Latin America, all books for undergraduates, or all the books published in Finnish in Finland. Approval plans, on the other hand, allow the library to examine the items before deciding to buy, and are thus not a firm order.

Each of these mechanisms has a role to play in effective and efficient collection development and clearly affects selection activities. When the librarian knows that the library needs everything on a subject or all of one type of information material, or can satisfactorily define the scope and depth of need, a standing or blanket order makes the best sense and frees selector time for more difficult decision-making activities. If there is less precise information available about the needs, but the librarian knows large numbers of titles will be needed, an approval plan may be the best solution; however, the selectors will be required to look over each shipment to decide what to keep and what to return.

Variations in Selection

This section covers some of the variations that develop in different institutional environments concerning selection practices. Given the universal nature of information and the diversity of institutional settings in which an information specialist may work during a career in information work, no one method of categorizing the environments is completely satisfactory. For convenience of presentation, the traditional categories of libraries are used here: academic, public, school, and special. There are great differences even within a category.

Academic Libraries

In the United States and many other countries, there are at least two broad types of postsecondary schools: vocational and academic. Publicly supported vocational programs in the United States are usually labeled "community" or "junior" college. However, most of these institutions have both vocational and academic programs. The academic program is roughly equivalent to the first two years in a college or university and is designed as a "transfer" program. Frequently the quality of education is as good as that of a four-year college. If the transfer program is to succeed in providing the equivalent of the first two years of a four-year bachelor's degree (undergraduate degree), then the scope of the program will need to be just as comprehensive as that of the university program.

Collection development officers in a community college library have a very challenging job. Not only must they be concerned about the academic programs, but they must give equal attention to the wide range of vocational programs. Unfortunately, from a cost perspective, it is seldom possible to find materials that are useful in both programs. Also, many vocational programs need more visual than print materials, which account in part for the fact that American community college libraries tend to be leaders in the use of audiovisuals (AV). It also means that the selection staff must know more about AV selection than their colleagues in other types of academic libraries.

Another factor is that most of the colleges have extensive adult or "continuing education" programs, which all too often have little or no relationship to the degree programs. It is true that most academic institutions offer some form of "adult" (nondegree) courses and programs. However, in most community colleges the library, or as it is often called, the learning resource center (LRC), is expected to handle all programmatic information material needs, and it is not uncommon for the university to have a separate "library" for the adult (nondegree) program. Given the diversity of subjects and levels of user ability, the community college library more resembles the public library than it does its larger relation, the university library.

Some help in establishing collection scope and size is available to the LRC. In 1979 the Junior College Library Section of the Association of College and Research Libraries (part of the American Library Association) published a "Statement on Quantitative Standards for Two-Year Learning Resources Programs."[1] While the statement does not indicate what to buy, it does help set some limits for what could be a "bottomless pit." It may also be useful in generating faculty, as well as administrative, interest in the collection and in selection activities. Faculty involvement in LRC selection work is desirable, just as it is in other educational settings, and is just as difficult to secure.

LRCs serve a heterogeneous community. Selection is usually item-by-item, with less use of blanket orders and approval plans than in other types of academic libraries. Collections generally contain at least a few items from all the standard educational formats. Selection personnel generally use a greater variety of selection aids than their colleagues in other types of libraries.

While college libraries serving primarily bachelor's degree programs are a very diverse group, each one individually serves one of the most homogeneous user groups. Only the small special library serving a company or research group is likely to have a more homogeneous service community. One characteristic of bachelor's degree programs is that, within a particular college, all the graduates have been exposed to the same "general education" program no matter what their major subjects have been. A program of core courses or curriculum means that there is less variety of courses at the first- and second-year levels. Less variety naturally also means that selection work for that aspect of the institution's activities will be less complex. Support of the curriculum is normally the primary objective of the college library collection. Some support of faculty research may be provided, but unlike the university environment, research is not greatly emphasized. With the curriculum as the focus for collection development activities, selectors have some very definite limits within which to work. Faculty members frequently play an active role in selection, at least more so than in the LRC or university context.

Most of the items selected for the American college library are current books in English. College libraries in general have fewer AV materials than do LRCs. Most will have an audio collection in music and some have art slides. As in all libraries, there is a movement toward greater use of AV materials in the college library; however, print formats still dominate the collections. Retrospective collection building (identifying and acquiring out-of-print items) is not a major activity in the college library. Almost every college library has its rare book room and may spend a very small percentage of its materials budget on rare book room items. Some have developed over a period of time a strong "special" collection in a narrow subject field. In such cases, retrospective buying would certainly take place. Generally, most of the out-of-print searching and buying centers on securing replacement copies of worn-out and lost books.

Because of their numbers (over 900 in the United States) and their long history, college libraries have had a series of standards, some quantitative and some qualitative. (A particularly good review of the standards and issues surrounding them is an article by David Kaser in *Library Trends*.)[2] Standards, while of some help in determining collection size, really do not have any influence in selection work, at least on the day-to-day aspects.

Without question the most widely used selection aid in American college libraries is *Choice* (published by the American Library Association). *Choice* was created to meet the specific needs of college library collection development officer(s) by reviewing publications aimed at the undergraduate market. Reviews are prepared by subject experts, so the quality of the content will be accurately addressed, while keeping in mind that the item is not intended for the researcher or scholar. With small staffs (a typical size is 10 to 15 people) few college libraries have sufficient subject expertise to evaluate all the potentially useful titles published each year, even with help from the teaching faculty. Because it reviews over 6,000 titles per year of "potential use by undergraduates,"[3] and is widely used as a selection aid, *Choice* has been studied by librarians to determine whether it is an effective aid in the sense that positively reviewed items receive more use than titles receiving "neutral" reviews. One recent study concluded that *Choice* "reviews appear helpful in identifying the most worthy titles, as those most likely to be used repeatedly ... titles appealing primarily to a more elite audience of specialists ought to be scrutinized if the selector is concerned about maximum use. The question of the level on which the book is written is an important one ... selecting strictly on the basis of probable popularity runs the risk of developing a collection which could be categorized as 'lightweight' academically."[4] The authors also note that a collection based on *Choice*'s "worthy" titles may or may not be a collection which will address the needs of the particular institution.

University and research libraries' interests and needs have tended to dominate the professional literature over the years, including that written about collection development. The domination arises from several types of numerical superiority. Though these libraries are not as numerous as libraries of other types, the size of their collections and number of their staff, as well as monies expended per year on operations, far surpass the combined totals for all the other types of libraries. University and research libraries have collections ranging from a few hundred thousand to over 10 million volumes. Tozzer Library (at Harvard University) is a research library of about 180,000 items, a small library in the world of research libraries, but it only collects in the fields of anthropology and archaeology. Like all research libraries, Tozzer spends a good deal of money on materials each year, does much work that is retrospective, and collects in most languages.

Collection development/selection work in university research libraries is more specialized than in any other type of library. Several individuals will be full-time collection development officers; in most other types of libraries, collection development is normally just one part of a person's duties. Looking at the history and development of American academic libraries, one can see a changing pattern in regard to who does the book selection. When the library is small and funds are limited, there is strong faculty involvement; in many cases the faculty are solely responsible. As the collection, institution, and budget grow, there is a shift to more and more librarian responsibility. At the university and research level subject specialists come back into the selection picture, but they are members of the library staff rather than the teaching faculty. Many if not most of the persons responsible for collection development in university and research libraries have one or more graduate degrees in some subject besides library science. Individuals are usually responsible for a specific subject or language area. There is no general method by which the universe of knowledge is divided up among the persons responsible. Local needs and historical precedent appear to be the determining factors. Some universities use such broad areas as social sciences or humanities, while others use geographic divisions (Oceania or Latin America) and still others use small subject fields (anthropology or economic botany) and languages (Slavic or Arabic). It is not uncommon to find a mix of all the methods.

A significant problem in large university and research library systems, with departmental/subject libraries, is coordination of collection development. Budgets may be large but there is always more material available than money to acquire it. Unintentional duplication is always a concern, but the biggest problem seems to be determining whose responsibility it is to collect in a given subject. As the number of persons involved increases and the scope of each person's responsibility gets smaller, the danger of missing important items increases. Working together, sending one another announcements, and checking with colleagues about their decisions become major activities for the university collection development officer.

University libraries make the greatest use of standing and blanket orders as well as approval plans. Use of such programs allows the selectors more time for retrospective buying and tracking down items from countries where the book trade is not well developed. Knowledge of one or more foreign languages is a must if one wishes to be a university-level collection development officer.

Public Libraries

Diversity is the primary characteristic of public library selection practices, diversity arising from the heterogeneous nature of the communities they serve. Communities of a few hundred people, with a small library open a limited number of hours per week with no professional or full-time staff, are not likely to copy the practices of the large urban library. Collection sizes range from several hundred items (Mancos, Colorado) to large research collections of millions of volumes (New York City).

Despite this variety there are some generalizations which apply to most public libraries. The service population is normally made up of many different, unrelated constituencies: persons from different ethnic groups, of all ages, with differing educational backgrounds and levels of skill and knowledge, and with a variety of information needs. Community need is most often the dominant factor in selection, all too often because funding and good sense will not allow any other choice. Librarians do the selecting, occasionally employing a committee format with patron involvement. Growth of the collection is modest since stack space is limited and removal of old, worn-out, or outdated materials frequently occurs to make room for new items. Most of the selected items are current imprints, with retrospective buying generally limited to replacements for lost or damaged books. In medium- and large-sized public libraries most of the common AV materials (audio and video recordings) will be collected to some degree. Perhaps the main difference between public libraries and libraries of other types in collection development is the strong emphasis on recreational needs as well as on the educational and informational side. Trade publishers count on a strong public library market for most of their new releases. Without the library market, prices would be even higher than they are, as only a fraction of the new books published will be strong sellers—much less make the bestseller lists.

For the larger libraries there are two important issues, speed and coordination. Most of the larger libraries are systems with a main library and one or more branches. The reading public likes to read new books while they are new and being discussed, not six to nine months after interest has died down, and often the interest is fleeting, especially in fiction. So, having the new books on the shelf, ready to circulate when the demand arises, is important in many public libraries. With several service points, a system needs to control costs. One way to help control costs is to place one order for multiple copies of desired items rather than ordering one now, another later, and still more even later.

Anticipating public interest is a challenge for the public library selector and would probably be impossible without a number of aids. Unquestionably the most important aid is the selector's inquiring, active mind and the commitment to read, read, read, as suggested earlier. Beyond those, one of the most useful aids is *Publishers Weekly* (*PW*). Reading each issue from cover to cover will provide a wealth of information about what publishers plan to do about marketing their new titles. Clues such as "30,000 first printing; major ad/promo; author tour," "BOMC Cooking and Crafts Club alternative," "Major national advertising," "Soon to be a CBS mini-series," or "Author to appear on the 'Tonight Show' " help the selector, who knows his or her service community, identify potentially high-interest items before the demand is there. *PW*'s information is based on publishers' stated plans and is well in advance of implementation, so there is time to order and process the items before the requests begin to roll in from the public. Needless to say, not all the highly promoted titles generate the interest hoped for by the publisher. Occasionally *PW* has an article that covers publishers' successes and failures.[5] By knowing the community and the publishers, in time a selector can become reasonably accurate at predicting the high-interest titles.

Another useful tool is the Greenaway Plan or a similar plan which automatically delivers a copy of each new book to the library immediately upon publication. With the book in hand and the information found in *PW*, selectors are usually able to pick out the titles that should be ordered in multiple copies to meet high demand. As noted in an earlier chapter, the McNaughton Plan is another way to meet high but short-term demand for multiple copies.

The need to coordinate order placement is one reason many public libraries use selection committees. If the committee has a representative from each service location, the problem of coordinating the orders is greatly reduced. In very large systems, such as the Los Angeles Public Library, with dozens of branches and mobile service points, total representation is not practical. When that is the case, some form of recommended buying list is generated and the service locations are asked to order from the list by a certain date. While not a perfect system, it does help achieve some degree of coordinated buying and control of costs.

For the small libraries, none of these problems exist. Rather, their problems involve finding some money and time to buy materials. Reviews are of vital importance to the small library to locate the best possible buys for the available funds. More and more public libraries, including the very smallest, are being linked together in cooperative networks of one type or another. Thus, small libraries are often able to draw on the expertise of the system for identifying appropriate materials and are able to use selection aids they could never justify having if they were on their own. Depending on the goal of the cooperative, the small library may even be able to gain a larger discount on the items purchased because many individual requests are combined into one large order. Even if it is part of a cooperative, for the small American public library, *Booklist* is the most important selection aid. Not only does *Booklist* contain recommended titles, but it attempts to identify particularly good buys, good in the sense that the items are above average for their type. *Booklist* also reviews a wide range of nonprint materials.

Another distinctive feature of public library collection development is an emphasis on children's materials. In many public libraries, children's books get the highest use. Because of concern for the children's welfare, almost all of their books are purchased on the basis of positive reviews and are then examined again when the library receives the items. When there are enough staff to specialize, usually the first specialist is for children's materials and services. Although there is some overlap between children's materials in schools and those in public libraries, it is not very great. In most countries, there are very different requirements for being a school librarian and for being a children's librarian in a public library.

Two other special features of public library collection development ought to be noted. One is that the public library, historically, has been a place to which citizens could turn for self-education materials. Self-education needs range from basic language/survival knowledge for the recent immigrant, to improving skills gained in schools, to maintaining a current knowledge of a subject studied in college. In addition to the true "educational" function of the preceding, there is the self-help/education aspect exemplified by learning how to repair a car, how to fix a sticky door, how to prepare a special meal, or how to win friends and influence people. Selecting materials for the varied educational wants and desires of a diverse population can be a real challenge and a specialty in itself.

The last feature of note is the selection of genre fiction, which public libraries are often expected to make available. Most of us only read and regularly keep up with a few types of fiction. Some librarians still believe genre fiction does not belong in the library, but in most public libraries genre fiction is actively collected. One of the problems for the selector of genre materials is that they are not widely reviewed; learning about types of fiction and the authors can be a problem. (It might be a good idea for all public librarians to have a course in "trashy" novels while in library school.) (A good book that can be of help in learning about such fiction is *Genreflecting: A Guide to Reading Interests in Genre Fiction*, 2d ed., by Betty Rosenberg.)[6] Although one may think all westerns are the same, Rosenberg's book points out that there are at least 33 distinctive themes, authors who specialize in just one or two of them, and readers who will devour any "range war book" but not touch a "mountain man" title. Learning about the different categories, and their authors, especially if one reads a few titles of each type, is not only fun, but useful, for working in a public library.

School Media Centers

Curriculum support is the predominant theme in media center (school library) collection development. Some similarities exist between community college, college, and school media center selection/collection development, since each has an emphasis on providing materials directly tied to teaching requirements and each uses instructor input in the selection process. An emphasis on current material, with limited retrospective buying, is also a common characteristic. Community college and school media centers share the distinction of having the greatest number and variety of AV materials in their collections.

Finally, school and community college media centers must serve an immense range of student abilities.

Although similarities do exist, there are also differences that may be great enough to outweigh them. Take curriculum support, for example. School media centers generally have very limited funds for collection development, in this matter much resembling the very small public library. With limited funds and limited staff (often there is only one, part-time professional on the staff), almost all of the money must be spent on items that directly support specific instructional units. Often two teachers teach the same unit in totally different ways, making it almost impossible for a single item to serve both teachers' requirements. Enrichment materials are all too frequently a luxury. An additional concern is that the center also must acquire and maintain the equipment for the various AV formats needed for the curriculum support, further limiting the funds available for books and "software." Even "supplemental" material is labeled enrichment, although most media specialists would prefer that this were not so. More often than not, it is a matter of not enough funds to meet the array of needs.

Perhaps selection practice is the area in which the differences are most clearly observed. All school media centers seek active input and participation of teachers, administrators, and in some cases, students, but many variations are found. What is sought is involvement of interested individuals, while the final responsibility for decision making remains with the media specialists. In some schools and school districts advisory committees are established to assist in the review and evaluation activities and to make recommendations for purchase. At the least, teachers and media specialist(s) review and select the items for purchase. Normally there is also some parent representation on the committee, and, where the adults are willing to listen and to act positively on some recommendations, students may have a place on the committee. Naturally, it is better not to have students involved if their views and ideas are consistently going to be ignored. Whatever the committee composition, it is the media specialist's responsibility to identify potentially useful items and prepare a list and/or secure examination or preview copies for group consideration.

Another technique is to notify teachers that certain materials in their subject areas are being considered, or perhaps are even available for review in the media center, and that their opinions would be valued input in the decision-making process. Obviously, this system has the potential for actively drawing all faculty members into the process, rather than just one or two who serve on the committee. Because this approach is less formal, the selection activities may move more rapidly, especially if there is a time frame for the faculty to submit comments. (Finding a time when all or most committee members can meet is, on occasion, an exercise in frustration and does slow the selection process.) The notification technique can be used with parents, if the school has regular parent-teacher association meetings and one is willing to give up part of an evening when there is a meeting. Also, "back-to-school nights" for parents can be employed to reach a larger segment of the parent population. (Many schools are now using a variation of this idea to display textbooks and other required materials early in the school year.) By providing annotations and reviews whenever they are available, as well as placing a "rating sheet" with each item, media specialists are able to secure meaningful parent involvement.

Without question, the role of the collection development/selection policy is greatest in school media centers. Because the media specialist normally is responsible for what is purchased and because more parents and others are actively concerned about both formats and contents of materials children will be exposed to, having clearly stated collection goals and selection criteria allows everyone to operate as efficiently (and safely) as possible. (Some parents and religious groups have strong objections to any format other than books and journals; it is not always content that is questioned.) School media center selections are probably the most closely monitored of all types of libraries. The type of library or information center that will most likely face the next challenge to an item in its collection is the school media center, as illustrated by an early 1986 announcement that the National Committee for Good Reading had released a "Reader's Guide to Non-Controversial Books," which listed items that would not be "offensive to any of the cultural or religious values in our society." It was intended for children, young adults and "discriminating" adults in the United States. The "publication" contained 10 blank pages.[7] Concern about "controlling," "influencing," "developing," or "expanding," children's minds (a number of other labels are also used) is what generates the challenges. Liberal and conservative pressure groups are equally involved in questioning why something is or is not in a collection. Policies and advisory committees are two means to reduce the problems.

Published reviews play a significant role in media center selection. Not infrequently, school districts secure published reviews and insist upon inspecting the items before making a purchase decision. Some of the most widely used sources of recommendation and reviews are ALA's *Booklist*, H. W. Wilson catalogs ("Children's Catalog," "Elementary School Catalog," and "High School Catalog," for example), *School Library Journal*, and *Bulletin of the Center for Children's Books*. Finding reviews providing adequate coverage of nonprint formats becomes a challenge; although *Booklist* and *School Library Journal* do contain some AV reviews, they cover only a small percentage of the total output. Information about grade level and effectiveness in the classroom is a special concern for the media specialist. Grade-level information is generally available but it is very difficult to locate classroom effectiveness data. In most cases, the time involved in gathering effectiveness data would be too great to make them useful in media center collection development. A good guide to selection sources is *Aids to Media Selection for Students and Teachers*, revised every few years.[8]

The term *media specialist* denotes a person who knows about all types of information formats and the equipment necessary for making effective use of the format. Today, at least in the United States, many of the school media centers are also the schools' computer centers. Selection of instructional computer software is a commonplace responsibility and, not infrequently, so is teaching students and staff how to use the computer and its software.

Building the school media center collection is probably both the most rewarding and the most frustrating of all the types of collection building. Normally the center serves a relatively small population and one gets to know each person as an individual. Frustration comes from having too little money to buy all the needed material, being understaffed, and its being difficult to find appropriate material and/or needed reviews. The frustration disappears when the student or teacher is happily surprised to find just what is wanted to complete a project.

Special Libraries/Information Centers

Almost any general statement about libraries and information centers in this "category" is inaccurate because of the diversity of environmental settings included. To some extent this is a catchall for everything that does not fit in the first three categories. As a result, numerically this category may be the largest, but it is also the least homogeneous. Dividing this category into three sub-classes—scientific-technical, corporate-industrial, and subject-research—allows some useful generalizations to be made. Even these subclasses are not always mutually exclusive. A hospital library can have both a scientific and a corporate orientation if it has a responsibility to support both the medical and the administrative staff. It can even have the flavor of a public library, if there is a patient service program. Some corporations establish two types of information centers, technical and management, while others have a single facility to serve both activities. A geology library in a university may have more in common with an energy corporation library than it does with other libraries in its own institution. Large, independent, specialized research libraries, such as the Newberry, Linda Hall, or Folger Libraries, are in a class by themselves; yet they have many of the characteristics of the large university library.

Depending upon which commercial mailing list is examined, the count of "special" libraries in the United States and Canada ranges from 12,000 to over 19,000. Despite their substantial numbers, special libraries have not influenced professional practice as much as one would reasonably expect. Their diversity in character and environment is one reason for their modest influence. Another reason is that libraries and information centers in profit-oriented organizations frequently are limited in their cooperative activities and ability to report new systems that they develop because of the proprietary nature of the information they work with. I do not mean that these libraries have not made important contributions nor engaged in innovative practices and developments, but merely that their circumstances often make it difficult or impossible for them to share information about their activities in the same manner as other libraries.

Having physical space problems is one rather widely shared characteristic of special libraries. Limited space for all services, but particularly for collection storage, is a frequent complaint of the special librarian. Although all libraries eventually have space problems, a special library is seldom expected to outgrow its assigned area. Weeding is, more often than not, a regular part of the special library's activity cycle. Having good information about the most useful "core" items for the collection and how long these items will remain useful is important. Special librarians and information officers have been able to make good use of data generated by bibliometric techniques in selecting the most-needed serials. Bradford's law, Lotka's law, Zipf's law, and citation analysis have all contributed to the effective operation of special libraries. I expect other libraries will make increasing use of these techniques as they too come under the economic and space pressures faced by the majority of special libraries. Two examples illustrate the use of bibliometric data: journal "half-lives" have been identified for many scientific fields. (For example, in physics the half-life is 4.6 years.) This means that, for physics, half of the references found in a current physics journal would carry a publication date within the last 4.6 years. The "impact," "importance," or "influence" of journals have been and are studied, and having determined which journals in a field are most frequently cited, one can decide which titles to acquire and keep. Like any statistical information, data from bibliometric studies are approximations, not 100 percent accurate, and while helpful in collection building/management, they are not intended to substitute for professional judgment. (An excellent review of bibliometrics is available in the Summer 1981 issue of *Library Trends.*)[9]

Special libraries tend to have collections that are very current and in terms of collection policy would be level 4 (research) but without the retrospective element. Despite the heavy emphasis on current materials, the best-known selection aids are of little value to the person(s) responsible for collection building in the special library. Most of the material acquired is very technical and of interest to only a small number of specialists; as a result there is no real market for review services. Recommendations of clients and a knowledge of their information needs are the key elements in deciding what to buy.

Information center is a reasonable label for most special libraries, as they collect many information formats not often found in other libraries. Patent and trademark information is an example of a class of information frequently acquired by special libraries. In some cases, regular searches are made for new information that may be of interest to the organization and, as is most typical, occasional searches are made for specific items. Two other classes of unusual information collected by some special libraries are well logs and remote sensing data. Well logs are records of drilling operations and are of interest to most energy companies involved in exploration. Remote sensing data take many forms but are normally derived from satellite sources; these data, depending upon their specific content, can be of interest to farmers, archaeologists, mining engineers, geologists, military officials, and others. Both of these formats are secured from specialized sources, are generally expensive (normally, cost is not the issue but access and speed of delivery), and require special handling. Many special libraries also handle "classified" information. The classified material may be from a government agency or take the form of internal documents that are important or sensitive in content. Staff members working with such information are usually "investigated" and given clearances before being allowed to handle the material. (An interesting book on the handling of "special" materials is *Top Secret/Trade Secret: Accessing and Safeguarding Restricted Information.*)[10]

Special library collections tend to be *now* collections. They are built for use immediately, not sometime in the distant future. (Historical material is secured through interlibrary loan.) Orders are often placed by telephone using credit cards to pay for the items. I have seen special librarians place international telephone calls to order a single item to be delivered by air express, with the cost of the telephone call and special delivery costs equaling or exceeding the cost of the item ordered. When that happens—and certainly it is not an everyday occurrence—it does give one a sense of how "valued" information has become for some organizations. Online database access is something that most special libraries provide, and unlike other libraries that tend to emphasize bibliographic databases, special libraries normally access numeric, bibliographic, and full-text services. A particular concern for today's special librarian is deciding when to join a database service for occasional access to information and when to acquire a hard copy of the same data. In time, this type of cost/benefit question will probably confront all librarians, but at present it is primarily an issue for the special librarian.

Needs assessment activities are also a regular part of the special library program, to a greater degree than in other types of libraries. Selective dissemination of information (SDI, a longstanding acronym not related to the

"Star Wars" concept of the popular press) is a technique often used in special libraries. By developing and maintaining user interest profiles, the library is able to continually monitor the information needs and interests of its service population, allowing more effective collection building. The technique also serves as a public relations activity. Every time a patron receives an SDI notification, he or she is reminded of the library's existence and, if the service is up-to-date, the value of the library. Normally SDI services are not effective with large service populations because they become too costly to operate; however, there are several commercial current awareness services that can be used in the same manner as the "custom" SDI service. The Institute for Scientific Information, Inc., is one such commercial organization offering some SDI-like services; they also publish a number of indexing and abstracting tools that many special libraries subscribe to (*Science Citation Index*, for example).

Selection Aids

Everyone involved in collection development recognizes the importance of bibliographies and review sources in building a library collection, no matter how often such tools are used in a specific library setting. It is possible to imagine a situation without published aids, but either the size of the library staff would have to increase dramatically or the number of items acquired would drop. What the aids provide is, to some degree, a kind of overview of the output of publishers and media producers. Imagine the problems that a library staff would have if no bibliographies or review sources existed. Each publisher and AV producer would flood the library with catalogs and announcements of its products; the development of a filing and retrieval system for that material would be a significant problem for the library. How many books exist on vegetable gardening? Going through thousands of catalogs and announcements to cull all relevant items would be very time-consuming. This merely underscores the fact that despite their shortcomings and the complaints that librarians have about specific selection aids, the aids are time-saving and essential if libraries are to function with any degree of efficiency.

A number of aids will be described along with a few representative titles. It is emphasized that the listing is selective, as there are literally hundreds of titles available in most of the categories for someone considering worldwide (or at least multinational) selection. All of the aids that follow will save time and frustration if one takes the time to study the titles in each one. As with any reference tool, the first step is to read the introductory material that the publisher or producer provides.

Six general categories of selection aids for books will be examined as well as some microform selection tools:*

1. current sources for in-print books;

2. catalogs, flyers, announcements;

3. current reviews;

---

*Serials and government documents are covered in separate chapters.

4. national bibliographies;

5. recommended, best, core collection lists;

6. subject lists;

7. microform selection aids.

The examples within each category are selective; to give complete, worldwide coverage to all the titles in each would require one or two books at least as long as this one.

Current Sources for In-Print Books

New books (those acquired during the year they were published) represent the majority of the materials acquired by most libraries. In some of the large research and/or archival libraries, this may not be quite the case, but even in such libraries, new books still represent a large percentage of the total annual acquisitions. Every country in the world with any significant amount of publishing has some publication that attempts to list that nation's books in print. (One source of information about selection aids and dealers for non-English-speaking countries is *Books in Other Languages*, published by the Canadian Library Association.)[11] Naturally, the degree of success varies, and access to such a list may be easy or difficult. For countries with a high volume of publishing (such as the United States, Great Britain, and other industrialized countries), there may be weekly listings of new books. (Examples are R. R. Bowker's *Weekly Record*, and Whitaker's *Bookseller.*) Lists of this type (in-print) normally provide information on author, title, publisher, place of publication, date of publication, and price. Beyond this minimum, there may be information about length, special features, series information, International Standard Book Number (ISBN), and sometimes cataloging information, including subject headings. The last item can be very helpful in selection, as too often the title of a book does not provide enough information to allow anyone to make an informed judgment about its content. More often than not, though, weekly lists facilitate only an author search; they are time-consuming if one is doing a subject search. Monthly lists are also common, either as the first listing or as cumulations of weekly lists. If a source is a monthly accumulation of weekly lists such as *American Book Publishing Record* (R. R. Bowker) or *Books of the Month* (Whitaker), it will contain the same information as the weekly listing but also provide several means of access—usually subject, author, and title. In a few countries, prepublication announcements are compiled in one source, such as *Forthcoming Books* (R. R. Bowker) and *Books of the Month* and *Books to Come* (Whitaker). (The latter combines current and future listings for a three-month period.) While such aids can be of some value in planning purchases of new books, two major factors limit their use: (1) announced books do not always appear on schedule, and (2) a few announced titles are never released.

For many countries, an annual list is the only list, or at least the only one that can be secured from countries with low new book outputs. Annual lists may range from only a few hundred pages to multivolume sets. All contain the basic bibliographic information required to order a specific book (author, title, publisher, date) and most include many of the other features listed above and provide author, title, and subject access. Examples of annual lists are *Books in Print* (R. R. Bowker), *Cumulative Book Index* (H. W. Wilson), *British Books in Print* (Whitaker), *Paperbacks in Print* (R. R. Bowker), *Cumulative Book List* (Whitaker), *Les Livres Disponibles* (Editions du Cercle de la Librairie), and *Libros Españoles en Venta* (Instituto Nacional del Libro Español). Almost every major language in which there is active publishing has an in-print book list.

Anyone concerned with collection development must remember that most "comprehensive" in-print lists issued by commercial publishers are not complete. In almost all cases, the listing is based upon titles or information sent in by the original publishers. Thus, if a publisher forgets or does not wish to send in the data on a title or group of titles, nothing can be listed. Naturally, since in-print lists are widely used as a buying tool, most publishers send in the information, as it provides a form of free advertising. Nevertheless, many smaller publishers do not appear in such works; it is not wise to assume that because a specific title is not in the national in-print list it is out-of-print or does not exist. Even if other titles by the same publisher are listed, it is wise to write to the publisher inquiring about the availability of the book needed. Some suspicious persons have suggested that a few publishers may be excluded from commercial in-print lists because of intercompany jealousies. To date no evidence suggests that this did or does happen. In countries where annual lists are produced from copyright deposit data, one has more confidence that the list is complete.

The national in-print list is thus an important tool in selection by virtue of its identifying new materials as they become available. Individuals involved in selection and acquisition work must be very familiar with these tools if they are to be effective in their work.

Weekly and monthly listings are frequently used as selection aids in the larger libraries, regardless of type, as reviews play a less prominent role in the selection decision-making process. Semiannual and annual listings are more widely used in small libraries because they allow the selector to see a broader spectrum of what was produced and help assure a better expenditure of limited funds. There is the danger that some items will already be out-of-print, but for most small libraries this is only a minor concern.

Catalogs, Flyers, and Announcements

Publishers market their products through catalogs and other forms of promotional material. Some publishers use a direct mail approach almost exclusively, and believe that national in-print lists bury their publications among too many others. They also believe that such in-print lists do not provide enough information to sell their books. Such publishers will distribute catalogs listing all their available products and, in addition, send out flyers and announcements of new titles. Even publishers who participate in combined in-print lists employ these sales methods.

Generally, such announcements contain more information about a book and its author(s) than do national in-print lists. When it is not possible to secure a review copy or find a published review, the catalog and flyers listing the book can provide useful selection data. Naturally such information must be used with caution. Very few publishers would lie about an item, but the purpose of the catalogs and flyers is to sell the merchandise; therefore, everything will be presented in the most favorable light. As the librarian gets to know publishers, he or she learns which ones are reasonably objective and which tend to "puff" their products more than the contents warrant.

Libraries that make heavy use of announcements, flyers, and catalogs for selection, as we do at Tozzer Library, must set up an efficient storage and retrieval system. In the past there have been commercial firms that attempted to collect publishers' catalogs and sell the collections to buyers such as libraries (for example, R. R. Bowker's *Publishers' Trade List Annual*). The process has become rather cumbersome, and the collections incomplete. Some years ago R. R. Bowker's *Books in Print* was based solely upon the information from the catalogs in *Publishers' Trade List Annual* (*PTLA*). Today this is not the case. Too many publishers could not afford to be in *PTLA*. Thus, fewer and fewer libraries buy it, depending instead upon their own filing system. Of course, only catalogs from publishers and dealers that are used on a regular basis are retained. (See also the section on bookseller catalogs, pages 237-47).

Current Review Sources

Wherever there is a flourishing book trade, there is usually an equally strong book-reviewing system. Book reviews can be divided into three general types: (1) reviews for persons making their living buying books (trade and professional booksellers and librarians), (2) reviews for subject specialists, and (3) reviews for the general public. Book selectors will use all three types, but the greatest use will be of trade and professional reviews. Some differences in emphasis do exist among types of libraries. As noted earlier, special libraries make the least use of reviews, but when reviews are needed the first two categories are given greatest credence, with a preference for the specialist reviews. Academic and school collection development personnel make extensive use of the first two types but seldom examine the popular reviews. Public libraries, on the other hand, frequently consult the mass market review sources along with the other types of sources.

Trade and professional reviews can be divided into two subcategories: (1) those designed to promote the books, and (2) those designed to evaluate the books. Although trade journals such as *Publishers Weekly* and *Bookseller* are aimed primarily at the bookseller (both wholesale and retail), librarians can and do make effective use of their reviews. In essence, the reviews serve to alert booksellers to new titles that are to be heavily promoted. Publishers have a reasonably good grasp of which titles will sell well and which will not; as a result they employ differential marketing, that is, not all titles are promoted in the same manner nor with equal funding. A potential good seller may receive extra promotional effort and funding in the hope that it will become a top seller. Bookstore owners want to know about such titles ahead of time in order to have enough copies to meet the demand, since bestsellers have relatively short life spans—high interest usually lasts for only a month or two. (Library patrons also want to read the bestsellers when they are bestsellers, not when the demand is down.) If selection personnel read the trade reviews, the bestsellers will be in their collections by the time interest peaks, rather than months later. Trade reviews do not solve all the problems of anticipating which new books will be in high public demand, but they do help. Regularly reading these reviews will help the librarian to identify the clues which help in discerning top demand items for the library.

Evaluative reviews prepared by librarians and by specialists for librarians are also extremely important in selection, especially in public and school libraries. These reviews appear in almost all library publications (*Library Journal, Wilson Library Bulletin*, and *LA Record*, for example). Normally, such reviews are both descriptive and evaluative; occasionally, they will also be comparative. Reviews of this type are particularly useful because they are prepared with library needs in mind. A relatively new selection aid in the United States for popular titles in Spanish is *Lector*. It is similar to *Library Journal* in format, since the reviewers are primarily librarians working with Spanish-speaking communities.

Despite the fact that many library publications contain book reviews, only a small percentage of the total publishing output for any year is reviewed. Some titles are heavily reviewed; others, never. An analysis of ten major American book review journals (both professional and for the general public) for the year 1976 showed the following totals of books reviewed:* *Choice*—6,402; *Library Journal*—5,819; *Booklist*—4,719; *Publishers Weekly*—4,184; *Kirkus Services*—4,050; *School Library Journal*—2,430; *West Coast Review of Books*—1,352; *New York Times*—1,186; *Bulletin of the Center for Children's Books*—798; *Horn Book*—429; and *New York Review of Books*—314. (Not all *NYRB* reviews concern new books.) The magnitude of the problem of coverage is clear when one realizes that at least 24,851 titles were published in 1976. The total number of reviews published in the 10 journals was 31,683. If there were no overlap (but it is known that overlap does exist) the average number of reviews per title would be 1.27. *Choice* probably covers the largest percentage of new books of primary interest to academic libraries. However, in just the fields of sociology and economics, 4,303 new hardcover titles were issued in 1976. Adding history (1,531 new hardcover titles), there would be only 568 reviews left for all other fields of academic interest, assuming that all economics, sociology, and history books were reviewed. A similar study today would produce the same basic results.

What are the implications of such a study? Three points stand out: (1) no one book review source will cover more than a fraction of the total output; (2) even if every book were to be reviewed, there would only be 1¼ reviews per title; and (3) it is very likely that a number of new titles are never reviewed. Even in countries such as Great Britain, where there is very high interest in the book trade and a strong tradition of reviewing, the basic fact remains that most books are seldom reviewed more than once, and a fairly large number are never reviewed.

Another limitation on the use of the reviews is that their appearance tends to be delayed. Most trade reviews appear on or before the publication date; most professional (library) reviews usually do not appear until several months after publication. One reason for this delay is that books are reviewed by librarians and subject specialists, one of the strong points of this approach. But first, a book must be sent to a journal's book review editor, who must identify an appropriate reviewer and send the book to that person. The reviewer may or may not be able to read and review the book immediately. Eventually, the review is sent to the editor, who will edit the text and schedule the review for publication. This is a complex process, but necessary if a number of librarians are to be involved in the review process.

Some professional journals focus on a particular type of library: for example, *School Library Journal, Choice* (academic), and *Booklist* (public and

---

*This analysis was done for the first edition of this book.

school). Naturally, there is some overlap of materials, and journal editors try to make their publications somewhat useful to all types of libraries. Nevertheless, they do have a primary emphasis, focusing on certain classes of books and using reviewers who are qualified to make value judgments about the materials covered.

Occasionally, a journal will have a policy of only publishing reviews of books that are recommended. A problem with this method is that one can never be certain whether a title did not appear because of a negative evaluation or because it was never sent for review. Just as the general professional review sources cannot cover every new book, neither can the specialty sources. If a library is dependent on, or required to use, published reviews, this drawback can be important. One can wait a long time before being certain that a book will not be reviewed, and will still be left wondering why no review appeared.

Competence of the reviewers is also an issue. Nonfiction titles require subject expertise if the content of the book is to be accurately evaluated. For general trade books, it is not so essential that the reviewer have an in-depth subject knowledge for every book reviewed. Once beyond the "introduction to ..." and average readers' guides, the need for depth in background increases until the level where the expert is reviewing another expert's book for just a few other experts in the field is reached. Most academic disciplines have one or two journals that publish scholarly reviews of books in that field. Expert reviews of this type could be, but seldom are, of great assistance in developing a collection. A major reason for this is that the reviews are not published soon enough; commonly, books reviewed in scholarly journals are one or two years old when the review appears. Such delays are unacceptable in libraries with patrons who need up-to-date material. Another factor is that scholarly books are frequently released in small quantities so that the item may be out-of-print by the time the review is published. The best source for the broadest coverage of academic titles from the United States is *Choice. Choice* reviewers are subject experts, whose names now appear with the reviews, and the reviews normally appear within a year of publication, often within three or four months. In order to provide wide coverage, the reviews are relatively short — one or two paragraphs; thus, depth is sacrificed to coverage and speed.

A final category of review sources is directed toward the general public (for example, *New York Times Book Review* and *Times Literary Supplement*). Anyone concerned with building a collection geared to current popular reading must examine these publications as a normal part of the selection process. Editors of popular book review sources must keep in touch with current interests and tastes in order to hold their readership. Because they can only review a very small percentage of the new titles, their selections are made with great care and an eye toward popular current interests. Reviews will be seen by thousands of readers and demand for the reviewed titles is likely to increase. Due to the need for being up-to-date and the fact that most of the reviewers are paid, most of the books that do get reviewed are covered within a month or two after publication.

The data on the number of book reviews published each year in only 10 journals make clear that the librarian will face a search problem if only reviews are used for selection purposes. (Where has that book been reviewed?) To some extent, indexing services that cover book reviews will help, but indexes of book reviews are of little assistance for the most current titles (from publication date to about eight months old). Not only is there the delay (described earlier) in publishing the review, but there is another delay in indexing the review journal and in publishing the index. However, for older titles, the indexes can be a major time saver. *Book Review Digest* (*BRD*) and *Book Review Index* (*BRI*) are two major American tools of this type. Another sign of the problem in review coverage of new titles is found in *Book Review Digest*. Each year *BRD* publishes citations to and summaries of 5,000 to 6,000 new books. A nonfiction title is included if and only if it is reviewed twice. *BRD* editors examine 70 leading journals and newspapers that have large book review sections. Even in this large number of potential sources for reviews, though, only 5,000-6,000 new books out of more than 24,000 are able to meet the inclusion criteria. In addition to the index publications that only cover book reviews, many of the general periodical indexes include book review citations, and these should be noted for future use. *BRI*, which does not include any annotations, lists the reviews that appear in about 325 journals and provides citations to 40,000-plus reviews each year. Even that number does not suggest that all new books could be reviewed twice. The price of gaining access to the citations is time. If one must make buying decisions quickly, *BRI* is of little assistance, since there are not only the usual delays in getting an item reviewed, but also the delays in the review journals' publication and in the indexing and publication schedule of *BRI*. Certainly *BRI* is a useful tool and seems to have overcome some of the early problems in its production and distribution.

Book reviews are useful for most libraries because the staff have insufficient time available to read and review all of the new books that might be suitable additions to the collection. Reviews must not be used as a substitute for local judgments; just because review X claimed that the book is great does not mean that the book will be great for the library. As the title of this section indicates, reviews are aids in selection, not the basis of selection. As the selector gains more and more familiarity with book review editors and with the reviewers' biases, these tools become more valuable as a source of useful information.

National Bibliographies

Up to this point, the discussion has focused on new (in-print) books. In time, however, almost every library will need to add some books that are not in-print. Retrospective collection development is a normal part of academic and research library collection programs. School and public libraries buy replacement copies of the books that wear out but are still used. Special libraries, as a class, do the least retrospective buying, but they do, on occasion, have to acquire out-of-print materials. (The sources for acquiring out-of-print books are covered in chapter 11.) However, before buying the material one must identify it. There are various sources for identifying authors, titles, publishers, and dates of publication of out-of-print items, but one major source is the national bibliography network.

Most countries with a book trade (except the United States) have some form of national bibliography. (For purposes of this book, a national bibliography is a listing of books published in a country or about a country.) One common feature of most of these bibliographies is that they are produced by nonprofit organizations—in many cases the national library or a very large research library. Some examples are the *British National Bibliography*, *Bibliographie de la France*, *Deutsche Bibliographie*, and *Gambia National Bibliography*.

Frequency of publication varies from weekly to yearly; and in some cases, it simply occurs whenever there is enough material to warrant issuing a volume. A few of these bibliographies are based in part upon books received by the country's copyright office (*British National Bibliography*, for example). In those cases, if it also includes out-of-print titles added to the library's collection, the bibliography serves as both an in-print and retrospective aid. A number of the national and large research libraries have published or are publishing their public catalogs in multivolume sets (the British Library, Library of Congress, Bibliothèque Nationale). If a selector has access to a full set plus the updated material, he or she has an almost complete record of official holdings of the library.

Because these libraries are so large, and in most cases, collect almost everything produced in and about their countries, the published catalogs are valuable bibliographic checking sources. They should be used to verify the existence of a particular work, and to locate a source for borrowing the item if one cannot acquire a copy. The *National Union Catalog* (*NUC*) volumes include entries for libraries other than the Library of Congress. (Note: *NUC* is not a true national bibliography, as it is not comprehensive in its coverage. The best one can do for current imprints is to use the *Weekly Record* and the Library of Congress CDS Alert Service.) These volumes contain information about other libraries holding a particular book, and in some cases, the book is not even in the Library of Congress collection.

All of the following information should be present in any of the existing national bibliographies: author, full title, publisher, place and date of publication, pagination, and form of main entry for the book in the library. Beyond this, in most cases, there is information about special features of the book — bibliographies, illustrations, charts, maps, either part of a series, scope notes, and subject information (the classification number and subject heading tracings). A few national bibliographies include the original price of the book.

Large academic and research libraries may use the current issues of *NUC, BNB,* and other national bibliographies as a selection aid. We use a variety of national bibliographies in selection work at Tozzer Library. For most libraries, national bibliographies are used to verify the existence of a title, rather than for selection. But no matter what the purpose is, they must be used with care. For example, both the United States and Great Britain have a reasonably comprehensive bibliographic network for new books. Several years ago, for use in another book, *Introduction to Technical Services for Library Technicians*, third edition (Libraries Unlimited, 1976), three books were searched through the basic American and British bibliographies: (1) *Publishers Weekly* (*PW*), (2) *American Book Publishing Record* (*BPR*), (3) *Publishers' Trade List Annual* (*PTLA*), (4) *Books in Print* (*BIP*), (5) *Subject Guide to Books in Print*, (6) *Paperbound Books in Print*, (7) *Cumulative Book Index* (*CBI*), (8) *National Union Catalog* (*NUC*), (9) *Bookseller*, (10) *British Books in Print* (*BBIP*), (11) Whitaker's *Cumulative Book List* (*CBL*), (12) *British National Bibliography* (*BNB*), and (13) *British Museum General Catalog*. The results are of some interest here. Of the books searched:

- all had personal author entries;

- all were monographs;

- two were available in both hardbound and paper covers;

- two of the books were American and one was British.

Among the bibliographies searched:

- although each title was searched through all available approaches in each bibliography (author, title, and sometimes subject), only two of the thirteen bibliographies searched listed all three books;

- American titles are slow to appear in British sources and vice versa;

- when a title is released in Great Britain and the United States at the same time, it appears in the trade bibliographies of both countries;

- subject entries varied even within the same bibliography;

- there is little consistency in the listing of series;

- when searching a library catalog, one must know that particular library's rules for establishing the main entry.

Best Books, Recommended Lists, and Core Collections

In the previous chapter we touched on the problem of generating lists of the "best of ..." or items recommended for purchase. They are useful aids when employed carefully. If there is any doubt that book selection is a subjective process, it should be dispelled upon looking over the number of titles that exist in this category. Titles such as *Public Library Catalog* (H. W. Wilson), *Books for Secondary School Libraries* (R. R. Bowker), *Books for College Libraries* (American Library Association), and *Opening Day Collection* (Choice) have some overlap, but also some differences. The differences arise from the purposes of the list makers and individuals who make the selection. Personal opinions vary, and these lists are either one person's opinion or a composite of many opinions about the value of a particular book.

Few specialists in collection development would claim that a library ought to hold any title just because it was on two or more recommended lists. If a list is something like basic books for undergraduate programs in mathematics, and is produced by a national association of mathematics teachers, and the library is at an institution with an undergraduate program in mathematics, there is reason to expect that a high percentage of the titles in the list would be in the collection, but not every title. Why not? A major reason would be difference in emphasis in the school's program; there may be no need for a particular title. Another factor is that often several equally good alternatives are available. A good list for collection development purposes will indicate alternatives.[12] A final factor is that the list is out-of-date the day it is published; new titles may have appeared that supersede the titles listed. Also, trying to get a copy of every title on a list can be very time-consuming. Unless there is agreement that it is important to secure every title, do not spend the time; retrospective buying requires considerably more time than buying in-print titles.

Subject Bibliographies

Subject bibliographies suffer from many of the same limitations as the "best" or "recommended" lists: currentness and selectivity. If the bibliography is prepared by one or more subject experts and contains critical evaluations of the items listed, it can be of great value in both selection and collection evaluation. The range of possible titles in subject areas is limited only by the imagination of the compilers. (A good review of subject selection aids for academic libraries is Patricia A. McClung's *Selection of Library Materials in the Humanities, Social Sciences, and Sciences.*)[13] In most broad fields, more than one bibliography has been published. Compare earlier titles to current titles. Where there have been multiple editions, check on the amount of change between editions. Do new editions merely add more titles or is there a real revision with older, superseded titles dropped and new assessments made of all the items? One should not depend upon published reviews but do one's own checking before using such a bibliography as a selection aid.

Using Citation Information for Selection

Many of the selection aids described above provide only the basic bibliographic information about an item. Based on only the citation information, thousands of titles are added to library collections each year. How do selection officers make their decisions from such limited data? Ross Atkinson has proposed a model for this process that in time may prove very useful. He based his model on the citation, "any string of natural language signs that refers to or represents, regardless of its textual location, a particular information source or set of sources."[14] Atkinson notes that every selector begins work with a very personal "I," the biases and knowledge base that each of us develops over time. The "I" is one element in his model. The citation is a "text" that the "I" reads and judges both from past experience and from the context of the citation. He proposes three general contexts; syntagmatic, supplemental, and resolution.

Bibliographic citations are created following conventions regarding the content and order of presentation. (More and more the ANSI Z39.29-1977 standard, American Standard for Bibliographic References, is being used in selection aids.) The standard order means there is a pattern of entry for different selection aids, and the order will provide "information" regarding the item cited (syntagmatic context). What this means is that with experience, one's judgment about an item may be altered by one element of the citation. If I were reading a citation about conditions on the Sioux reservations in South Dakota, I would make different judgments about the content of the item, depending upon whether the citation included "Washington, D.C., 1986" or "Pine Ridge, S.D., 1977"; likewise for a title about apartheid depending upon whether it was from "Johannesburg, 1985" or "Maseru, 1985." Other examples of how an element in order could modify a judgment are: a title implying comprehensive or comparative treatment of a broad or complex subject with its pagination indicating a much shorter book than would be reasonable for the topic; or a book on Soviet intentions in Afghanistan authored, say, by Edward Evans rather than by Mikhail Gorbachev. Certainly, this "context" relates to all the factors writers on selection have been discussing for years: accuracy, currentness, bias, style, etc., but what Atkinson did was provide a framework for understanding how the process operates.

If the citation string includes subject descriptors, the modification in judgment can be profound (supplemental context). An entry in the *Weekly Record* may seem appropriate for Tozzer Library until one encounters the subject heading "juvenile." Without the supplemental context, it is possible and even probable that some inappropriate items will be selected because there is not enough information. (This is a good reason to follow Ranganathan's rule to know the publishers; even then one may be fooled occasionally.) Subject headings and classification numbers in selection aids are assigned by a person who also makes a judgment about the content of the item, and normally only one class number is given. Another person might form a different opinion about the item and assign other headings and classification numbers. If a selector uses several sources with overlapping coverage and which also supply subject assignments, some additional information may be gained; however, more often than not a judgment is made based on only one source. Another type of supplemental information is the source in which the citation appears. In national bibliographies, there are no value judgments made by the compilers regarding the merits of an item, whereas in a publication such as *Booklist* all the items listed are recommended. Thus each selection aid carries with it a form of "supplemental context." And, as Atkinson notes, a patron request may be the supplemental information that determines the decision, regardless of any other contextual information.

"Contexts of resolution" is Atkinson's last category, which ties in the selector's personality. This context is made up of three elements, "archival," "communal," and "thematic," which are related to a selector's attitudes, knowledge, values, perceptions, and total personality. He defines "archival" as the selector's knowledge of the collection and its strengths and weaknesses; "communal" refers to the knowledge of the clientele and their interests; and "thematic" is the selector's knowledge of the totality of current output on a topical (theme) area. How these three elements interact is a function of the selector's background, values, and personality as well as of the information environment in which the person works. Atkinson suggests that one of the elements will dominate most of the time. For a school media center or industrial center setting, the communal context would most likely dominate. At Tozzer Library the archival context is the most important. In a public library environment, where funds are scarce and getting the best for the monies available is essential, the thematic context is likely to be the most influential.

The Atkinson model is useful as a way of thinking about selection, and in time, with more research, it may become part of a true theory of selection. Every beginning selector should read his article.

Summary

Although this has been a lengthy discussion, only the high points and basic issues of book selection could be covered. Learning to be a book selector is a lifelong process, and the items listed in the bibliography provide further leads to material on various aspects about this challenging, exciting, and rewarding area of information work.

Notes

[1] Junior College Library Section, Association of College and Research Libraries, "Statement on Quantitative Standards for Two-Year Learning Resources Programs" (Chicago: American Library Association, 1979).

[2] David Kaser, "Standards for College Libraries," *Library Trends* 31 (Summer 1982): 7-18.

[3] "Introduction," *Choice* 1, no. 1 (March 1964).

[4] J. P. Schmitt and S. Saunders, "Assessment of *Choice* as a Tool for Selection," *College & Research Libraries* 44 (September 1983): 375-80.

[5] "The Red and the Black," *Publishers Weekly* 227, no. 16 (19 April 1985): 26-30.

[6] Betty Rosenberg, *Genreflecting: A Guide to Reading Interests in Genre Fiction*, 2d ed. (Littleton, Colo.: Libraries Unlimited, 1986).

[7] National Committee for Good Reading, "Reader's Guide to Non-Controversial Books" (1986).

[8] *Aids to Media Selection for Students and Teachers* (Indianola, Iowa: National Association of State Educational Media Professionals, n.d.).

[9] *Library Trends* 30, no. 1 (Summer 1981). Edited by William Gray Potter.

[10] Ellis Mount and Wilda B. Newman, *Top Secret/Trade Secret: Accessing and Safeguarding Restricted Information* (New York: Neal-Schuman, 1985).

[11] *Books in Other Languages* (Ottawa: Canadian Library Association, 1970).

[12] A good example is *Basic Library List: For Four-Year Colleges*, 2d ed. (New York: Mathematical Association of America, 1976).

[13] Patricia A. McClung, *Selection of Materials in the Humanities, Social Sciences, and Sciences* (Chicago: American Library Association, 1985).

[14] Ross Atkinson, "The Citation as Intertext: Toward a Theory of the Selection Process," *Library Resources and Technical Services* 28 (April/June 1984): 109-19.

Further Reading

General

Atkinson, R. "The Citation as Intertext: Toward a Theory of the Selection Process." *Library Resources and Technical Services* 28 (April/June 1984): 109-19.

Batt, F. "Folly of Book Reviews." In *Options for the 80s*, M. D. Kathman and V. F. Massman, 277-89. Greenwich, Conn.: JAI Press, 1981.

Cline, G. S. "Application of Bradford's Law to Citation Data." *College & Research Libraries* 42 (January 1981): 53-61.

D'Aniello, C. "Bibliography and the Beginning Bibliographer." *Collection Building* 6 (Summer 1984): 11-19.

Fitzgibbon, S. A. "Citation Analysis in the Social Sciences." In *Collection Development in Libraries*, pt. B, edited by R. D. Stueart and G. B. Miller. Greenwich, Conn.: JAI Press, 1980.

Furnham, A. "Book Reviews as a Selection Tool for Librarians: Comments from a Psychologist." *Collection Management* 8 (Spring 1986): 33-43.

Hamlin, J. B. "The Selection Process." In *Collection Development in Libraries*, pt. A, edited by R. D. Stueart and G. B. Miller. Greenwich, Conn.: JAI Press, 1980.

Katz, B. "Who Is the Reviewer?" *Collection Building* 7 (Spring 1985): 33-35.

Ryland, J. "Collection Development and Selection: Who Should Do It?" *Library Acquisitions: Practice and Theory* 6, no. 1 (1982): 13-17.

Stiffler, S. A. "Core Analysis in Collection Management." *Collection Management* 5 (Fall/Winter 1983): 135-49.

Academic

Danton, J. P. *Book Selection and Collections: A Comparison of German and American University Libraries.* New York: Columbia University Press, 1963.

Dickinson, D. W. "Rationalist's Critique of Book Selection for Academic Libraries." *Journal of Academic Librarianship* 7 (July 1981): 138-43.

Junior College Library Section, Association of College and Research Libraries. "Statement on Quantitative Standards for Two-Year Learning Resources Programs." Chicago: American Library Association, 1979.

Kaser, David. "Standards for College Libraries." *Library Trends* 31 (Summer 1982): 7-18.

Macleod, B. "Library Journal and Choice: A Review of Reviews." *Journal of Academic Librarianship* 7 (March 1981): 23-28.

McClung, P. A. *Selection of Library Materials in the Humanities, Social Sciences, and Sciences.* Chicago: American Library Association, 1985.

Miller, W., and D. S. Rockwood. "Collection Development from a College Perspective." *College & Research Libraries* 40 (July 1979): 318-24.

Schmitt, J. P., and S. Saunders. "Assessment of *Choice* as a Tool for Selection." *College & Research Libraries* 44 (September 1983): 375-80.

Public

Books for Public Libraries, 3d ed. Edited by C. Koehn. Chicago: American Library Association, 1981.

Haighton, T. *Bookstock Management in Public Libraries.* London: C. Poingley, 1985.

Scheppke, J. B. "Public Library Book Selection." *Unabashed Librarian*, no. 52 (1984): 5-6.

Serebnick, J. "Book Reviews and the Selection of Potentially Controversial Books in Public Libraries." *Library Quarterly* 51 (October 1981): 390-409.

Swope, D. K. "Quality versus Demand: Implications for Children's Collections." In *Festschrift in Honor of Dr. Arnulfo D. Trejo*, 66-73. Tucson, Ariz.: Graduate Library School, University of Arizona, 1984.

School

Altan, S. "Collection Development in Practice in an Independent School." *Catholic Library World* 54 (October 1982): 110-12.

Collection Management for School Library Media Centers. Edited by Brenda H. White. New York: Haworth Press, 1986.

England, C., and A. M. Fasick. *ChildView: Evaluating and Reviewing Materials for Children.* Littleton, Colo.: Libraries Unlimited, 1987.

Hearne, B. G. *Choosing Books for Children: A Common Sense Guide.* New York: Delacorte Press, 1981.

Miller, M. L. "Collection Development in School Library Media Centers: National Recommendations and Reality." *Collection Building* 1 (1987): 25-48.

Reeser, C. "Silk Purse or Sow's Ear: Essential Criteria in Evaluating Children's Literature." *Idaho Librarian* 34 (October 1982): 157-58.

Selecting Materials for School Library Media Centers. Compiled by D. J. Helmer and J. J. Mika. Chicago: American Association of School Librarians, 1985.

Woodbury, M. *Selecting Materials for Instruction.* 3 vols. Littleton, Colo.: Libraries Unlimited, 1979-1980. (Volume 1, *Issues and Policies*; Volume 2, *Media and Curriculum*; Volume 3, *Subject Areas and Implementation*).

Special

Basic Business Library: Core Resources. Edited by B. S. Schlessinger. Phoenix, Ariz.: Oryx Press, 1983.

Byrd, G. D., et al. "Collection Development Using Interlibrary Loan Borrowing and Acquisitions Statistics." *Medical Library Association Bulletin* 70 (January 1982): 1-9.

Dalton, L., and E. Gartenfeld. "Evaluating Printed Health Information for Consumers." *Medical Library Association Bulletin* 69 (July 1981): 322-24.

McCleary, H. "Practical Guide to Establishing a Business Intelligence Clearing House." *Database* 9 (June 1986): 40-46.

Parker, R. H. "Bibliometric Models for Management of an Information Store." *Information Science* 33 (March 1982): 124-38.

6

Producers of
Information Materials

Producers of information materials can be divided into two broad categories: (1) those who produce printed matter (books, periodicals, newspapers, microforms, etc.) and (2) those who produce audiovisual matter, including electronic. The first portion of this chapter examines the production of printed material (publishing) and concludes with audiovisual production. With each passing day, the distinction between the two categories becomes less and less clear. Where should one place a producer of an audiotape of someone reading a complete Agatha Christie novel or a company that provides an abstracting service in both hard copy (paper) and online? This chapter presents a general examination of some of the important characteristics of production in both categories. Enough depth will be attained, however, to provide a reasonable picture of what these groups do and how they go about this work.

Various writers have been predicting a "paperless" society, office, or library for some time. For example, Frederick W. Lancaster has written extensively on this topic (a relatively recent compilation of his work is *Libraries and Librarians in an Age of Electronics*).[1] To date, books, newspapers, journals, and other printed materials have failed to die as had been predicted. It seems unlikely that they will die in the near future, and they still represent the largest proportion of materials available through most libraries and information centers. A major reason for this is that paper copies are still the least expensive means of distributing large quantities of information to a large number of people. A second important reason is that many people are uncomfortable with technology-based information sources, as well as the fact that people still like to read in bed, on the subway, at the beach, and other places where technology-based systems are at least inconvenient, if not impossible, to use.

Why Know about Publishing?

What is publishing? The question is simple, but it is one whose answer is long and complex, reaching far beyond the activities of book publishers, which is what most people think of when they hear the term. Publishing involves many different people and activities: there are the creators of the materials (writers and performers), the editors and manufacturers, and the distributors and salespeople.

In response to the question, "Why bother with details of the trade?" several responses come to mind. When one is going to work day in and day out with an industry, even if one is just buying its product(s), some knowledge of that industry will make everyone's life a little easier. An understanding of the trade's characteristics—such as what determines the price of an item, how products are distributed, and what services one can expect—all improve understanding and communication between producers and buyers. Under the best of circumstances, a great deal of communication exists between the library and the trade regarding orders.

All this knowledge provides some understanding, if not sympathy, on the librarian's part for the problems of the producers. Publishers who depend upon library sales know (or should know) a great deal about library problems and operations, but a number of jokes circulate among publishers about how uninformed librarians are about the trade. The present strained relationship between libraries and publishers has occurred partly because neither group really understands nor is trying to understand the other's position. (For instance, copyright, discussed in chapter 18, is an area of great controversy.) Yet, we also know that when two parties discuss problems with mutual understanding of the other's position, the working relationship will usually be more pleasant. Each is more willing to make an occasional concession to the other's needs, which can in turn foster mutually beneficial alliances.

Book selection and collection development courses in library schools usually touch only lightly on publishers and their problems, teachers claiming insufficient time to give more coverage. And somehow, courses in the history of the book trade seldom have time to deal with the contemporary situation—it is not yet history. Most schools do not have a place in their curriculum for a course in contemporary production, and if they did, most students would not have time for it in their course of study. But for this reason, these same students are lacking information that could prove invaluable to them on a basic level, since knowing what happens in publishing can affect the selection process. First, it aids in identifying the most likely sources of materials—that is, which ones among thousands of producers are most likely to have what is needed. Second, by keeping up-to-date with what is happening in publishing, one can anticipate changes in quality and format. Third, librarians may be able to influence decisions about what is published, provided that the publisher knows that the librarian is knowledgeable about what is involved in developing profitable books.

Obviously, most publishers are primarily concerned with making a profit, which includes getting a reasonable return on the money that they invest in producing books, periodicals, and newspapers. Quality and service do matter, but publishers are not in existence to provide quality materials and exceptional services at a constant loss, as some librarians (and patrons) seem to believe. They are in *business*, and are not there just to meet personal information needs when those arise. Publishers must make a profit in order to stay in business, and to do this, they must produce materials that are marketable to a fairly large audience.

Thus, librarians should be among the first to discard the stereotype of the publisher as a retiring, highly sophisticated literary person interested only in creative quality, just as publishers should abandon the view of the librarian as a woman with her hair in a bun, wearing horn-rimmed glasses, and with a constant "shush" on her lips.

What Is a Publisher?

What is a publisher? A simple answer is that the publisher supplies the capital and editorial assistance required to transform manuscripts into books. (Two exceptions to this are vanity and subsidy presses, discussed later in this section.) Generally, publishers in Western countries perform six basic functions. They

1. tap sources of materials (manuscripts);

2. raise and supply the capital to make the books;

3. aid in the development of the manuscript;

4. contract for the manufacturing (printing and binding) of the book;

5. distribute the books—including promotion and advertising;

6. maintain records of sales, contracts, and correspondence relating to the production and sale of books.

One misconception about publishers is that they actually print books. Printing, though, is seldom a function of a major publisher, as publishers enter into a contract with an independent printer for the production of each book. A printer does *not* share in the risk of the publisher and the author in the production of a book. Printers are paid for their composition of type, presswork, and binding regardless of how many or few copies of the book are sold.

In the past, a book's publisher and printer were often one and the same, as can be seen in a number of excellent histories of publishing and the book trade. A thumbnail sketch of a basic pattern in their development is pertinent. The pattern seems to be worldwide and does have an impact on acquisition and selection work. In the history of publishing, there appear to be three stages of development. These stages have occurred both in Europe and America, and they also appear in developing countries as each evolves its own publishing and book trade.

During stage one, the publishing, printing, and selling of the product are combined in one firm, and often in one person or one family. The early "giants" in Europe acted as publisher, printer, and "retail" bookseller—Froben, Schoffer, Manutius, Caxton, and others. When one examines American publishing history, the same pattern appears on the eastern seaboard and moves west with the frontier; names such as Franklin, Green, and Harris fall into this period. Publishing in developing countries exhibits the same evolutionary pattern, which is in large measure a function of how the society has organized its economic, educational, and human resources. In developing countries, though, limited resources, technical skills, and very small markets make it unfeasible, and in many cases impossible, to have specialty publishers in all fields.

From a collection development point of view, stage one development presents many interesting challenges. Large research libraries buy materials from around the world, but developing countries seldom have anything resembling a national bibliography, much less a trade bibliography (mainstays in identifying important titles). As if this were not challenge enough, most publishers operating at a stage one level do not print a large number of copies of their books. In many cases they take orders *before* the book is printed. When this happens they normally print just a few more copies than the number for which they have orders. Many collection development officers have experienced the frustration of having an order returned with the comment "unavailable, only 200 copies printed." The story of the book being out-of-print on the day it was published has a basis in fact, and it frequently occurs in areas where publishing is at the stage one level.

During stage two, specialization begins, with firms emphasizing either publishing or printing. A few firms are established with a single emphasis; again, the factors creating this situation are directly related to economic, educational, and human resources. Better education should and does mean that there is a greater market for books among both individual and institutional buyers. The retail trade usually develops at the same time because the reading public is often widely dispersed and requires outlets across the country. A single outlet in the major population center of the country is no longer adequate. Examples from this early period in American publishing are John Wiley, George Putnam, and the Lippincott Company. In 1807, Charles Wiley joined George Putnam in a bookstore operation in New York City. Over the following 150 years, the heirs of the two men built up two of the leading publishing houses in the United States. The Lippincott Company started in 1836 as a bookstore and over the years shifted in emphasis to publishing.

When bookstores begin to develop, trade bibliographies must be created through which publishers inform bookstores of what is to be or has been published. Collection development librarians expend a great deal of energy in tracking down such systems in those developing countries where the book trade has reached stage two. The usual procedure is to establish a good working relationship with one of the bigger bookstores in such an area and then to work through that shop. This may entail signing an agreement to spend a certain amount of money each year with the firms, but it will ensure much better coverage, and usually better service, than working through individual publishing houses.

The third stage is the complete separation of the three basic functions, as publishers drop their printing activities. For example, John and James Harper started out as printers in 1817. Today, Harper and Row is one of the leading publishers in the United States, but it ceased its printing activities years ago. (Some of the last major publishers to retain printing plants as part of their operations are McGraw-Hill and Doubleday.) By the time this final stage is reached, all the trappings we see in present-day U.S. publishing are evident: specialty publishers, literary agents, trade journals, sales personnel, jobbers and wholesalers, and so forth. Normally there is something resembling a national bibliography as well as a trade bibliography, both of which are essential for collection development work.

Canadian, U.S., and European publishers have gone through two other changes since they reached the third level. Before 1950, most publishing houses were family owned or privately held firms. With the rapid and widespread expansion of the educational materials market, especially in the U.S., most publishers found it impossible to raise enough capital to expand adequately. Slowly at first, and then with increasing frequency, publishers "went public": they sold stock in the firm to the general public. Going public brought about a number of changes in the publishing field, both good and bad. On the positive side, new materials were produced and more services were offered. On the negative side, there was an increased emphasis on profitability, and perhaps a decline in overall quality. The problems were neither as great nor as bad as the doomsday prophets predicted. Certainly, publishers faced a new responsibility to show investors a profit. Under the new arrangements, profitability became more and more important to the now-public publishing houses.

As more and more money was poured into education in the late 1950s and early 1960s, educational publishing became increasingly profitable. High profitability made publishing an area of interest for large conglomerates looking for diversification opportunities, and large electronics and communication firms began to buy up publishing houses — RCA, IBM, Xerox, Raytheon, and General Electric, for example. One interesting combination today is Time-Life, Inc., and General Electric's General Learning Corporation. This group has controlling interest in Little, Brown (trade publisher), Silver-Burdett (school textbook publisher), Peter H. Roebuch (television and educational films), New York Graphics, Alva Museum Replicas, Seven Arts Society, Book Find Club, and five publishing houses in England, Spain, Mexico, and France. There are a number of other "giants" of this type. (Two excellent articles on the merger trend are Celeste West's "Stalking the Literary-Industrial Complex" and a special report "The Question of Size in the Book Industry.")[2]

The potential impact of these new combinations, which control a very high percentage of the total annual sales, is great. If nothing else, it will mean that market potential will take on even greater importance when publishers select manuscripts to publish. Anyone with a little imagination can build a horrible vision of the future of publishing by contemplating this danger. To date, little evidence exists that any real change has come about in the quality of books being produced, but the potential danger is there. Selection and acquisition librarians should be among the first to note any significant changes, provided that they are aware both of what is happening in the publishing field and of the implications of these changes.

Changing economic conditions have caused some slowdown in the merger activity. Many of the companies are now divesting themselves of their publishing holdings. Xerox Corporation, for example, sold many of its publishing holdings, including the R. R. Bowker Company. For others, the changing nature of the production and distribution of information fits nicely with their electronic-broadcasting interests. Only time will tell what significance these changes will have.

A fourth stage is also developing — electronic publishing. Publishers are quickly entering the electronic age in the area of information delivery. Some publishers offer the information in two or more formats — print and electronic — while a few offer some information in an electronic format alone. There are predictions that a large percentage of scholarly and research material will be solely distributed in electronic forms. A report issued in mid-1984 describes a project, cosponsored by the Council on Library Resources, and intended to develop an industry (publishing) standard and create guidelines for the preparation and processing of manuscripts by computer.[3] Although the project's focus is on preparation and processing, ultimately there will be implications for dissemination. At almost the same time, volume 1, number 1, of the *Electronic Text Consortium Newsletter* appeared.[4] Electronic publishing is the storage of numeric, text, and graphic material in a computer and the distribution of material by telephone, satellite, cable, or broadcast transmissions. End users gain access to their material through computers or special decoder terminals. Numerous experiments have been conducted using different delivery systems in several countries: Canada, France, Japan, Sweden, the United Kingdom, and the United States, to name but a few. Perhaps the driving force behind the movement toward electronic publishing is word processing systems and writers' rapid acceptance of these systems. Publishers see this fact as a way to help contain costs. In the first chapter, it was noted that governments have been taking an increasing interest in the electronic transmission of information. In the United States, it appears likely there will be some government regulation, at least of those systems that employ videotext or teletext, by the Federal Communications Commission. Certainly, in other countries there will be strong government involvement in any such system because radio, television, and telephone systems are usually government controlled. Should book and other paper-based communication services die, as some predict, there is every reason to be concerned about intellectual freedom and the free expression of divergent points of view because the computer systems offer an easily controlled distribution network.

Types of Publishers

In the preceding paragraphs the terms *trade*, *house*, and *specialty publishers* were used. *House* is a term that goes back to the period when publishing was a family, or at least a very personal, operation. *Trade* publishers are those that produce a wide range of titles, both fiction and nonfiction, having a wide sales potential. Names such as Harper and Row, Knopf, Doubleday, Macmillan, Little, Brown, Thames and Hudson, and Collins Harvill are typical of the general trade publisher. Trade publishers frequently have divisions that resemble specialty publishers—children's, elementary-high school (Elhi), paperback, technical, reference, and so forth. *Specialty* houses restrict their output to a limited area, subject, or format. Their audience is smaller and often more critical of the product than is the case with the trade publisher's audience. There are a number of categories of specialty houses: textbook (Elhi and college level), paperback, children's, microform, music, cartographic, and subject area.

Textbook publishers, especially at primary and secondary school levels, are in one of the highest risk areas of publishing. Most publishers in this area develop a line of textbooks for several grades, for example, a social studies series. Preparation of such texts requires the expenditure of large amounts of time, energy, and money. Printing costs are high because school texts usually involve the use of color plates and expensive presswork. This means that the investment will be high before there is a chance of recovering the cost. Of course, if enough school districts adopt a text, profits can be great, while failure to secure adoption can mean a tremendous loss. Bigger textbook firms (Ginn and Scott, Foresman, for example) have a number of different series to help ensure a profit or at least to provide a cushion against loss. Why would anyone take the risk this type of publishing involves? A look at the amount of money spent on textbooks each year provides one answer — $2589.7 million in 1984. By carefully planning a series with a great deal of educator cooperation and by focusing on marketing, profits can be enormous. Sales representatives for a trade publisher have a number of potential markets — bookstores, libraries, and wholesalers. Each successful visit will mean the sale of a few copies of each title; the adoption of one textbook could mean a thousand copies sold of a single title. Because of the nature of school textbook adoption practices (a process usually occurring once a year), textbook publishers can reduce their warehousing costs, thus adding to their margin of profit. During the past five years American school textbook publishers have faced increased pressure to change the content of their publications from a variety of special interest groups (see chapter 19).

Subject specialty houses have some of the same characteristics as textbook houses. Their market is restricted and easily identifiable; focused on a limited number of buyers, they can achieve an excellent return. Art (Abrams), music (Schirmer), scientific (Academic), technical (American Technical Society), law (West Publishing) and medical (Saunders) books often require expensive graphic work, which increases the cost of production. While there is a higher risk in specialty publishing than in trade publishing, it is much lower than that which textbook publishers face. Occasionally complaints arise, especially in the law and medical fields, that too much control is in the hands of a very few publishers, but it seems questionable whether more publishing houses in either field would change the picture significantly.

Vanity presses differ from other publishing operations in that they receive most of their operating funds from the authors whose works they publish (an example is Exposition Press). They always show a profit and never lack material to produce. They offer editing assistance for a fee, and print as many copies of the book as the author can afford. Distribution is the author's problem. While providing some of the same functions as other publishers, they do not share the same risks.

Private presses are not usually business operations in the sense that the owner(s) expects to make money. (Examples are Henry Morris, Bird, and Poull Press.) In many instances, the owner(s) do not sell the products they produce — instead, they give them away. Most private presses are owned by individuals who enjoy fine printing and experimenting with type fonts and design. As might be expected, when the end product (often produced on hand presses) is given away, the number of copies is limited. In the past, many of the developments in type and book design originated with a private press. Some of the most beautiful examples of typographic and book design are from private presses. Most private presses are operated as an avocation rather than as a vocation.

Large research libraries often attempt to secure copies of private and vanity press items. By knowing local publishers, persons in the acquisitions department can make their work easier. Authors who use vanity presses frequently give local libraries copies of their book(s), but such gifts usually arrive with no indication that they are a gift. As will be seen in the section on processing, books without packing slips or invoices cause problems. If the staff knows the local vanity and private presses, a great deal of time can be saved by quickly identifying such possible gift items.

Academic scholarly publishers are normally subsidized, not-for-profit organizations. More often than not, they are associated with academic institutions (University of California Press), museums (Museum of the American Indian Heye Foundation), research institutions (Battelle Memorial Institute), or learned societies (American Philosophical Society). These presses were originally established to produce scholarly books. Generally, scholarly books have a very limited appeal, and a commercial (profit-making) publisher is faced with three choices when evaluating a manuscript: (1) publish it and try to sell it at a price to ensure a recovery of costs; (2) publish it, sell it at a price comparable to commercial titles, and lose money in the process; or (3) do not publish the item. Either of the first two options will cost the publisher money and for that reason, most commercial publishers will *not* publish the book. Because of economic factors and a need to disseminate scholarly information regardless of cost—even if it must be done at a loss—the subsidized (by tax exemption, if nothing else), not-for-profit press was created. As publishing costs have sky-rocketed, it has even been necessary to have entire books subsidized, almost in the manner of a vanity press.

Some commercial publishers have raised questions about the validity of the subsidized press. They claim that any work that does more than break even should be offered to commercial publishers. They suggest that this could be done through an auction process; if no commercial publishers bid on the title, it could remain with the scholarly press. Their reasoning is that the scholarly presses (usually, only university presses are the target) are publicly supported by tax monies and/or tax-exempt. Furthermore, they are not supposed to be making a profit. This idea was more the result of a peak in academic library purchases of scholarly works during a period of high funding than it was the result of a desire on the part of commercial publishers to publish scholarly books. To some extent, the scholarly presses may have caused some of these criticisms by publishing works that would and could have been published by a commercial house. Governments subsidize most of the scholarly presses either by direct payments or by tax-exempt status. Yet, as costs rise, the presses are pressured by their funding agencies to at least break even on the majority of books, or to have a few "money makers" to carry the losers.

The role of the scholarly press in the economical and open dissemination of knowledge is critical. Every country needs this type of press in some form. Without such arrangements, important works with a limited appeal will seldom be published. Certainly, there are times when a commercial house will be willing to publish a "loser" because it is thought to be very important, but reliance upon that type of willingness will, in the long run, mean that many important works will not be published.

Government presses are, as a class, the world's largest publishers. The combined annual output of government publications—international (UNESCO), national (Government Printing Office), regional and local (Los Angeles)—dwarfs the commercial total. In the past, government publications were thought to be of poor physical quality, uninteresting, and generally a problem. Today, some government publications rival the best offerings of commercial publishers. Most government publishing activity goes well beyond the printing of legislative hearings or actions and of occasional executive materials. Often, national governments publish essential and inexpensive, frequently free, materials on nutrition, farming, building trades, travel, and a wealth of other topics. (See chapter 8 for more detailed information about government publications.)

Paperback publishing can be divided into two types: quality trade paperbacks and mass market paperbacks. A trade publisher may have a quality paperback division or may issue the paperbound version of a book through the same division that issued the hardcover edition. These titles are distributed in the same fashion as the hardcover books. Mass market paperback publishers are only concerned with the publication of paperback books, and the distribution of mass market paperbacks is very different from other book distribution. They are priced very low, and they are put on sale anywhere the publisher can get someone to handle them. The paperback books on sale in train and bus stations, airline terminals, corner stores, and kiosks are mass market paperbacks.

People talk about the "paperback revolution," but it is hard to think of it as a revolution. Certainly the softcover book has had an impact on publishers and on a few authors' incomes; and some readers seem unwilling to accept a hardcover version when the smaller, more compact size is more convenient to use. A paperback version of a hardcover edition may be released by the original publisher or by a paperback house through the purchase of paperback rights. Using a paper cover rather than a hard cover does not, however, reduce the actual unit cost of a book by more than $0.20 or $0.30, depending upon the size of the printing. The reason the price of a paperback is so very much lower is that in most cases it first appeared in hardback form. This means that many of the major costs in production have already been absorbed. The title has already sold well in hardback, and probably has made a profit for the publisher. Since many of the editorial costs are already recovered, it is possible to reduce the price. Furthermore, the reduced price should help sell more copies, which in turn can help push the price still lower. Naturally, original paperbacks require the same costs, except for the cover material, as a hardcover title.

Books with paper covers have been produced for a long time, at least since the nineteenth century. In some countries this is the standard format. The major difference is that most people only think of the mass market paperback as a paperback. The emphasis on very popular, previously published titles — issued in new and colorful covers and sold at a low price — is apparent. Those are the elements of the paperback revolution, not the paper cover nor even the relatively compact form. Nor has the paperback created a whole new group of readers, as some overenthusiastic writers claim. It has merely tapped an existing market for low-cost popular books.

Paperbacks are, or can be, an important element in collection development. If they are not treated as if they were hardcover items, they can supply multiple copies of popular works at a relatively low cost. If the paperback is purchased as a multiple copy — expendable — item, libraries can make limited collection development funds go a long way toward providing breadth and depth by means of this material which is more readily available for the user.

Newspaper and periodical publishers are still a different class of publisher. For the most part, book publishers depend upon persons outside their organization to prepare the material that is eventually published. Newspaper and periodical publishers are exceptions, in that they retain reporters and/or writers as members of their staffs. Of course, there are exceptions to the exception. For instance, some popular (and most scholarly) periodicals are made up of articles written by persons not employed by the organization publishing the journal. In general, in the field of newspaper or periodical publishing, one finds the same range of activities as in the book field. In other words, there are commercial publishers of popular materials, specialty publishers, children's publishers, scholarly/academic publishers, and of course, government publishers. They share the same characteristics as their book publishing counterparts, and sometimes are divisions of book publishing organizations.

Supplying current information is the primary objective of this type of publisher, in addition to securing enough income to keep operating. As far as currency in book publishing is concerned, one can assume that most of the material in a majority of books was prepared at least six to twelve months prior to the publication date. The newspaper or periodical format provides the means for more rapid publishing, anywhere from two to three months to less than one day. (A major exception are the scholarly and academic periodicals and newsletters that frequently are from one to two or more years behind in publishing articles that have been accepted.) In order to give the community the most current information available, then, the library must acquire those newspapers and/or periodicals that suit the community's needs and interests. The problems concerning control and selection of these materials will be covered in chapter 7; here, the main point about them is their currency when compared with books.

Two other types of publishing activities should be noted: *associations* and *reprint houses*. Professional and special interest groups and associations frequently establish their own publishing houses (American Library Association, Library Association). They may only publish a professional journal, but frequently they may also issue books and even audiovisual materials. The operating funds come from the association but the group hopes to recover its costs. Because associations are often tax-exempt, their publishing activities are very similar to those of scholarly presses: limited-appeal titles, relatively small press runs, relatively high prices, and at least indirect government subsidies. Some associations do not have formal publication staff and use volunteer members; they contract with a commercial publisher to print their journal, conference proceedings, and so forth. Association publications, whether published by the organization itself or by contract, can provide the library with numerous bibliographic control headaches. Titles are announced as forthcoming but never get published. Often the publications are papers from meetings and conventions (the transactions of ..., or proceedings of ...); such publications frequently change title two or three times before they appear in hardcover and often do not find their way into trade bibliographies.

Reprint publishers, as the name implies, are concerned with reprinting items no longer in print. Most of the sales for reprint houses are to libraries and scholars, and many of the titles that these publishers reprint are in the public domain (i.e., no longer covered by copyright). The other major source for reprinted material is the purchase of rights to an out-of-print title from another publisher. Although many of the basic costs have already been covered, reprints are expensive because of their very limited sales appeal. (In the past, some reprints would be announced with a prepublication flyer or order form; later a number of these titles would be reported as canceled. Some suspicious persons suggested that such cancellations were related to a lack of prepublication orders.) Sometimes reprints provide as many, if not more, bibliographic headaches for libraries than association titles do. Despite many problems, reprint houses are an essential source of titles in collection development programs concerned with retrospective materials.

Small presses are important for some libraries. Small presses are often thought of as "literary" by some people, including librarians. Anyone reading the annual "Small Press Round-Up" in *Library Journal* could very reasonably conclude the same thing. The reality is that small presses are as diverse as the international publishing conglomerates. Size is the only real difference, as far as functions and interests are concerned.

Small Press Record of Books in Print annually lists between 15,000 and 17,000 titles from about 1,800 small publishers.[5] Many of the publishers are one-person presses operating out of a spare room or garage and publish only one book per year. An examination of the listings in SPRBIP will show that a full range of subjects is covered and that there are both book and periodical small presses. An assumption that the content of small press publications is poor is incorrect. Small presses do not produce, proportionally, any more worthless titles than do the large publishers. Often it is only through the small press that one can find information on less popular topics. (Two examples of books from small presses are Ruby-Fruit Jungle by Rita Mae Brown and the Boston Women's Health Book Collective's Our Bodies, Ourselves.) Another factor is economics: the large publishers have high costs and need substantial sales in order to recover their costs, while a small press can often produce a limited market book at a reasonable cost and still have reason to expect some profit.

From a collection development point of view, small presses represent a challenge. Generally, new releases are difficult to track down. Len Fulton of Dustbooks has tried to provide access, and he has succeeded to a surprising degree, given the nature of the field. However, waiting for his annual (SPRBIP) may take too long because small presses are frequently moved about and their press runs are short (limited quantity); so by the time the press is located, the book is no longer available. In essence, very few small presses are part of the organized trade or national bibliographic network. Very few of these presses advertise and even fewer of their titles are reviewed in national journals. Lack of reviews is not the result of book review editors discriminating against small press publications; rather, it occurs because small presses have not sent copies to be reviewed.

In the past few years, collection development librarians who are interested in small presses have had some commercial help. Quality Books of Northbrook, Illinois (a vendor known as a source of remainder books) has become active in the distribution of small press publications. Although they stock books from only a small percentage of the presses listed in SPRBIP (about one-fifth), the fact that they do stock the items is a major feature. Most jobbers will say that they will attempt to secure a specific title for a library if they do not stock the publication. A librarian could easily devote too much time to an effort to track down a single copy of a $10.95 list price item from an "obscure" small press. All librarians interested in small presses, collection development, and access to information need to keep their collective fingers crossed in the hope that Quality Books will find its operation sufficiently profitable and that it will continue to offer the service. (For more information on distributors and vendors, see chapter 11.)

It is hoped that this very brief overview of some of the major types of publishing houses and what they do has whetted an appetite to learn more about the field. If so, excellent starting points would be Chandler B. Grannis's What Happens in Book Publishing? and Gerald Gross's Editors on Editing and Publishers on Publishing (see "Further Reading").

Some of the reasons librarians need to know about the producers whose products we buy have been pointed out. Different classes of publishers perform different functions. Knowing which publishers are good at what helps to speed up the selection process because some publishers are known for quality material — well written, organized, edited, and produced as a durable, physical book. Also, it must be pointed out that the wide range of activities in which different groups of publishers engage makes it clear why each class of publisher has different manuscript selection procedures, marketing methods, and discount schedules.

Functions of Publishing

Publishing consists of five basic functions, and they apply equally to print and "nonprint" materials: administration, editorial, production, marketing, and fulfillment. All five functions must be successfully carried out if the organization is to survive for any length of time. Just because the organization is established as nonprofit, it does not mean there is any less need for success in any of the five areas. Administration is concerned with overseeing the activities, ensuring the coordination, and making certain there are adequate funds available to do the desired work.

It is in the editorial area that decisions are made about what to produce. Here, ideas for books, manuscripts, articles, proposals, or other items are discussed and reviewed. Large book publishers develop "trade lists" (publications that have been or will be produced) with the objectives of achieving a profit and avoiding unnecessary competition with other publishers. Book selectors ought to learn something about the chief editors in the major publishing houses with which they deal. The reason seems clear: the editors' opinions about what is good and bad determine what will be available. It is possible to meet editors at library conventions, discuss problems, make suggestions, and thus influence what happens in the coming years. This activity is only possible when librarians know the editors, and understand both their importance in a publishing house and something about the nature of the book trade in general. In addition, librarians can provide valuable marketing information to editors and publishers, again provided that they understand something of the industry beyond its products.

Securing and reviewing manuscripts is a time-consuming activity for most editors. Based on a range of guesses concerning the number of manuscripts reviewed for each one accepted, the "average" seems to suggest that approximately nine-tenths of all manuscripts are rejected after the first examination. After the first complete reading, still more manuscripts are rejected. Even after careful reading by several people, all of whom have favorable reactions, a manuscript may still not be published. Three common reasons for this are: (1) the title will not fit into the new list, (2) the sales potential (market) is too low, and (3) the cost of production would be too high.

Considerations in regard to a company's "trade list" or list of books are very important. The "annual list" is the group of books that a publisher has accepted for publication and plans to distribute over the next six to twelve months. The "back list" comprises books published in previous years and still available. A strong back list of steady selling titles is the dream of most publishers. Editors spend a great deal of time planning their lists. They do not want to have two new books on the same topic appear at the same time unless they complement one another. They want a list that will have good balance and strong sales appeal. Some consideration must also be given to past publications that are still in print.

Librarians and readers often complain that commercial publishers are exclusively, or at least overly, concerned with profit and have little concern for quality. What is forgotten is that publishing houses are businesses and must show a profit if their operation is to continue for any length of time. Even if the presses or publishers are governments, they must try to recover their costs in some manner, and those costs are constantly increasing. In time, even government publishers are forced to ask the same question—is this manuscript really worth producing if it will not even recover the production costs? As costs skyrocket, the answer, more and more often, will be no. What society asks of publishers is to undertake the risk of production and assume that, in some manner, their living needs will be taken care of. A capitalist system involves the right to make a profit on the use of capital. When one can make almost as much "profit" by placing capital in a no-risk savings account as by risking the loss of all of it in a publishing venture, only the compulsive gambler or altruist will *try publishing.* For noncapitalist systems, the decision whether to continue publishing is eventually determined by the willingness of people to continue to underwrite the expense— only society can make that decision, but usually health, safety, and the general good come ahead of books in social priorities.

Production and marketing join with editorial to decide on the final details for the publication. Most published items can be packaged in a variety of ways and employ an equally diverse pricing pattern. Some years ago, the Association of University Publishers released an interesting book entitled *One Book Five Ways* (see "Further Reading"). The book provides a fascinating picture of how five different university presses would handle the same project. In all five functional areas the presses would have done things somewhat differently, from contract agreement (administration), copyediting (editorial), physical format (production), pricing and advertising (marketing), to distribution (fulfillment). Production is concerned with issues such as page size, typeface, number and type of illustrative material, and cover design—as well as with typesetting, printing, and binding issues.

Marketing is concerned with all aspects of promoting and selling the product. How many review copies will be sent out and to what review sources is a decision usually made in the marketing department. Where, when, or if an ad is to be placed is the responsibility of the marketing department, and all these decisions have an influence on the cost of the items produced. Many small publishers use direct-mail (catalogs, brochures) to market their books. Publishers' sales representatives visit stores, wholesalers, schools, and libraries. When salespeople visit the library or information center, they keep the visits short and to the point. Each visit represents a cost to the publisher and the cost will in turn be recovered in some manner—most often in the cost of the material produced. One activity that most marketing units are responsible for is exhibits. For library personnel, convention exhibits are one of the best places to meet publishers' representatives and have some input into the decision-making process. From the publishers' point of view, if the conferees go to the exhibits, conventions can be a cost-effective way of reaching a large number of potential customers in a brief period of time. Librarians should also remember that the fees exhibitors pay to have a booth help underwrite the cost of the convention.

Fulfillment activities are those needed to process an order as well as those connected with the warehousing of the materials produced. In many ways, fulfillment is the least controllable cost factor for a publisher. Libraries and information centers sometimes add to the cost of their purchases by requiring special handling of their orders. Keeping "special" needs to a minimum can help keep prices in check. Speeding up payments to publishers and vendors will also help slow price increases, because the longer a publisher has to carry an outstanding account the more interest has to be paid. Ultimately, each increase in the cost of doing business is passed on to the buyer, so whatever the purchaser can do to help publishers control their fulfillment costs will also help their collection development budgets.

Despite the best efforts of publishers, for various reasons some publications do not sell as well as expected. When this happens, sooner or later the material will have been disposed of—remaindered. A decision by the U.S. Internal Revenue Service has influenced press runs and the speed with which warehouse holdings are remaindered (*Thor Power Tool Decision*). A remaindered item is sold for a small fraction of its actual production costs. Before this decision was rendered, businesses would normally "write-down" the value of their inventories (warehouse stock) to a nominal level at the end of the tax year. This practice would result in a paper loss in the value of the inventory which could then be deducted from the company's income—reducing the tax liability. Now such a reduction can be taken only if the material is defective or was offered for sale below actual production costs. Under the previous method, publishers could still find it profitable to keep slow-selling titles in their warehouses for years. Thus far, efforts to get an exemption from the ruling for publishers have been unsuccessful. At first the ruling increased the number of remaindered books, but now most publishers have cut back on the size of their print runs in an attempt to match inventories to sales volume. More often than not, this means higher unit costs and retail prices. Despite all the problems for the field, total sales income for book publishing has increased steadily: 1972—$3,177,200, 1977—$5,142,200, and 1983—$8,592,000.[6]

Data on annual sales amounts can be found in a variety of sources: *Publishers Weekly*, the *Bowker Annual of Library & Book Trade Information*, Standard and Poor's *Industry Surveys*, etc. Anyone concerned with collection development must make use of statistical data on publishing in order to develop intelligent budgets and work plans. Statistical data on the number of new titles, paperbacks, reprints, etc., can be useful in planning the work load for the next fiscal year—for example, perhaps more staff will need to be hired if the volume of acquisitions is to go up. The two most accessible sources for publishing statistics for U.S. publications are *Publishers Weekly* (*PW*) and the *Bowker Annual* series. Data in both of these sources, and almost all other printed statistical data on publishing, come from the American Publishers Association (APA). Remember that the statistics represent information drawn from APA members, and *not all* publishers belong to the group. In fact, a great many small and regional publishers do not belong.

Annually, two issues of *PW* report this statistical information for the previous year. One issue (normally in February) contains the "preliminary" figures; sometime in the late summer (August or September), the revised figures are released. (The reason for the delay in the final figures is that returns from bookstores and wholesalers cannot be determined quickly.) The *Bowker Annual* information is a condensation of the *PW* reports, but because it is a hardcover volume, considerable delay in reporting the information is inevitable. For small libraries, which do not need to subscribe to *PW*, and for libraries in which the most current cost information is not required, the *Bowker Annual* is a very adequate source.

Publishers use a number of different distribution outlets, selling directly to individuals, institutions, retailers, and wholesalers. Distribution is a major problem for publishers and libraries because of the variety of channels and what their implications are for acquiring a specific publication. Each channel has different types of discounts and is accessed through different sources. Figure 6.1 illustrates in a general way the complexity of the system. Production and distribution of information materials, whether print or nonprint, is made up of many different elements, all interacting with one another. Writers and creators of the material can and do distribute their output in several ways: directly to the community or public, to agents who in turn pass it on to producers, or directly to the producers. Agents may be approached by producers who are seeking writers for specific projects that are thought to be potentially profitable. Producers use a great variety of channels to distribute their publications to the end consumer.

Fig. 6.1. Distribution system.

Most publishers use all these sales channels. Wholesalers, direct mail, and retail store operators act as middlemen; a retailer may buy from the jobber or directly from the publisher. Each seller will have different discounts for different categories of buyers, ranging from 0 to more than 50 percent. Not only are there a great many choices available to the buyer, but the sources compete with one another. All of these factors combine to push up the cost of distributing a publication, which in turn increases its list price. With multiple outlets, with different discounts, and with different credit conditions, the publishing industry has created a cumbersome, uneconomical distribution system.

Selling practices vary from title to title as well as from publisher to publisher; however, a few generalizations can be made. Advertising will help a good book but it seldom, if ever, makes a success out of a poor book. Publishers use both publicity and advertising, which are two different marketing devices. An interview with the author or a review of the book on a national radio or television program are examples of publicity. Generally free, such publicity will do a great deal for the sales of a book. However, the book's topic or its author was thought to be of national interest, or it would not have been selected for attention. Changes in current events can change a slow-moving book into a top seller overnight, something that no amount of advertising can do.

Advertising is done in several ways. First, trade advertising is employed, usually directed toward retail outlets rather than individual buyers. Second, an effort is made to get the book reviewed by major professional and general review media. Third, announcements are placed in professional journals, where the emphasis is on reaching individual buyers, both personal and institutional. Fourth, "cooperative" advertisements ("co-op ads") are placed in the book review sections of many newspapers. They are cooperative in the sense that both the publisher and a retail store pay for the advertisements. Finally, for books with a defined audience for which there is a good mailing list, the publisher may use a direct mailing campaign. Librarians may expect some patron requests to be generated by such efforts.

This brief overview points out some of the most basic elements in publishing. It is intended to start a collection development novice thinking about the trade. The next section presents a discussion of audiovisual producers. Unfortunately, because of their diversity, it is not possible in a limited space to parallel the discussion of print publishing.

Producers of Audiovisual Materials

Any attempt to generalize about audiovisual producers is bound to be superficial; nevertheless, some attempt must be made at sketching in a general picture. Media producers are a very diverse group working with a great many formats (audio recordings, film, filmstrips, video, models, etc.). The following discussion is an attempt to cover all of those audiovisual formats, but it would require a full-length book to describe all the individual variations and exceptions. The reader is reminded that this is to be taken as an overview, not as an analysis of individual media.

Media producers enjoy substantial sales every year to schools and libraries. Indeed, this market is almost the sole sales outlet for the majority of media producers. (Two major exceptions are audio and video recordings.) The audio recording industry is the major source of "other media" for most libraries. Recorded music collections are a common feature of libraries and reflect the fact that a large segment of the general population buys and/or listens to music. In terms of sales, however, libraries and other institutions represent only a fraction of the music industry income. Video recordings are also being added to many library collections, both educational recordings and theatrical film recordings. The motion picture video cassette sales are far larger to the general public than to libraries but in terms of educational video the library is the primary market (including school media centers).

One important fact to remember about almost all media, with the exception of books and filmstrips, is that they are generally group-based and group-paced. Films, videotapes, audiotapes, and some other media require the user to follow the material presented at a fixed pace — the pace of the machine involved. In addition, most media are geared to the average ability and level of knowledge of the target audience. A good number of educational media are designed with group presentation and a teacher in mind, and since libraries do have an educational function, they should have educational media available. While individuals working alone can benefit from the material, they will find it of limited value because it was designed for a different use.

This, then, is the first major difference between book publishers and media producers. Media producers market a product designed primarily for group use. Book publishers market a product designed primarily for individual use. This difference in product use has had a significant influence on the distribution system employed by each of the two. Media producers place a heavy emphasis on direct institutional sales; book publishers do use this method, but outside the textbook field it is not the primary source of sales.

One very important but generally overlooked characteristic of media production is the question of authorship. Books are usually the result of the intellectual effort of one or two persons who then try to find a publisher. Textbook publishers frequently commission books. (Perhaps in the age of merger, this approach is becoming more common.) In media, the process is reversed. Normally, the producer will generate the ideas and seek the necessary persons to carry out the project if it cannot be handled by the company's staff. *This means that the producers have almost total control over what will appear.* It is true as well that book publishers have the final say in what will be published. The difference is that the book publisher receives hundreds of manuscripts and ideas for books to consider each year, and is thus exposed to ideas and needs that otherwise might be overlooked. In addition, even if one publisher rejects a manuscript, there is always the chance that another may pick it up. In essence, the book field has a tradition of being a free marketplace for ideas, whereas this concept is almost nonexistent in the media field. Although this may seem to be a very subtle difference, it does have an impact on the type of material produced and, in turn, upon the library's collection.

Despite these considerations, the media field is often viewed as the field of independence and freedom, an image that arises in part from the relatively low cost of entry into it. One hears many stories about the individual who started off with a few thousand dollars and some equipment and is now a major producer. One does not hear about the thousands of others who tried and failed. Mediocre equipment and a low advertising budget usually mean a mediocre product and few, if any, sales. The opportunity is there, but the chances of success are only slightly better than for any other business venture. As noted, almost anyone may become a media producer. To become a "producer" of 35mm slides (educational, art, travel, and so forth), one needs only a 35mm camera and some money for advertising. Success is *not* likely, but this is all that one needs to become a "media producer" and to be listed in a directory of media sources. In general, the start-up capital (money required to begin operations) is much lower than would be necessary for a book publisher. Good quality professional media production equipment is exceedingly expensive; however, many of the so-called producers do *not* invest in quality equipment. They depend upon commercial laboratories and hope for the best.

Because of a lack of materials and the pressure to have media in schools and libraries, it has been and still is possible to sell copies of extremely poor quality materials because they are all that is available. Purchases are made on the basis of need in curriculum or subject areas rather than on the basis of quality, so in this instance, the problem of quality versus need becomes acute. The need may be present, and the money available, but not qualified producers. Yet, a lack of quality equipment does not keep some persons from trying to produce something to take advantage of the situation. There is nothing wrong with starting off in this way, if it is the only alternative available; and there is constant pressure from buyers on the producer to improve quality. If, after a reasonable period of time for development, there is no improvement, buyers must stop purchasing material, since continuing to buy it will only ensure continued poor performance. (Note: it is not just media producers whose products lack quality, as was illustrated by the Gille family incident in the early 1980s—a family who engaged in extensive but questionable publishing activities.)

Another characteristic of media producers is that their products have a fairly high cost per unit of information conveyed. Many media items can be characterized as single-concept materials. (Single-concept films are a special class of educational films that deal with a very narrow concept, such as cell division, and are usually very short, three to four minutes long.) Books, on the other hand, have a low cost per unit of information. For example, no single film, videotape, audiotape, or set of 35mm slides can convey the same amount of information about American Indians as one 300-page book. This feature of the media has great importance for selection, since not every medium is ideal for every purpose. Librarians must know the advantages of each and select and acquire items on this basis.

Generally, media products cost more per copy than do books. Color, 16mm sound films with a 20-minute running time have an average cost of over $300 per title—close to $20 per minute; today there is a choice of film or video cassette. Sets of 35mm slides will range from $5 to over $100. All media producers have found the most profitable item to be some combination of 35mm filmstrips and a sound track (phonograph record or audiotape is the usual system). In general, the "kit" combinations of media are high-profit items. Prices on such combinations run from $20 to over $100. Also, they are the perfect medium for "building-level" materials—that is, developing media collections around curriculum needs, over a period of time. Because of this cost factor, selectors normally can buy only a few items each year, thus making the selection process very important.

While book publishers use a multitude of outlets to sell their products, media producers use very few. With the exception of audio and video stores and a very few map shops, there are *no* retail outlets for "other media." There are no media-of-the-month clubs (although there are some music and video clubs available), few mail-order houses, and no remainder houses (except for records and some 8mm films). Even wholesalers dealing with all media are few and far between. The main source, and in some cases the only source, is the producer. Because the producers are the basic source, collection development personnel must spend an inordinate amount of time and energy in maintaining lists of producers' addresses. Without such records, schools and libraries would almost have to halt their acquisition of "other media." However, since many producers are small and move frequently, updating of addresses is a constant problem for the library. It also means that directories more than 12 months old must be used with great caution.

The one advantage to this situation is that the market for media is clearly identifiable: schools and libraries. Like the specialty publisher, the media producer is better able to focus advertising and sales activities on a small area with a very good chance of success. Trade book publishers use a broad spectrum of advertising sources, newspapers, periodicals, flyers, radio, and television. In general, the trade publisher must take a shotgun approach, while specialty publishers and media producers should have a much better idea of their market.

Books and other media are both easy to copy. The difference is in the cost of the item, because media items are normally more expensive. Most institutions having the capability to use media also have the capability to duplicate that material. Most producers are concerned about this problem because media buyers normally request materials for preview, and previewing can be an opportunity for copying. Awareness of this potential danger may account for the general absence of wholesalers in the media distribution system. The media for which this danger is greatest are tapes (video and audio) and 35mm slides.

The majority of media producers are small businesspersons without a large capital reserve. For the small media producer, cash flow is a real problem. Anything that the library can do to help the small media firm keep its costs down will help to keep the unit cost of products down as well — for example, using cooperative previewing and keeping order and billing procedures simple.

One other important characteristic of the media field is the speed with which its technology changes. This characteristic is a central problem for everyone concerned with the field — both producers and consumers. Improvements in equipment constantly make existing equipment almost obsolete, and occasionally a new format may, in fact, make equipment obsolete. Because of the volatile nature of the field, many users, with good reason, are reluctant to invest heavily in equipment. For the producer the problem is greater; it means deciding rather quickly whether to go with the new or stay with the old. Staying with the old too long may cut the producer out of the field because of licensing, franchising considerations, or simply not keeping up-to-date. On the other hand, moving too soon may use up capital on a change that does not last. Book publishing can have some of the same problems, but only when the publisher is involved in large-scale printing operations. Printers are more likely to be faced with the problem of changing equipment and technology than are publishers.

Figure 6.2 provides an overview of the basic differences between book publishers and media producers, differences that do have an impact on collection development. Again, the reader is reminded that what is represented are broad generalizations and that there are many exceptions.

	Media Producers	Book Publishers
Audience	Individual as part of a group	Individual
Idea authorship	Company generated	Free agent generated
Use	Group and sequential equipment paced	Self—non-sequential
Cost per concept	high	low
Selection process in library	usually group	individual
Cost to enter field	relatively low	relatively high
Inventory	low	high
Market	more clearly defined	highly variable
Potential sales volume	low	medium
Cost per copy	relatively high	relatively low
Ease of copying	easy to copy/high sales price	easy to copy/low sales price
Distribution	mostly single source	multiple source
Changes in format and equipment	very rapid with high obsolete rate	relatively slow

Fig. 6.2. Media producers—book publishers.

Types of Media

Up to this point, the discussion has focused on some of the main characteristics of the media field. In this section the focus is on the various types of media, with a few notes about their potential use in the library. Chapter 9, on media selection, discusses the value and use of media in the library for the adult audience.

Any list of all available media is bound to be out-of-date by the time it is published. New technologies and new combinations of older forms seem to appear daily. Just when one thinks that the latest developments have been identified and a decision to invest money in the equipment and software has been made, a new, even more exciting and potentially valuable format appears. With these limitations in mind, the following is offered as an extensive but not exhaustive list of media useful in the library:

- Audiotapes (single and multiple track)

- Films (8mm and 16mm, including single concept)

- Filmstrips (with and without sound)

- Flat pictures (photographs, illustrations, original art work, posters, etc.)

- Games (usually educational, but some libraries offer a variety of recreational games)

- Globes (terrestrial and celestial)

- Laser formats (including holograms)

- Maps (flat and relief)

- Microforms (all types)

- Mixed media packages (kits)

- Opaque projector materials (commercial and locally produced)

- Phonograph records (all speeds)

- Printed music (performance and study scores)

- Programmed learning materials (machine and printed book formats)

- Realia

- Slides (35mm and 4x4)

- Specimen collections

- Video formats (including kinescopes)

- Working models (full and scale)

Considering this range of material alone, and remembering the special aspects of the media trade, one can understand why collection development in media areas presents some special problems.

Audiotapes and phonograph records are often thought of together because of the commercial music business, and commercial music (including classical) has had a place in libraries for some time. One problem has been the tendency of most libraries to handle only one speed of phonograph record—currently 33⅓ rpm, even though the 45 rpm is also very popular with young people and many adults. The commercial music trade is reasonably well controlled in a bibliographic sense; certainly there is more control than in any other nonbook format. Audiotapes and compact disks are increasing in popularity in the commercial music field, as anyone walking the streets of a large city will have observed, and they have a special value in the language field. While language learning is always facilitated by hearing the proper sounds, the phonodisc does not allow the learner to hear his or her own pronunciation. Dual track tapes, with an instructor's voice on a nonerasable track and a learner's recording track, increase learning efficiency. Another advantage is that the same tape can be used repeatedly with minimum wear.

Films are also a popular format, at least in public and school libraries. In the past libraries with film collections emphasized the 16mm format; today it is the video cassette. Theatrical films are gaining in popularity as libraries compete in the home entertainment market. Access to theatrical films is reasonably easy because of the number of retail video stores and their need to have "bibliographic" control. Documentary film access is fairly good in the sense that there are a number of guides available. However, independent filmmakers come and go with great speed—many never get listed in guides, and others remain in the guides long after they have gone out of business. Keeping up on changes in the independent filmmakers' field could become a full-time occupation for a person if serious collecting is a goal.

Filmstrips, as noted earlier, have become one of the most popular formats with producers, primarily because they have a very low production cost and a high profit margin. Many book publishers have ventured into the media field in this format. Sometimes it is the first and only additional format; more often, it leads to other varieties. By and large, this format is still geared to the primary and secondary school market, and bibliographic control of this format is always focused on that market. Even the material designed for the school market has potential value in the self-education of adults, if it is made available to the general user.

Flat pictures have been available in the library vertical files for years, although use of these materials was usually confined to schoolteachers and students. With the introduction of rental collections of art reproductions and even original paintings and prints, as well as a choice of frames in some cases, the flat picture audience has expanded to include most adult patrons. Many libraries have found that these materials provide one of the most popular services they can offer. Aside from a few UNESCO publications, there is little or no control in this field. Selectors and acquisition staff must learn about producers and maintain files of catalogs in order to secure these materials.

The idea of buying educational games for library collections is only beginning to develop in the United States, yet libraries in the Nordic countries have been lending recreational games for years. It is strange that when lending music seems natural for libraries, and when there is a general acceptance of lending art (at least of reproductions), the lending of games is frowned upon. Could it be that most music collections are predominantly classical and art collections include only "good" art? One problem may be that the issue has not been discussed, and that access to games is difficult. Until more institutions enter the game-buying market, there will be little incentive to improve control. This means that a library wanting to buy games must develop its own file of sources and catalogs.

Globes and maps, although different in form and requiring very different handling, are normally secured from the same source. In the past, most libraries have had a small collection of maps and perhaps one or two globes. At the present time this picture is changing. There is an increasing variety of globes available—smooth and in relief—and in small sizes that make them true study aids. Increased leisure time has caused a great increase in interest in maps of recreational areas for boaters, campers, and hikers. However, control of map production is very uneven. There are not too many commercial sources of maps, and these are easy to identify. Unfortunately, the largest producers of maps are governmental agencies, and while federal agency maps are reasonably well controlled, for state and local agencies there is no central means of access. Large-scale local maps are not often produced by the national government, so local sources are very important. So once again, it becomes a matter of the acquisition department developing its own lists.

Laser technology and its place in the library and information field is just being explored, and the potential for holograms is tremendous. As a storage unit of printed information, the hologram far surpasses the microformats. A few technical and research libraries now have small collections of holograms, and most, if not all, of these have been produced in research and development units of companies or in engineering departments of universities; however, no published list of sources exists for holograms. News notes of available holograms in technical and scientific journals provide the only means at this time of learning what is on the market. Perhaps the hologram's greatest potential is in combination with other formats rather than as a separate form.

Next to recordings, microforms are probably the most common audiovisual format in libraries. Because of their popularity as a compact storage medium for printed materials, bibliographic control is good. Until recently, there was little or no new material appearing initially in microform, since it has been and still is used to secure copies of out-of-print books, archival material, and unique items. Microform is used as a means of storing material in a compact form, and recently it has been used to disseminate research reports to a large audience at a very low unit cost. Some firms now exist that "publish" only in a microformat: their inventory consists of the original copy, and they generate another copy when they receive an order. This format will no doubt grow in importance, if for no other reason than that its storage capability and the ease with which "hard copy" can be made. The low cost per unit is another reason that this format will grow in popularity. A variation is the COM (computer output microform), which is usually a microfiche that has been created from computer files. We use such a system in Tozzer Library to produce *Anthropological Literature*.

Two very popular mixed media packages are filmstrips with a sound track and 35mm slides with a sound track, both of which are primarily educational packages. Some producers put together packages that include printed matter (workbooks or texts), records, and filmstrips or slides. Slides, 16mm films, separate sound tracks, holograms, and video material have been combined, but the cost of these packages is relatively high. Many of the packages appear to have been put together with little consideration of their combined effectiveness. Thus, as with any medium, librarians must know the strengths and weaknesses of the form and acquire only those that meet their specific needs. The educational mixed media packages are reasonably well controlled and are listed in many guides. Often the package will be listed in every guide under each form, that is, a filmstrip and record kit will be listed both in filmstrip guides and record guides.

Transparencies and/or opaque projector materials are directed primarily at schools. Of all the media, this form is the most group-oriented, designed to aid in the presentation of graphic material to small- and medium-sized groups. While an individual can use the material, it has no advantage over flat pictures. A library could obtain materials related to adult education classes, especially in the science fields. Plainly, this material has very limited value to the individual user and is not likely to be found in many public or academic libraries. There are a number of guides to educational transparencies.

One rather surprising void in public and academic libraries is printed music. When both recorded music and books about music are available, why is it so difficult to secure the score? Cost is one possible explanation, but then most other media cost more than books. Difficulty in handling (storage and checking in the parts) may be another aspect of the problem, but other media are also "difficult" to handle in some way. Certainly music publishers' catalogs are available, and there is a real need in the community.

Programmed learning materials, working models, specimen collections, and realia are intended mainly for schools (primary and secondary). While a few items are useful for adults who are studying a subject on their own, they are bought by most public libraries only in order to supplement school library resources. A number of catalogs and guides to these items exist.

Slowly gaining in popularity for general library use are 35mm slides. Although slide collections have existed in a few libraries for many years, slides have been directed at teachers rather than the general public. Because of the popularity of 35mm photography and availability of home projection equipment, many libraries find that a slide collection quickly becomes one of the most popular materials in the library. Perhaps the greatest problem in collecting slides is the large number of sources of highly variable quality. One must be certain to check each slide for quality, especially color, purity, and durability; this makes the acquisition process very time-consuming.

Video formats are probably one of the most promising forms for information dissemination. The two formats that are most likely to be used are videotape and disk. One of the newest developments in video is the disk format, which is similar to a disk phonograph record, as it uses a vinyl base with the image embedded in the surface. While the disk may be the future direction for video, at the present time, two incompatible disk systems are being developed. Laser disk technology is also being explored by the Library of Congress as a means of storing printed material. One of the big advantages of videotape is the relative ease with which the same image can be given a new sound track. Many different languages can be used with the same image. I know of one case in the United States, where a library produced a series of videotapes on how to tune up a truck. After producing the master visual tape they produced copies with English-, Spanish-, and several American Indian-language sound tracks. (One can do this with 16mm sound film as well, but the cost is very high.)

Unfortunately for media producers, there is no source similar to the Grannis book on publishing that would explain the field in depth. One must search for information on each format in a variety of sources—educational (including library-related), technical, and commercial.

Producers' Problems and Collection Development

Although we have looked at only a few of the most basic problems of information materials producers, even that discussion has taken up a fairly large number of pages. Collection development personnel need to understand some of the important issues and problems facing producers, since those factors will inevitably have an impact on the library. Rising costs create problems for everyone, but publishers and media producers have some special problems. Information producers experience pressure from two sides. On the one hand, the rising costs of materials and labor put pressure on them to raise the prices of their products. On the other, if they do raise prices, they must realize that this may cut more deeply into sales than the increase itself. The consumer must meet basic needs first, and—during periods of inflation—meeting basic needs cuts into funds available for luxury items. For the majority of individual buyers, books and media are one of the first items to be cut or reduced.

Institutional buyers will continue to need to buy materials but they face several problems. All of the producers are likely to increase their prices over a relatively short period of time. A fixed materials budget over a two- or three-year period, in combination with increasing costs of materials, means that the library will buy fewer items each year. A second problem is that most institutions are not given large budget increases during inflationary periods. What increases they do receive usually do no more than keep pace with inflation; thus, for all practical purposes, the budget is static. These two factors combine effectively to cut the number of items purchased, and producers must carefully weigh these concerns before raising prices. This in turn forces them to be more and more selective in regard to the items they do produce—few, if any, money losers will be carried.

Resource sharing between libraries is being widely discussed. During periods of tight budgets, many libraries actively cooperate rather than just give lip service to the concept. Sharing resources will help ensure that copies at least will be available, even if not on a convenient basis; however, such cooperation means an overall decline in the market for producers. How to handle this market decline and the related concept of resource sharing have been knotty problems for producers and librarians for a long time. Librarians are concerned with how to achieve real resource sharing, while producers worry about how to react to the new system should it materialize. One approach for the producers is to tie the issue to the concept of copyright, which will be discussed in chapter 18; it is mentioned here to illustrate how complex the issues are.

If producers could simplify their distribution system, they could achieve significant savings. Why should the general consumer (individual or institution) be able to purchase an item directly either from the producer, a wholesaler, or retailer? The system as it now operates is cumbersome and costly. For book publishers, it is currently a matter of having a typical marketing system (producer to wholesaler to retailer) but at the same time, this system allows *any* individual customer access to any level of the system to make a purchase. Media producers, on the other hand, use a direct sales method in most cases. Both systems are costly for everyone. The book system requires complex handling procedures at each level because of different classes of customer. The media system, with single-item orders to be shipped to numerous locations, runs up the cost of placing and filling an order. The impact on collection development is that more money goes into paperwork and administrative procedures, and less is available for collection development. Both producers and librarians must worry about this problem.

Perhaps the most difficult question concerns the right to use knowledge resources, or rather how they may be used. As noted, copyright has become a central issue between librarians, educators, and other users of knowledge resources on the one hand, and the producers on the other. Yet, without copyright, there is little incentive for anyone to produce a work. The problem is how far society can go to provide and protect such incentives and still ensure adequate access to material at a fair price. Libraries want fairly open, free access and use while producers want limited free access. This issue, of course, has, or will have, an important role to play in determining how a collection can be developed.

Notes

[1]Frederick W. Lancaster, *Libraries and Librarians in an Age of Electronics* (Arlington, Va.: Information Resources Press, 1982).

[2]Celeste West, "Stalking the Literary-Industrial Complex," *American Libraries* 13 (May 1982): 298-300; "The Question of Size in the Book Industry," *Publishers Weekly* 214 (31 July 1978): 25-54.

[3]*Electronic Manuscript Project: Task One Requirement Study* (Washington, D.C.: Association of American Publishers, 1984). EMP Document no. 2.

[4]*Electronic Text Consortium Newsletter* 1, no. 1 (1984). San Diego, Calif.: The Center for Communication, San Diego State University.

[5]*Small Press Record of Books in Print* (Paradise, Calif.: Dustbooks, annual).

[6]*The Bowker Annual of Library & Book Trade Information* (New York: R. R. Bowker, 1974, 1979, and 1985).

Further Reading

General

Arthur Anderson Company. *Book Distribution in the United States.* New York: R. R. Bowker, 1982.

Dave, R. *The Private Press*, 2d ed. New York: R. R. Bowker, 1983.

Dessauer, J. P. *Book Publishing: What It Is, What It Does*, 2d ed. New York: R. R. Bowker, 1981.

Electronic Publishing and the UK: Prospects, Economies and Constraints. London: British Library, 1986.

Grannis, C. B. *What Happens in Publishing?* 2d ed. New York: Columbia University Press, 1967.

Gross, G. *Editors on Editing.* New York: Grosset, 1962.

_____. *Publishers on Publishing.* New York: Grosset, 1961.

Lancaster, F. W. *Libraries and Librarians in an Age of Electronics.* Arlington, Va.: Information Resources Press, 1982.

Melinat, C. H. *Librarianship and Publishing.* Syracuse, N.Y.: Syracuse University Press, 1963.

Oakeshott, P. *Impact of New Technology on the Publication Chain.* London: Pontish Library, 1983.

One Book Five Ways. Los Altos, Calif.: William Kaufmann, Inc., 1977.

Small Press. Westport, Conn.: Meckler Publishing, 1983- .

Academic

Day, M. P. "Electronic Publishing and Academic Libraries." *British Journal of Academic Librarianship* 1 (Spring 1986): 53-70.

Graham, G. "Adversaries or Allies?" *Scholarly Publishing* 14 (July 1983): 291-97.

Lustig, S. "UK Academic Library Purchasing Patterns." *The Bookseller* 4208 (16 August 1986): 646-50.

National Enquiry into Scholarly Communication. Baltimore, Md.: Johns Hopkins University Press, 1979.

Public

Eaglen, A. B. "Publishers' Trade Discounts and Public Libraries." *Library Acquisitions: Practice and Theory* 8, no. 2 (1984): 95-97.

Harper, T. "Public Library and Small Presses." *Show-Me Libraries* 34 (October 1982): 8-9.

Johnson, P. "What Publishers Should Know about the Public Library." *Publishers Weekly* 211 (28 March 1977): 40-42.

School

Roginski, J. W. "When the Publisher Calls: Children's Libraries and Telephone Sales." *School Library Journal* 32 (October 1985): 98-101.

Scilken, M. H. "Children's Book Discounts—Are You Getting Ripped Off?" *Unabashed Librarian* 35 (1980): 12.

Special

Krupp, R. G. "Issues in Acquisition of Science Literature." In *Special Librarianship*, 492-99. Metuchen, N.J.: Scarecrow Press, 1980.

White, H. S., and B. M. Fry. "Economic Interaction between Special Libraries and Publishers of Scholarly and Research Journals." *Special Libraries* 68 (March 1977): 109-14.

7
Serials

Journals, magazines, periodicals, and serials are labels that are used by individuals when writing or talking about the subject matter of this chapter. Often the terms are used interchangeably and no great misunderstandings result from the imprecise usage. The *American Library Association Directory* provides the following definitions:

> *Serial*—"a publication issued in successive parts, usually at regular intervals, and, as a rule, intended to be continued indefinitely. Serials include periodicals, annuals (reports, yearbooks, etc.) and memoirs, proceedings, and transactions of societies."

> *Periodical*—"a publication with a distinctive title intended to appear in successive (usually unbound) numbers of parts at stated or regular intervals and, as a rule, for an indefinite time. Each part generally contains articles by several contributors. Newspapers, whose chief function it is to disseminate news, and the memoirs, proceedings, journals, etc. of societies are not considered periodicals."[1]

Definitions in general dictionaries have more overlap: *journal*—"a periodical publication especially dealing with matters of current interest—often used for official or semi-official publications of special groups"; *magazine*—"a periodical that usually contains a miscellaneous collection of articles, stories, poems, and pictures and is directed at the general reading public"; *periodical*—"a magazine or other publication of which the issues appear at stated or regular intervals—usually for a publication appearing more frequently than annually but infrequently used for a newspaper"; *serial* — "a publication (as a newspaper, journal, yearbook, or bulletin) issued as one of a consecutively numbered and indefinitely continued series."[2] Throughout this chapter the term *serials* will be used, as it represents the broadest spectrum of materials of interest here.

For many patrons serials are the most important source of printed information. Serials generally contain the most current information about a topic, although some of the professional society serial publications are very slow to appear. Currency is an important factor, and providing a system which allows patrons to determine the latest issue received is important in most libraries. Related to currency is the frequency of updating information. Very few monographs are ever updated and for those titles that do go into second or more editions, the updating interval is normally several years. For serials, the update interval can be very short; daily in the case of most newspapers. Articles in a serial are short and focus on a fairly narrow subject; thus readers with very specific information needs frequently find that serials provide the desired data more quickly than in monographic publications. Finally, serials are often the first printed source of information about a new subject or development. People use serials as a source for learning about new "things" while they use monographs to gain a broader or deeper knowledge of a subject they first encountered in a serial.

Selection of Serials

A decision to subscribe to or place a standing order for a serial is a much bigger decision than for a monograph. Several factors account for the difference. Unlike the monograph, a serial normally implies a long-term commitment, year after year after year. Subscriptions require renewals, but under some vendor plans (e.g., Till Forbidden — TF), the renewal is automatic, without any further decision from the collection development staff. When the subscription renewal requires a positive decision from the library, there is a greater chance that the serial holdings will reflect the current interests of the patrons. With a TF system or standing order, there is a greater chance that inappropriate serials will continue to be paid for and continue to be added to the collection.

Because of the long-term commitment, the cost of the subscription becomes almost a fixed feature of the budget and each year takes an increasing proportion of the total materials budgets. Chapter 12 (fiscal management) provides more information about this problem, but in general, serial prices have been increasing at a much higher rate than general inflation. Thus each year the amount of money required even to maintain the present serials will increase at a rate higher than many libraries are able to sustain, and still maintain the same level of monographic acquisitions.

Another "fixed" cost is processing. When a monograph is ordered and received, it is a one-time cost. Serials have an ongoing receiving cost as well as ordering and renewal costs. "Claiming" missing issues is a normal part of maintaining a serials collection. Each issue is recorded when it arrives in the library and when a number is skipped a claim is made to the publisher. Acting promptly on claims is important because serial publishers print runs only slightly larger than the number of subscribers. Serial publishers know a certain percentage of issues sent out will go astray in the mail and print extra copies to cover the expected claims. However, at times the number of claims is greater than copies available. When that happens, a number of unlucky librarians receive out-of-print notices. The closer the claim is to the publication date, the greater the chances are of receiving the missing issue. Serial "check-in" should be done the day the items arrive. In a library with a large serials list, one or more persons may devote all their time to processing serials. Clearly, each new serial adds to the work load on an ongoing basis.

By their nature, serials arrive in successive issues, normally in paperback form. If they are to be kept for long periods of time and relatively heavy use is expected, serials are "packaged" for more convenient handling. One method is to store or package the loose issues in a cardboard or metal container (sometimes referred to as a "Princeton File") that keeps a limited number of issues together in a vertical position. This allows the loose items to be more easily shelved with bound materials. On the container there is enough room to record a title and issue or volume number of the items in the box. The other common package treatment is to bind the serials. Whichever choice is made, there is an ongoing cost to "package" each serial, year after year. A third alternative, microformat storage, is available, but it too represents additional expenses.

Serials are not only taking up an ever-increasing percentage of the total funds available for collection development, they are also occupying a greater portion of the available storage space. A year's worth of a weekly magazine may use as much as a foot of storage space when it is bound. As space becomes scarce, the decisions about what to keep and for how long become more and more difficult. Because of the "current" nature of most serials, the older holdings are often prime candidates for remote storage/access. (See chapter 14.) After the first decisions about storage are made, future space needs and weeding decisions become increasingly complex and take more time, and can lead to conflicts between staff and patrons.

An important consideration in serials selection is how the patron gains access to the information each issue contains. Going through each issue is not efficient, and few patrons are willing to do this. Many serials produce an annual index, but this is of no help with the current issues. An entire "industry" has developed around the problem of providing access to serials. A variety of indexing and abstracting services now provide services that assist in locating information in serials. Naturally, most of these services are expensive and are a "hidden" cost of building a serials collection. Although Tozzer Library's circumstances are atypical, it does provide an illustration of the nature of the problem. We receive over 1,200 serial titles each year. If we did not do our own indexing, we would have to spend over $20,000 per year in indexing and abstracting services and still only achieve 83 percent coverage of our serial holdings. One question is, should one subscribe only to serials that are indexed in commercial services? If a library subscribes to an unindexed title, does it do anything to help patrons locate information in the new serial? Specialized (subject) indexing services can also lead to patron requests for titles indexed in the service but not held by the library. The library is then faced with the choice of adding yet another title to the serials list, increasing the work load on the interlibrary loan (ILL) department, or having unhappy patrons. The ILL choice as a means of not subscribing may be influenced by copyright law provisions (see chapter 18) concerning the frequency with which one may legally borrow serials titles.

Serials also have a tendency to increase the volume of photocopying activities. Because serial articles tend to be short, many people prefer to photo-copy the article and consult the material at their leisure. Also, many libraries do not allow serials, or at least journals, to circulate, which also tends to promote heavy photocopying. The level of library or information center photocopying is also a legal/copyright issue. While photocopying of monographs is also covered by copyright law, it is the serials photocopying that has been and is the major concern.

Finally, if a library is not starting a subscription with volume 1, number 1, the librarian must also make a decision regarding "back issues" or volumes. Are the back files needed? If so, where can the files be placed? Some serial publishers will have full runs available, but most will not. Titles that are widely held by libraries may be available from reprint houses. Backfiles tend to be expensive, they may often be difficult to find, they may require binding, and they certainly will take up valuable shelf space.

Given all of the above factors, it is clear why the serials selection decision is a major decision. Yet all too often it is treated as being no different than a decision to acquire a monograph. Even if all of the above factors are considered, one other issue must be kept in mind. Serials can and do change over time. New editors, governing boards, and/or owners make major and minor shifts in the content and orientation of their serial publications. The major shift in emphasis is usually well publicized. Selectors will become aware of shifts and can reassess the serial. A more difficult shift to identify is the slow shift over a number of years. The final result may be a greater difference in content than a well-publicized "major" change, but few people will be aware of the situation. Periodic examination of incoming serials by the selection officers is an excellent method for checking on changes in emphasis.

What Is a Serial?

About 10 years ago, Fritz Machlup and others developed an 18-part classification system for serials.[3] The discussion that follows is based on this classification system, which appears to cover all types of serials. One of the categories is "other serials, not elsewhere classified" and in the last six years of discussing this classification system with a variety of people, I have not learned of a serial that would not fit into one of the other 17 categories.

One category is "annual, semi-annual, quarterly or occasional reports of corporations, financial institutions, and organizations serving business and finance." Academic libraries serving business and management programs frequently need to acquire this type of serial. Some corporate libraries also actively collect this serial category. Most of the reports that are available to libraries and information centers are free for the asking. Some organizations will add a library to their distribution list while others will only respond to a request for the current edition. Collecting in this area has been and still is very labor-intensive, in the sense of maintaining files and correspondence, especially if one collects much beyond the large national corporations. Certainly, having a computer system that has both word processing and mailing list capabilities will make collecting somewhat less tedious, but will not reduce the need constantly to monitor the program. Corporations issue annual reports every month of the calendar year. Often the annual report is tied to an annual meeting of the management board, owner, or stockholders which, in turn, frequently is related to the month in which the organization was originally established. It may be difficult to find a satisfactory vendor for this serials category, except for 10-K reports to the Securities and Exchange Commission that are available on microfiche from Disclosure, Inc. A good discussion of the vendors that do offer annual report assistance can be found in Judith Bernstein's "Corporate Annual Reports: The Commercial Vendors."[4]

A related category is "annuals, biennials, occasional publications, bound or stapled, including yearbooks, almanacs, proceedings, transactions, memoirs, directories and reports of societies and associations." Serials in this class are widely collected by academic, special, and large public libraries. The more libraries that collect a particular society's or association's publications, the more likely it is that a commercial vendor will handle a standing order for the material. Although it will be possible to secure some of these serials through a vendor, a significant number can only be secured directly from the society.

Two other labor-intensive collecting categories are (1) "superseding serial services (each new issue superseding previous ones, which are usually discarded) including telephone directories, airplane schedules, catalogs, loose-leaf data sheets, etc.," and (2) "nonsuperseding serial services bound, sewn, stapled, or loose-leaf, including bibliographic and statistical data." Most of the materials in these classes must be acquired directly from the publisher. Superseding serials are important but present a problem: important because people need the correct or current information, and a problem to keep track of and sometimes to secure. Airline schedules, current hotel guides, and other travel-related "serial" sources have been something of a problem for libraries to acquire in the past. Often the publishers would only sell the material to a qualified travel agency. As more and more corporations handle staff travel on their own, it has become easier for libraries to subscribe to such services. In many corporations the library or information center is expected to maintain current travel information. In the United States since the "break up" of AT&T, libraries have found it more difficult and expensive to secure telephone directories outside their immediate area. Looseleaf services are particularly important in American law libraries and accounting firms. Proper filing and discarding can be of critical importance in such an environment because incorrect information can be very costly to a firm (perhaps the clearest way to identify the cost of not having the right information at the right time). With the looseleaf service, making certain that all sections that have been released are received is also important.

Nonsuperseding serials are less of a problem and some are available from serial jobbers. However, most of the materials in this class tend to be rather expensive and must be ordered directly from the publisher. Indexing and abstracting services fall into one of these two classes. All types of libraries need a few of these reference serials. As the serial collection grows, there is an increasing demand from patrons for more indexing and abstracting services.

Newspapers, another serial category, are widely held in all types of libraries, with the exception of elementary school media centers. Almost every small public library receives the local newspaper and one or two newspapers from some nearby communities. Large public and academic libraries try to have some national and foreign newspaper coverage. Serial jobbers handle subscriptions to major newspapers for libraries. Thus it would be possible to place one order with a jobber such as Faxon or EBSCO for almost all the major newspapers from around the world. Selectors and collection development officers will need to set a "value" on the newspapers' content at the time the order is placed, in the sense of how much demand or need exists to have the latest issue in the shortest possible time. For example, the *London Times* is offered in a variety of packages (and of course, costs): daily (airmail edition) by air freight, daily airmail edition by airmail (the most expensive), daily regular edition by air freight, and daily regular edition in weekly packets (least expensive) and a microfilm edition. *The New York Times* has even a wider variety of editions and modes of delivery: city edition, late city edition, national edition, New York edition, and large-type weekly. As is clear, it is not just a matter of entering a subscription to "the newspaper." Depending on the library's clientele, a certain edition and delivery method will provide the right service at the least cost, but determining the right combination takes more time than selecting a book.

Newspapers present special storage and access problems. Display of recent issues can take up a large portion of a "current issues" area when a library has several newspaper subscriptions. For research libraries, long-term storage is a problem. Bound newspapers tend to be very large, heavy, and awkward to handle. The quality of newsprint paper is poor and presents preservation problems. Today, most libraries use a microformat for back issue storage, but this adds to the overall subscription cost because most newspapers control the microfilming of their publication. Access is also a problem, except for the very largest newspapers, because indexing services tend to cover only the best-known papers and may be slow to be published.

Newsletters, leaflets, news releases, and similar materials are of major importance for some libraries and represent another serial category. Special libraries are the most likely to become involved in the ongoing collecting of this class of serial. Most of the items in this class are very inexpensive and often are free. Time and effort are required to identify the sources and get on the appropriate mailing lists. Libraries in marketing and public relations firms are likely to be very active collectors of this type of material. Any library operating in a disturbed-reactive or turbulent information environment (see chapter 1) is likely to collect heavily in this class.

Machlup defined two broad groups of serials—magazines and journals, each with several subcategories—as periodicals which are "published more than once per year."[5] Magazines are the mass market serials and the ones that almost any serial jobber will handle for a library. Machlup divided magazines into five categories: "newsweekly or monthly magazines"; "popular magazines (fiction, pictures, sports and games, travel and tourism, fashion, sex, humor, comics, etc.)"; "magazines for popularized science, social, political and cultural affairs, etc."; "magazines for opinion and criticism (social, political, literary, artistic, aesthetic, religious, etc.)"; and "other magazines not elsewhere classified." It is easy to think of magazine titles in each of these categories, with perhaps the exception of the last one. "Other magazines ..." are published by many organizations and even governments for a general or mass market and serve to promote, to a greater or lesser extent, those groups' services or products; these magazines also contain articles of general interest that are not related to the organization in any direct manner. An example is the magazine, published for the airline, found in the seat pocket on an airplane. Magazines in the last category are seldom handled by serial vendors and are not widely collected by libraries.

Journals are also divided into four subcategories, with one category divided into two smaller units: "nonspecialized journals for the intelligentsia well-informed on literature, art, social affairs, politics, etc."; "learned journals for specialists—primary research journals and secondary research journals (reviews, abstracts, literature surveys, etc.)"; "practical professional journals in applied fields, including technology, medicine, law, agriculture, management, library science, business, and trades"; and "parochial journals of any type but addressed chiefly to a parochial audience (local, regional)." Again, most titles in these categories are available through vendors, although some of the more specialized learned journals must be ordered directly from the publisher. Parochial journals are usually direct-purchase items; local history and archaeological publications are examples of this class of serial.

The final serial category identified by Machlup was "government publications, reports, bulletins, statistical series, releases, etc. by public agencies, executive, legislative and judiciary, local, state, national, foreign and international." As the next chapter addresses government documents, no further discussion of this category is needed here.

Identifying Serials

Serials employ a different bibliographic network than that used by monographs. Very few of the selection aids for books provide coverage of serials. There are several general guides to serial publications, as well as specialized guides. Reviews of serials are few and far apart. In the past, this was not such a problem when publishers would supply several free sample copies for the library to examine. Today many publishers charge for sample issues and while that money depletes the funds for subscribing to serials and adds to the time to acquire, it is useful to get sample issues before committing the library to a new serial.

Three useful general guides are *Ulrich's International Periodicals Directory* (R. R. Bowker), *Irregular Serials & Annuals* (R. R. Bowker), and *Standard Periodical Directory* (Oxbridge Communications). They are all arranged by subject and entries provide all the ordering information. Ulrich's annuals are updated by *Ulrich's Quarterly. Standard Periodical Directory* covers American and Canadian titles and has a reputation for providing the best coverage of publications with small circulations, lesser known organizations, and "processed" materials. Other general guides are *Guide to Current British Journals* (London: Library Association), *Swets Info* (Lisse, Netherlands: Swets Subscription Service), and *Brown Quarterly Serial Bulletin* (Godalming, England: Stevens and Brown).

Newspapers, newsletters, and serials published at least five times a year can be identified in guides such as *IMS Ayer Directory of Publications* and *Willings Press Guide* (Thomas Skinner Directories). For literary publications one should use *International Directory of Little Magazines and Small Presses* (Dustbooks), *MLA International Bibliography* (Modern Language Association), and *L'Année Philologique* (Societe International de Bibliographie Classique).

All of the above, with the exception of *Ulrich's Quarterly*, are of limited value in identifying new titles because they are annuals, which means the information is at least several months old. As noted earlier, serials change in a variety of ways (titles, frequency, editorial policy, and so on), and keeping up with existing titles is enough of a problem without adding the need to identify newly created serials. The best source of information for serials acquired by American libraries is the Library of Congress's *New Serial Titles* (*NST*), which now reflects data in OCLC. The data in *NST* are based on a cooperative effort—*Con*version of *Ser*ials or CONSER. Some sense of the number of serial titles one will need to consider is conveyed by the fact that in 1981 there were 339,000 CONSER records in OCLC; in 1986 there were more than 865,000. If one can justify costs, online systems provide the most current information. Certainly OCLC is one source, as are BRS and DIALOG. The latter services have information from *Ulrich's*. Such services are current but very costly; $75.00 per hour is not an uncommon charge, so one must be certain that the speed and currency are truly needed. Some serial vendors also supply new serial titles information online.

Writing, or using, a review of serials presents certain difficulties. Because serials change so much, the only completely accurate assessment can be made after the serial has ceased and all the issues can be examined. Serials that are reviewed are usually the popular magazines rather than learned journals. All that one should expect from a review of a serial is an accurate description of the content of the issue(s) at hand; as much information about the purpose, audience, and editorial policy as the reviewer can identify; information about publisher, price, frequency, and other technical matters; and, if appropriate, comparisons to other related serials. Unfortunately, even some of those limited data may be lacking, as it is sometimes difficult to determine purpose and editorial policy, even with the volume 1, number 1, issue in hand. Information about the publisher is less important in serials selection than with monographs because many times the serial is the only publication, and only time will reveal the publisher's reliability.

One publication, *Serials Review* (Pierian Press), does provide some reviews of serials prepared by serials librarians and occasionally by subject experts. The journal is both a reviewing journal and a professional journal for serials librarians; thus, as much as half of an issue is devoted to articles about serials. An important feature of *Serials Review* is that "established" serials are reviewed along with new titles. This policy helps the librarian monitor changes in editorial policy of titles to which the library has already subscribed.

Library Journal (R. R. Bowker) also has a regular section on new periodicals. Each issue contains brief annotations on six to ten new titles. Because of the breadth of coverage, most types of libraries will find some titles of interest "reviewed" in the course of a year. Bill Katz has been the editor of the *Library Journal* (*LJ*) periodical section and every few years he compiles a book, *Magazines for Libraries: For the General Reader, and School, Junior College, College, University and Public Libraries*.[6] He covers between 6,000 to 7,000 titles and, of course, all the titles are recommended.

New Magazine Review (New Magazine Review) is designed to help public librarians select appropriate new serials. Choice (Association of College and Research Libraries) features a column, "Periodicals for College Libraries." Another way to see new titles is to check at book and serial exhibitor booths at professional association meetings.

Serial Vendors

For most libraries, it is not economical to place serial subscriptions directly with the publisher. The amount of work required to monitor expiration dates, place renewals, and approve payments over and over again for each title is too great. In a sizable serials collection, some titles must be treated as direct orders; however, if most orders are placed with a serials jobber this will free up time for other problem-solving activities related to serials.

Serials jobbers tend not to handle monographs just as book jobbers tend not to handle serials. *Tend* is the key word here, given the variety of serials, and especially in the area of annuals and numbered monograph series, lines become blurred and jobbers overlap. Given the nature of serial publications, one will be better served by an experienced serials jobber than by a friendly and willing book jobber who offers to handle the serials list along with book orders. Many serials librarians have found it best to use domestic dealers for domestic serials and foreign dealers for foreign titles. Picking a foreign dealer can be a challenge; for American libraries ALA's *International Subscription Agents* is very helpful. The latest edition (1986) lists 289 agents and provides information about countries and regions covered, types of material serviced, catalogs or listings provided to customers, notes about special services (standing orders for monographs, for example), and name and address. Even with the guide, it is advisable to ask other librarians about their experience with the dealers being considered. If the librarian cannot identify anyone using a dealer, he or she might start by placing one or two "test" subscriptions with the dealer and increase the volume of business if service is satisfactory.

Service is what one is looking for in a serials vendor. In the past, the library may have received a discount on serials subscriptions but today it will probably be necessary to pay a service charge based on a percentage of the total subscription price. Generally, an agent will receive a discount from the publishers it handles (it is also convenient for the publishers to deal with one billing/ordering source). The service charge to the libraries is usually the difference between the agency's costs and a "reasonable" profit and the publisher's discount.

What does the customer receive beyond the basic advantage of one order, one invoice, and one check for multiple subscriptions? Automatic renewal by a vendor saves library staff time, and when the invoice arrives there is still the opportunity to cancel titles no longer needed. There may be multiple-year subscription rates that will save money. Information about discontinuations, mergers, changes in frequency, and other alterations is a standard service for a serials jobber. The jobber is more likely to learn of changes before a library does, especially if the jobber has placed hundreds of subscriptions with the publisher.

Some assistance is provided in claiming (missing issues, breaks in service, damaged copies, and so forth). Several of the larger American subscription agents (for example, Faxon and EBSCO) have fully automated serial systems that libraries use to handle their serials management programs. In such cases the claims are automatically generated. With manual systems, most vendors offer two forms of claims: one is to notify the agency, who in turn contacts the supplier; or, as an alternative, the agency supplies forms for the library to use for directly contacting the publisher. Assistance in claiming has become more important in the past 10 to 15 years as more and more popular market publishers use "fulfillment centers." In essence these centers serve as a publishers' jobber, that is, a center handles a number of different publishers' titles by receiving, entering subscriptions, and sending out the copies to subscribers. For such centers, the mailing label from the publication is the key to solving the problem and, until recently, few libraries worried about serial mailing labels. In any event, the subscription agency is often more effective in resolving a fulfillment center problem than is a single library.

Management information is also a service serial vendors offer. Their information regarding price changes can be most useful in preparing budget requests. (A sample of this type of data appears in figure 12.4, p. 258). Other types of management information that may be available, often at an extra cost to be sure, are reports that sort the subscription list by subject or classification category accompanied with the total amount spent for each grouping, or (if there are a number of funds) a record of how many titles and how much money was charged to each fund.

A good place to learn of the variety of service available, and who is offering what, is to attend national meetings of various library associations. Representatives of most national serial vendors, as well as a number of foreign vendors, are at the ALA annual conventions. They will supply more than enough promotional material to fill a suitcase. Collecting the information, making comparisons, and talking with other librarians about their experiences with different vendors is the best way to go about selecting a vendor for one's library.

Cooperation in Serials Work

As should be clear by now, serials are complex, and managing them in the collection is a demanding and time-consuming job. No library is able to acquire and keep all the serials that its patrons need or will at some time request. Knowing who has what serial holdings is important to serials librarians and anyone involved in interlibrary loan activities. The CONSER project and *NST* help in identifying holdings in American and Canadian libraries. It is interesting to note that despite the long-time concern about serial holdings, it was not until early 1986 that the United States could come up with a national standard for serials holding statements (ANSI Z39.44; for other ANSI standards see p. 218). The standard now provides for the same data areas, data elements, and punctuation in summary holding statements in both manual and automated systems.

Although the Center for Research Libraries (p. 349) is much more than a cooperative serials program, CRL serial holdings have been effective in holding down the amount of duplication of low-use serial titles in American and Canadian research libraries. Bibliographic utilities, such as OCLC and RLIN, that have serials holdings as part of the database, provide a type of union list service that H. W. Wilson's old *Union List of Serials* performed so well in the past. To some extent, even vendor-based systems offer a form of union listing. While it is possible to use such union lists and shared holdings to cover some low-use serial requirements, the librarian must be certain he or she is in compliance with copyright regulations (see pp. 376-85) before deciding not to buy.

Issues and Concerns

Low-use serials and interlibrary loans have been a concern of the field for some time. (Often several libraries in close proximity to one another duplicate subscriptions to serials that are seldom used. This may reduce the overall range of titles available to the library users.) Off and on in the United States there are discussions, and even some research, on the feasibility of establishing an American equivalent of the British Library Document Supply Centre (formerly British Library Lending Division). Usually referred to as "National Periodicals Center" (NPC), the concept has met with generally strong support from libraries and information centers and strong vocal opposition from publishers and the "information industry." Such a center might well meet the needs of both sides if it ever is created. That is, many libraries might find it economical to pay a reasonable fee for articles as needed. (One can go beyond the copyright law limits if proper fees are paid.) It is conceivable that for low- and perhaps even moderate-use serials, the fee payments to such a center could be less than all the costs attendant upon subscribing, receiving, storing, and servicing the title in a library. Naturally, this presupposes the continuation of the paper-based serial, because in an online system many costs would be removed. Producers might find such a system also provided better revenues and control than exist under the present Copyright Clearance Center (CCC) system, in that NPC would actually house serials and send out copies on demand. CCC is a record-keeping-payment-disbursement operation and does not have a collection of documents.

Continued growth in the number of serials and their spiraling costs are two issues of grave concern, especially in regard to the scholarly journals. Areas of knowledge are being constantly divided into smaller and smaller segments and the number of persons interested in the smaller topics decreases with each division. Costs of producing a special interest journal rise, no matter how many or how few people are interested in reading about the subject. After a certain cost level is reached, the number of individual subscribers drops quickly. Usually any price increase to individual subscribers designed to offset lost subscription revenue only makes the problem worse. Increasingly, the publishers have gone to a "dual pricing" system, one price for individuals and another, higher price (often double or triple the individual rate) for "institutions" (read library). The publishers' premise is that an institutional subscription serves the needs of many readers and therefore a higher price is justified. If taken to a logical, if foolish, conclusion, publishers would demand that libraries keep track of the number of readers for each serial and pay an annual "service" fee based on that number. Before dismissing the idea as unrealistic, consider two things. First, for years libraries have been paying an annual "service fee"/subscription to H. W. Wilson for its periodical indexes based on the number of journals indexed that the library subscribes to. Second, some countries, including Canada, now have a lending fee—a fee paid to the author for each circulated use of his or her book in a public library (see pp. 389-90). An interesting ethical question for librarians in general and collection development personnel in particular: is it ethical for a library to accept a "gift" from an individual on a regular basis—of a journal which has a high dual rate subscription?

Notes

1*ALA Glossary of Library and Information Science.* Edited by H. Young (Chicago: American Library Association, 1983).

2*Webster's Third New International Dictionary* (Springfield, Mass.: G & C Merriam Co., 1976).

3F. Machlup, et al. *Information through the Printed Word* (New York: New York University, 1978).

4Judith Bernstein, "Corporate Annual Reports: The Commercial Vendors." *College & Research Libraries News* 47 (March 1986): 178-80.

[5]Machlup, et al., *Information through the Printed Word.*

[6]William Katz and Linda Sternberg Katz, *Magazines for Libraries*, 5th ed. (New York: R. R. Bowker, 1986).

Further Reading

General

Bourne, R. *Serials Librarianship.* London: Library Association, 1980.

Clasquin, F. F. "Financial Management of Serials and Journals through Core Lists." *Serials Librarian* 2 (Spring 1978): 287-97.

Hamaker, C., and D. Astle. "Recent Pricing Patterns in British Journal Publishing." *Library Acquisitions: Practice and Theory* 8, no. 4 (1984): 225-32.

International Subscription Agents, 5th ed. Chicago: American Library Association, 1986.

Katz, W. W., and L. S. Katz. *Magazines for Libraries*, 5th ed. New York: R. R. Bowker, 1986.

Lee, S. *Serials Collection Development.* Ann Arbor, Mich.: Pierian Press, 1981.

Machlup, F., et al. *Information through the Printed Word.* New York: New York University, 1978.

Osborn, A. D. *Serial Publications: Their Place and Treatment in Libraries*, 3d ed. Chicago: American Library Association, 1980.

Serials Automation for Acquisition and Inventory Control. Edited by W. G. Potter and A. F. Sirkin. Chicago: American Library Association, 1981.

Serials for Libraries, 2d ed. Edited by J. V. Ganly and D. M. Sciattara. New York: Neal-Schuman, 1985.

Taylor, D. C. "Love-hate Relationship of Librarians and Publishers of Serials." *Drexel Library Quarterly* 21 (Winter 1985): 29-36.

Tuttle, M. *Introduction to Serials Management.* Greenwich, Conn.: JAI Press, 1983.

_____. "North American Prices for British Scholarly Journals." *Library Acquisitions: Practice and Theory* 10, no. 2 (1986): 89-96.

Academic

Gorman, M. "Dealing with Serials." *Serials Librarian* 10 (Fall/Winter 1986): 13-18.

Miller, R. H., and M. C. Guilfoyle. "Computer-assisted Periodicals Selection." *Serials Librarian* 10 (Spring 1986): 9-22.

Peters, A. "Evaluating Periodicals." *College & Research Libraries* 43 (March 1982): 149-51.

Stagg, D. B. "Serials in a Small College Library." *Library Resources and Technical Services* 29 (April/June 1985): 139-44.

Stankus, T. "Serials Librarian as a Shaper of Scholars and Scholarship." *Drexel Library Quarterly* 21 (Winter 1985): 112-19.

Tomajko, K. G., and M. A. Drake. "The Journal, Scholarly Communication and the Future." *Serials Librarian* 10 (Winter 1985/86): 289-98.

White, Herbert S. "Differential Pricing." *Library Journal* 111 (1 September 1986): 170-71.

Public

Boyer, R. E. "Serials in the Small Public Library." *Library Resources and Technical Services* 29 (April/June 1985): 132-38.

Falk, G. "Increase Your Budget by Convincing Users to Adopt-a-Magazine." *Library Journal* 110 (15 June 1985): 34.

Katz, W. *Magazine Selection, How to Build a Community-Oriented Collection.* New York: R. R. Bowker, 1971.

School

Bury, J. M. "Management of Periodicals in a Small School LMC." In *Collection Management for School Library Media Centers*, edited by Brenda White, 313-49. New York: Haworth Press, 1986.

Clark, M. P. "Young Adult and Children's Periodicals: Selections for the School Media Center." *Serials Review* 7 (October 1981): 7-24.

Drott, M. C., and J. Mancall. "Magazines as Information Sources." *School Media Quarterly* 8 (Summer 1980): 240-44.

Richardson, S. M. *Magazines for Young Adults: Selections for School and Public Libraries.* Chicago: American Library Association, 1984.

Thomas, J. L. "Periodicals in the Schools: Is the Investment Worth It?" *California Media and Library Educators Association Journal* 2 (Winter 1979): 10-11.

Special

Amir, H. J., and W. B. Newman. "Information: Unlimited Demands — Limited Funds." *Collection Management* 3 (Spring 1979): 111-19.

Bernstein, J. R. "Corporate Annual Reports: The Commercial Vendors." *College & Research Libraries News* 47 (March 1986): 178-80.

Cawkell, A. E. "Evaluating Scientific Journals with Journal Citation Reports." *American Society for Information Science Journal* 29 (January 1978): 41-46.

Harrison, T. W., and A. P. Miller. "Online Interactive Serials Management at Marathon Oil Company." *Journal of Library Automation* 12 (September 1979): 283-87.

Segal, J. A. "Journal Deselection: A Literature Review and an Application." *Science and Technology Libraries* 6 (Spring 1986): 25-42.

Shalini, R. "Journal Acquisition and Cost Effectiveness in Special Libraries." *International Library Review* 13 (April 1981): 189-94.

8

Government Publications

Introduction

Government documents form a mysterious and frequently misunderstood part of a library's collection. Because of their unique nature, they can frighten and confuse librarian and patron alike. Yet they can also constitute one of the most current and vital parts of any collection, as well as provide a wealth of information on virtually any topic. Government documents can be identified by a number of labels, such as government publication, official document, federal document, agency publication, legislative document, or presidential document. They can be housed in a number of different places in the library, ranging from a separate collection containing nothing but governmental documents to complete integration into the general collection. They can be fully cataloged, partially cataloged, or uncataloged, and can be classified by anything from the Library of Congress Classification System or the Superintendent of Documents system to local classification systems. Finally, they can be included or excluded from numerous indexes, card catalogs, and other resources for locating materials.

To add to the confusion created by the diverse management of documents, the documents themselves have only one universal trait. All documents are the publication of an official government body. Thus, all of them have corporate rather than personal authors, which in turn often causes patrons to have difficulty locating a specific publication in the public catalog. Documents can come in any size, shape, or medium. There are books, technical reports, periodicals, pamphlets, microforms, posters, films, slides, photographs, and maps, to name but a few of the possibilities. They have no special subject focus, since they are the product of many diverse branches and agencies of government. However, they do tend to reflect the concerns of the agency that produced them. Predictably, a document produced by the U.S. Department of Agriculture (USDA) will probably deal with an agriculture-related subject, such as livestock statistics, horticulture, or irrigation. The relation may even be less direct, since USDA also publishes information concerning nutrition, forestry, and home economics as a part of its mission. However unusual they might appear to be, most government publications are connected in some way with the purpose and function of their publishing agencies, and all are official publications of the agencies or branches of government.

Of course, any confusion about the nature of government publications may be compounded by the fact that any level of government may issue an official document. Although national government documents are frequently the only official publications easily identified or treated as government publications, all other levels of government—local, regional, state, foreign national, and international—also produce official publications which are properly considered government documents. Though national government documents are the most numerous and important in the library's collection, the other levels of government publication are also valuable and useful. Of course, any library may choose to include only one type or level of document in its "government documents" section, or it may include several together. But no matter what management decision is made, it does not change the fact that a government document is the official publication of an official government agency.

The inherent diversity of government agencies and their publications combines with the diversity of management techniques concerning government documents to create a bibliographic schizophrenia in regard to government publications. However, this immense body of information, at a modest cost, makes government publications a worthwhile information resource for collection development.

Government publications come from all branches, divisions, and levels of government. They embrace the universe of information and ideas, and there are few subjects outside the scope of government publication. They provide reasonably priced current information on geography, history, space science, statistics, education, environmental matters, earth science, legislation and Congress, banking, business, nutrition, forestry, communication, economics, demographics, weather, cancer research, television, libraries, floods and other hazards, women and minorities, agriculture, cars, regulations, standards and specifications, and virtually any other subject imaginable.

The cost of government publications varies among the different levels of government and varies according to purchase plans or depository agreements. However, most government publications are quite reasonably priced. For example, U.S. law states that federal documents may not be sold for a profit. The price is set by statute to recover cost of publication and overhead. This can lead to remarkable bargains for collection development. Where else could a major reference tool like the annual directory of the federal government—including names, addresses, organizational charts, and brief descriptions of the mission and activities of each agency—be purchased for $15.00?[1] Other levels of government follow a similar philosophy concerning pricing and distribution of their documents. This makes government publications a remarkably cheap way to expand segments of a collection.

Though price and subject area coverage offer attractive features, the variety in level of documents within any subject area also offers many advantages for collection development. The USDA may publish information on nutrition ranging from bilingual pamphlets to sophisticated studies of nutritional composition of foods. NASA (National Aeronautics and Space Administration) publishes a variety of documents ranging from space science for school children to extremely technical studies of space flight and the possibilities of extraterrestrial life. Information on most government-related subjects is available at a surprising number of reading and use levels and can serve the needs and interests of most age groups.

Perhaps the most attractive feature of documents is their timeliness. They frequently provide the most current information available on popular topics.

Types of Documents

United States Federal Documents

Federal publications are issued by the executive, judicial, and legislative branches as well as by executive cabinet-level agencies and independent agencies. Executive documents are issued by the Office of the President or the Executive Office of the President. Although presidential statements, reorganization plans, and executive orders are the most widely discussed publications, there are many others. Two sources for identifying such publications are *Code of Federal Regulations—Title 2 (President)* and *Weekly Compilation of Presidential Documents*. Presidential commission reports also are part of this class of publication, along with the *President's Budget* and the *Economic Report of the President*. Such documents are valuable for academic and general interest purposes and most large and medium-sized public and academic libraries collect some if not all of them. School media centers may also collect those publications related to curriculum concerns.

Cabinet-level departments (Department of Agriculture or Interior, for example) are made up of administrative units such as agencies and bureaus. Almost all of these units issue reports, regulations, statistics, monographs on subjects under their jurisdiction, and often educational and public relations materials as well. Some sample titles include: *U.S. Statistical Abstract, Yearbook of Agriculture, Handbook of Labor Statistics*, and *Smokey the Bear Coloring Book*. All types of libraries will find publications of interest from the various units. Special libraries will collect many of the technical publications. Academic libraries normally collect heavily in this area, while media centers and public libraries tend to be rather selective. One source of information about "popular" publications in this class is *Guide to Popular U.S. Government Publications*.[2] In addition to cabinet-level "agency" publications there are a number of independent agencies which also publish a similar range of items. The Tennessee Valley Authority, Federal Reserve Board, and Central Intelligence Agency are examples of independent agencies.

Cabinet-level and independent agency publications constitute the core of the widely collected federal documents. Many of the departments and subunits publish periodicals intended for the general reader which are very popular with patrons. Media centers may find these agencies a good source of inexpensive, high-quality visual materials.

Judicial documents are not as numerous as those from the other two branches of government. The best known and most important title is the *Supreme Court Reports*, which contains the opinions and decisions of the Justices of the Supreme Court on the cases they have heard. (Note: lower federal court decisions are published by private commercial publishers and are not government documents.) Although large legal libraries must have the *Supreme Court Reports*, other libraries may find that there is an interest in the set for historical, political, or personal reasons. As a result, many of the larger public and academic libraries acquire a set for the general collection, even when there is a good legal library nearby.

Congressional publications are second in number and popularity only to the executive publications. In addition to the text of proposed and passed legislation, these publications include materials documenting various aspects of House and Senate deliberations. Floor "debates" are recorded in the *Congressional Record*, assessments of the need for legislation will be found in congressional committee reports, testimony before congressional committees will appear in *Hearings of* or *on* ..., and there are also several important reference books in this class: *Congressional Directory, Senate Manual,* and *House Rules.*

The *Congressional Record* (*CR*) provides a semiverbatim transcript of the proceedings on the floor of each house of Congress — semiverbatim, because it is possible for a congressperson to add or delete material in *CR*. Thus, it cannot be considered an accurate record of what did or did not transpire on the floor on a given day. Many libraries, including large public libraries, find that there is a strong demand for *CR*.

House and Senate committee hearings offer a surprising wealth of material for libraries. Because such hearings normally involve a subject that has some degree of controversy, one source will contain the pros and cons on the subject, as well as what groups support or oppose the proposed legislation. Also, the hearings often contain the first detailed published report on topics under consideration in Congress. While such hearings may have immediate interest for patrons, they are also important for scholars of legislative history.

Reports which accompany bills out of committee form another important information resource for libraries. These documents provide the recommendations concerning the proposed legislation and the background on the need for it. Often these reports are central in interpreting the law once the bill is passed. As is discussed in chapter 18, many of the present practices regarding the U.S. Copyright Law are based on such reports.

Laws of the United States are first published as "slip opinions." They next appear chronologically in *Statutes at Large* and finally are codified in the *U.S. Code*. For most nonlegal libraries, the *U.S. Code* is the more useful publication because it provides subject and "popular" name access, in addition to placing a specific law in the broad context of other laws on the same subject.

The *Congressional Directory* provides biographical information and current addresses for members of Congress, plus useful information about the executive and judicial branches of government. As such, it is a basic reference work and is acquired by many libraries. Any library with patrons having an interest in or doing business with the federal government should have a copy. The congressional procedure manuals are less widely collected but do help patrons to have a better understanding of the federal legislative process, and assist them in following legislation that they are concerned about.

Because of the special congressional publication methods and formats, many collection development officers think of these publications in terms of all or nothing. Certainly it is possible and appropriate for many libraries to get everything, all the items mentioned above plus many others. But it is also reasonable and possible to select one or two series, such as *Reports* or *Hearings*. It is also possible to collect by subject, for example all the congressional publications on the elderly or native Americans. In many cases, especially in the smaller library situation, it may be necessary only to acquire a few items of very high local interest.

Federal publications are an important source to consider for current information at a modest price. It is not a matter of all or nothing, any more than it is a matter of acquiring all or none of the books and serials on a given topic. Learning more about federal publications and their content will pay dividends in meeting the information needs of a library's community in a timely and cost-effective manner.

State and Local Governments

These documents are generally of limited availability. Within the last decade most states in the United States have established or passed legislation to establish depository programs roughly paralleling the federal depository program (see pp. 185-88). These programs distribute varying quantities and percentages of state agency publications to designate state document depositories in formats varying from paper to microfiche. The quantity of publications distributed, the format, and the completeness of the depository collection, as well as the types and numbers of designated depository libraries, vary from state to state. Some states have relatively few depositories, while others have extremely liberal depository programs. A few states allow selection of documents for collection development, while others distribute everything on an all-or-nothing basis. In some states only paper copies of their documents are provided, while others follow the Government Printing Office's lead in making microfiche the preferred format. What service is provided also varies, and may include centralized bibliographic control and a classification system for the documents. Some states carefully select depository materials for distribution, while others provide as comprehensive a collection as possible. Out-of-state libraries may or may not become depositories because some states require depositories to be in-state libraries with a certain profile.

Depository practices and requirements differ considerably from state to state. Consulting the statutes of any particular state will usually provide the frequency and the statutory framework of the depository program. The state library can usually provide more detailed information about its state depository program—a list of depositories, sales and acquisition information, as well as information as to whether documents are available from a central source or must be acquired from individual agencies.

Historically, the most effective method for acquisition of state and local documents has been through direct agency contact. Documents of great public interest traditionally have been produced and sold by individual agencies, at or near cost. Complimentary copies are often available for libraries. The greatest problem in acquisition of state documents has been the short press run, which results in state documents being out-of-print practically before they are off the press. Although state and local agencies are usually quite happy to provide copies of their publications if available, they rarely keep standing orders, deposit accounts, and other conveniences for libraries. Acquisition usually is possible only on a case-by-case basis, which is time-consuming and frustrating. Frequently the only reason a library knows of a timely document is because a newspaper article mentions it or a patron requests it.

Since the relatively recent advent of state documents depository programs, bibliographic control of state documents has improved. Inclusion of state documents and local documents in a variety of computer-searchable, bibliographic databases has also increased control of documents and has led to greater public exposure and use. However, selection guides have almost always been nonexistent for state and local documents. They normally have consisted of an assorted collection of checklists and random catalogs. State library checklists of new acquisitions, the very incomplete Library of Congress *Checklist of State Documents*, as well as occasional lists or indexes produced for frequently demanded, isolated collections (state Geological Survey materials and agricultural experimentation publications most notably, as well as occasional legislative studies or special gubernatorial panels or commission indexes) are the traditional means of identifying relevant state publications. With the advent of state depository programs, some states also provide a catalog and index of their publications. Though these state productions are frequently inadequate because of budgetary constraints, they offer significant improvement over the past.

Privately published indexes, such as CIS's *Statistic Reference File* (*SRF*), which contains a large section of state government published statistics, and the *Index to Current Urban Documents*, offer both bibliographic control of state and local documents and an optional microfiche collection which may be purchased and which corresponds to the index. Given the poor bibliographic control of state and local documents generally, these sets, though expensive, sometimes offer the best cost-effective option for collection development.

In general, local government publications offer even fewer selection tools and less bibliographic control than state publications. However, some major publications of special interest, such as long-range county plans, or demographic studies, or virtually anything with local impact, get local publicity. Complimentary copies are often available to local libraries, or are available at minimal cost. The problem of acquisition roughly parallels those of state documents—no agency mailing lists or standing orders, no effective acquisition options (deposit account for example). Furthermore, there is the need to negotiate individually with agencies to acquire reports and short-run publications. The strategic problems are almost identical to those for state documents, without the advantage of the state documents depository programs. In many communities, the central public library becomes an unofficial local documents depository and it may offer support to other libraries seeking local documents.

International Documents

Publications of international agencies also vary in availability and acquisition procedure. Major international agencies, such as the United Nations (UN) and its affiliates (agencies like UNESCO, the World Bank, Food and Agriculture Organization, International Monetary Fund, and World Health Organization) may offer liberal international depository programs for their publications. Others, such as the Organisation for Economic Cooperation and Development (OECD), offer a heavily discounted purchase plan in lieu of a true depository agreement. The larger agencies normally produce a variety of checklists and archival lists. However, only the UN produces its own comprehensive index on a regular basis. The others produce sporadic catalogs and lists. Unfortunately, since the 1950s, the UN index has not included the publications of its affiliates. Thus, bibliographic control, including purchase information, is in fact only officially available for the UN publications. Regional or smaller agencies offer less-sophisticated bibliographic control and sales assistance. They closely parallel the situation with state documents, where standing orders or mailing lists are difficult to establish, and each individual purchase or acquisition requires a specific request and some negotiation.

The international document collection development situation has benefited from the existence of UNIPUB, a private distributor which collects international documents, creates catalogs, and offers them for sale from a central facility. It offers a unique opportunity to build an international documents collection from a variety of agencies and provides all the conveniences found in the trade book field — standing orders, sales catalogs and subject pamphlets, deposit accounts, and a central sales office.

Like state and federal documents, international documents have profited from inclusion in computerized bibliographic databases. Privately published indexes, such as CIS's *IIS* (*Index to International Statistics*) and *IBID*, are among the tools creating some degree of bibliographic control and collection development assistance. As with CIS's state and federal documents program, *IIS* offers companion fiche collections.

Foreign National Documents

Almost every national government issues a few documents each year. Most developed countries have a government publications program that rivals that of the United States. They publish the required documents reporting on their activities as well as informational and educational materials. Generally the publications are issued by a central agency similar to the U.S. Government Printing Office, and this eases acquisition problems. In order to gain an overview of government publishing programs in 20 countries with the highest output, one should consult J. J. Cherns's *Official Publications: An Overview.*[3]

Very few countries offer depository arrangements for foreign libraries. It may be possible to set up deposit accounts with some agencies; however, variations in exchange rates often cause problems. One method that often works, if one wishes to buy a substantial number of publications from a country, is to arrange to have a bookdealer or vendor in the country purchase them. This approach generally results in a higher acquisition rate than can be managed at long distance, especially in countries where there is limited or poor bibliographic control. As might be expected, there is a wide variation in bibliographic control, from almost total to nonexistent. Anyone involved in an extensive foreign publications collection development program should read the bimonthly *Government Publications Review*, published by Pergamon Press (see "Further Reading"). Pergamon Press also has a series (Guides to Official Publications) that is steadily increasing its coverage on a country-by-country basis. Books in this series provide useful acquisition information.

Each type of document has its own place in collection development and each has special acquisition problems, possibilities, and advantages. Depository programs offer free documents, but may be unavailable because of requirements needed to qualify for depository status. Or perhaps a library may not wish to assume depository responsibilities in order to acquire documents. A wide variety of options, from individual purchases to book selection plans, are available to nondepository libraries.

GPO and Other Official Publishers

Official publication is accomplished in a variety of ways. A government can establish and operate its own presses, or it can contract out some or all of its publishing needs. It can also employ a central publication office, which is responsible either for actual publication or the contracting of actual publication of documents with private printers. This office may also be responsible for bibliographic control and sales to some extent. The central office may even oversee depository libraries, if they exist. On the other hand, there may be no central office for control and coordination of government publications. In that case, publications may be the responsibility of various departments and agencies, or may be contracted out wholesale. Sales programs and depository library programs would be the exception rather than the rule in such a system.

The U.S. Government Printing Office (GPO) offers a fairly advanced, centralized operation under the aegis of the Joint Committee on Printing of Congress and the watchful eye of the Public Printer of the United States. Though the Superintendent of Documents, who is the Public Printer's assistant, oversees most library-related functions, it is the Public Printer who retains a more than titular position in regard to the actual business of government publication.

The GPO is the world's largest printer. The quantity of materials it must print in order to perform its statutory duties calls for even more than it can do in its on-site printing shop in Washington, D.C. Just the daily publication of the *Congressional Record* and the *Federal Register* would challenge the capabilities of normal printers, and the GPO prints many, many more items daily. As a result of the demands of publishing for the three branches of the government, including the numerous cabinet-level departments and independent agencies, much work is either contracted out or done in the "field" printing plants around the United States.

The GPO is obviously much more than just a printer. It offers many varieties of service to the government, libraries, and the public. It is a central collection point for all federal publications. Title 44 of the *U.S. Code* requires that all agency publications be provided to the GPO for cataloging and distribution to depository libraries. In the past, agencies largely ignored their statutory duty when it was inconvenient—for example, when they needed to avoid the cost of a press run long enough to meet the needs of the deposit program. Today, compliance has improved significantly. There will always be a body of "fugitive literature," which the GPO has never seen and will never see, even though it lives on as footnotes in reports and dissertations. However, this figure has dropped from 25 percent of all government publications in 1965 to 5 percent in 1985.

The GPO runs a depository program for making the publications of the government available to the public. Under this program, libraries willing to meet specific requirements are sent free documents on the condition that they will house them and make them accessible to the public. The GPO is charged with the administration of this system, including selection of depositories, materials to be sent to depositories, depository inspections (to be certain that the depositories act in accordance with Title 44 and the depository programs), solving problems for depositories, and dealing with libraries which no longer wish to be depositories. It must issue standards and guidelines as well.

The GPO runs a sales program, which makes available to the public for a statutorily set price any documents which it feels have market potential or should be of great public interest. The sales program includes selection of documents, pricing, handling orders, managing eight regional GPO bookstores, and providing them with hand-selected, popular merchandise.

The GPO runs a comprehensive bibliographic control program, whose mission is to identify, catalog, and classify *every extant* government publication. Perhaps to the outside observer, the *Smokey the Bear Coloring Book*, a five-page promotional item of no long-lasting value, may not seem to deserve this treatment, but the GPO's mission statement indicates that it must be cataloged, classified, and distributed to depository libraries which have selected the item number covering such publications. While this example represents an extreme, it indicates how seriously the GPO views its mission to collect, catalog (by AACR2 since 1976), and classify (by the Superintendent of Documents system) all available documents. Documents are now given full cataloging and entered into OCLC. Each document is assigned a classification number within the Superintendent of Documents classification system. Only after all of this has been done can documents be mailed to depositories or made available to the sales program. Even if, for some reason, a publication is not destined to go into the depository program, the GPO maintains a strict requirement that it be allowed to catalog and classify the document and enter it into the *Monthly Catalog of United States Government Publications* unless it has a security classification. The requirement of bibliographic control is one of the oldest statutory requirements of the GPO, going back to 1895, when the *Documents Catalog* was initiated as a comprehensive bibliographic record of government publications.

Other official publishers do not necessarily follow the GPO's lead. HMSO (Her Majesty's Stationery Office) functions as Great Britain's central publication bureau, and most former British possessions follow suit. European countries follow long-established traditions, which vary greatly. Developing countries tend to have no central publications bureau at all, since that is customarily one of the last arms of government to appear in the evolution of a modern government.

Bibliographic Control

United States federal publications have reasonably good but not complete bibliographic control. For retrospective purposes, *Poore's Descriptive Catalogue of Government Publications, 1774-1881*; *Ames' Comprehensive Index of Publications of the United States Government, 1881-1893*; *Checklist of United States Public Documents 1789-1969*; and *Congressional Documents: Tables and Indexes, 1789-1893* provide pretwentieth-century coverage. Since 1898 the *Monthly Catalog of United States Government Publications* has been the basic listing of GPO output. Unfortunately not all government agency publications are produced by the GPO. Some of these agencies issue sales catalogs on a fairly regular schedule. If close to comprehensive coverage is desired, it will be necessary to consult a number of sources and write numerous letters. However, for most libraries the *Monthly Catalog* will be adequate. Publications for sale (in-print) are listed in GPO's *Publication Reference File* (*PRF*). Any library buying federal publications should probably buy *PRF* (microfiche) and use it in the same way as *Books in Print*. It provides price, Superintendent of Documents classification number, stock number (essential for purchase from the GPO), bibliographic information, and a brief description of each publication. Thorough indexing makes it a very easy selection and acquisition tool to use.

Libraries that buy only a few popular titles will probably find *New Books* and/or *U.S. Government Books* (both are free) sufficient to identify appropriate items for the collection. Public libraries will find *Consumer Information Catalog* (*CIC*) an excellent source for rapid identification of government consumer information. Many of the items listed in *CIC* are free and may be secured from the Consumer Information Center located in Pueblo, Colorado. (The Center has been charging a processing fee for two or more free titles.)

The National Technical Information Service (NTIS) issues *Government Reports Announcements and Index*. NTIS is the source for the majority of reports prepared under government contract, including many such reports listed in the *Monthly Catalog*. It is also, on occasion, able to provide copies of out-of-print GPO publications. The future of NTIS as a source of low-cost government publications is uncertain. There have been extensive discussions about the possibility of converting it to a commercial (profit) organization. Should that happen many libraries, particularly special libraries, would find that their acquisition funds would be stretched too far to meet the essential needs of their collections.

Acquisition

Libraries acquire their government documents in a variety of ways. Some assume the responsibilities of depository collections if this option is available to them. Others purchase documents to match a collection profile. Some have standing orders through official or commercial vendors, while others purchase documents individually or acquire most of their documents free of charge.

The federal depository system is the most common depository system in the United States, with over 1,000 participating libraries. Most states and some international agencies also have depository library systems which are characterized by different degrees of sophistication. The core of the depository arrangement is an agreement between the library and the government publishing body, which provides publications free of charge; in return, the library makes them available to the general public. The depository agreements may allow great latitude in management decisions concerning the depository documents, but the agreements usually require public access.

Another major method of acquisition is purchase through the agency's official sales program, which may or may not be done on a standing order basis. Some commercial jobbers and bookstores do deal in documents, and some booksellers, especially used or rare booksellers, have documents as a part of their stock.

Of course, documents are often available free of cost from issuing agencies and congressional representatives. They are also available as gifts or exchanges from libraries that have held them for the statutory period and wish to dispose of them, or from libraries with extra nondepository or gift copies.

Retrospective Collections

Much of the value of a larger, long-established documents collection revolves around its historical research significance. A historical collection containing old congressional serial set volumes, Smithsonian American Ethnography Bureau publications, early Army Corps of Engineers reports and surveys, State Department surveys, and countless other documents of the United States offers a rare treasure for the scholar, subject specialist, statistician, or curious researcher. Such a collection contains valuable and fascinating primary documents of great public and scholarly merit. However, most functioning documents collections are not in this category, nor should they be.

Most depository libraries collect current documents. This is appropriate, since the primary use of documents focuses on timeliness. In fact, "selective" status allows a collection to be exclusively a current documents collection. Libraries may weed unwanted depository documents after a statutory period of five years' retention, provided they follow proper procedures. This is neither an uncommon nor a bad policy when the decision is made on the basis of an analysis of community needs, clientele, space, money, and geographic or regional availability of historical resources. However, for the library that chooses to develop retrospective historical collections, the rewards are substantial.

The major bibliographic tools necessary to deal with pre-1962 publications (chosen because this date marks the beginning of the modern depository program) were mentioned in the section on bibliographic control. Each source serves a different function. *Poore's Descriptive Catalogue* and *Ames' Comprehensive Index* describe historic documents but provide little more than bibliographic verification information. *Poore's Catalogue* purports to be comprehensive, but is a rather incomplete catalog of nearly a century's worth of government publishing. *Ames' Index* offers bibliographic identification and serial set identification where possible, which makes it at least marginally functional as a bibliographic finding tool as well as for verification. The *Monthly Catalog* in its pre-1962 format is a clumsy tool. However, it is the basic catalog for GPO publications. It began as a sales catalog, and in the 1920s, Superintendent of Documents classification numbers were added, making it a valuable finding tool as well as a verification tool. The *Documents Catalog (1898-1940)* was originally envisioned as the basic bibliographic catalog for U.S. government publications. It eventually ceased publication, and its place was taken by the faster *Monthly Catalog*. Cumulative subject and title indexes for the *Monthly Catalog* are available from commercial publishers.

The Federal Depository System

The federal depository system has been in effect in some form since Congress first distributed the serial set to libraries in the early nineteenth century. The federal depository system of today evolved slowly. By the early twentieth century, a number of depositories had been created, but no bibliographic control (in the sense of a catalog and classification system) existed. Through the first half of the twentieth century, the federal government and depository libraries struggled with growing quantities of documents, mediocre bibliographic control, and an increasing need for the information the documents contained. Finally, the

Depository Library Act of 1962 was passed, creating the system of depository libraries we know today and statutorily defining their relationship to the GPO.

The depository library system provides the most logical acquisition method for libraries that qualify for depository status. Under Title 44 of the *United States Code*, several types of libraries may qualify for depository status. Public and academic libraries which are open to the public may be designated depository libraries by federal legislators. Judicial libraries, federal agency libraries, and law school libraries may also qualify for depository status. Corporate or nonfederal special libraries and school media centers are almost excluded by definition from depository status. Depository libraries usually share the characteristic that they serve either the general public or a branch or agency of government. Most are chosen to serve the largest possible public audience. The criteria for their selection includes their willingness to participate in the depository program, to commit resources to it, and to make documents available to the general public at no cost or without impediment. Additional criteria are concerned with geographic location and the presence or absence of other depositories in the area.

The federal government, through the GPO, distributes documents of all three branches of the government free of cost to the depository library. The library must provide staffing, processing, maintenance, and minimal public service; however, few other restrictions are placed on the management or arrangement of the depository collection. The library may use any cataloging and classification system it wishes. Additionally, most libraries are free to choose their own collection profile from the enormous range of documents available for selection — these libraries can choose as many or as few types of documents as they wish. Though the *Guidelines for Depository Librarians* suggests a minimum of 18 percent of available selections, this suggestion is not rigidly enforced. Libraries select documents by item number and have the opportunity to alter their selections on a quarterly basis. Item numbers are a moderately broad grouping of documents by general area of interest. A single item number may include any combination of monographs, series, and periodicals, as well as maps, posters, and other formats. It provides a convenient way to select documents in groups rather than by individual title.

In the past, item numbers consisted of large and unwieldy groups of documents designed for the GPO's convenience rather than the library's collection development needs. Currently, the documents are grouped under much more specific numbers and actually provide a reasonably effective collection development tool. In addition, being able to change selection by adding or dropping numbers on a quarterly basis facilitates collection development. It makes it possible to select a set of documents for inspection and quickly deselect them if they are not suitable for the library's collection. Though the library must maintain all documents selected for a statutory period of five years, it may avoid acquiring long runs of unwanted documents by changing depository profile on a quarterly basis. And it may dispose of the unwanted parts of the collection after a mandatory five-year retention period. Though caution in selection always pays (because it is always easier to add selections than deselect), the flexibility of the GPO with regard to collection profiles significantly aids selection officers in acquiring suitable materials for a specific library.

Most libraries are able to select their acquisitions from the full range of documents offered through the depository program, and are not restrained by required acquisitions. These libraries form the backbone of the depository system, and are called "selective depositories," because of their ability to selectively acquire and dispose of documents through the depository program. A second type of depository library exists. Each state may have a maximum of two "regional" libraries. These libraries, chosen for both research strength and willingness to serve as regional resources, agree to receive all publications available through the depository program and hold them permanently, and provide ILL service for the region as well. Since "regional" status is voluntary, not all states have two or even one "regional" library. A list of current depositories is available through the *Monthly Catalog* and several other sources, including the GPO and individual congressional offices.

Along with the depository collection, the GPO provides bibliographic control in the form of a comprehensive index, the *Monthly Catalog of United States Government Publications*. The GPO also provides a centrally controlled classification system, the Superintendent of Documents system – an agency-based classification with alphanumeric classification and punctuation. The GPO also provides AACR2 cataloging for all documents indexed in the *Monthly Catalog*. Although no library is compelled to use any of these features, they make depository procedure, as well as collection development and maintenance, much easier.

The GPO and Sale of
Government Publications

Not all federal publications are available for purchase through the GPO – only those chosen for the sales program. These are usually documents which have been screened and evaluated for their sales potential and their public interest. These documents are produced in quantities sufficient for sale and enter the GPO's sales mechanism.

The GPO operates regional bookstores, as well as a sales office in Washington, D.C. Publications which have entered the sales program may be purchased from either the central GPO sales office or the regional bookstores. The bookstores are located in several cities, including Denver, Houston, and Atlanta.

Publications listed in the *Publications Reference File* (*PRF*) may be ordered individually or collectively from the GPO's sales office or purchased through the regional bookstores. GPO deposit accounts are available to minimize purchasing problems. These accounts may also be used for NTIS purchases, and NTIS accounts may be used for GPO purchases. Additionally, major credit cards may be used to purchase GPO publications from Washington, D.C. and regional bookstores.

Prices are usually quite reasonable. For example, the *1986 Congressional Directory* costs less than $25.00. This pricing is no accident. According to law, government publications cannot be sold for profit. They are limited to cost of publication and overhead.

The GPO sales office offers a series of subject bibliographies based on the current *PRF*. They republish them regularly, updating them by adding new publications and deleting those that are "out-of-print." These are particularly useful as acquisition tools for libraries which have particular subject interests or strengths, or for libraries which have limited access to the *Publications Reference File*. They provide patrons with ordering information and an idea of the availability of documents that they might wish to acquire. The GPO sales office also creates a series of sales brochures and catalogs. These range from catalogs to fliers and are available through the GPO sales office and bookstores. Since mailing lists are expensive to maintain, the GPO requires occasional purchases in order to assure continued receipt of the catalogs.

Other Sources for Federal Documents

Jobbers, academic and commercial bookstores, and out-of-print dealers do occasionally handle federal documents as a regular part of their stock or as special order purchases. Jobbers and purchase plans may suit the library whose needs are easily profiled, but which cannot or will not become a depository. Bookstores and rare book dealers may meet the acquisition needs which are more specialized or require relatively few orders per year.

Some congressional publications, such as hearings and committee prints, and a few agency publications can be obtained directly by contacting local or Washington, D.C. offices of congressional representatives. Obviously, this is not an appropriate acquisitions technique for large quantities or standing orders, but it can be quite effective for current issues or special subject publications. It is especially effective for acquisition of information about current legislation or information covering a wide range of subjects. School and media centers should take advantage of this source of free government documents. The best method for acquiring recently out-of-print or nonsales publications is to contact the issuing agency directly. The *U.S. Government Manual* provides an annual list of addresses and telephone numbers for the major and minor agencies of the federal government. Individual contact can produce copies of many federal documents, often free of charge.

Notes

[1] *1986 U.S. Government Manual* (Washington, D.C.: Government Printing Office, 1986).

[2] LeRoy C. Schwarzkopf, *Guide to Popular U.S. Government Publications* (Littleton, Colo.: Libraries Unlimited, 1986).

[3] J. J. Cherns, *Official Publications: An Overview* (Oxford: Pergamon Press, 1979).

Further Reading

General

Cherns, J. J. *Official Publications: An Overview.* Oxford: Pergamon Press, 1979.

Government Publications Review. New York: Pergamon Press, 1974- .

Hernon, P., and G. R. Purcell. *Developing Collections of U.S. Government Publications.* Greenwich, Conn.: JAI Press, 1982.

International Documents for the 80's: Their Role and Use. Edited by T. D. Dimitrov. Pleasantville, N.Y.: UNIFO, 1982.

Moody, M. "State Documents: Basic Selection Sources." *Collection Building* 7 (Spring 1985): 41-44.

Morehead, J. *Introduction to United States Public Documents*, 3d ed. Littleton, Colo.: Libraries Unlimited, 1983.

Robinson, W. C. "Evaluation of the Government Documents Collection." *Government Publications Review* 9 (March 1982): 131-41.

Smith, B. E. "British Depository Arrangements for Official Publications." *Government Publications Review* 4, no. 2 (1977): 123-26.

Academic

Bailey, E. C. "Access to Federal Documents in Small Non-depository Academic Libraries." *Government Publications Review* 8, no. 5 (1981): 405-10.

Gray, C. J. "Sources for Legislative Histories and Status Reports." *Show-Me Libraries* 34 (September 1983): 29-34.

Heim, K. M., and M. Moody. "Government Documents in the College Library." In *College Librarianship*, edited by W. Miller and D. S. Rockwood, 214-32. Metuchen, N.J.: Scarecrow Press, 1981.

Hernon, P. "Academic Library Reference Service for Publications of Municipal, State and Federal Government." *Government Publications Review* 5, no. 1 (1978): 31-50.

Public

Blasdell, L. M. "Government Publications and the Small Public Library." *Texas Libraries* 39 (Winter 1977): 172-79.

Documents to the People. Chicago: American Library Association, 1972- .

Morehead, J. H. "Between Infancy and Youth: Children and Government Serials." *Serials Librarian* 4 (Summer 1980): 373-79.

School

Dickmeyer, J. N. "U.S. Government Documents Belong in School Media Centers." *Indiana Media Journal* 3 (Spring 1981): 23-26.

Jay, H. L. "Government Documents and Their Use in Schools." In *Collection Management for School Library Media Centers*, edited by Brenda White, 295-312. New York: Haworth Press, 1986.

Schwarzkopf, L. C. *Guide to Popular U.S. Government Publications.* Littleton, Colo.: Libraries Unlimited, 1986.

Smallwood, C. *A Guide to Selected Federal Agency Programs and Publications for Librarians and Teachers.* Littleton, Colo.: Libraries Unlimited, 1986.

Smelser, L. B. "Government Publications in Secondary School Libraries in Minnesota." *Government Publications Review* 6, no. 4 (1979): 373-81.

Special

Morehead, J. H. "Corporate and Government Annual Reports." *Serials Librarian* 5 (Winter 1980): 7-14.

Sauter, H. E., and R. H. Rea. "Place of Research/Classified Reports in a Special Library." In *Special Librarianship*, edited by E. B. Jackson, 509-20. Metuchen, N.J.: Scarecrow Press, 1980.

Schmidt, F. "Technical Reports and Non-depository Publications." *Government Publications Review* 9 (November 1982): 545-55.

Schmidt, F., and H. W. Welsch. "Acquisition Guide: Technical Reports and Other Non-GPO Publications." *Government Publications Review* 8, no. 4 (1981): 175-79.

9
Audiovisual
Materials

With each passing year the distinction between books and audiovisuals becomes more blurred — blurred in the sense that the contents of books and serials are preserved, not in a paper copy but in a microformat. Information that once was available only in printed book form is now made available in several forms, including book, microfiche, and online. Book publishers, and especially publishers of scholarly journals, are thinking about and, in a few cases, publishing, their material electronically (access through online databases and a CRT). As a January 1986 issue of *The Wall Street Journal* indicated, "much more than music lies in the future for compact disks."[1] Many publishers expect to use compact disk (CD) packages for "reference"-type material. The Library of Congress is experimenting with the use of laser disks (a related but different technology) to store the contents of brittle books. The compact and laser disks can hold thousands of pages of text, thus providing significant storage cost savings. Add to this video/ teletext and machines capable of "reading" aloud standard typefaces (Kurzweil Reading Machine), and one begins to realize that the integration of information technology described in chapter 1 is becoming a reality. Collections are beginning to reflect the changes, even those academic libraries that have been the least active in audiovisual collection building.

My basic philosophy is that the library's most important products are information and service. If one accepts this philosophy, then the library collection must consist of more than books. Books are, and will be for some time, the least expensive method of conveying large amounts of detailed information to a large number of persons at a given time. Television may reach millions of persons at one time, but it does not convey *detailed* information except in the most exceptional circumstances. A major consideration in building an information collection is how to convey the right information at the right time to the public at the least cost.

Books are only useful to persons who are literate. Depending upon what area of the world one is in, the percentage of persons who are "literate" ranges from 1 to 100 percent. For a great portion of the world, less than 50 percent of the population can be considered literate. Even in countries where very high literacy rates are reported (such as the United States), there is a difference between what is reported and the true literacy rate. In the United States, great concern is expressed in many areas about functional illiteracy; persons may have gone through the required educational system (12 years of schooling) but are not able to read beyond the level reached by the third or fourth year of schooling. Many colleges and universities are worried about the inability of entering students to read and write, and there seems to be a growing difference in the United States between young people's ability to use and understand the spoken, as opposed to the written, word.

For many purposes, textual material is not the best or even the reasonable method for conveying the "message." Collections of graphic and audio materials for teaching, research, and recreation are becoming accepted as appropriate and useful. Some people still view these materials as less "intellectual," or as toys or for purely recreational purposes, and resist adding such formats to a collection. However, as the number of people who have used a number of formats in learning about a subject increases, so does the pressure to have all appropriate formats in a collection.

Microforms

Where do microformats belong—with books or with audiovisuals? Probably in both places. However, in this text they are after the book section aids and before audiovisual aids. Most of the guides to microform materials cover microfilms and microfiche that contain printed information.

At several points in the text we have discussed retrospective collection development. One of the problems in that activity is finding a "hard" copy of all of the items that one might wish to add to the collection. Usually, if one waits long enough (perhaps years) the book or periodical volume can be found in an out-of-print shop. Sometimes the need for the item is too great to wait. If reprint dealers do not have the item, then a microform copy may be the answer.

Another reason for using microformats is to save space, especially with low-use back files of serials. (A back file or back run is a set of older volumes of a current serial subscription; for example, if a library's current issues of *Newsweek* are from volume 92, volumes 1-91 would represent the back file for *Newsweek*.) When a library has long runs and the use of the material is low, it may be wasting space by keeping the physical volumes in the library. A serial that occupies several hundred feet of shelving may be reduced to less than a foot of space when converted to a microformat. Naturally, there is a trade-off in space; the more material there is in microformat, the more equipment is needed in order for patrons to use the material. Some serial librarians use a microformat for back files of popular titles that have a high incidence of mutilation or a habit of disappearing. Not many persons have microform readers in their homes, at least not yet; and if the library has a reader-printer (a device that allows a person to read the microform and, when he or she wishes, to push a button and receive a hard copy of the material being read), loss and mutilation drop.

One major drawback to using microforms to any major degree in collection development is patron resistance. Many persons claim that they cannot read anything on a microformat, that it gives them headaches, and causes eyestrain and other problems. Occasionally, someone will say it causes nausea. *None* of these has been established as a significant physiological problem arising from extended use of microformats. In most cases where the only source for the information is microform, an individual is able to use the material without a problem arising. Admittedly, it takes time to get used to using microforms — it is harder in some formats, such as reels, to locate a specific portion of text than when one has a book in hand. If the equipment is not properly maintained the image quality will be poor and will cause eyestrain; and equipment does break down and malfunction at times.

Despite these problems it will become necessary to use more and more microformats as time goes on. The major factor in this increased use will be economic: new library buildings will be harder to secure; the prices of hard copies of older materials keep going up; and library book and materials budgets remain about the same or increase at a rate less than the inflation rate. Thus it is important to know the guides to microformats. Two guides to "in-print" micro-formats are *Guide to Microforms in Print* (Microform Review) and *National Register of Microform Masters* (Library of Congress). Both titles try to be inter-national in scope, cover both commercial sources of supply and noncommercial ones (for example, libraries and historical associations), and cover over 16 types of microformats. In the *National Register* only U.S. supplies are covered, but the actual material available is international in scope. *Microform Market Place* (Microform Review) is an international directory of micropublishing, including microform jobbers. A major source for reviews of microform series, both current and retrospective, is *Microform Review* (Microform Review). Major producers have extensive catalogs of what they have available, and it is necessary to keep a file of their catalogs because it is even less common for micropublishers than for book publishers to contribute information to the "in-print" guides.

General Evaluation Factors

To a degree, the same factors that determine inclusion or exclusion of books apply to other formats. Obviously, factually incorrect items should not be acquired, and materials that are badly organized and presented are equally un-acceptable. If the quality of a book is difficult to assess, with other media the problem is magnified. All of us have gone to a film and enjoyed it, only to hear some of our friends claim that it is "absolutely *the* worst film" they had ever seen. Thus, subjectivity is a great problem. Basically, the issues of authority, accuracy, effectiveness of presentation or style, and value and usefulness to the community are as valid for all other formats as they are for books.

Before embarking upon a program to develop a media collection, one should carefully evaluate each potential format in terms of its unique utility to the service community. Each format has its strong and weak points, and similar information may be available in a variety of formats. Following are some general guidelines for assessing the strengths and weaknesses of various forms.

Formats that involve motion (such as 8mm, 16mm, and 35mm films and videotapes) are among the most expensive. Therefore, an important question to ask is whether motion really adds that much information. There are films in which there is no motion at all, or if there is motion, it may not be relevant to the content. For example, many "educational" films and videotapes simply alternate shots of one or two persons talking to one another or to the viewers; there are no other graphics (or at least no graphics that require this expensive mode of presentation). On the other hand, hundreds of pages can be read and dozens of still photographs of cell division viewed, but the reader may not yet really understand how cell division takes place. A short, clearly photographed film combined with a good audio track can sometimes produce a quicker, more accurate understanding of the process than hours of reading can achieve.

Detailed study is sometimes most effectively carried out with the use of still pictures, charts, and/or graphs. Another advantage is that the cost of producing and acquiring these formats is much lower than for those that involve motion.

With both motion and still graphic formats, color is an important consideration. Color reproduction is more costly than black-and-white; so what must be considered is whether the color is necessary or just pleasing. In some instances it is absolutely necessary. Certainly, anything that attempts to represent the work of a great artist must have excellent color quality. Excellent color quality is often also necessary with a great many medical and biological materials.

Audio formats can also provide greater understanding and appreciation. One's reading of a poem is never the same as hearing the poet recite it. We all know that tone, emphasis, inflection, and so forth, can change the meaning of a printed text dramatically. On a different level, there are literally millions of persons in the world who cannot read music scores and yet get great enjoyment out of hearing music. Audio recordings also should be considered for any collection if there are persons to be served who are visually impaired. "Talking Books" can be an important service for such persons.

Other general factors are cost, flexibility and manipulation, and, of course, patron preference. Cost is a consideration in almost all major decisions in collection development; however, audiovisual formats often require expensive equipment in addition to rather expensive software. Cost factors need to be considered in light of what type of equipment patrons own — film or slide projectors, videotape players, tape decks, and record players. If the patrons do not own the necessary equipment, can the library supply it free of charge, or on a rental basis? Should the library buy the equipment and allow its use only in the library? The librarian must also consider *what* patrons like and use. Libraries ought not to get into the position of attempting to change patron format preferences when the community is not *known* to be actively interested in a particular format. Thus, both cost and patron preference become significant in deciding what to buy or not to buy.

Flexibility and manipulation are interrelated. How and where can the format and equipment be used? Some equipment can be used to produce local programs as well as to play back commercial software. Others, such as videotape equipment, will allow both motion and stop-action use, or even more sophisticated, instant replay. These features may be necessary, nice, or just gimmicks, depending on the local situation. Ease of operation is also important; can a person quickly learn to operate the equipment or does it take extensive training to use it properly?

Although it is not exhaustive, figure 9.1 provides an overview of the basic factors in planning a comprehensive media collection. It is important to remember that the statements are general and that there are exceptions to almost every one. (See also figure 6.2, page 154, which compares media to books.)

Medium	Motion	Visual	Aural	Flexibility	Manipulation	Cost if Purchased	Cost if Produced in Library	Cost of Equipment
16 mm film	yes	yes	yes	Equipment heavy but portable Darkening required Re-sequencing not feasible	Larger, smaller, slower, faster	high	med.-high	high
Records	no	no	yes	Good portability Shipping & re-sequencing easy	Slower, faster on occasion	low	not feasible	low-mod.
Tape recording	no	no	yes	Excellent, particularly cassettes Re-sequencing, editing, & shipping easy	Slower, faster on occasion	low	low	low-mod.
Paintings & art prints	no	yes	no	Easily circulated	none	low-high	framing & mounting— low-mod.	n/a
Video-cassettes	yes	yes	yes	Depends on distribution system Re-sequencing, editing, shipping not feasible Limited to no. of programs available	Larger, smaller, slower, faster	high	medium	mod.-high
Television— commercial or closed circuit	yes	yes	yes	Portability limited Shipping easy Re-sequencing not feasible	Larger, smaller, slower, faster	high	mod.-high	mod.-high
Overhead transparencies	rarely	yes	no	Very portable Re-sequencing, editing, & shipping easy	Larger, smaller	low-mod.	low	mod.
Filmstrips with/without recording	no	yes	possible	Very portable Darkening req. for group use Re-sequencing not feasible	Larger, smaller	low-mod.	low	low-mod.
Simulations & games	n/a	n/a	n/a	Usually very portable	n/a	low-high	low-mod.	n/a
Computer-assisted, managed instruction	yes	yes	no	Limited to location of terminal	Larger, smaller, slower, faster	high	high	high
Graphics, charts, posters, maps	no	yes	no	Depends on size	Larger, smaller	low	low	n/a
3 dimensional objects, realia, models, globes	on occasion	on occasion	yes	Depends on size & shape	Larger, smaller	low-high	low-mod.	n/a

Adapted from a classroom handout, with permission of instructor, William Speed.

Fig. 9.1. Comparison of audiovisual materials.

Selection Criteria

Once a library has decided to follow the acetate path, how are appropriate items selected? There are three general factors to consider (content, technical aspects, and format) and there are also criteria for each format. In a short chapter only the highlights of the selection criteria can be included. The problems involved in putting together effective audiovisual programs for the library must be ignored. Programming (that is, use of material) is important in deciding what to acquire, and a number of articles and books have been written on this topic, some of which are listed in the bibliography at the end of this chapter. Some of the programming questions include: Will the medium be used in a formal instructional situation? Will it be used only for recreational purposes? Will it focus on an audience of adults, children, everyone? Will it be used in the library with someone from the staff or an "expert" in the field to guide group discussions before or after its use? Will the library be joining a formal network (for example, 16mm film networks are popular); sharing with other libraries the use of the material?

Content Factors

Content is the first concern in the selection of any format. Samples of the types of questions that should be asked appear below. Audiovisual selection tends to be done by a group rather than by one individual (especially in the case of expensive formats), which usually means that some type of evaluation form will be employed in the process. No matter what specific questions are on the form—and not all items listed in this chapter will be on any one form—all of the items listed below should be considered:

1. What is the primary purpose(s) of the item? If there is a user's guide included, does it provide a specific answer to this question?

2. Given the purpose(s) of the item, is the length of the program appropriate? An item can be too short, but more often than not, they are too long.

3. Is the topic a current fad or is it something that is likely to have long-term interest? (Long-term interest and lasting value are not always one and the same).

4. Is the material presented in a well-organized fashion?

5. Is it easy to follow the story line?

6. If the item is of relatively short duration and is an attempt to popularize a subject, does it do this with sufficient accuracy—sufficient in the sense that the simplification process does not cause misunderstandings or, worse, create misrepresentation?

7. When was the material copyrighted? Copyright information can be difficult to find for some formats. Motion picture films usually provide this information somewhere in the credits, often in roman numerals. Generally speaking, there is no national bibliographic description standard for the various media. Sales catalogs may or may not provide the date of production. Unfortunately, a large number of very dated products are—or have been—sold as if they were currently produced.

8. Will the visuals or audio date very quickly? In many educational films the subject matter is important but the dress of the actors makes it seem old-fashioned. If such films are not presented as historical films, the true purpose may be lost to most viewers. Audience attention is easily drawn away from the real subject. Needless to say, this ties into the need for copyright information.

9. How many uses could be made of the material, in addition to those identified by the producer? Naturally, if there are a number of ways to use the format (with different types of programs or audiences), it is easier to justify spending money on the item.

Technical Factors

Technical issues will vary in importance from format to format, but some general considerations apply to a number of forms. In most instances, judging technical matters is less subjective than many other selection criteria. On the other hand, it will take time and guidance from experienced selectors to develop a critical sense of these facators. This process will take longer for media than for books because school systems traditionally have emphasized literature, and to a degree everyone who completes 12 years of schooling has been exposed to some of the great works of literature. Most individuals entering the field of library and information work are usually even more attuned to good literature, well-manufactured books, and the various methods of literary review and criticism than the average person. Today we may be more exposed to television, film, and recordings than to books, but very few of us are exposed to the methods for assessing the technical aspects of these formats. This fact is evident when film and television awards are made—the general public is only interested in the best film or program and performance categories; yet there are usually three times as many awards for technical aspects (direction, production, special effects, cinematography, and so forth).

The following questions should be asked:

1. Are the visuals, assuming that there are visuals, really necessary?

2. Are the visuals in proper focus, the composition effective, the shots appropriate? (These questions need to be asked because out-of-focus shots, strange angles, and jarring composition may be used to create different moods and feelings.)

3. Is the material edited with skill?

4. Does the background audio material contribute to the overall impact?

5. Is there good synchronization of visuals and audio?

6. How may the format be used — small or large group viewing, or both? In a darkened, semilighted, or fully lighted room?

Format Factors

Many of the format factors are identified in figure 9.1. Additional factors to consider are:

1. Is the format the best one for the stated purposes of the producer?

2. Is the format the least expensive of those that are appropriate for the content?

3. Will the carrier medium stand up to the level and type of use that the library would give it?

4. If it is damaged, can it be repaired? (locally or by producer), or must it be replaced? Does it require maintenance, and if so, what kind?

5. What type of equipment is required to use the medium? How portable is it and how heavy?

It is possible to group all audiovisual materials into six broad categories. Again, some general questions can be asked about each category.

Still pictures (slides, filmstrips, transparencies, microformats, flat pictures, and art reproductions):

1. Does the lack of movement cause the viewer to misinterpret the original meaning?

2. How accurate is the color reproduction? Is the color necessary?

3. Are the mountings/holders compatible with existing library equipment?

4. For filmstrips and microforms, is the sequence of frames logical and easy to follow?

5. If there is an audio track, does it aid in understanding the materials?

6. Are microformat images readable when enlarged? What is the reduction ratio that has been employed? Can it be used in equipment that will allow the user to make a copy of single frames as desired?

7. Is the ratio of pictures to narration appropriate? (A frequent problem with slide or tape programs or narrated filmstrips is too few illustrations; this often results in a product that seems to last too long.)

Motion pictures (35mm, 16mm, 8mm films, video formats—most of these are available in reel-to-reel, cartridge, and cassette configurations):

1. Does the motion add to the message?

2. Are variable speed capabilities (fast, normal, slow, stop) used effectively?

3. Is the running time appropriate to the content? Too long? Too short?

4. If it is a recreational film using either performers or animation, has that fact caused a problem in presenting an accurate picture of the true events?

5. Has the sound been properly synchronized with the visual materials?

Audio recordings (disks or tapes):

1. How much use can the format withstand without distorting the quality of the sound?

2. How easily damaged is the format?

3. Does the recording provide coverage of the full range of sound frequencies?

4. Is there any distortion of the sound?

5. Was the recording speed held constant? (This is seldom a problem with major producers but it can be significant with those who do not produce many recordings.)

6. If the recording is multiple channel, were the microphones properly placed to ensure a balanced recording?

7. Was the recording site suitable for the purposes or was it a matter of convenience? (For example, if the goal is to produce an excellent recording of a musical composition, then a recording studio or a concert hall with excellent acoustics and no audience is the best location—not a concert. With "live" performances one should not expect the best sound quality.)

Graphic materials (maps, charts, and posters):

1. Has there been an attempt to convey too much information? (Maps and charts can become so complex as to be almost unusable if too much information is included on any one item.)

2. Are the symbols employed standard ones or are they unique to the particular item?

3. Is the printing of high quality? (When color is employed, especially with maps, the presswork must be of high quality or all the efforts of the cartographer are wasted.)

4. Is the scale appropriate for the library's needs?

5. How durable is the paper or cloth on which the information is printed?

6. Can a user determine the intended message with a single look?

7. Is the surface treatment appropriate—glossy, semiglossy, etc.?

Three-dimensional objects (models, realia, dioramas, and globes):

1. Are objects of less than life size reproduced in an appropriate scale?

2. Is the scale sufficient to illustrate the necessary details?

3. When horizontal and vertical scales must be different, is the distortion so great as to create a false impression?

4. Are the colors used accurate in terms of the original object?

5. Are the objects constructed of materials that will stand up to the type of handling that they will receive in the library?

Other formats (simulations, games, self-guided instruction formats, computer software):

1. Can a patron understand the directions without assistance from the library staff and/or does the item require training to set up and use?

2. Does the system allow for a variety of speeds in learning?

3. If it is a computer system, does the system cover areas that cannot be handled as effectively in any other format?

4. Does the program use an operating system available in the library?

5. Is the computer program reliable in normal use? (Does it "boot" accurately? Does it run without mistakes?)

6. Is the program clear and logical?

7. What "help" menus are available?

8. How much user interaction is required?

9. How long does it take to complete the program? Will the length cause problems of access to the computer?

10. Will the patron be able to take the item home or must it be used in the library?

11. If it must be used in the library, will it be available anytime the library is open, or just during certain hours?

12. Are the right answers predictable in a manner that prevents true learning?

13. If it is a printed system, are there additional answer sheets available or will the library have to produce extras?

These are but a few of the considerations that must go into the selection of audiovisual formats. Just as there are few, if any, universal questions to raise about selecting books, so it is with audiovisuals. Each library will develop its own selection criteria as it gains experience in the field.

Previewing

As noted earlier the actual selection process of audiovisual materials is often a group rather than individual activity. This is particularly true of films and video formats. To some degree it is the cost of the decision rather than the usual collection development factors that brings this about. In essence, making a mistake on a 20-minute sound, color, 16mm film has more serious economic consequences for the library budget than most single mistakes with a book, a transparency, or a sound recording. A sound color film will cost anywhere from $300 to $500. As we have seen, the criteria for selection tend to be highly subjective. As a result, it is safer to get multiple opinions about a possible purchase. An audiovisual selection committee is the typical mechanism employed for securing such multiple points of view.

How does the book selection committee—rather common in public and school libraries—differ from the audiovisual selection committee? Audiovisual selection committees usually function as a true group decision-making body. Materials being considered for purchase are normally previewed by the entire group; films (both motion pictures and filmstrips) and video formats are viewed in their entirety. A group discussion usually takes place after each screening and each person expresses a reaction to and an evaluation of the item. Everyone sees the same material and group interaction ends in a decision to buy or not to buy. Sometimes the product is rerun several times when there are strong differences in opinion.

Book selection committee meetings normally operate on a more individual basis. That is, each person is assigned certain books to review and report on, including indications of what published reviews of the book have said. A brief synopsis is given and a purchase recommendation is made. There may be or may not be an extended discussion of the recommendation. In any case, only one (or perhaps two) person(s) on the committee will have examined the book in detail — examined rather than read completely, because most libraries do not have enough professional staff time to allow for the complete reading of every book purchased. In some library systems the selection process is conducted solely on the basis of published reviews, bibliographic data, and the knowledge the selectors have of various authors, editors, and publishers. Very few libraries can afford to (or should) select films and video formats on the basis of published reviews alone.

Another important difference is the sequential nature of films and video formats. It is not really possible to skim a film as one does a book; the film must be run at its normal speed in order to get the proper impression. A 20-minute film requires 20 minutes of preview. Simple arithmetic tells us that in an eight-hour work day a maximum of twenty-four 20-minute films could be viewed. A book selection committee that only discussed twenty-four titles in eight hours of meetings would be considered something of a disaster. Realistically, though, no group can preview twenty-four films in eight hours, as the figure does not provide for discussion time between films or for breaks. It is possible that with three playback units one could actually run twenty-four films, but it would require someone to do nothing but set up one playback unit after another—it does require a few minutes to thread and rewind. Finally, it is not feasible to have people sit and view materials for four straight hours; they need a break. All of this means that a more realistic figure would be somewhere between ten to twelve audiovisual items per day could be evaluated.

Standardization of the evaluation process is probably a long way away in the media field, but several professional associations have attempted to bring some order to previewing by developing evaluation forms. Until such time as a library decides to commit a major segment of its materials budget to audiovisual forms, librarians can save effort by using one of the association forms. Some of the forms are the UNESCO Film Appraisal Information Form, the Educational Film Library Association form, the Council on International Nontheatrical Events, Inc. (CINE) film rating sheet, and the Educational Product Report evaluation form (this latter form covers more than motion picture formats).

Not only do audiovisual formats cost more to buy, they also cost more to select. The two combined cost factors can be significant. Thus, one cannot conclude that just because a library does not have a collection of films or video materials, there is necessarily a reluctance to accept new formats. A significant difference exists between reluctance and the lack of money and qualified staff to select the newer formats. The only question should be whether the monetary factor is being used as an excuse to avoid trying out other media.

Audiovisual Selection Aids

Despite the desirability of previewing audiovisual materials, published evaluations (especially when combined with previewing) are important in this field. Each year there is a little more progress toward bibliographic control of the field, including reviews of most formats. Perhaps when multiple published reviews of most formats are available, there will be less and less need for hundreds of audiovisual librarians to spend hours and hours in preview screening rooms.

At this time, no comprehensive source for audiovisual materials similar to *Book Review Digest* or *Book Review Index* exists. *Media Digest* (National Film and Video Center) has developed into the best source for locating reviews in all formats.

Identifying potentially useful audiovisual materials also represents a problem. One series of indexes from the NICEM group (National Information Center for Educational Media) focuses on educational materials; however, as they have a rather broad definition of education, the publications are useful to all types of libraries and are constantly revised. Some of their basic publications are:

Index to 16mm Educational Films
Index to 35mm Educational Filmstrips
Index to 8mm Motion Cartridges
Index to Overhead Transparencies
Index to Educational Audio Tapes
Index to Educational Records
Index to Educational Slides
Index to Educational Video Tapes
Index to Producers and Distributors

Other NICEM indexes exist, and they also have several subject indexes on current topics such as ecology and ethnic studies. Access Innovations, Inc., recently purchased the NICEM indexes and promises even more publications. With these tools one can locate basic descriptive information (producer, title, source) and a brief annotation about the content and grade level, and in this regard, the series is not unlike many other tools. That is, they describe rather than analyze or critique the materials covered. Lacking critical evaluations, then, a media librarian must still preview items. The NICEM series is in many ways the closest thing that the audiovisual field has to an equivalent of *Books in Print*. The NICEM indexes are also accessible online through DIALOG under the database name AV-ON-LINE.

Another service, Educational Media Catalogs on Microfiche (EMCOM), also provides a form of "in-print" list. It includes 100-plus microfiche which contain a very large number of audiovisual distributors' catalogs. It is probably as comprehensive a source as any, and is updated every six months. Because access is by vendor, one has to spend more time searching for material on a topic and format than with the NICEM indexes. Although an expensive service, it does relieve the library of having to file hundreds of vendor catalogs and trying to keep them up-to-date.

A major problem in the field is its vast size and diversity. As a result, very few aids are published annually that cover more than one or two formats. One must also be alert to the fact that this field changes very quickly. Indeed, the field is so volatile that although the titles and dates of publication of the aids identified in this chapter were correct at the time the chapter was written, there is no assurance that they will reflect the state of the art by the time this book is published (and that time frame is only a few months). With that caution in mind, the following is offered as a selective list of guides, aids, and review sources. Books include:

Audio Video Market Place: A Multimedia Guide. New York: R. R. Bowker, 1969- . (annual).

Bensinger, C. *Consumer's Handbook of Video Software*. New York: Van Nostrand Reinhold, 1981.

Computer-Readable Databases: A Directory and Data Source-book. Chicago: American Library Association, 1978- . (irregular).

Data Acquisitions: 1982. Storrs, Conn.: Roper Center, 1982.

Data Base Directory. White Plains, N.Y.: Knowledge Industry Publications, 1984.

Datapro Directory of Online Services. Deltran, N.J.: Datapro Research Corporation, 1982- . (irregular).

Directory of Computerized Data Files. Washington, D.C.: Government Printing Office, 1982.

Film File. Minneapolis, Minn.: Media Referral Service, 1980- . (annual).

Guide to Microforms in Print. Westport, Conn.: Meckler Publishing, 1975- . (annual).

Limbacher, J. L. *Feature Films on 8mm, 16mm and Videotape*, 8th ed. New York: R. R. Bowker, 1985.

Microform Market Place. Westport, Conn.: Meckler Publishing, 1974- . (biennial).

Miller, E. E., and M. L. Mosley, eds. *Educational Media and Technology Yearbook*. Littleton, Colo.: Libraries Unlimited, 1973- . (annual).

New Serial Titles. Washington, D.C.: Library of Congress, 1953- . (annual).

Sive, M. R. *Selecting Instructional Media: A Guide to Audio-visual and Other Instructional Media Lists*, 3d ed. Littleton, Colo.: Libraries Unlimited, 1983.

Video Source Book. Syosset, N.Y.: National Video Clearing House, 1979- . (annual).

Journals (review sources) include:

APDU Newsletter (Association of Public Data Users)

Booklist (American Library Association, 1905-)

Channels of Communication Choice (Myles Fuchs, 1981-)

Datapro (Datapro Research Corporation, 1982-)

EFLA Evaluations (Educational Film Library Association, 1946-)

ESRC Newsletter (Economic and Social Research Council, London, 1967-)

Film Library Quarterly (Film Library Information Council, 1967-)

Filmmaker's Review (Columbia University, 1976-)

High Fidelity (ABC Leisure Magazines, 1951-)

Instructional Innovator (Association for Educational Communications and Technology, 1956-)

Library Journal (R. R. Bowker, 1876-)

Media & Methods (American Society of Educators, 1964-)

Microform Review (Meckler Publishing, 1972-)

National Preservation Report (Library of Congress, 1979-1980)

Resource Center Index (Association for Information and Image Management, 1974-)

School Library Journal (R. R. Bowker, 1954-)

Stereo Review (CBS Magazines, 1958-)

Video Times (Publications International, 1984-)

Wilson Library Bulletin (H. W. Wilson, 1914-)

Although the preceding lists of sources are intended to provide a general overview, there is a slight emphasis on films. One reason for this is historical: after microforms and phonograph records, motion picture films are the most commonly held audiovisual forms in libraries. Also, 16mm films cost significantly more than either of the other two formats, making previewing all the more important. Because of film's popularity, cost, and longer history of use, film review and evaluation have had more time to become established. Increased popularity of other formats will in time make it economically feasible to publish journals covering just one form.

Ordering Audiovisuals

For all practical purposes, ordering materials in the formats discussed in this chapter is the same as that used for books and serials, with only a few exceptions. One difference is that most of the orders will be made directly to the producer because there are no general AV jobbers as there are for books and serials. The other exceptions are related to those items acquired after preveiwing.

There is a major difference between review copies of books and preview copies of other media. With books, if the purchaser likes what he or she sees, the library keeps it, pays the invoice, and perhaps orders multiple copies at the same time. For a number of reasons (risk of loss, damage, and so forth), audiovisual preview copies are requested from the supplier, viewed, and then *returned*. (A few film vendors now ship an approval copy with 10 percent discount if the library buys the film.) Also, almost all filmstrips are sent on approval. It is becoming very common for the vendor to charge a preview fee. Suppliers only have a few preview copies of each title available, so this means that in most cases, one must *schedule* the preview copy well in advance. Normally, a librarian will write to the producer or supplier asking for preview copies of titles X, Y, and Z, and list a number of alternative dates. This becomes an issue when previewing with a group, which may cause additional scheduling problems. One must also know when specific items will be available for previewing. A preview file thus becomes a very important aid in the selection process; it should contain a listing of each title requested, the dates requested, when it is scheduled for previewing, and the result of the preview.

Several other factors should be kept in mind. The preview copy will probably have been used before; therefore, the quality will not be as high as that of a new copy. If one can determine from the supplier how often the preview copy has been used, it is possible to gain an insight into the durability of the product. In assessing this information (assuming that it can be acquired) the librarian must remember that the copy has been handled by persons who are more skilled in using the medium than is the average library patron.

If the decision is made to buy the item, the preview copy is generally returned and a new print ordered. When the new print is received, it should be screened to be certain it is: (1) a new print, (2) the same item as the film ordered, and (3) technically sound—check for breaks, make certain that the sound track is coordinated with visuals, and that the film has been properly processed. Generally, other media are not mass produced in the same manner as are books; sometimes they are just produced on an "on-demand" basis. That is, the producer has several preview copies and a master copy; when an order arrives the master copy is used to produce a new print. Thus, there is no assurance that the preview copy accurately reflects the quality of the print that the library will receive.

With some formats there may be another decision to make: to buy or rent. Normally, vendors charge 10 percent of the list price as their rental fee. If there are doubts about the level of demand, it may be best to rent a copy. (Ten usages in five years would be more than enough to justify buying the item.) One should not forget when calculating the cost that it will be necessary to include staff time in preparing the rental forms as well as time allotted for the mailing and handling costs. In many cases, with film, video, and computer software, the library is not "buying" the item in the same sense that it can purchase books and serials. Often there is an agreement form the library must sign which spells out what may or may not be done with the item. These agreements cover duplication, resale, and, in some cases, place and type of use allowed. Vendors do enforce these agreements and they are legal contracts, so the librarian must understand what it is that is being signed. If something is not clear or a clause should be changed, the librarian should discuss it with the vendor and the library's legal counsel *before* signing.

Equipment Issues in Selecting Audiovisuals

Part of the expense of developing an audiovisual collection is in buying and maintaining the equipment required for use of the various formats acquired. Increasing standardization in equipment means that the problem of compatibility is not as great as it once was, but newer formats always go through an early stage in which there are competing and incompatible lines of equipment. In those cases in which the library must buy such a format—that is, before standardization has occurred—the librarian should select the equipment line that has the greatest number of available titles. One should not believe more than one-quarter of what the sales representative says about plans for the future development of a strong line of titles. Look at what is, not what may be.

Over the last 15 years, video formats (tapes, cassettes, disks) have been developed and marketed. The BETA and VHS cassette systems (incompatible with one another) have been established in the home market. A "newer" system, the RCA disk system, appeared and failed. New disk technologies are under development and are making their way into institutions if not into homes. From a technical point of view, the disk systems are better than the cassettes. How long will the cassette last as a major home video system? No one knows, but a lot of public libraries have invested heavily in video cassettes and the circulation figures indicate a strong demand in 1986. Also in developmental stages are hologram programs (a laser technology), which may make *both* tape and disk video obsolete.

The above example illustrates two points: (1) standardization takes time to accomplish (assuming that is possible), if ever; and (2) the media field is always changing. These two factors combine to make equipment buying hazardous, and to some extent, they keep libraries from building collections outside the areas of sound recordings (records and tapes) and films (filmstrips, 8mm, 16mm).

Several annual guides to equipment are available:

Audio Visual Market Place: A Multimedia Guide (R. R. Bowker) is really a directory of manufacturers and distributors. It includes only the briefest description of the types of equipment and the names and addresses for additional information.

The Audio-Visual Equipment Directory (National Audio-Visual Association) is much more detailed than *A-V Market Place*. Whenever possible, each piece of equipment will have information on its technical details, operation, and price, and is usually accompanied by a photograph. The list is as comprehensive as possible but does depend upon manufacturers and distributors to supply the information, in much the same manner as *PTLA*. The content is descriptive, not evaluative.

EPIE Gram: Equipment and *EPIE Gram: Materials* (Educational Products Information Exchange) provides monthly assessments of materials and equipment. For equipment, technical data are provided, while for materials, the reviews are similar to other AV review sources with the addition of a little more technical emphasis.

Library Technology Reports (American Library Association) provides, from time to time, useful evaluations of equipment for the media library (record players, filmstrip projectors, and microform equipment have all appeared). The *Reports* are published as a looseleaf service and include, in addition to reports on new products, articles on the use of a specific type of equipment, as well as testing and evaluation information. Unfortunately, the LTR program is not well supported, so no attempt is made to be comprehensive or necessarily to update information previously published. The *Reports* and LTR program are very useful and it is too bad that more support cannot be found to develop them more fully.

Information on 16mm film projectors, 35mm slide projectors, and phono-record and tape player/recorders is also available in popular magazines. The major drawback to these sources is that the evaluation is normally made in terms of home or personal use, rather than institutional. Institutional use requires the same ease of operation as home use; however, the equipment must be much more durable and designed to withstand misuse. Most popular magazines do not examine durability in this light.

All of this means that the selector can do his or her homework in the above sources, and perhaps visit a showroom or convention to examine the equipment and see it demonstrated. But the final decision is the selector's. Before signing a purchase order for the equipment, any prospective buyer should spend some time and effort in locating a library or educational institution that already has the equipment. Talking with individuals who have used equipment on a day-to-day basis is the best insurance against getting equipment that is continually breaking down. One should find out how easy or how difficult it is to get parts when the unit does go down. Can local technicians repair the unit or must it be returned to the manufacturer? If informants say that in their experience, the equipment has proved to be durable, reliable, and easy to maintain, it may be what the library needs. If they say less than that, perhaps more searching will save time and trouble in the long run.

Summary

This chapter has tried to convey the fact that building a media collection for the library is a time-consuming activity and an expensive undertaking. It probably has done that, but it was *not* intended to convey the message: do not bother with audiovisual materials. Previewing and seeking out published evaluations of hardware and software do take time. Beyond the cost in time is the cost of the equipment and software. Also, new formats seem to appear every day, threatening to make one or two existing formats obsolete. On the other hand, photography (still and motion), radio, and television have not made the book or any other format obsolete, despite pronouncements of the forthcoming demise of this or that medium. Each new format is capable of doing certain things that no other format can do, but each also has its limitations, and as a result, supplements rather than replaces other formats. What is also clear is that there are different preferences in seeking and enjoying information. If the library is to be responsive to the total community, it must build a collection of materials that reflects that community's variety of interests and tastes.

Notes

[1] *The Wall Street Journal*, 24 January 1986, 23.

Further Reading

General

Barrette, R. P. "Selecting Digital Electronic Knowledge: A Process Model." *School Library Media Quarterly* 10 (Summer 1982): 320-26.

Binder, M. B. *Videotext and Teletext: New Online Resources for Libraries.* Greenwich, Conn.: JAI Press, 1985.

Block, D., and A. Kalyoncu. "Selection of Word Processing Software for Library Use." *Information Technology and Libraries* 2 (September 1983): 252-60.

Calmes, A. "New Confidence in Microfilm." *Library Journal* 111 (15 September 1986): 38-42.

Craig, J. "Evaluating Materials: A System for Selection of Non-print Materials." *Media Spectrum* 9 (1982): 5-6.

Ellison, J. W. "Non-print Selection: A Combination of Methods." *Catholic Library World* 54 (October 1982): 119-21.

Hannigan, J. A. "Evaluation of Software." *Library Trends* 23 (Winter 1985): 327-48.

Line, M. B. "UAP and Audiovisual Materials." *IFLA Journal* 12 (May 1982): 91-103.

Melin, N. "The Book on Library Uses: CD-ROM." *CD-ROM Review* 1 (October 1986): 36-38.

Microforms in Libraries: A Manual for Evaluation and Management. Edited by F. Spreitzer. Chicago: American Library Association, 1985.

Nugent, W. R. "Optical Discs—An Emerging Technology for Libraries." *IFLA Journal* 12 (August 1986): 175-81.

Saffady, W. *Video-Based Information Systems.* Chicago: American Library Association, 1985.

Sive, M. R. *Media Selection Handbook.* Littleton, Colo.: Libraries Unlimited, 1983.

Veaner, A. B. *Evaluation of Micropublications.* Chicago: American Library Association, 1971.

Weihs, J., S. Lewis, and J. Macdonald. *Nonbook Materials: The Organization of Integrated Collections,* 2d ed. Chicago: American Library Association, 1980.

Academic

Colby, E. K. "Is the Academic Library's Non-print Collection Incidental to Learning?" *Catholic Library World* 49 (March 1978): 335-37.

DeGennaro, R. "Shifting Gears: Information Technology and the Academic Library." *Library Journal* 109 (15 June 1984): 1204-9.

Sirkin, A. F. "Academic Libraries Struggle to Provide Video Services." *American Libraries* 11 (October 1980): 572-74.

Smith, D. G. "Media Resources in College Libraries." In *College Librarianship*, edited by W. Miller and D. S. Rockwood, 205-13. Metuchen, N.J.: Scarecrow Press, 1981.

Wiener, P. B. "A Library Is as Great as Its Film Collection." *Catholic Library World* 57 (March/April 1986): 233-34.

Public

Harlan, P. "Videotapes in Libraries: Principles and Realities." *New Jersey Libraries* 15 (Summer 1982): 13-15.

Intner, S. S. "Access to Media: Attitudes of Public Librarians." *RQ* 23 (Summer 1984): 424-30.

Josey, E. J., and J. B. Spear. "Survey of Media Resources in Public Library Systems and Two-Year Colleges." *Bookmark* 38 (Summer 1980): 456-70.

Koepp, D. P. "Map Collections in Public Libraries: A Brighter Future." *Wilson Library Bulletin* 60 (October 1985): 28-32.

Lettner, L. L. "Videocassettes in Libraries." *Library Journal* 110 (15 November 1985): 35-37.

Lewis, S. "Nonprint Materials in the Small Library." *Library Resources and Technical Services* 29 (April/June 1985): 146-50.

Palmer, J. W. "Future of Public Library Film Service." *American Libraries* 13 (February 1982): 140ff.

School

Aaron, S. L., and P. R. Scales, eds. *School Library Media Annual*. Littleton, Colo.: Libraries Unlimited, 1983- .

Berry, J., and J. C. Thomas. *Current Trends in Media for Children*. Minneapolis, Minn.: Dennison, 1982.

Brown, L. G. *Core Media for Elementary Schools*, 2d ed. New York: R. R. Bowker, 1978.

_____. *Core Media for Secondary Schools*, 2d ed. New York: R. R. Bowker, 1979.

Emmens, C. A. *Children's Media Market Place*, 2d ed. New York: Neal-Schuman, 1982.

Pillon, N. B. *Reaching Young People through Media*. Littleton, Colo.: Libraries Unlimited, 1983.

Sive, M. R. *Selecting Instructional Media: A Guide to Audiovisual and Other Instructional Media Lists*, 3d ed. Littleton, Colo.: Libraries Unlimited, 1983.

Special

Connolly, B. "Laserdisk Directory—Part I." *Database* 9 (June 1986): 15-26.

_____. "Laserdisk Directory—Part II." *Database* 9 (July 1986): 39-50.

Gasaway, L. N. "Nonprint Works and Copyright in Special Libraries." *Special Libraries* 74 (April 1983): 156-70.

Rydeskey, M. M. "Audiovisual Media: Special Library Asset or Bane?" In *Special Librarianship*, edited by E. B. Jackson, 521-29. Metuchen, N.J.: Scarecrow Press, 1980.

Wagers, R. "Online Sources of Competitive Intelligence." *Database* 9 (June 1986): 28-38.

10
Acquisitions

Acquisitions work involves locating and acquiring the items identified as appropriate for the collection. Only in the smallest libraries are the same people likely to be doing both selection and acquisition work. As the size of the library increases, so does the complexity of selection and acquisition work, which usually results in two separate yet interrelated units.

Selection personnel and the acquisitions department must have a close, cooperative work relationship in order to be effective. Poor coordination will mean wasted effort, slow response time, and high unit costs. Coordination can only be achieved when all parties involved in the work understand the processes, problems, and utility of each other's work. Beyond the obvious purpose of supporting overall library objectives, the acquisitions department has both specific library-wide goals and departmental goals. Library-wide goals can be grouped into five very broad areas: (1) develop a knowledge of the book and media trade (discussed earlier), (2) aid in the selection and collection development process, (3) process requests for items to be added to the collection, (4) monitor the expenditure of collection development funds, and (5) maintain all of the required records and produce reports regarding the expenditure of funds.

By disseminating information from book publishers and from media producers and vendors, the acquisitions department aids in the selection process. Collections of publishers' catalogs, prepublication announcements, and book-dealer catalogs are maintained in most acquisitions departments. Information regarding changes in publishing schedules, publishing houses, and new services is also collected. Many departments serve as central clearinghouses for this type of information for the entire library. Indeed, in larger libraries, the department sometimes operates a limited SDI system by routing information to selectors, based on each individual's subject or area of responsibility.

Processing requests for materials involves a number of activities to ensure that the library acquires the needed items as quickly and inexpensively as possible. Time and money would be wasted if requests simply were forwarded to a publisher or vendor. Inaccurate information, duplicate requests, unavailable material, and other similar problems would generate unacceptable costs for both the library and the supplier (and would probably cause considerable ill will). Each acquisitions department develops its own set of procedures to reduce problems of this type, and while there are hundreds of variations, the basic process is the same: preordering, ordering, receiving, fiscal managing, and record keeping.

Acquisitions departments also have internal goals. Four common goals are: (1) to acquire material as quickly as possible; (2) to maintain a high level of accuracy in all work procedures; (3) to keep work processes simple, so as to achieve the lowest possible unit cost; and (4) to develop close, friendly working relationships both with other library units and vendors. Internal goals are important in the achievement of the broader, library-wide goals discussed earlier, since all of the department's decisions regarding internal goals will have some impact on other operating units in the library.

Speed is a significant factor in meeting patron demands and determining patron satisfaction. Many patrons want their material "yesterday," and an acquisition system that requires three or four months to secure items already in the local bookstore will create problems in public relations. A system that is very fast but has a high error rate will increase operating costs, and waste time and energy for both departmental staff and suppliers. In many medium- and large-sized libraries, studies have shown that the costs of acquiring and processing an item are equal to or greater than the price of that item. By keeping procedures simple, and by periodically reviewing work flow, the department can aid the library in providing better service. Speed, accuracy, and thrift should be the watchwords in acquisitions departments.

Staffing

Staffing patterns play an important role in the successful achievement of departmental and library goals. Thoughtful staff planning will go a long way toward providing efficient service. Efficient staffing is usually accomplished by using four classes of employees: (1) professionals, (2) library/media technical assistants, (3) clerks, and (4) part-time help. Persons in each category supply certain skills and knowledge required for the optimum operation of the department.

Librarians provide in-depth knowledge of library operations and the book and media trades. They should set departmental objectives and goals, prepare operating plans, develop policies, and supervise the operation of the department. They also carry out tasks that require special skills or knowledge, such as verifying out-of-print requests or checking rare or special collection items. If the acquisitions department does not have any selection responsibility (and very few do), there is little need to have a large number of professionals on its staff except in the very largest departments. A high percentage of the department's activities can be handled by technicians and clerks – if the work has been properly planned.

Library/media technical assistants (LMTAs) are staff who have had some training in librarianship. Many LMTAs are staff graduates of community college library technician training programs and also hold a bachelor's degree. When staff members have both a bachelor's degree and the one-year library assistant degree, they have a background similar to a library school graduate. Considerable use should be made of this category of employee in planning work in an acquisitions department. Acquisition work does require a knowledge of librarianship, yet it is rather structured and routine. LMTAs have enough background to operate effectively while not being so highly educated as to waste skills and education in such tasks. Typing and filing activities should be assigned to clerical and part-time staff.

What follows is an overview of acquisition functions. Details regarding the nonprofessional aspects of this work can be found in the latest edition of *Introduction to Technical Services for Library Technicians.*[1]

Request Processing

The first step in acquisition work is to organize the requests to acquire an item. The form of the request can vary from an oral request or a scrawled note on a napkin from the local coffee shop to a completed formal request card. Eventually, all requests are organized so that efficient searching can be carried out. Each library will have its own format and method of recording the requests; frequently a blank form that the requestor is asked to complete is used.

Typical categories of information normally asked for are author, title, publisher, date of publication, edition, price, number of copies, and requester's name. Other information frequently requested includes series, vendor, fund to be charged, and approval signature. For any person not familiar with library or book trade practice, the most confusing item on such a request card is the space entitled "date/year." The most frequent assumption by patrons is that the library is interested in the date on which the request card was filled out, rather than the date on which the item was produced or published. Anyone with acquisitions department experience knows how often this item is confused. If the form specifically calls for "date of publication," there will be no problem. Patrons often request items already in the collection because they do not know how to use the public catalog. People occasionally combine or confuse authors' names, titles, publishers, and so on. Therefore, bibliographic searching is the next step in acquisition work.

Preordering

Bibliographic verification or searching consists of two elements. First is the establishment of the existence of a particular item—verification. Second is the establishment of the need for the item by the library—searching. In verifying, the concern is with the author, the correct title, the publisher of the work, and other necessary ordering data. Searching is concerned with whether the library already owns the item, whether it needs a second copy or multiple copies, and whether the item already has been ordered but not received.

Which step should one start with? The answer will depend upon the collection development system employed by each library. It is true that all requests will have to be searched. It is also true, however, that not all request cards have sufficient information to do this accurately. If the majority of request cards are filled out from bibliographies, dealer catalogs, publishers' flyers, by book selection personnel, then searching may be the most efficient way to start. When a large percentage of the selections are from nonlibrarians, it is advisable to start with the verification process.

One of the major problems for a searcher is the question of author (main entry) entry. Some selectors, usually nonlibrarians, know very little about cataloging rules of entry. Even bibliographers may not keep up-to-date on rule changes. Knowing something about main entry rules as well as how the standard bibliographic list works, including the most complete entry, will save searchers time. It will be necessary for the professional staff to train new searchers, if the new person has no prior experience. Corporate authors, conference papers, proceedings, or transactions are the most troublesome to search. If the files in the acquisitions department are maintained by title rather than main entry, it may be possible to reduce bibliographic training to a minimum. Titles seldom change after the item is published; main entries, on the other hand, may change several times between the time the item is selected and the time it is on the shelf. Main entry searching requires a greater knowledge of cataloging rules, which in turn requires more time for training searchers and more time spent in searching.

If the author main entry search procedure does not verify between 60 and 90 percent of the items, the procedure should be examined carefully, as it is probable that either the requests lack adequate information or the wrong tools are being searched. For the remaining items, a title search should verify most if not all the remaining requests. Occasionally, an item cannot be located in any source; when this happens, it is best to contact the requester, who may have some additional information.

If the requester cannot provide further information, a subject search may produce a verification. The success rate of subject searches is generally low for a number of reasons. Some bibliographies do not provide subject access, thus making it impossible to search all the commonly used bibliographies. Another reason, and a more critical one, is that the assignment of subject is somewhat arbitrary, and even with a work in hand, two individuals may very well provide two different subject categories for the same title. A searcher must look under as many subjects as seem likely and still can never be certain that all the appropriate headings were examined. Because of its low success rate, subject verification should be used as a last resort for items urgently needed.

Occasionally, it will be necessary to examine three or four sources in order to establish all of the required order information. One may quickly find the author, title, publisher, date of publication, and price, but it may be difficult to find information determining whether or not the item is in a series. Failure to identify series information may lead to duplication—one copy received on a series standing order and another copy from a direct order. *Books in Series ... in the U.S.* (R. R. Bowker) is of help, but as the title indicates, it is limited to the United States (nevertheless it covers 37,619 series with over 326,688 titles).[2] Both verification and searching procedures, though, involve the use of a number of bibliographic tools, the major categories of which were described in chapter 5. Book dealer catalogs are another helpful source (see chapter 11).

There are several files to check in order to establish the library's need for the selected item. The most obvious place to start is with the public catalog. A checker should look first under the assumed main entry; if the results are negative and there was some doubt as to validity of the main entry, then a title search should be made. Some librarians suggest that checkers begin with the title because there are likely to be less variation and doubt. In some libraries, a number of other public catalogs must be searched. Audiovisual materials, phonograph records, government documents, serials, collections in special libraries, or subject areas (such as fine arts) often are only found in separate catalogs. Other public service files to be examined are those for lost, missing, or damaged items (replacement files). The checker would not examine all of these files for all items, but merely for those popular items not marked "added copy" or "replacement."

In the technical service area, several files must be checked to determine whether the item is being processed. Technical service units tend to maintain a number of files that, to some degree, duplicate one another. Normally three files must be consulted, if the department has a manual system: the in-process file, the verified requests file (items waiting to be typed on order forms), and the standing order file. The in-process file represents books on order, books received but not yet sent to cataloging, and books in the cataloging department. The standing order file represents items to be received automatically from a supplier. Usually these items are in publishers' series, and it is important that the checker examine the standing order file after establishing that an item is in a series. Online systems are now available in many libraries to speed up the preorder checking. *Books in Print* is available online and other commercial bibliographical selection aids are likely to follow suit over the next few years. Bibliographic utilities such as OCLC, WLN, and RLIN also provide large bibliographic databases that can be and are used in verification and searching activities. Finally, automated acquisition systems and public catalogs may also be available to establish the library's need for an item. In a few libraries, a person responsible for preorder activities may be able to do 90 percent or more of the work at one terminal merely by logging on and off of different systems. Searchers, even in that situation, have to learn as many if not more procedural rules as when working with printed sources, as each online system has a special way of handling its search sequence.

Ordering

Five major methods are employed to acquire materials for the collection: firm order, standing order, approval plan, deposit or gift, and exchange. Each method has a useful role to play in developing a collection in an efficient, cost-effective manner. In most large- and many medium-sized libraries, orders are computer generated and stored electronically, thus reducing the volume of paper associated with ordering activities. For a few libraries there is no order form for current trade books, as the entire order process is handled electronically and the record of the order is "stored" in both the library's and supplier's computers. Some time in the future this may be the way all libraries place all their orders; however, for thousands of libraries the "paperless" order is far from reality. There are only a few libraries today that collect in a variety of information formats and place all their orders in a paperless manner. Regardless of the method used to order material, the vendor must be given enough information to assure shipment of the correct materials: author, title, publisher, date of publication, price, edition (if there are various editions), number of copies, order number, and any special instructions regarding invoicing or methods of payment. Also, more and more suppliers are asking for the International Standard Book Number (ISBN) or International Standard Serial Number (ISSN). In time the "ISN" may be all that is required, because it is a unique number representing a specific journal or a specific edition of a specific title.

A useful publication that all aspiring collection development officers should read is *Guidelines for Handling Library Orders for In-Print Monographic Publications* (1984), published by the American Library Association. Written by the Bookdealer-Library Relations Committee of Resources and Technical Services Division, it reflects the needs of both groups and contains recommendations for establishing and maintaining good working relationships. One suggestion is that libraries use the American National Standards Institute Committee Z39's 3-by-5-inch "single title order form." At the present time, there is no equivalent standard for electronic order transmission; however, Committee Z39 is working on such a standard.

Another standard of ANSI Committee Z39 is the "Standard Address Number" (SAN). Like the ISBN, the SAN is a unique number (seven digits) which identifies each address or organization doing business in the American book trade. For example, Tozzer Library's SAN is 344-8568; Bro-Dart, 159-9984; Libraries Unlimited, Inc., 202-6767. Perhaps in time all that will be necessary to order a title electronically will be to key in three sets of unique numbers, the ISBN or ISSN, and the SANs for the supplier and the buyer. Again, such ease of ordering is some way off, if it ever comes. Nevertheless, these unique numbers can be useful as a cross-check for accuracy, if for nothing else. SANs are being published in a variety of sources—for example, the *American Library Directory*, since its 33rd edition, has provided the library SAN numbers.

The multiple copy (fan-fold) order form is commonly used. These forms are available in a number of formats, containing from four to as many as twelve copies. The 3-by-5-inch size is standard in the United States. Normally, each copy is a different color for easy identification, but no standard dictates a particular color for a certain purpose. A minimum of four copies is typical in libraries: (1) an outstanding order copy, (2) a dealer's copy, (3) a claiming copy, and (4) an accounting copy. The number of potential uses seems to be limited only by the imagination of the librarians. In some libraries, two copies are sent to the dealer, while three or four may be kept in the in-process file. In the past, some libraries used one copy to order catalog cards from either the Library of Congress or a commercial cataloging service. Today such use is diminishing, as more and more libraries use only online cataloging systems such as OCLC. In some larger systems, where selectors are not in close contact with the acquisitions department (as in academic libraries where faculty members do much of the selecting), an "information" copy is sent to the selector.

The outstanding order copy is one of the most important because of its many uses. It is essential that this be a clear, readable copy which is filed in either the outstanding order or in-process file. Often the in-process file contains several copies of the order. For example, when the order is sent, the in-process file might receive five slips. The first represents on-order status, two for possible claims, one for cataloging, and the final one remains in the file, indicating that the book is being processed but is not yet ready for public use. When the book is received, all slips except the in-process slip are removed. When the book is ready for circulation, one slip from cataloging is returned to the acquisitions department to signal the removal of the in-process slip. Presumably, at this point a set of cards will be filed in the public catalog indicating that the book is now available for the public.

Claiming and handling supplier reports is one of the more time-consuming and frustrating aspects of the order function. Most multiple copy order forms have slips for these purposes. Purchasers have every reason to expect American commercial publishers, or vendors supplying titles from such publishers, to deliver or report on the status of the order within 90 days. For American noncommercial publishers (for example, university presses or professional associations) an additional 30 days (120 days total) is common for delivery or a report. Western European titles, delivered to the United States, normally require 180 days and from countries with a developing book trade, a year or more is not uncommon. When there is an active collecting program from developing countries, one must expect a certain percentage of nonresponse. Learning when "long enough" is long enough to wait takes experience. Tozzer Library recently received a monograph from Bolivia that had been ordered over five years ago.

When dealing with an American publisher, allowing for the normal two-way postal time, it is reasonable to send a second claim in 60 days if no response has been received. Many order forms have a printed note stating "cancel after XXX days." Although such statements are legally binding, it is recommended that a separate cancellation notice be sent. Certainly the cancellation should not take place before the normal response time has passed, unless there are unusual circumstances, such as unexpected reductions in the budget. Unfortunately, over the past 10 to 15 years such cuts have taken place and most vendors have been cooperative about making the adjustments. By establishing a regular cancellation time line, libraries, whose funds must be expended within a fixed period, can avoid (or reduce) the last-minute scramble to cancel outstanding orders and to order instead materials that can be delivered in time to use the funds.

Vendors should respond with a meaningful report when they cannot fulfill an order, within a reasonable period. One less-than-helpful report that was and occasionally still is used is "temporarily out of stock" (TOS). How long is temporarily? What is/has been done to secure the item? Poor or inaccurate reporting does cost the library money, as Audrey Eaglen pointed out in "Trouble in Kiddyland: The Hidden Costs of O.P. and O.S."[3] In periods of rapid inflation, each day the funds are committed but unexpended erodes buying power because producers and suppliers can and do raise prices without notice. Recommended vendor reports are "not yet received from publisher" (NYR), "out-of-stock, ordering" (OS ordering), "claiming," "canceled," "not yet published" (NYP), "out-of-stock, publisher" (OS publisher), "out-of-print" (OP), "publication canceled," "out-of-stock indefinitely" (treat this one as a cancellation), "not our publication" (NOP), "wrong title supplied," "defective copy" and "wrong quantity supplied." Once one learns just how long a vendor takes to supply items first reported in the recommended manner, it is possible to make an informed decision regarding when to cancel and when to wait for delivery.

Before the order is placed, several important decisions must be made: which acquisition method is to be used; what source of supply is to be tapped; and if the item is to be purchased, where the money is to come from. The remainder of this chapter explores the methods of acquiring materials. Chapter 11 concerns vendors, when and how to use them, and what to expect from them. Chapter 12 covers the fiscal side of acquisition work.

For most current items the firm order is the only logical method to use. It is often the best method for the first volume in a series, even if the selectors are thinking about ordering all the items in the series. A distinction should be made between "thinking about" and "planning on" when considering series items. When the publisher and/or editor of the series is well established it is probably best to go ahead with the standing order. If there is some question about suitability or context, a firm order or approval-copy order for the first volume is probably a better choice. While standing orders (sometimes also called blanket orders) can save ordering paperwork by automatic delivery of each new volume, they must be reviewed periodically to assure that the material is still appropriate for the collection. (Review of standing orders and approval materials is normally the responsibility of the selector(s), not the acquisitions department.)

Deciding to use the gift or deposit method of acquisition will almost always mean a delay in receiving the desired item(s). Verification may establish that the item is a government publication which may be received as part of a depository program or it may be a new government series which should be set up on a depository basis. In either case, one would not issue a firm order, but should notify the requester so he or she can decide what to do. Sometimes a library user or board member donates certain materials on a regular basis, making it unnecessary to order the item, if there is no immediate demand for the material. Occasionally, a series or set of items is advertised that would be appropriate but costs so much that regular funds should not be used. Seeking out a donor to assist with, if not fully pay for, the purchase is not unheard of, but again there may be extended delays. Most often this takes place with rare book and special collection items. An active (also well-to-do) Friends of the Library group may be the answer to a special purchase situation. (Friends groups, used judiciously, can significantly expand the collection and stretch funds.)

Gifts and Deposits

Acquisitions departments are usually the ultimate recipients of unsolicited gifts of books, serials, and sometimes other materials (including a variety of molds and insects) that well-meaning people give to the library. Both solicited and unsolicited gifts can be a source of out-of-print materials needed for replacement, extra copies, and the filling of gaps. The collection development policy statement on gifts will help process the material more quickly.

Searching gifts is important, because the library cannot afford to add unnecessary items, and processing and storage costs *must* be considered. But it cannot afford to discard valuable or needed items. Older books may be carefully checked, as variations in printings and editions determine whether an item is valuable or worthless. (Second or third printings normally lessen the value of a work.) This must be done by persons with extensive training and experience in bibliographic checking.

Only a small percentage of gifts will be added to the collection. In larger libraries, gifts are rejected if they are already in the collection, but if they are accepted, this means a rather high cost per item added. Careful training and efficient work procedures will help keep the unit cost as low as possible, but it will still be higher for gifts in comparison with purchased items. This also means that the library is confronted with the problem of disposing of a great many unwanted items, which is usually the responsibility of the exchange unit.

There are two basic types of exchange activity: the exchange of unwanted duplicate materials, and the exchange of new materials between libraries. Exchange of new materials is usually confined to large university or research libraries; in essence, cooperating institutions trade their publications. At Tozzer Library we have exchange agreements with several hundred organizations. They send us the publications their organizations produce and we send them Peabody Museum publications. Often this method is the only way one can acquire an organization's publications. Occasionally, this system is employed to acquire materials from countries in which commercial trade operations are limited or restricted in some manner. Where government trade restrictions make buying and selling of foreign publications difficult or impossible, the cooperating libraries acquire (buy) their local publications for exchange. Exchanges of this type are very complex and difficult to manage and should be used as a last resort. There is better quality control when trading for known organizational series or titles than when the choice of which publications the organization is to send is left to chance. Exchanges are established through formal agreements between the cooperating organizations. They do play a role in developing comprehensive subject collections.

Disposition of unwanted gift materials is an activity that almost every library engages in at some time. One method is to list the unwanted items and mail the list to exchange units in other libraries, and the first library to request an item gets it for the shipping cost (usually book rate postage). This method is very time-consuming.

Another method is to arrange with an out-of-print dealer to take the items, usually for a "lot," rather than a per item price. Cash is generally not involved; instead, credit is extended by the dealer to the library in the amount agreed upon. The credit is then used when buying materials from the dealer. This system will work when the library has specialized materials the dealer wants and it is known that the dealer will stock enough useful material that the credit will be used up within a reasonable time. (Anything over 18 to 24 months is too long.)

Holding a book sale is yet another method of disposing of unwanted material, and one gaining in popularity as dealers resist the credit memo system. Staff must choose the materials to be sold, establish a "fair" price, find a suitable location, and monitor the sale. Depending on the volume of gifts, annual or semiannual or monthly sales may be justified. Sales can be an excellent Friends of the Library project and will save some staff time. A few libraries have opted for the "ongoing sale" when staff and space are limited but a high volume of gifts are received. Gifts can be processed and disposed of more quickly, storage space is not tied up, and a small amount of revenue is generated, which, one hopes, goes into the collection development fund.

Order Placement and Receiving

After the method of acquisition is decided (as well as vendor and funding source), an order number is assigned to assist in "tracking" the order. It is simply a matter of checking the last order number and assigning the next number in the sequence. With that taken care of, the order is prepared and sent to the supplier.

Receiving orders, although not difficult, must be carefully planned. As strange as it may seem, the careful unpacking of shipments can save everyone in the department a great deal of time, energy, and frustration. One of the first steps in the unpacking process is to find the packing slip and/or invoice. A packing slip lists (or should list) items in a particular shipment; an invoice is an itemized bill, which is required before a business office will issue a voucher or check. The invoice may or may not accompany the shipment. No matter which format is used (packing slip or invoice), the person unpacking a shipment may spend time playing "Who has the packing slip?" Most vendors conveniently attach a clearly marked envelope containing the slip to the outside of one of the boxes.

Unfortunately, a few vendors seem to delight in hiding the slip in the strangest places: one technique is to enclose the slip inside one of the items, while another favorite hiding place is in the bottom of a box under a cardboard bottom liner. If no slip is found, it is essential to keep the items separated from other materials in the receiving area. Mixing shipments can create seemingly endless problems.

Each item should be checked against the packing slip as it comes out of the shipping container. This serves to check what the shippers think they sent against what the library actually received. Boxes go astray in shipment, items are overlooked in packing rooms, and sometimes items disappear from the library before they are processed. Checking the physical condition of each item is also important because defective materials need to be returned for credit or replacement. Some of the more common receipt problems are listed below.

1. The wrong edition is received. (Note: the checker must be aware of the difference between an edition and a printing. A new edition indicates that the item has been changed — material added and/or deleted; a new printing merely indicates the item was reprinted with no change.)

2. Items ordered are not received.

3. Items not ordered are received.

4. Too many copies of an item are received.

5. Imperfect copies are received.

Imperfections can be of many kinds. With books, some of the typical problems are missing or blank pages, or improperly collated texts. Audiotapes should be checked for gaps, blank tapes, and proper speed of recording. Film items should be examined for proper developing. Many times a film is "fogged," "streaked," or spotted with hypo residue. Any imperfect book or item can be returned for replacement.

After determining that the shipment is complete, "property marking" takes place. As noted above, sometimes items disappear, so the sooner items are property identified (stamped or embossed for example), the more difficult it will be for them to disappear.

Vendors are usually good about accepting returns of unwanted items, even when it turns out to have been the fault of the library — if the material is unmarked. A library must be a very good customer before it will get credit for a "mistake" that has been property marked. Property marking takes many forms. Books are usually stamped on the fore-edge and on the title page. (Naturally rare books are handled differently.) When a library is required to "accession" items, the number is recorded in the book and in the accessions book. (Accessioning is a system of assigning a unique number for inventory control to each item purchased.)

Films often have a special leader attached, which has the name of the library imprinted in it. If an accession number is used, the leader is perforated with that number. Phonograph records may have the label on the record stamped, as well as a stamp on the record jacket. Cassette items may have a special label attached, or may have the library name and accession number engraved into them.

The last step in processing a received order is approval of the invoice for payment. Normally, this may be approved only by the head of the department or that person's representative. The approval of payment is made only when the order is "complete" (that is, when all items have been accounted for). When the invoice is approved, the bookkeeper passes this information to the agency that actually writes the check. Rarely does a library itself write such checks; it is done by the governing agency.

In this chapter we have touched upon only the basic activities and problems in acquisition work. The three following chapters cover vendors and suppliers, fiscal management related to collection development, and an overview of some of the automated acquisitions systems available as of early 1986.

Notes

[1]Marty Bloomberg and G. Edward Evans, *Introduction to Technical Services for Library Technicians*, 5th ed. (Littleton, Colo.: Libraries Unlimited, 1985).

[2]*Books in Series ... in the United States ...*, 4th ed. (New York: R. R. Bowker, 1985).

[3]Audrey Eaglen, "Trouble in Kiddyland: The Hidden Costs of O.P. and O.S.," *Collection Building* 6 (Summer 1984): 26-28.

Further Reading

General

Eaglen, A. "Trouble in Kiddyland: The Hidden Costs of O.P. and O.S." *Collection Building* 6 (Summer 1984): 26-28.

Guidelines for Handling Library Orders for In-Print Monographic Publications, 2d ed. Chicago: American Library Association, 1984.

Kennedy, G. A. "Relationships between Acquisitions and Collection Development." *Library Acquisitions: Practice and Theory* 7, no. 3 (1983): 225-32.

Kovacic, M. "Acquisition by Gift and Exchange." In *Acquisition of Foreign Materials for U.S. Libraries*, by T. Samore, 37-41. Metuchen, N.J.: Scarecrow Press, 1982.

Lane, A. H. *Gifts and Exchange Manual*. Westport, Conn.: Greenwood Press, 1980.

Leonhardt, T. W. "Collection Development and Acquisitions: The Division of Responsibility." *RTSD Newsletter* 9, no. 6 (1984): 73-75.

Magrill, R. M., and D. J. Hickey. *Acquisitions Management and Collection Development in Libraries*. Chicago: American Library Association, 1984.

Miller, B. C. "Placing and Tracing Orders in a Dynamic Acquisitions Process." *Collection Management* 3 (Summer 1979): 233-46.

Samore, T. *Acquisition of Foreign Materials for U.S. Libraries*, 2d ed. Metuchen, N.J.: Scarecrow Press, 1982.

Academic

Archer, J. D. "Preorder Searching in Academic Libraries." *Library Acquisitions: Practice and Theory* 7, no. 2 (1983): 139-44.

Diodato, L. W., and V. P. Diodato. "Use of Gifts in a Medium-sized Academic Library." *Collection Management* 5 (Summer 1983): 53-71.

Kilton, T. D. "Out-of-Print Procurement in Academic Libraries." *Collection Management* 5 (Fall 1983): 113-34.

Neikirk, H. D. "Less Does More: Adapting Preorder Searching to On-line Cataloging." *Library Acquisitions: Practice and Theory* 5, no. 2 (1981): 89-94.

Sewell, R. G. "Managing European Automatic Acquisitions." *Library Resources and Technical Services* (October 1983): 397-405.

Public

O'Brien, J. M. "Acquisition Process in Public Libraries in the 1980s." *Illinois Libraries* 62 (September 1980): 634-37.

Steinbrenner, J. "Cost Effectiveness of Book Rental Plans." *Ohio Library Association Bulletin* 49 (April 1979): 5-6.

Schools

"Ordering Procedures." In *Media Program in the Elementary and Middle Schools*, edited by J. J. Delaney, 126-44. Hamden, Conn.: Shoe String Press, 1976.

Special

Byrne, N. "Selection and Acquisition in an Art School Library." *Library Acquisitions: Practice and Theory* 7, no. 1 (1983): 7-11.

Dickson, L. E. "Law Library Book Orders." *Law Library Journal* 73 (Spring 1980): 446-50.

Koenig, M. E. D. "Expediting Book Acquisitions." *Special Libraries* 65 (December 1974): 516-17.

Moore, E. "Acquisitions in the Special Library." *Scholarly Publishing* 13 (January 1982): 167-73.

11

Distributors and
Vendors

Three major problems for materials producers were identified in chapter 6: (1) economics, (2) copyright infringement, and (3) distribution. A knowledge of distribution is essential for developing the most cost-effective collection of information materials. Wholesalers, retailers, and remainder houses are major sources of material for the library collection. Often several different sources can supply the same item. Is there an important difference between sources? What services are available? For example, if one is looking for a book published last year, it is possible to acquire a copy from many of the sources. Would it matter which one? How likely is it that all would have the book? For that matter, what function does each perform?

Jobbers and Wholesalers

Librarians generally refer to *jobbers* or *vendors* rather than wholesalers. There is a technical difference between a wholesaler and a jobber,* but for purposes of collection development, it does not matter. Jobbers purchase quantities

---

*Jobber — "1. One who buys merchandise from manufacturers and sells it to retailers. 2. A person who works by the piece or at odd jobs." Wholesaler — "a person who sells *large* quantities of goods to a retailer." Drop shipper — "a person who orders materials from manufacturers after receiving an order from a retailer (library). Unlike jobbers and wholesalers, a drop shipper does not have a stock of materials, just a telephone."

of books from various publishers; in turn they sell copies to bookstores and libraries. Because they buy in volume they receive a fairly high discount (reduced price) from the publishers. When the jobber sells a book, the purchaser receives a discount off the producer's list price, but it is much lower than the discount that the jobber received. For instance, if the jobber received a 50 percent discount from the producer, the discount given the library will usually be between 15 and 20 percent. If the library or bookstore had ordered the book directly from the publisher, the discount could have been as high or perhaps even higher.

Discounting is a complex issue in any commercial activity, and it is highly complex in the book trade. Every producer has a discount schedule that is slightly different, if not unique. Some items are net (no discount); these are usually textbooks, scientific technical titles, or items of very limited sales appeal. "Short" discounts are normally 20 percent; these items are also expected to have limited appeal but with more potential than the net titles. "Trade" discounts range from 30 to 60 percent or more; items in this category are normally high demand items, or high-risk popular fiction. One thought is that by giving a very high discount for fiction, bookstores will stock more copies and thus help promote the title. Jobbers normally receive 50 to 60 percent discounts, primarily because of their high-volume orders (hundreds of copies per title rather than the tens that most libraries and independent bookstore owners order).

Recently, jobbers have encountered financial problems in the form of rising costs and declining sales. A number of publishers are requiring prepayment or have placed jobbers on a "pro forma" status, where prepayment is required and credit extended on the basis of the current performance in payment of bills. Much of the credit/order fulfillment extended by publishers depends upon an almost personal relationship with a jobber. This means that for libraries the selection of a jobber must be made with care. It is *not* inappropriate to check a prospective jobber's financial status (through a rating service such as Dun and Bradstreet). Indeed, it is recommended that this be done by the library, since so much depends upon its choice of jobber.

What Can Jobbers Do?

Why buy from an indirect source that charges the same or a higher price than the direct source would? *Service!* Jobbers provide a very important service in that they can save a library a significant amount of time and money. Although jobbers do not give high discounts, the time saved by placing a single order for 10 different titles from 10 different publishers, instead of 10 different orders, more than pays for the slightly higher price. Other savings can result from the "batch effect" of unpacking only one box and authorizing only one payment. Most jobbers also promise to provide fast, accurate service. It is true that a few publishers, if they accept single-copy orders (and most do), handle these orders more slowly than they do large orders. But it is also true that jobbers do not always have a specific title when it is wanted, which also means that additional time must be allowed to secure the desired item.

"Items in stock will be shipped within 24 hours" is a typical claim of jobbers. Can and do they make good on the claim? Generally, yes; however, the key phrase is "in stock." Frequently, there are delays of three to four months in receiving a complete order because some titles are not in stock. When talking with jobbers, *do not* become impressed by numbers quoted in their advertising: "more than 2 million books in stock." What is important to know is how many *titles* and which *publishers* are represented. For various reasons, economic and/or personal, some publishers will refuse to deal with a particular jobber. Three important questions must be asked of any jobber before a library contracts for that firm's services:

1. Will you give me a list of all the publishers that you do not handle?

2. Will you give me a list of series that your firm does not handle?

3. How does your firm handle a request for a title not in stock?

The answer to the first question is difficult to get. Sales representatives want to say they can supply any title from any publisher, with only minor exceptions. However, libraries in the same system may be given different lists, at the same time, by different sales representatives from the same firm. The issue is important and must be resolved if the acquisitions department is to operate effectively. Sending an order for a title from a publisher that the jobber cannot handle only delays matters. In some cases the jobber will report back that they are trying to secure the item; this often results in a later report of failure, making the acquisition process even slower. Buying directly from the publisher is the best approach to this problem, *if* one knows which publishers are involved.

Questions 2 and 3 are also important in terms of speed of service. Some jobbers will order a single title from a publisher when it is not in stock. Others say that they will do this (and they do); but they may wait until they have received multiple requests before placing the order; by placing a multiple-copy order they will receive a better discount. For the library, the delay may be one to several months, because it will take that long for the jobber to accumulate enough individual requests for the title to make up an order of sufficient size. Jobbers who do place single-copy orders for a customer usually offer a lower discount. Again, the acquisition staff must weigh service and speed against discount. Occasionally, a jobber will have a title in stock after the publisher has listed the item as being out-of-print (o.p.). On occasion a jobber can supply o.p. material, and a few jobbers will even try to find o.p. items for their best customers. This is a special service which is never advertised and is given only to favored customers.

Beyond fast, accurate service, jobbers should provide personal service. A smooth working relationship with anyone, including a jobber, depends on mutual understanding and respect. When that is achieved, it is much easier to solve problems when they arise, even the difficult ones. The jobber, because of the smaller base of customers, normally can give answers more quickly than can a publisher's customer service department. Even the small account customer receives careful attention (in order to hold the account), something that seldom happens with publishers.

No single jobber can stock all of the in-print items that a library will need. Most large firms, however, do carry the high-demand current and backlist items. The book trade folklore says that 20 percent of the current and backlist titles represent 80 percent of the total sales. All of the good jobbers try to stock in their warehouses the *right* 20 percent. Some are more successful than others. Bookstores will find this concept very useful for maintaining a stock of best-sellers. Libraries, on the other hand, must acquire a broader range of titles. Thus the opinion of bookstore owners about the best jobbers in an area is useful only if it is supported by the experience of librarians.

One problem with a limited stock jobber is in invoicing and billing procedures. A small jobber may ship and bill for those items in stock, then back order the remainder. In this case, when the invoice is sent, the shipper expects to receive payment for the partial fulfillment of the order. However, some library systems are only allowed to pay for complete orders. Every item is either received or canceled before a voucher (check) is issued. This procedure can cause problems for small jobbers and/or libraries. Very few are able or willing to wait for payment until a particular order is complete. For small libraries with small materials budgets, the problem is to find a jobber who will accept complicated procedures and delays despite a low volume. It is becoming harder to find such firms, and libraries are attempting to get their funding authorities to simplify ordering and payment procedures.

Jobbers may handle thousands of different publishers and may maintain an inventory of over 200,000 titles. One useful service that many large jobbers offer is a periodic report on the status of all of a library's orders. Many provide a monthly report on all items not yet shipped. Each back-ordered item is listed and the reason for its unavailability is included. If the reporting system (status report) is properly organized, it can save both librarian and jobber a lot of letter writing and filing. Most large jobbers offer a flexible order and invoicing system — that is, they try to adapt to the library's needs, rather than force it to use their methods.

Status reports have been and remain an area of concern for acquisition and collection development staff. Almost everyone in the field has felt frustration with the reports. Does the report from a jobber that a book is o.p. really mean the book is out-of-print? It should, but occasionally, writing to the publisher may result in having the item in hand in less than 30 days, and this happens often enough to keep doubts alive about the quality of jobber reports. Perhaps two of the most frustrating reports are out-of-stock (o.s.) and temporarily out-of-stock (t.o.s.). Just what these two reports mean varies from jobber to jobber. The basic meaning is clear — the book is not about to be shipped. Beyond that basic information, however, there is doubt. How long will it be out-of-stock? Some cynics have suggested that these reports really mean "we are waiting until we get enough orders from buyers to secure a good discount from the producer" and the difference between the two reports is that t.o.s. means "we expect to have enough soon" and o.s. means "don't hold your breath." Those interpretations are much too harsh, but it does indicate that there are problems with the quality and content of the reporting system. (It must be noted that not all blame for faulty reporting lies with jobbers; the producers also change their minds after reporting a status to a jobber.)

Does it really matter how accurate the reports are? Yes, it does matter and the result can have an impact on collection development. An item on order encumbers (sets aside) funds to pay for it when it is received. The precise cost of the item cannot be determined until it is received, and one hopes to set aside just slightly more than the total cost. Most libraries and information centers have annual budgets and operate in systems where some monies not expended in a given year must be returned to the funding authority (not carried forward into the next year). Having large sums of money tied up (encumbered) in outstanding orders that may not be delivered before the end of the fiscal year can mean a very real loss for the collection, and in a sense the library loses twice: the item ordered is not received and the money is lost.

Another problem is the paperwork involved in cancellations and reordering. Numerous estimates have been made regarding the cost of normal office paperwork; they range from about $4.00 for a "simple" two-paragraph business letter, to over $21.00 for placing an order, and even more depending on the complexity of task, the organization, and what cost elements are included. No matter how costs are calculated, there are staff time, forms, letters, and postage involved in every cancellation. While these costs are not usually taken from acquisition funds, it still is a loss in the sense that the order did not result in receiving the desired material.

Finally, the library does lose some buying power the longer the funds are encumbered. Unlike money in a savings account which is earning a small amount of interest each day, encumbered funds lose a small amount of purchasing power each day. If inflation is rapid or if one is buying foreign books and the currency's value is fluctuating widely, losses can be large. Producers can and do raise their prices without notice, and in times of inflation one can count on regular price increases. So the less time funds are encumbered, the more purchasing power the library has. Thus the accuracy of the reports is important; if an item (o.p., o.s., or t.o.s.) cannot be delivered in time, the order can be canceled and the funds used for something that can be delivered. Monitoring of vendor performance in report accuracy and speed of delivery can help control the problem.

The services described above should be the ones offered to libraries and retail bookstores by a jobber, although most jobbers interested in selling to libraries offer a variety of other services. A typical jobber, beyond supplying books at wholesale prices, may offer libraries some or all of the following services:

- Cataloging/processing services
- Continuation services
- Approval plans
- Book rental plans
- Other media
- Library furniture
- Library supplies

As this list suggests, the jobber attempts to offer a library most of the supplies and services necessary for its operation.

Many small libraries, and perhaps in the future, large libraries, may find it beneficial to buy their books already processed. A study may show this approach to be very cost-effective, provided that the public service staff and users find that the material supplied is adequate. Normally the technical services offered by jobbers allow the library a number of choices. "Processing kits" — catalog cards, pockets, labels, jackets, etc. — can be purchased, with the library staff then completing the processing routines. Completely processed, ready-for-shelf services can also be secured. Because several different classification systems are widely used in the United States, a jobber will offer processing for all the major systems. In some areas such as the Nordic countries, there are central acquisition, cataloging, and processing services that most if not all public libraries use to acquire and prepare their stock. Flexibility is essential in these services; yet, in order to make them cost-effective (profitable) for the jobber, there must either be a high degree of uniformity or at least a high sales volume for each variation. Thus one can expect to receive a degree of personalized customer service but not custom processing.

Standing orders or continuations are a problem for most libraries. Publishers start a "series" with a number of books, each with a different number. Often such a numbered series will last for many years. Ordering each title will waste staff time, assuming the library wants the entire series. Most jobbers offer some type of standing order plan—the automatic shipment of each new title in a series. Status reports on standing orders are as important as in regular orders. If the jobber includes all orders in the status report, this will save everyone time; next best is a regular, monthly, bimonthly, quarterly, or other standard interval standing order status report. Any reputable dealer will explain just how much service to expect. Certainly, no single jobber will be able to handle all standing order needs, and some titles can only be secured on a direct order or membership basis. Nevertheless, jobbers can provide excellent service for a high percentage of a library's needs.

Most book jobbers offer only a monographic continuation service. For journals and other serials, a serials jobber is better. A basic difference is that serials jobbers seldom offer any service except order placement. As with monographic continuations, some journals and serials must be ordered directly. All of the questions asked of a book jobber should be asked of the serials jobbers. Of special concern here should be the size of the discounts or handling charges the firm employs. If one order is placed once a year for hundreds of serial titles, a large amount of library staff time will be saved. When the firm provides fast, accurate service and a good reporting system, both the library and the jobber will benefit. (More about serials jobbers appears in chapter 7.)

Public libraries and others serving popular reading interests want speedy delivery of current bestsellers. Various programs have been devised to assure prompt shipment of such items. Some years ago an American public librarian, Emerson Greenaway, came up with the idea of placing a standing order with publishers for one copy of each trade book, to be delivered on publication date. Eventually this idea developed into the "Greenaway Plan," and today one sees many variations of this basic concept. The Greenaway Plan is a contract between a library and one publisher. Some jobbers compete in this area by offering either date-of-publication approval copies or prepublication lists. The basic purpose of all of these schemes is the same: to be able to select titles in advance, so as to be able to anticipate patron demand for multiple copies.

One jobber, Bro-Dart, offers a rather unusual service—the McNaughton Plan—to help solve the problem of providing an adequate number of high-demand titles. Most libraries have suffered from the problem of high demand for a very popular book, the demand lasting only a few months. Should the library buy many copies and discard all but one or two after the demand dies down, or buy just a few copies and take reservations? The McNaughton Plan offers another alternative: rent multiple copies for the duration of the high-demand time. Actually, Bro-Dart describes it as a leasing program. This plan is geared to high-demand items that are selected by Bro-Dart's staff; one cannot order just any book; it must be on their list. Saving occurs in several areas: there are no processing costs because the books come ready for the shelf, and the leasing fee is considerably lower than the item's purchase price. Patrons will also be happier about shorter waiting times for the high-interest books. All in all, anyone involved in meeting recreational reading interests will find the program worth looking into. Educational libraries may use it to stock a variety of materials for recreational reading without taking too much money out of the book fund.

What Does a Jobber Expect from the Librarian?

The preceding pages describe what can be expected from the jobber. But a librarian also has certain obligations in maintaining a good working relationship with the jobber. Simply stated, a jobber's profit is based on the difference between the cost of the merchandise and the sales price. Any different from any other business? Basically no. However, there is a major difference in that any buyer can buy directly from the materials producer, which is seldom true in other fields. A further difference is that all buyers can determine for themselves what the maximum price should be by checking "in-print lists," such as *Books in Print*, or with the publisher. With every buyer knowing what the maximum price is, including any discount from the publisher, the jobber must at least match that price and provide superior service in order to hold customers.

Volume buying and selling is the only way that a jobber can hope to make a profit. Efficient plant operations and low overhead can help, but no matter how efficient the operation, it may fail without a high volume. One order for 15 or 20 titles in quantities will result in a very high discount for the jobber, perhaps as high as 60 percent. Even after giving a 20 to 25 percent discount to the library, the jobber is left with a comfortable margin with which to work. Unfortunately, that type of order is usually the exception rather than the rule. More often the jobber's discount is 50 percent. A smaller margin is still acceptable if all the items sell. But all of them do not! Yes, there is something called "returns" (where a publisher buys back unsold books). Returns normally result in credits against the current account or future purchases. Seldom do they result in a cash return for book jobbers.

Because jobbers are dependent upon volume sales, they must know their markets fairly well to project sales and to order for stock accordingly. Thus, when the jobber representative stops by, it is not mere public relations or, necessarily, an attempt to sell more books, but an attempt at determining the customer's plans for collection development. The collection development librarian should take time to talk to the person and explain new programs and new areas to be worked on. It is important to ask about what is available in the field, even if one thinks one knows; the answers may be surprising. One should ask what the firm could do to supply the items: is it a field they carry as part of their normal inventory, or would items have to be specially ordered? Such discussions take time, but will result in better service. Some librarians dump their problem orders on the jobber and then order the easy items directly from the publisher in order to get the maximum discount. Nothing could be more short-sighted. Without the income from the easy, high-volume items, no jobber can stay in business. Someone is needed to work on the problem order, and most jobbers will try to run down the difficult items; but they should be given the easy orders as well. Almost all of the problems facing the jobber involve cash flow. Lack of cash has been the downfall of many businesses, and it becomes critical for jobbers if they handle only problem orders; staff expenses go up, but income does not. Financial failure of jobbers would mean higher labor costs for most acquisitions departments as a result of having to place all orders directly with the publishers.

Whenever possible, the library should use the order format that is best for the jobber, and not plead legal or system requirements for a particular method of ordering unless it absolutely cannot be changed. Most jobbers, and publishers, go out of their way to accommodate the legal requirements of library ordering procedures. If libraries could come closer to a standardized order procedure, jobbers could provide better service, since they would not have to keep track of hundreds of variations. If *all* paperwork is kept to a minimum, everyone will benefit. While most jobbers will accept a few returns from libraries, even if the library is at fault, returns create a lot of paperwork. If an item truly serves no purpose in a library's collection, perhaps it would save time and money to accept the mistake and discard it rather than return it, assuming mistakes are infrequent. (This refers to items sent in error, not defective ones. Any defective copy should be returned.)

Finally, invoices should be paid promptly, not held any longer than necessary. Most library systems require at least two approvals before payment will be made: first, the library's, then, the business officer's. Some have three or more offices involved. The collection development officer should know the system, from approval to final payment. If it takes longer than six weeks, a new jobber should be given that information. And jobbers should be told when a change occurs in the system. Most jobbers would like to be paid within 30 days since they are on a 30-day payment cycle with publishers.

Jobbers provide a valuable service to libraries. Given a good working relationship, both parties benefit. Following is a summary of the basic factors at work in establishing such a relationship.

What libraries expect from jobbers:

- Large inventory of titles

- Prompt and accurate order fulfillment

- Prompt and accurate reporting on items not in stock

- Personal service at a reasonable price

What jobbers expect of libraries:

- Time to get to know what the library needs

- Cooperation in placing orders

- Keeping paperwork to a minimum

- Prompt payment for services

There are a number of jobbers offering their services to American libraries. Some of the larger and/or more active firms in marketing their programs are Bro-Dart, Baker and Taylor, Ingram, Gordons, Ballen, Coutts, and Blackwell North America. Most of these firms offer a variety of services, including some automated order placement and fulfillment services. Several offer information about average price increases which can be helpful in budget preparation. To find jobbers outside the United States there are *Books in Other Languages*, published by the Canadian Library Association, and R. R. Bowker's *International Literary Market Place*.[1]

Retail Outlets

How Do New Bookstores Operate?

New bookstores — stores selling new books, not stores that just opened — are interesting places to visit, whether or not one is responsible for collection development. Many librarians started haunting bookshops long before they became librarians. If there is a bibliographic equivalent to alcoholism, many librarians have it. "Bibliomania" is defined as "excessive fondness for acquiring and possessing books."[2] Most bibliomaniacs (librarians included) cannot stay out of bookshops and consider it a great feat of willpower and self-control if they manage to leave one without buying a book or two.

Bookstore owners would be happy if a high percentage of the general population suffered from bibliomania. In the United States, they do not. In fact, Americans seem to have been inoculated with a most effective vaccine. On a percentage basis, book buyers are a minority group in most countries, although their actual numbers might be large. Because of this, bookstores generally have to exist in somewhat special environments and operate in a certain way. While most people have undoubtedly visited many bookshops innumerable times, one should make a special visit to at least two stores in order to answer some specific questions. What are the conditions (environmental and operating) necessary for a good bookstore? How are materials displayed and marketed? What is for sale in the shop? How wide a range of materials is available? And, could this shop be of any real value in collection development?

One consideration for any bookstore owner is location. Many owners live and work in the community for a long time before they open their stores. Just as the person responsible for successful collection development in a library needs to know the community, so does the bookstore owner. He or she also needs to be known and respected in the community. The dream of finding a quaint little town somewhere to retire to and then open up a small bookshop is one that many librarians harbor. Most use it as a nice daydream for the bad day in the library. Of those who go further and try to implement the idea, very few succeed. Those who do are located in communities they know and are known in as a result of frequent visits and extended stays. A successful bookshop is a busy, people-oriented organization. It is not a quiet retreat for persons who do not like working with people, anymore than is a library. Furthermore, it requires physical work on the part of the owner, and a fairly large population base to support the required volume of sales.

The population base is a key consideration in determining where to locate a bookstore. The American Booksellers Association suggests that a minimum population for a "books-only" store is 25,000 persons. Thus, large cities are the most likely locations for books-only shops. The smaller the community, the less likely it is that a books-only store will survive. Cultural activities in a large city help stimulate interest in reading. In major cities, it is even possible to find a variety of specialized bookstores (foreign language and subject matter). Smaller communities adjoining a good-sized academic institution provide the primary exception to what has been said above about size.

The educational level of the population is another factor in store location. As the average level of education in a community rises, so do the chances of a bookstore's succeeding with a smaller population base. College graduates represent the largest segment of bookbuyers. Where a high concentration of college-educated persons lives near a large shopping center, one is likely to find a bookstore.

Shopping centers are considered one of the most desirable locations for a bookstore—if there is a lot of foot traffic. A store tucked away in a remote corner of the busiest center is not likely to do well. If bookstore owners had to survive solely on the basis of individuals seeking a particular book, there would be even fewer stores than now exist. A store catering to the tastes of middle- and upper-income persons also increases its chance of success, because a high percentage of book sales results from impulse buying, which requires a location where the bookseller can stimulate the impulse in persons who can afford to indulge themselves. It frequently happens that one goes into a bookstore looking for just one book or "something to read" and walks out with three or four paperbacks. Bookstore owners depend on such impulse buying.

There are striking similarities between successfully operating a bookstore and a library. Both require a solid knowledge of the community; if libraries could select sites as do bookstores, library circulation would skyrocket. A public library branch in the center of Stockholm provides an instance of an almost ideal bookstore location: on a shopping mall, in the center of the main business district, with a high volume of foot traffic, and near a concourse to a main subway station. This particular branch is the most active of all the service points in a system where high use is the norm.

Store owners attempt to stimulate buyers through a variety of sales methods. Some lures are employed in store windows and entryways, providing clues about the basic stock before a customer enters. Only very large shops can afford ads on a weekly basis in newspapers, and radio and television advertising costs are prohibitively high for most owners. For most, an occasional newspaper ad and a good storefront display are the best they can do in promoting business.

One can make a fair assessment of a shop through its windows without walking in the door—an assessment of the type of material within, not necessarily of the level of service. Observing is not the same as casually looking. One can look closely, but without some guidelines he or she may not know what to look for or how to interpret what is seen. The following broad generalizations can serve as the most basic of guidelines, providing a foundation upon which to build as one gains experience.

An owner has two basic methods available for promoting a store through its windows: one is to focus on a particular topic or on a few bestsellers; the other is a "shotgun" approach—a wide variety of titles appealing to a wide range of interests. Using a little imagination, some nonbook props, and a good supply of books, very interesting window displays can be created. The inactive reader may be stimulated to come in and buy the promoted title but will seldom pause to examine other titles in the store. Generally, the display will lead to a good sale of the promoted title or subject, but most buyers, especially those interested only in a certain topic, will not return to the store until another equally striking window on that topic is created.

"Shotgun" window displays are less likely to attract the nonactive reader. They will stop a reader, if they are well done. A jumble of books in the window will not do the job, but a wealth of titles using some basic graphic techniques will. This type of window is known to attract the steady book-buying customer. Such individuals are as likely to buy four or five titles as one, and all of them may be impulse purchases—impulse in the sense that the buyers did not come into the store looking for the specific titles purchased.

If a store has consistently striking windows featuring the latest top sellers, this very likely reflects the orientation of the total book stock. Almost everything in such a store will have a proven track record. Backlist titles that have had steady sales (dictionaries, cookbooks, home reference items, and "classics") will comprise the majority of items in stock, plus stacks of "in" titles and tables piled high with discount and "gift" books. Though shops of this type may be willing to order single titles, there will be little advantage for the library. Almost the only reason for a library to patronize such a store is for the discount (remainder) books they offer.

There is a remote chance that the independent store owner (nonchain) would begin to special order items for the library. In smaller communities this may be the only type of store available. If the library were to buy $10,000 worth of books each year from the store, this would probably be an adequate incentive for the owner to shift emphasis. (For a great many small libraries $10,000 would be 10 years' worth of purchases.) It will still be possible for the store's regular patrons to find their favorite types of books there, and perhaps it will draw in some new steady customers as a result of the change.

If a store's windows do not provide enough clues, looking in the door can provide another quick visual check. Tables of books with signs such as *Top Twenty!*, *55% to 75% Off!*, or *Giant discounts!* are almost certain to announce a store of limited value to a library, especially if most of the window displays have favored the latest and best sellers. A store with a good, wide range of stock cannot afford to devote much floor area to such sales methods. All stores will have sales from time to time—books that have not sold and may be past their return date, some remainders—and of course there is always the preinventory sale. However, the store that is always having a "sale" is never really having a sale and seldom is of value to libraries.

Another quick visual check should be for sideline items in the store. A new bookstore selling only new books needs a minimum community population of 25,000, but almost all bookstores now sell at least a few sidelines: greeting cards, stationery/office supplies, posters, art supplies, magazines and newspapers, calendars, games, and so forth. Why the sideline? It is difficult to make a good living just selling books because there are few buyers and the margin of profit on books is much smaller than that on sideline items.

For purposes of comparison, let us briefly consider the possible profits on books, a complex subject given the different discount arrangements available to booksellers. Publishers offer the same general discounts (trade, long, short, new, mass market) to bookstores as they give to jobbers. Long discounts (40 percent or more) are given on most trade books, except paperbacks. In the case of very large orders (multiple copies), discounts of 50 percent are possible, and very occasionally, 60 percent. Normally the discount is 40 percent and even then there is often a required minimum number of copies (five or more) to receive this amount. A few publishers offer 33 to 40 percent off on an order of 10 different single titles—the Single Copy Order Plan (SCOP). Librarians ordering a sizable number of single copies from one publisher may find bookstores very willing to place such orders. However, it is important to remember that such an agreement requires the bookseller to *prepay* and to do all the paperwork. Thus, if the library is slow issuing payments, only large bookstores can afford to carry its accounts.

Some stores will order short discount (20 to 25 percent) items but add on a service charge. If enough short discount items are needed from a single publisher, most stores will handle the order without a service charge. On a $20.00 book with a 25 percent discount, the bookstore has only a $5.00 margin to work with. By the time the clerical and record keeping costs are taken out, the owner is very lucky if the transaction has not cost the store more money than was taken in.

Of the two general classes of paperbacks — quality and mass market — quality paperbacks generally sell for more than $5.00 and are only found in bookstores. (The term does not necessarily apply to the content of the book.) Mass market books are those in drugstores, grocery stores, airports, and so forth, that usually sell for around $3.00 to $4.00. Most publishers give a long discount on quality paperbacks when they are ordered in groups of five to ten or more. A store must order 25 to 50 assorted titles of the mass market type to begin to approach a 40 percent discount. Orders for less than that amount will get discounts of 25 to 35 percent.

The book distribution system in the United States is very cumbersome and adds unnecessarily to the cost of books. A simplified system would benefit everyone. Perhaps the best illustration of the complexity of the system is in the area of discounts, returns, billings, etc. Each year the American Booksellers Association (ABA) publishes a 500-page guide entitled *ABA Book Buyer's Handbook*. Pity the poor bookseller, confronted with all of the other problems of a bookstore, who also must work through a mass of legal forms and sales conditions for purchasing from various publishers. It does create extra work for the bookseller and publisher, and they undoubtedly pass their costs on to the final buyer.

Thus, when a sideline item offers a 70 to 80 percent discount, it is not surprising to find a mixed store; as much as 30 to 40 percent of the *total* store income is derived from nonbook sales. Indeed, such sales have become so important to the average bookstore that the ABA now issues a *Sideline Directory*. A store that devotes more than one-third of the available floor space to nonbook items probably will not be of much use to a library for developing collections, and such calculations should enter into the librarian's observations. In addition to quick visual checks, some acquaintance with its personnel will provide further information about a store, although more and more shops are forced to use a self-service arrangement as labor costs rise. Most self-service orientations emphasize paperbacks, sidelines, and very popular trade books. Obviously such stores offer little that will be of value to the library.

In general, the new bookstore can be a valuable means of acquiring new books. Carrying out visual inspection of the local shops and discussing the library's needs with their owners is an important link in the selection and acquisition program. Unfortunately, most libraries are not located in major metropolitan areas where there are a number of bookstores. Many are lucky if there is one bookstore in the community. Although the chances of a major portion of the library's book buying going to such small stores is slight, the possibility ought to be explored. (The reason this type of bookstore is not a likely source is that the store will probably have a very small stock, and then predominantly of the bestsellers, many sidelines, and very small staff, perhaps only the owner and one or two assistants.)

Out-of-Print, Antiquarian, and
Rare Book Dealers

Allowing for some overlap, there are two broad categories of secondhand bookdealers. (It should be noted, though, that most dealers of the following types do *not* like to be called "secondhand dealers.") One type is concerned primarily with o.p. books; that is, with buying and selling used books. These books often sell at prices that are the same as or slightly higher than when they were published. The other category of dealer is concerned with rare, antiquarian, and/or "special" books (fore-edged painted, miniature, or private press, for example). Prices for this type range from around $10 to several thousand dollars per item. (It is possible to distinguish between antiquarian and rare book dealers, but even dealers use the terms interchangeably. A "pure" antiquarian dealer would only deal in books 100 years old or more, whereas a rare book dealer could have a book only a few months old but unusual in some way other than its age — for example, one of the 100 copies printed and signed by a famous person.) Some overlap occurs between the two categories, but a dealer generally tries to specialize in one area or the other, and often further specializes in limited subject areas, for example, Western Americana, children's books, military history, medicine, or preseventeenth-century items.

If the variety of stores dealing in new books is wide, the range for out-of-print dealers is almost infinite: from an individual working out of a house or apartment with almost no stock and functioning as a book agent, to the conventional small shop, to the exclusive Beverly Hills rare bookshops visited by appointment only. The vast majority are somewhere near the lower middle of this spectrum — small shops in very low-rent areas. Because of this diversity, it is difficult to make many generalizations about this group. Sol Malkin paints a cheery picture of at least part of the out-of-print trade:

> Imagine a separate book world within the world of books where dealers set up their businesses where they please (store or office, home or barn); where the minimum markup is 100 percent; where they can call upon 5,000 fellow dealers throughout the world and a stock of over 200 million volumes, practically from the beginning of the printed word; where books are safely packed and mailed with no extra charge for postage; where there is no competition from the publishers and discount houses; where colleagues help one another in time of need to provide fellow dealers with a unique service that makes customers happy all the time — an ideal imaginary book world that never was nor ever will be? Perhaps ... but the above is 99 percent true in the antiquarian book trade.[3]

Libraries can function without using new bookstores, but they must use the o.p. and antiquarian dealer. Replacement copies will always be needed. Often they are no longer in-print and can only be found in o.p. stores. Retrospective buying is almost always confined to this category of shop, although it is possible to buy directly from private collectors.

Almost every library will have occasion to use the services of these dealers. However, there are variations in use. Collection development officers working with large research collections may spend a significant portion of their time engaged in retrospective collection development. Changes in organizational goals and programs may result in developing whole new areas of collecting, both current and retrospective materials. Public libraries also buy from o.p. dealers, especially for replacement copies and occasionally for retrospective collection building. School libraries make limited use of this distribution system; scientific and technical libraries rarely need to worry about acquiring retrospective materials.

Several directories to antiquarian or rare bookdealers provide information about specialties, and anyone concerned with selection and acquisition needs to get to know these directories (for example, *American Book Trade Directory*). Some major metropolitan areas have local directories or guides to special bookshops. In any case, a person will find it worthwhile to develop a card file on the local shops. The file can provide quick information about *real* specialties, search services, hours, and so forth. One can often go to a shop that advertises itself as a Western Americana store only to find the "specialty stock" very, very limited and/or overpriced; still, the shop can be studied and its true specialties and general pricing policy estimated. Maintaining this private directory can prove to be well worth the time required to keep it up-to-date. This is not to say that the published sources are worthless. However, owners change emphasis and their stock does turn over and is subject to local economic conditions that often change faster than published sources can be updated.

Many acquisition librarians and book dealers classify out-of-print book distribution services into three general types: (1) a complete book service, (2) a complete sales service, and (3) a complete bookshop. The first two may be operated in a manner that does not allow, or at least require, customers coming to the seller's location. All contact is by mail and telephone. The owner may maintain only a small stock of "choice items" in a garage or basement. In type 1, a dealer actively searches for items for a customer even if they are not in stock, by placing an ad in a publication such as *AB Bookman's Weekly*. Sales service (type 2) is just what the name implies: a dealer reads the "wanted" sections of book trade publications and sends off quotes on items in his or her stock. Such services seldom place ads or conduct searches for a customer. The last (type 3) is a store operation where "in person" trade is sought; stores of this type often engage in type 1 and type 2 activities as well. Given the unpredictable nature of the o.p. trade, it is an unusual store that can afford not to exploit every possible sales outlet.

AB Bookman's Weekly (or *AB*, as o.p. specialists refer to it) is a weekly publication devoted solely to advertising from dealers either offering or searching for particular titles. Publications of this type are an essential ingredient in the o.p. book trade, since they serve as a finding and selling tool. Without services like this the cost of acquiring an o.p. item would be much higher, even if a copy could be located without the service.

One characteristic of o.p. and rare bookshops is that they both require a high capital investment in a book stock that may not sell immediately. Most owners feel very lucky if total sales for a year equal 1½ times the total stock. Indeed, some items may never sell and most will remain on a shelf for several years before a buyer appears. Lacking the return rights of the new bookstore owner, then, a used or rare bookstore owner must be careful about purchases and have relatively inexpensive storage available.

Because of the factors of high investment and low turnover, most owners locate their businesses in a low-rent area. Rare and antiquarian shops can sometimes exist in high-rent areas, but in such locations the buyer will pay a premium price for the books. Shops in high-rent areas generally grew with the area and seldom resulted from an owner's decision to move into a high-rent area. I know of several attempts to start antiquarian shops in high-rent areas in Los Angeles that failed, despite locations that had a high volume of foot traffic, well-to-do customers with higher-than-average education, and a large university only a few blocks away.

One requisite for an out-of-print dealer is a reputation for honesty, service, and fair prices. To gain such a reputation requires a considerable period of time in this field. Unfortunately, most newcomers do not have adequate capital to carry them through this period if they locate in a high-rent area. As a result most o.p. shops are located in the less desirable areas in a community. This means that a person looking for such shops must make a special trip to visit them. Out-of-the-way, low-rent quarters for such a store also mean that there will be very little walk-in trade (someone just passing by). This in turn means most customers come looking for specific items and are less likely to be diverted to something else. Sideline items are seldom found in these shops, although a few may have some used phonograph records, old photographs, or posters. Owners can only hope that they have the right items to spark some impulse book buying in the true bibliophile.

One element in the o.p. trade seems very mysterious to the outsider and even to librarians who have had years of experience with these dealers. How *do* they determine the price they ask? As Sol Malkin indicated in the earlier quotation, there is at least a 100 percent markup, but how much more? One may find a book in an o.p. store with no price on it, take it to the salesperson (often the owner), ask the price, and receive, after a quick look, the answer, "Oh, yes. That is X amount." Sometimes the amount is lower than expected, other times much higher, but most of the time it is what was expected. Some salespersons seem to be mind readers, to know exactly how much a customer is willing to pay. Another quotation from the Sol Malkin article sums up the outsider's feeling about pricing in the o.p. trade: "Many new book dealers think of the antiquarian bookseller as a second-hand junkman or as a weird character who obtains books by sorcery, prices them by cabalistic necromancy, and sells them by black magic."[4]

It may appear that magic is the most essential ingredient in successful o.p. operations. Actually, it is not very mysterious after three central issues concerning this trade are understood: the source of supply, the major sales methods, and the way prices are set. Once these are known, most of the mystery disappears, but for those who enjoy the o.p. trade, the magic remains. With an excellent memory, a love for books, the ability and time to learn books, enough capital to buy a basic stock of books, and finally, the patience to wait for a return on the capital, anyone can become an o.p. bookseller. Sources and sales methods will be discussed before we turn to the necromancy referred to by Malkin, only to find it nonexistent as such.

The question of pricing is determined to a large degree by the answers to the questions of supply and sales. The o.p. dealer has several sources of supply but only two consistently produce new stock. One major source is to buy personal or business collections. Placing an ad in the telephone directory ("I buy old books") will generate a number of inquiries. Two of the most frequent reasons for a private collection's coming into the market are household moves and the settling of estates. Except for outstanding private collections of a well-known collector, most dealers will not enter into a bidding contest. They may come to look at a collection, but only after determining by telephone that it is very large and has some potential value. After an examination they make a flat offer with a take-it-or-leave-it attitude. A person who has no experience with the o.p. trade will usually be very surprised and disappointed at how low the offer will be. After one or two such offers a prospective seller might conclude that there is a conspiracy of o.p. dealers to cheat owners out of rare items.

Nothing could be further from the truth. Experienced o.p. dealers know how long most of the items they have bid on will occupy storage space in their shops. They also know how few of the seller's "treasures" are more than personal treasures. Grandfather's complete collection of *National Geographic* from 1921 to 1943 may be a family heirloom but to most o.p. dealers it is so much fodder – for the $0.25/each table.

Time is the central theme in the o.p. trade. In time every edition of a book will become o.p.; in time the vast majority of the world's printed materials should be returned to pulp paper mills for recycling; in time the few valuable books will find a buyer. But when is that time? Knowing the time factor as well as they do, o.p. dealers must buy for as little as they can or they will go out of business. Knowledgeable dealers know the local and the national market; therefore, it is not surprising that several bids on the same collection are almost identical. They read the same trade magazines, they see the same catalogs, and to some extent they see the same local buyers. If they are to stay in business they must know the market.

Walk-in sales are generally only a small segment of o.p. sales income. Mail-order sales are the major source: buying and selling items through publications such as *AB* and catalogs. Most dealers prepare catalogs of selected items in stock and mail them to dealers, libraries, and book collectors. Often the catalog will list only one type of material (for example, Western Americana, European history, first editions, or autographed books); at other times it will list a variety of titles that the dealer hopes will appeal to many different buyers.

Just as the contents of catalogs vary, so do the quality of the item descriptions and the care taken in preparing the catalog. Some catalogs are faded or smeared mimeographed or dittoed sheets that are almost impossible to read; when an entry is legible it only gives the author, title, date, and price. At the other end of the spectrum are catalogs that are so well done and contain so much bibliographic information that research libraries add the catalog to their bibliography collection. A catalog of high quality is encountered less and less frequently now, and the trend is likely to continue because of rising costs. In order to recover the cost, it is necessary to sell the catalog to buyers who are not regular customers, which also usually means that the prices for all of the items in the catalogs will be rather high ($100 and up).

When a librarian sees a catalog that contains something the library needs and can purchase, he or she should *run*, not walk, to the nearest telephone and call in the order. It will probably be too late, but the telephone is almost the only chance of getting the item. A mailed order is almost certain to arrive too late. Out-of-print folklore says that if one librarian wants an item so do 30 other persons. This means a certain amount of competition among buyers.

Dealer catalogs and magazines such as *AB* provide both a sales mechanism and a major means of establishing prices. If an o.p. dealer in London offers an autographed copy of the first edition of Richard Adams's *Watership Down* for £10, other dealers will use this information as a guideline in setting prices for copies of the book that they have in stock. An unautographed copy of the first edition would be offered for something less than £10, assuming that both copies were in approximately the same physical condition. Other editions, including foreign first editions, would also sell for less. The foreign first editions might come close to the English first edition in price, but the *first* first usually commands the highest price.

Prices, then, are based upon a number of interrelated factors: (1) how much it costs to acquire the item; (2) the amount of current interest in collecting a particular subject or author; (3) the number of copies printed and the number of copies still in existence; (4) the physical condition of the copy; (5) any special features of the particular copy (autographed by the author and/or signed or owned by a famous person, for example); and (6) what other dealers are asking for copies of the same edition and same condition. Without question, the current asking price is the major determining factor — given equal conditions in the other five areas — thus making sales catalogs and *AB* major pricing tools.

A few further facts about the condition of o.p. books are important for beginning librarians to know because these bear directly on price. Most o.p. books are sold on the basis "as described" or "as is." If there is no statement about the item's condition it is assumed to be "good" or better. A common statement in catalogs is "terms — all books in original binding and in good or better condition unless otherwise stated." An example of such a condition statement can be seen in figure 11.1. The examples of o.p. dealer catalog entries (figures 11.1, 11.2, 11.3, and 11.4) should be studied carefully.

No. 275 Autumn 1986

American & European History
Art, Science, Philosophy, Etc.

Unless otherwise noted, books are 12mo or 8vo, bound, and in good second-hand condition. Prices are net; carriage extra. **Send no money; you will be billed.** Pennsylvania residents are liable to the 6% sales tax. All bills are payable **only** in U.S. dollars, drawn on a U.S. bank, or by postal money order.

William H. Allen, Bookseller

2031 Walnut Street **Philadelphia, Pa. 19103**
(Area Code 215) 563-3398

A. Anderton, James. **The Protestants Apologie for the Roman Church, by John Brereley, Priest.** St. Omar 1608. 4to. New half morocco. Small piece out of corner of title-page. $150.00
The author, a Roman Catholic controversalist and probably a priest, quotes passages from the works of Protestants which admit the claims of the Roman church.

B. Bacon, Sir Francis. **The Elements of the Common Lawes of England, branched into a double tract.** 1639. Old calf, one cover detached. Small piece torn from one margin. Name cut from title. $200.00
The third issue of this work, containing Bacon's proposed restatement of English law.

C. Bible. Whole. **The Self-interpreting Bible: containing the sacred text of the Old and New Testaments.** With marginal references by John Brown. New York 1792. Folio. 20 engr. pl. by Doolittle, A. Godwin, & others. Old leather, front cover detached, 2 leaves, the margins of which are quite frayed, supplied. Some tears into text. $300.00
The second illustrated Bible printed in America.

D. ——. **Biblia, das ist: die ganze goettliche Heilige Schrift alten und neuen Testaments.** Reading, Pa. 1805. 4to. Old calf, quite worn, stitching on spine torn, leather partly covered with scotch tape. Contents very good. $65.00
The fourth edition of the Bible in German printed in America.

E. Bilson, Thomas, Bp. **The True Difference betweene Christian Subjection and Unchristian Rebellion: wherein the princes lawful power to command for truth, and indeprivable right to beare the sword, are defended against the popes censures and the Jesuits sophismes.** 1586. Royal coat-of-arms on verso of title. Lacks first blank. Stamped leather of the 19th century. One joint starting. $200.00
A defense of the English Reformation and an assertion that the English Church is the true Catholic Chjurch.

F. Bungus, Petrus. **Numerorum mysteria ex abditis plurimarum disciplinarum fontibus hausta.** Paris 1618. 4to. Vellum, one joint cracked, edges mouse-eaten. Worm-holes in corner of about 150pp. Title-page mounted. $125.00
The author, a Catholic theologian, devoted much of the work to the mystical number 666 which he equated with Luther, thus proving that he was the Antichrist. Other sections are devoted to other numbers in which he found mystical powers.

Fig. 11.1. William H. Allen, Bookseller. Reproduced by courtesy of William H. Allen.

30

6431 (Cont.) with a full description of the Sudd, and of the measures which have been taken to clear the navigation of the river.'

6432 GIDEIRI, Y.B.A. A Guide to the Perciform Fishes in the Coastal Waters of Suakin. K.U.P., 1968. Oblong 8vo., pp. 52, illus., a v.g. copy.   £8.50

6433 GLADSTONE, P. Travels of Alexine. Alexine Tinne 1835-1869. John Murray, 1970. Bds., pp. xii, 247, illus., 2 maps, v.g. in rubbed d.w.   £12.50

6434 GREENER, L. High Dam over Nubia. Cassell, 1962. Illus., maps, v.g. in d.w.   £5

6435 GWYNN, C.W. Imperial Policing. Macmillan, 1934. pp. ix, 366, 13 maps; a working copy only with front hinge weak and bds. spotted and creased; internally good.   £8.50

6436 HAKE, A.E. The Story of Chinese Gordon. Remington, 1884 rep. (1884). Port. frp., plate, 2 folding maps, orig. dec. cloth gilt; 2 vols., and a very good set.   £65

6437 Ditto, another set, both vols. first edn.; cloth rubbed and faded, o/w good.   £45

6438 HAKE, A.E. The Story of Chinese Gordon. With additions, bringing the narrative to the present time. Worthington, N.Y., 1884. Orig. pict. cloth gilt, t.e.g., frp., illus., pp. 358, a v.g. copy.   £25

6439 HALLAM, W.K.R. The Life and Times of Rabih Fadl Allah. Stockwell Ltd., Ilfracombe, 1977. Bds., pp. 367, 3 mpas, illus., a v.g. copy in d.w.   £15

6440 HARTMANN, Dr. R. Reise des Freiherrn Adalbert von Barnim durch Nord-Ost-Afrika in den Jahren 1859 und 1860. Georg Reimer, Berlin, 1863. Lge. 4to., orig. cloth, pp. xvi, 651, XI, + appendix of 111 pp.; tinted lithographic frp., 28 woodcut illus. in the text, (some full-page), 2 other plates, sketch map, 2 folding maps; some foxing to text and fore-edge, faint waterstain to bottom margin, (but not affecting the text), and a v.g. clean copy. With the accompanying Atlas : Reise in Nordost Africa, 1859-1860. Skizzen nach der Natur gemalt von Adalbert Freiherrn von Barnim und Dr. Robert Hartmann. Oblong folio, (48 x 32 cms.), orig. cloth, cold. lithographic title-page, double page panorama, 23 other lithographic plates, (of which nine are cold.), by W. Loeillet after sketches by the author and von Barnim, an exceptionally fine copy.   £2500
        Hartmann, a naturalist who ended his career as Professor of Anatomy at Berlin University, accompanied the young Baron A. von Barnim on the latter's journey to the Sudan. Crossing the Bayuda Desert from Old Dongola to Khartoum, they continued up the Blue Nile valley via Sennar to Fazughli. After von Barnim died of fever at Roseires, Hartmann took the body to Europe for burial. The work he later produced about this ill-fated tour ranks with those of Tremaux and Lejean as one of the most beautifully produced travel books relating to the Sudan in the mid-Nineteenth Century. Far from being a simple description of the tour, it is a primary source for the period, a major and immensely detailed contribution to the study of Sudan's natural history and ethnography, particularly regarding the Upper Blue Nile, Dar Funj and Sudan-Ethiopian borderlands. The quality of the text is matched by that of the accompanying plates, illustrating the natural history, landscapes and peoples en route, and of which this copy is an exceptional example.

6441 HASSAN, Y.F. & DOORNBOS, P. The Central Bilad Al Sudan. Tradition and Adaptation. Essays on the Geography and Economic and Political History of the Sudanic belt. K.U.P., Sudan Library Series No. 11, 1977. Sm. 4to., wraps, pp. v, 316, maps, tables etc., a v.g. copy.
                                                                                                       £15

6442 HENDERSON, K.D.D. Sudan Republic. Benn, 1965. Cloth, pp. 233, 2 maps, (1 folding), a v.g. copy.   £22.50
        In the series 'Nations of the Modern World' ; provides a good general survey of the later Condominium period and early years of the independent Sudan.

Fig. 11.2. Oriental and African Books catalog sample. Reproduced by courtesy of Oriental and African Books.

ANTHROPOLOGY & TRAVEL

THEORETICAL & COMPARATIVE
AFRICA
MIDDLE EAST
ASIA
AUSTRALASIA & PACIFIC
AMERICAS & CARIBBEAN
POLAR REGIONS
EUROPE
ADDENDA

THEORETICAL & COMPARATIVE

1   BANTON (Michael) - Race Relations. Tavistock Pubs., 1967. Pp. xiv+434,
    brown clothgilt, d-j. (snagged). VG. (Analyses of the history and oper-
    ation of different patterns of racial tension.)   £10

2   BETTANY (G.T.) - Red, Brown & Black Men & Their White Supplanters / The
    Inhabitants of America & Oceania. Ward Lock, n.d. (c.1890.) Pp. xi+221,
    numerous ills., grey pictorial clothgilt. Lacks 1 page, o/w VG. Manners,
    customs, racial characteristics and drawings of many tribes.   £10

3   BINDER (Pearl) - Magic Symbols of the World. Hamlyn, 1972. Pp. 127, ills.
    (some coloured), cloth, silvergilt. VG in worn d-j. (Study by artist
    Fellow of the R.A.I. discussing fertility symbols, magical protection
    of body and dwelling, family and livelihood, death and afterlife.) £4.50

4   BOISSEVAIN (Jeremy) - Friends of Friends: Networks, Manipulators and
    Coalitions. Oxford, Blackwell, 1974. Pp. xv+285. Tan clothgilt. Fine,
    in d-j.   £9.50

5   CHAPPLE (Eliot Dismore) & Carlton Stevens Coon - Principles of Anthropology
    New York, Holt, 1947, reprint. Pp. xii+718, blue cloth, VG. (Includes
    operational method, development of personality, symbolism.)   £14

6   COON (Carleton S.) - The Hunting Peoples. Book Club Associates, 1974, rpt.
    Pp. 413, maps, ills., brown clothgilt. VG in chipped d-j.   £9

7   COTLOW (Lewis) - In Search of the Primitive. Robert Hale, 1967 (first Eng-
    lish edn). Pp. 454, col. & b/w plates. Green clothgilt. Bumped at base
    of spine. Good, in chipped d-j. (Ituri Forest pygmies, Watusi, Masai,
    Babira, Jivaro, Matto Grosso Bororo, Yaguas, Eskimo.)   £8

8   DOUGLAS (Mary) - Evans-Pritchard: His Life, Work, Writings & Ideas. Har-
    vester Press/Fontana, 1980. Blue clothgilt, d-j. Mint.   £6

9   DOUGLAS (Mary) - Purity & Danger / An Analysis of the Concepts of Pollution
    & Taboo. Routledge & Kegan Paul, Ark Paperback, 1984. (First pub. 1966.)
    Pp. 188. Paperback, fine.   £2.75

10 DOUGLAS (Mary) - Natural Symbols / Explorations in Cosmology. Barrie &
    Jenkins, 1978, 2nd edn, rpt. Pp. 218. Black clothgilt, d-j. VG.   £7.50

11 EPSTEIN (A.L.) Ed. - The Craft of Social Anthropology. Intro. Max Gluckman.
    Tavistock Pubs., 1969, rpt. Pp. xx+276. Contributors include Mitchell,
    Barnes, Turner, Marwick. Paperback; signature, some scuffmarks and
    scratched erasing on back cover - o/w clean and fresh.   £6

12 EVANS-PRITCHARD (E.E.) - Social Anthropology. Cohen & West, 1960, rpt.
    Pp. vii+134, blue cloth, d-j. (embrowned). Good.   £6.50

Fig. 11.3. Janice Bowen catalog sample. Reproduced by courtesy of Janice
Bowen.

- Dec. 6, 1879. Volume I, nos. 1-18 complete. Elephant folio, bound in original cloth, pictorial gilt on front cover. Illus. An interesting collection including military reminiscences of various wars, especially the Civil War, each issue 16 pages in length. Very scarce. (V27-20774) 125.00

MCKENNEY AND JACKSON ON INDIANS

847. [NEW YORK] McKenney, Thomas L. *DOCUMENTS AND PROCEEDINGS RELATING TO THE FORMATION AND PRO-GRESS OF A BOARD IN THE CITY OF NEW YORK FOR THE EMIGRATION, PRESERVATION, AND IMPROVEMENT OF THE ABORIGINES OF AMERICA.* N.Y.: Vanderpool & Cole, 1829. 48pp. Sewn. First printing. S. & S. 39083. Includes a lengthy address by McKenney, an address from Pres. Andrew Jackson to the Creek Indians, an address from John H. Eaton to John Ross and the Cherokees, the Constitution of the Indian Board for the Emigration, Preservation, and Improvement of the Aborigines of America, and a report by Eaton on the Indians in Georgia. Exceedingly rare, with very fine content. (V27-20797) 125.00

848. [NEW YORK] Murphy, William D. *BIOGRAPHICAL SKETCHES OF THE STATE OFFICERS AND MEMBERS OF THE LEGISLATURE OF THE STATE OF NEW YORK.* N.Y., 1861. 298pp. Original cloth. First edition. A nice copy of the principal reference work on the state legislature of the Civil War's first year. (V27-20731) 35.00

849. [NEW YORK] *THE NEW YORK DEMOCRACY AND VALLANDIGHAM: THEY ENDORSE THE TRAITOR AND WINK AT THE TREASON.* N.p., 1861. 4pp. First printing. "By the time of his return to Ohio he was suspected of treasonable intent and had become one of the most unpopular and most bitterly abused men in the North....Whatever his policy at any time, he advocated it with the ardor and sincerity of a fanatic. In 1871 he was retained as counsel for the defendant in a murder case and while demonstrating the way in which the victim had been shot he mortally wounded himself." (V27-20638) 20.00

850. [NEW YORK] [WEST POINT] *WEST POINT LIFE: AN ANONYMOUS COMMUNICATION, READ BEFORE A PUBLIC MEETING OF THE DIALECTIC SOCIEY, U.S. MILITARY ACADEMY, MARCH 5, 1859.* N.p., 1859. 16pp. Original printed wrappers. In verse form, this fascinating pamphlet details the intense social life at West Point on the eve of the Civil War with amusing accounts of balls and dances and courtships, as well as learning soldiering. George A. Custer and many other future generals were at the Point at this time. (V27-20811) 65.00

851. [NEW YORK] Wilkins, William, et al. *ADDRESS OF THE FRIENDS OF DOMESTIC INDUSTRY, ASSEMBLED IN CONVENTION, AT NEW YORK, OCTOBER 26, 1831, TO THE PEOPLE OF THE UNITED STATES.* Baltimore, 1831. 44pp. Much on developing American industry and on cotton mills. With a complete list of the delegates. S.& S. 5637. (V27-15106) 25.00

852. Nicollet, Joseph Nicolas. *REPORT INTENDED TO ILLUSTRATE A MAP OF THE HYDROGRAPHICAL BASIN OF THE UPPER MISSISSIPPI RIVER.* Wash.: SD237, 1843. 237pp. Calf and boards. First edition. Huge folding map in facsimile by J. C. Fremont. Holliday 820: "Scarce and most interesting." Howes N152. Buck 339: "The report contains also a sketch of the early history of St. Louis." Graff 3022. Wagner-Camp 98: "Nicollet gives many details regarding his expedition to the upper Missouri in 1839 with Fremont." Overlooked by Clark. (VW1-5101) 100.00

853. Noble, Samuel H. *LIFE AND ADVENTURES OF BUCKSKIN SAM, WRITTEN BY HIMSELF.* Rumford Falls, Maine, 1900. 185pp. Original cloth. Fine copy. Frontis. Recollections of his travels throughout the world. His hunting trips, being captured by Indians in South America, and his experiences with Custer during the Civil War. (VW5-12817) 100.00

854. [NORTH CAROLINA] *AN ACT TO INCORPORATE THE NORTH CAROLINA TRANSPORTATION COMPANY.* [Raleigh], 1866. Broadside, 1p., octavo. Creating a steamboat company for the Chesapeake Canal. (VW14-6601) 15.00

855. [NORTH CAROLINA] Alderman, Ernest H. *THE NORTH CAROLINA COLONIAL BAR [AND] THE GREENVILLE DISTRICT, BY E. MERTON COULTER.* Chapel Hill: Univ. of N.C., [1913]. 56pp. 1st ed. Orig.ptd.wrp. Articles in the Sprunt Historical Series (Vol.13 #1). (VW14-15868) 35.00

856. [NORTH CAROLINA] Arthur, John P. *WESTERN NORTH CAROLINA: A HISTORY (FROM 1730 TO 1913).* Raleigh, 1914. 709pp.+errata. First edition. Illus. An early scholarly survey. CWB II, 210: "Sheds light on civil and military affairs [during the Civil War]." Thornton 317. Howes A342. (VW14-9597) 100.00

857. [NORTH CAROLINA] *A BILL CONCERNING THE FAYETTEVILLE & CENTRE PLANK ROAD COMPANY.* Raleigh, 1854. 4pp. (VW14-2-6595) 15.00

858. [NORTH CAROLINA] *A BILL TO IMPROVE THE PUBLIC ROADS IN NORTH CAROLINA.* Raleigh, 1850. [8]pp. (VW14-6596) 15.00

859. [NORTH CAROLINA] *A BILL TO INCORPORATE THE FAYETTEVILLE AND NORTHERN PLANK ROAD COMPANY.* Raleigh, 1850. [8]pp. (VW14-6594) 15.00

860. [NORTH CAROLINA] Boyd, William K. [ed.]. *SOME EIGHTEENTH CENTURY TRACTS CONCERNING NORTH CARO-LINA.* Raleigh, 1927. 508pp. Illus. Facs. Index. An excellent scholarly edition of 14 early North carolina-related printed sources, including politics, religion, economics, Indians, and law. Boyd provides and introduction and good notes for each work. Scarce. (VW14-9598) 65.00

61

Fig. 11.4. The Jenkins Company catalog sample. Reproduced by courtesy of The Jenkins Company.

All of the catalogs are examples of the basic catalogs that a librarian concerned with retrospective buying would check. The sample from the William H. Allen catalog represents more expensive materials but is still well within the limits which a beginner might select. All the catalogs give information about the condition of the items offered. What does the "t.e.g." indicate about item 6438 in the Oriental and African Books catalog, or what is the difference between "VG" (very good) (item 3) and "fine" (item 9) in the Janice Bowen catalog, or between "exceedingly rare" (item 847) and "scarce" (item 852) from The Jenkins Company?

"T.e.g." means top edges gilt. Some of the meanings will come only from knowing the particular dealer, but some guidance can be found in books such as John Carter's *ABC for Book Collectors* and *The Bookman's Glossary*.[5] (New editions of such works appear periodically but any edition will be suitable to start with.) Carter provides illuminating and entertaining notes about dealer adjectives describing the condition of a book:

> *General.* – As new, fine, good, fair, satisfactory (a trifle condescending, this) good second-hand condition (i.e., not very good), poor (often coupled with an assurance that the book is very rare in any condition), used, reading copy (fit for nothing more and below collector's standard), working copy (may even need sticking together).

> *Of exterior.* – Fresh, sound (probably lacks 'bloom'), neat (implies sobriety rather than charm); rubbed, scuffed, chafed, tender (of *joints*), shaken, loose, faded (purple cloth and green leather fade easily), tired (from the French *fatigué*), worn, defective (very widely interpreted), binding copy (i.e., needs it).

> *Of interior.* – Clean, crisp, unpressed, browned (like much later 16th century paper), age-stained, water-stained (usually in the depreciating form, 'a few light waterstains'), foxed (i.e., spotted or discolored in patches: often 'foxed as usual', implying that practically all copies are), soiled, thumbed (in the more lyrical catalogue notes, 'lovingly thumbed by an early scholar'), and (very rare in English or American catalogues, but commendably frank), washed.[6]

A careful review of the sample catalog pages herein will reveal many of these terms. The terms are subjective. What one dealer describes as fine another may call good. Buy on approval whenever possible, especially from a dealer that is being used for the first time.

Because dealer catalogs are so important and the manner in which they describe an item's condition is central to a buying decision, I worked with a student on an "experiment" in describing some out-of-print books. The student worked for an antiquarian bookdealer and helped prepare sales catalogs. Three items that were to appear in one of the dealer's catalogs were selected for the study. The bookdealer's description of each book for the upcoming catalog was one element in the study. Two other antiquarian dealers who worked in the same subject areas were then given the three items to describe as if they were going to list the books in one of their catalogs. In addition, the books were given to two librarians (both were in charge of a large rare book collection in major research libraries) who were also asked to describe the condition of each item. Five major "conditions" (water stains, mildew, tears, and so forth) were identified in each book by the student and me before the items were described by the dealers and librarians. Both librarians noted all of the "conditions" for each book and gave precise information. By combining all three dealers' descriptions all the conditions were noted for each item but no one dealer described all the conditions for all the items. It was also interesting, but not surprising, to see that the dealer descriptions tended to down play the faults. One would expect this since their goal is to sell the item. Professional associations (such as the American Library Association) and antiquarian dealer associations often attempt to work out guidelines to help reduce the tensions that often develop between libraries and dealers as a result of catalog descriptions. In the United States there is the *Code of Fair Practice for Dealers and Librarians*, which is worth reading and using as a standard when working with new dealers.

This section, like the one on new bookstores, can only outline briefly some of the more significant points about the retail book trade. It has provided some basic information upon which one can continue to build while buying and collecting books for oneself or a library.

Other Media Retail Outlets

Due to the variety of their formats and purposes it is not possible to generalize about retail outlets for other media. Many of the formats are acquired directly from their producers, as noted in chapter 9, or from an educational media jobber. Others are handled as a sideline or minor element in a store actually specializing in another service.

The most common retail outlets for "other media" are the record shop and video store. Many small communities that do not have a bookshop have a record shop and a video outlet. One reason for their popularity is that each record has a relatively low sales price (video cassettes are often rented) and a fairly large market exists for both formats. The top 20 recordings (records and tapes) of popular music may outsell the top 20 books by a 20-to-1 margin, at least in the United States.

Other than record shops, it is almost impossible to describe other media retail outlets, primarily because there are so few that it is hard to generalize. There are a few map shops in larger cities, most metropolitan areas have at least one sheet music store, and there are museums that sell slides and art reproductions. Educational models and games may be purchased from teacher supply stores. Microforms are generally purchased from their producers. In chapter 9 sources were discussed in more detail.

The distribution system for books and other library materials is varied and complex. One must know something about the system before beginning to develop a library collection. This chapter has provided *highlights* of what one needs to know. It is just the beginning of a long, enjoyable learning process. Jobbers, bookdealers, and media vendors are more than willing to explain how their work is affected by library activities when they know that a librarian has taken time to learn something about their operations.

Notes

[1]*Books in Other Languages* (Ottawa: Canadian Library Association, 1976); *International Literary Market Place* (New York: R. R. Bowker, 1966-).

[2]*Random House Dictionary of the English Language* (New York: Random House, 1967), 145.

[3]Sol Malkin, "Rare and Out-of-Print Books," in *A Manual on Bookselling* (New York: American Booksellers Association, 1974), 208.

[4]Ibid.

[5]John Carter, *ABC for Book Collectors*, 4th ed. (New York: Knopf, 1970); *The Bookman's Glossary*, 6th ed. (New York: R. R. Bowker, 1983).

[6]Carter, *ABC for Book Collectors*, 67-68.

Further Reading

General

Bonk, S. C. "Toward a Methodology of Evaluating Serials Vendors." *Library Acquisition: Practice and Theory* 9, no. 2 (1985): 51-60.

The Bookman's Glossary, 6th ed. Edited by Jean Peters. New York: R. R. Bowker, 1983.

Gilbert, D. L. *Complete Guide to Starting a Used Book Store*. Chicago: Chicago Review Press, 1986.

Grant, J. "Librarian and the Purchasing Function." *Library Acquisitions: Practice and Theory* 9, no. 4 (1985): 305-6.

Kim, U. C. "Purchasing Books from Publishers and Wholesalers." *Library Resources and Technical Services* 19 (Spring 1975): 133-47.

Kuntz, H. "Serials Agents: Selection and Evaluation." *Serials Librarian* 2 (Winter 1977): 139-50.

Martin, S. "Ordering after Selection." *The Bookseller* 4218 (24 October 1986): 1674-78.

Oulton, A. J. "Measuring Book Supply Efficiency." *The Bookseller* 4206 (2 August 1986): 493-95.

Stephens, A. "British National Bibliography — Aims and Uses." *The Bookseller* 4219 (31 October 1986): 1780-85.

Tyckoson, D. A. "On the Convention Circuit." *Technicalities* 4 (September 1984): 14-15.

Who Distributes What and Where, 3d ed. New York: R. R. Bowker, 1983.

Academic

Baumann, S. "An Extended Application of Davis' Model for a Vendor Study." *Library Acquisitions: Practice and Theory* 9, no. 4 (1985): 317-29.

Evans, G. E., and C. W. Argyres. "Approval Plans and Collection Development in Academic Libraries." *Library Resources and Technical Services* 18 (Winter 1974): 35-50.

Issues in Acquisitions: Programs and Evaluation. Edited by S. H. Lee. Ann Arbor, Mich.: Pierian Press, 1984.

Reidelbach, J. H., and G. M. Shirk. "Selecting an Approval Plan Vendor." *Library Acquisitions: Practice and Theory* 7, no. 2 (1983): 115-25.

_____. "Selecting an Approval Plan Vendor, Part 2." *Library Acquisitions: Practice and Theory* 8, no. 3 (1984): 157-202.

_____. "Selecting an Approval Plan Vendor, Part 3." *Library Acquisitions: Practice and Theory* 9, no. 3 (1985): 177-260.

Schmidt, K. A. "Capturing the Mainstream." *College & Research Libraries* 47 (July 1986): 365-69.

Public

Tuttle, M. "Magazine Fulfillment Centers." *Library Acquisitions: Practice and Theory* 9, no. 1 (1985): 41-49.

School

Eaglen, A. B. "Book Wholesalers: Pros and Cons." *School Library Journal* 25 (October 1978): 116-19.

Stafford, P. "One-Stop Shopping with Your Paperback Wholesaler." *School Library Journal* 32 (September 1985): 39-41.

Special

Rouse, W. B. "Optimal Selection of Acquisition Sources." *Journal of the American Society for Information Science* 25 (July 1974): 227-31.

Stave, D. G. "Art Books on Approval: Why Not?" *Library Acquisitions: Practice and Theory* 7, no. 1 (1983): 5-6.

12

Fiscal
Management

Controlling expenditures and securing adequate funding are part of the activities involved in collection management. Generally, monies spent on materials for the collection constitute the second largest expense category for libraries and information centers. Traditionally, in American libraries, salaries have represented the largest percentage of the total budget, followed by the materials ("book") budget, and finally, all other operating expenses. While the sequence remains the same today, the percentage for materials has become smaller. Although percentages vary, as well as circumstances, the basics remain the same, regardless of the type of information environment and the size of the collection. As is often the case, most of the literature on the topic of collection budgeting reflects a large research library orientation, but the same issues exist in other libraries. Most of the ideas and suggestions contained in such articles, however, can be applied in other settings.

Over the past 20 years or so there has been a more or less constant pressure on the materials budget in most libraries, which has resulted in a fairly steady decline in the percentage of the total budget spent on acquiring items for the collection. If one compares the total amount of money expended on materials in a library in 1966 with the current level of funding, the total amount available today would be considerably higher. Unfortunately, the total amounts available do not tell the entire story. When one looks at how much material is acquired for the money, one sees that the increase in the number of acquisitions is not proportional to the increase in the amount of funding. During the 1970s, many libraries, along with many other organizations, were confronted with budgets that some persons called "steady state," and others, "zero growth," and still others, "static." Generally, budgeting of this type was based on the previous year's inflation rate. An average inflation rate, like all averages, contains elements that increased at both above and below the average rate.

Problems in Fiscal Management

During that period collection development staffs were faced with several problems. Book and journal prices generally rose at a rate above the average inflation rate, as measured by the Consumer Price Index (CPI). If the national average was calculated at 10 percent and the materials budget was increased by 10 percent, the collection development staff could only hope to maintain the previous year's acquisition rate—the increase would not account for the current year's inflation. Unfortunately, publishers often increased prices at a rate higher than the national average. The result was that most libraries experienced some decline in acquisition rates in general. Serial prices increased more rapidly than did monographic prices. In order to maintain serial subscriptions, monies had to be taken from book funds, thus further reducing the number of monographs that could be acquired. Libraries eventually started canceling subscriptions. Thus, differential inflation rates and the use of national average rate as the basis for calculating budgets contributed to declining acquisition rates for many libraries.

A few specific facts help to document the magnitude of the problem. During 1984 American libraries spent three times the dollar amount expended in 1972, yet they acquired 3.87 percent *fewer* books than in 1972. Joan Neuman, director of METRO and a member of the Book Industry Study Group, states that library expenditures on materials for the collection are expected to increase by 7.1 percent per year, while each year there will be a 1.4 percent drop in the number of items purchased.[1]

A second problem was and is that the materials budget is very vulnerable in periods of tight budgets. Expenditures on materials are to some extent "discretionary," in that (in theory) one would not *have to* buy an item this year. Salaries of the staff are set for the year and staff reductions are rare in libraries, unless the entire organization is threatened with closure. Utility bills (an operating expense) must be paid if the library is to remain open. Some of the other operating expense items are also "discretionary": pens, pencils, paper, typewriter ribbons, and so on. Small savings may be achieved in cutting back in such areas, but for most libraries the operating expenses (o.e.) seldom represent more than 15 percent of the total budget. With utility costs taking up a significant portion of the total o.e., there is little left to cut. The reality is that the monograph materials budget is the only place where significant cuts can "easily" be made. All too often the long-term impact of such decisions is not given enough consideration, and the other choices appear to be even less acceptable.

What happened in collecting in the 1970s was a shift in emphasis from monographs to maintaining subscriptions. Today that shift is slowly being reversed, and through careful budget preparation, funding authorities appear to be more willing to accept differential budget increases that closely reflect actual expense experience. If nothing else, the problems of the 1970s have caused collection development officers to become better planners and to develop more accurate methods for calculating budgetary needs; in essence they have more credibility with funding authorities.

Several topics are covered in this chapter: (1) library accounting systems (a brief discussion), (2) estimating costs of materials, (3) allocating funds available,

(4) monitoring expenditures (encumbering), and (5) special problems. The reading list at the end of the chapter provides some suggestions for further study.

Library Fund Accounting

The vast majority of libraries and information centers are part of not-for-profit organizations. Being not-for-profit makes some difference in how the financial records are maintained, particularly when contrasted with profit-making organizations. For libraries that are part of a governmental jurisdiction, most revenues are received through an annual budget. Collection development officers must have accurate information about the monies potentially available, and need accurate data to assist in the preparation of budget requests. The funding authorities review the budget requests and authorize certain levels of funding for various activities. The two most common forms of income for such libraries are appropriations (monies distributed by the governing body to its agencies to carry out specific purposes) and revenue generated by the library as a result of fees and fines.

Because of the nature of the financial activities, certain accounting terms and concepts are different for the not-for-profit organization (NFP). Nevertheless, the basic accounting rules and practices do apply. One special term for NFP accounting is *fund accounting*. (Fund accounting has been defined as "a set of self-balancing account groups.") Another difference is that the profit-oriented bookkeeping system equation uses assets, liabilities, and equity; in NFP the elements used are assets, liabilities, and fund balance. One of the equations for NFP bookkeeping is that *assets* must equal *liabilities* plus the *fund balance*; another is that the *fund balance* is the difference between *assets* and *liabilities*. Substituting *equity* for *fund balance* would make the equation one for a profit organization. A difference between these equations is that an increase in fund balance carries with it no special meaning, whereas an increase in equity is a positive signal in a profit organization. Other terms, such as *debit, credit, journalizing, posting,* and *trial balance* are used in the same manner, no matter what type of organization is involved.

In most libraries the major fund is the operating fund. Other funds may be endowment and physical plant funds. The operating funds are the group of accounts used to handle the day-to-day activities of the library for a given time, usually one year, covering such items as salaries, book purchases, and utility bills. Within the fund there may be two categories of accounts, restricted and unrestricted. Restricted accounts may only be used for very specific purposes. Collection development/acquisition staff often must work with such accounts (frequently referred to as funds but in the monetary rather than accounting meaning). More often than not, these accounts are the result of monetary gifts or donations to the library by individuals who wish the money to be used for definite, often narrow purposes. (Sometimes gifts are for current use and sometimes for an endowment intended to generate income indefinitely. The income from the endowment is then used.) We have several such accounts at Tozzer Library, one of which may only be used to buy materials on biological anthropology. When the restrictions on the use of the monies are too narrow, it is difficult to make effective use of the monies available. Most collection development officers prefer unrestricted book accounts (used for any appropriate item for the collection) or restricted accounts that are broad based.

The purpose of the accounting system is to assure the proper use of monies provided and to make it possible to track expenditures. That is, every financial transaction is charged to some account, and a record exists of what the transaction involved. With a properly functioning fund accounting system, it is possible to tie every item acquired to a specific account and to verify when the transaction took place. Having a good accounting system, one that can easily provide accurate reports about all financial aspects of collection development activities, is a great planning aid. It takes time to understand accounting systems, but they must be understood if one wishes to be an effective and efficient collection development officer. A good book to consult on this topic is G. Stevenson Smith's *Accounting for Libraries and Other Not-for-Profit Managers.*[2]

Estimating Costs

Several factors influence the funding needs for collection development. Changes in the composition of the service community may have an important impact in either a positive or negative sense (see chapter 2). Another factor is changes in the scope and/or depth of collecting, as is any change in emphasis on retrospective collecting (see chapter 3). The two factors that come up year in and year out are the price of material and inflation.

As noted earlier, libraries have had some problems in establishing the credibility of funding needs for collection development. While a good accounting system will assist in justifying budget requests, additional data about book expenditures are necessary. One example of the problems caused by inflation, stable budgets, and rapidly rising prices for materials (and perhaps also limited credibility), is what happened to the acquisition rate for the University of California (UC) library system between the mid-1960s and 1970s. In the mid-1960s, the UC library system was adding over 650,000 volumes per year; by the mid-1970s the rate had fallen to below 520,000. Libraries of every type and size experienced similar problems.

Although data on price increases had been available for some time, it was during the 1970s that significant efforts were made to create useful library indexes measuring rates of change. A subcommittee of the American National Standards Institute, the Z39 Committee, was able to develop guidelines for price indexes.[3] This standard was revised in the early 1980s and is an important source to consult when developing a price index for a library, which is what many larger libraries have done. Another effort in this area is the work of the Library Materials Price Index Committee (Resources Section, Resources and Services Division of ALA). For some time, this group has produced a price index for American materials and some international publications.

The most recent data will be found in journals, while "historical" data appear in the *Bowker Annual.* Using a table in the *Bowker Annual* may be adequate for some purposes, but one needs to understand that the information is almost two years old. Preliminary data for books listed in the *Weekly Record* can be found, after the end of a calendar year, in *Publishers Weekly* (often in a late February or early March issue). Final data appear some months later (sometimes not until September or October). The major problem with the published indexes is that when one must prepare a budget request, up-to-date data may not be available because of the delay in publication. Vendors sometimes provide the most current data; for example, Coutts Library Services, probably the most current, issued their *Cumulative Blanket Order Statistics* for 1 February 1985 to 31 January 1986 on 7 March 1986. Naturally, given the company's orientation toward American and Canadian academic libraries, the index has limited value for many libraries. (Figures 12.1 and 12.2 illustrate the type of data available from Coutts, while 12.3 illustrates information from Blackwell North America for the same type of material but for a slightly different time period.) It is also possible to secure information about serial subscriptions from a vendor (figure 12.4). Figure 12.5 provides an illustration of all the problems discussed above as reflected in the Library of Congress. The sources used at Harvard are listed on pages 271-73.

For libraries that purchase a significant number of foreign publications, there is a need to estimate the impact of exchange rates. Buying power can be sharply affected by changes in the rate(s). For example, in January 1985 the pound sterling was at 1.1470 (U.S.), by January 1986 it was up to 1.4810 (U.S.), while the Canadian dollar went from .7720 to .7390 (U.S.). Although it is impossible to predict the direction and amount of fluctuation in the exchange rates for the next 12 months, some effort should go into studying the past 12 months and an attempt should be made to predict apparent trends for the future. Naturally one must have good data on the amounts spent in various countries during the past year. Knowing what country the item was purchased in may not be the important information, but rather the country of the source it was purchased from. If the library uses a vendor such as Harrassowitz, prices will be in Deutsche marks regardless of the country of origin of the item purchased. Once the data are collected, they can be used as a factor in estimating the cost of continuing the current acquisition levels from the countries the library normally buys from.

```
AMERICAN IMPRINTS                                            PAGE 1
                            COUTTS
                 CUMULATIVE BLANKET ORDER STATISTICS
                    FOR JAN 26 85 TO JAN 31 86

            CLASSIFICATIONS            QUANTITY LIST PRICE AVERAGE COST
            ---------------            -------- ---------- ------------

   AC      COLLECTIONS                     2       27.90      13.95
   AG      DICTIONARIES                    1      140.00     140.00




AMERICAN IMPRINTS                                            PAGE 4
                            COUTTS
                 CUMULATIVE BLANKET ORDER STATISTICS
                    FOR JAN 26 85 TO JAN 31 86

            CLASSIFICATIONS            QUANTITY LIST PRICE AVERAGE COST
            ---------------            -------- ---------- ------------

   QK      BOTANY                        106     5234.53      49.38
   QL      ZOOLOGY                       185     7974.42      43.10
   QM      HUMAN ANATOMY                  48     1626.95      33.89
   QP      PHYSIOLOGY                    409    30814.93      75.34
   QR      MICROBIOLOGY                  165     9843.43      59.67
   R       MEDICINE - GENERAL            166     5650.15      34.04
   RA      PUBLIC ASPECTS OF MEDICINE    217     8780.89      40.46
   RB      PATHOLOGY                      80     4592.00      57.40
   RC      INTERNAL MEDICINE             738    36627.50      49.63
   RC/BF   NEUROLOGY AND PSYCHIATRY      321    10143.21      31.60




AMERICAN IMPRINTS                                            PAGE 5
                            COUTTS
                 CUMULATIVE BLANKET ORDER STATISTICS
                    FOR JAN 26 85 TO JAN 31 86

            CLASSIFICATIONS            QUANTITY LIST PRICE AVERAGE COST
            ---------------            -------- ---------- ------------

   UD      INFANTRY                        1       16.95      16.95
   UF      ARTILLERY                       8      227.45      28.43
   UG      MILITARY ENGINEERING           22      481.50      21.89
   V       NAVAL SCIENCE - GENERAL         5      134.80      26.96
   VA      NAVIES                          9      371.20      41.24
   VB      NAVAL ADMINISTRATION            1       16.95      16.95
   VG      MINOR SERVICES OF NAVIES        1       12.75      12.75
   VK      NAVIGATION: MERCHANT MARINE     7      215.80      30.83
   VM      NAVAL ARCHITECTURE              6      167.35      27.87
   Z       BIBLIOGRAPHY. LIBRARY SCIENCE 251     9632.60      38.38

                                        TOTAL      TOTAL    AVERAGE
                                        BOOKS      AMOUNT     PRICE
   PRICES IN AMERICAN DOLLARS           21789   731442.92     33.57
```

Fig. 12.1. Coutts Library Services, cumulative blanket order statistics for Jan 26 85 to Jan 31 86: American Imprints. Reproduced by courtesy of Coutts Library Services.

FRENCH CANADIAN IMPRINTS   PAGE 2

COUTTS

CUMULATIVE BLANKET ORDER STATISTICS
FOR JAN 26 85 TO JAN 31 86

	CLASSIFICATIONS	QUANTITY	LIST PRICE	AVERAGE COST
ML	LITERATURE OF MUSIC	3	66.95	22.32
N	VISUAL ARTS	8	125.40	15.68
NA	ARCHITECTURE	1	15.00	15.00
NB	SCULPTURE	2	34.45	17.23
T	TECHNOLOGY	1	17.00	17.00
TN	MINING & METALLURGY	2	15.00	7.50
TP	CHEMICAL TECHNOLOGY	1	20.95	20.75
TX	HOME ECONOMICS	16	215.25	13.45
U	MILITARY SCIENCE – GENERAL	1	19.95	19.95

	TOTAL BOOKS	TOTAL AMOUNT	AVERAGE PRICE
PRICES IN CANADIAN DOLLARS	794	11605.29	14.62

ENGLISH CANADIAN IMPRINTS   PAGE 4

COUTTS

CUMULATIVE BLANKET ORDER STATISTICS
FOR JAN 26 85 TO JAN 31 86

	CLASSIFICATIONS	QUANTITY	LIST PRICE	AVERAGE COST
TK	ELECTRICAL ENGINEERING	4	90.35	22.59
TL	MOTOR VEHICLES.AERO&ASTRONAUT	6	130.85	21.81
TN	MINING & METALLURGY	8	357.95	44.74
TP	CHEMICAL TECHNOLOGY	1	80.00	80.00
TR	PHOTOGRAPHY	18	301.20	16.73
TS	MANUFACTURES	3	70.20	23.40
TT	HANDICRAFTS. ARTS & CRAFTS	8	96.14	12.02
TX	HOME ECONOMICS	50	687.01	13.74
U	MILITARY SCIENCE – GENERAL	7	214.85	30.67
UA	ARMIES	5	52.05	10.41
UB	MILITARY ADMINISTRATION	1	19.95	19.95
UC	MAINTENANCE & TRANSPORTATION	1	7.50	7.50
UF	ARTILLERY	5	134.90	26.78
UG	MILITARY ENGINEERING	12	252.60	21.05
V	NAVAL SCIENCE – GENERAL	4	76.45	17.11
VA	NAVIES	6	144.70	24.12
VD	NAVAL SEAMEN	1	0.75	0.75
VK	NAVIGATION. MERCHANT MARINE	3	67.85	22.62
Z	BIBLIOGRAPHY. LIBRARY SCIENCE	66	1746.50	26.46

	TOTAL BOOKS	TOTAL AMOUNT	AVERAGE PRICE
PRICES IN CANADIAN DOLLARS	3314	59289.61	17.89

Fig. 12.2. Coutts Library Services, cumulative blanket order statistics for Jan 26 85 to Jan 31 86: French Canadian Imprints. Reproduced by courtesy of Coutts Library Services.

TOTAL APPROVAL PROGRAM COVERAGE (07-01-84/06-30-85) Page 1a-1
PRIMARY SUBJECT COVERAGE

| | | U.S. & CANADIAN | | | | | |
| | | NEW | | | REPRINT | | |
CODE	SUBJECT	# OF BKS	TOTAL LIST	AVG LIST	# OF BKS	TOTAL LIST	AVG LIST
0110	Societies div	7	391.85	55.97			
0120	Meetings	2	51.45	25.72			
0125	Museums	2	100.95	50.47			
0130	Exhibitions	1	27.50	27.50			
0135	Holidays, dates, etc.	4	84.89	21.22			
0140	Awards, prizes	3	106.50	35.50			
0150	Genl reference works div	47	2,038.09	43.36			
0302	Fine arts	5	82.25	16.45	1	22.95	22.95
0310	Primitive art div	17	651.75	38.33			
0320	Native American art div	20	507.55	25.37			
0340	Western Asiatic art div	3	235.00	78.33			

TOTAL APPROVAL PROGRAM COVERAGE (07-01-84/06-30-85) Page 1a-11
PRIMARY SUBJECT COVERAGE

| | | U.S. & CANADIAN | | | | | |
| | | NEW | | | REPRINT | | |
CODE	SUBJECT	# OF BKS	TOTAL LIST	AVG LIST	# OF BKS	TOTAL LIST	AVG LIST
7820	Land & land use div	28	814.90	29.10	1	55.00	55.00
7826	Water conservation div	20	569.10	28.45			
7835	Nature conservation	10	238.35	23.83			
7839	Forest conservation	2	13.00	6.50			
7852	Wildlife conservation div	60	1,810.41	30.17			
7865	Recreation areas mgt	9	231.25	25.69			
7878	Marine resources	7	216.85	30.97			
7891	Mineral resources div	10	346.50	34.65			
8102	Veterinary medicine	3	91.85	30.61			
8125	Veterinary science div	14	821.50	58.67			
8150	Laboratory animals	4	134.90	33.72			
8175	Veterinary med & surgery	28	1,657.45	59.19			
8402	Career books	3	26.85	8.95			
8407	Architecture as career	2	24.66	12.33			
8409	Art as career	4	55.56	13.89			
8412	Business as career	9	97.31	10.81			
8415	Communications as career	3	26.85	8.95			
8418	Computer science as caree	4	40.19	10.04			
8421	Crafts & trades as career	1	9.95	9.95			
8427	Economics as career	1	5.95	5.95			
8433	Engineering as career	2	34.70	17.35			
8436	Entertainment as career	1	7.16	7.16			
8439	Government as career	3	23.06	7.68			
8445	Law as career	2	13.11	6.55			
8458	Mathematics as career	1	5.95	5.95			
8461	Medicine as career	2	31.90	15.95			
8473	Photography as career	1	9.95	9.95			
8477	Psychology as career	1	5.95	5.95			
8483	Recreation as career	1	7.16	7.16			
8499	Other specific career boo	5	36.17	7.23			
9226	Fiction authors: Fu-				1	6.00	6.00
	TOTAL...................	28,528	859,624.02	30.13	779	17,939.70	23.02

Fig. 12.3. Blackwell North America, total approval program coverage (07-01-84/
06-30-85), primary subject coverage. Reproduced by courtesy of Blackwell North
America.

```
EBSCO BUILDING
RED BANK, NJ 07701    /201/ 842-3600    /TELEX 132-404/
HISTORICAL PRICE ANALYSIS BY TITLE CODE                 03/10/86    PAGE 1

RB  81549-00

TOZZER LIBRARY
HARVARD UNIVERSITY
21 DIVINITY AVE
CAMBRIDGE MA        02138
```

TITLE CODE	TITLE	FREQ	SUB	PRICE 1982 FEB	PRICE 1983 FEB	% INCR	PRICE 1984 FEB	% INCR	PRICE 1985 FEB	% INCR	PRICE 1986 FEB	% INCR	TOTAL INCREASE	%
007233005	ACTA ANTHROPOGENETICA	QR	01	50.00	100.00	100.0	100.00	00.0	100.00	00.0	100.00	00.0	50.00	100.0
007320005	ACTA ARCHAEOLOGICA /DENMARK/	AN	01	34.79	38.67	11.2	35.38	08.5-	35.16	00.6-	44.98	27.9	10.19	29.2
021566007	AFRICA-TERVUREN /SURFACE MAIL/	QR	01	15.18	14.04	07.5-	12.73	09.3-	11.28	11.4-	14.51	28.6	.67-	04.4-
021747019	AFRICAN ARTS /WITH INDEX/	QR	01	21.00	21.00	00.0	23.00	09.5	23.00	00.0	23.00	00.0	2.00	09.5
022493001	AFRICAN STUDIES	SA	01	22.87	19.00	16.9-	16.98	10.6-	19.83	16.8	18.48	06.3-	4.39-	19.1-
030423007	ALABAMA ARCHAEOLOGICAL SOCIETY MEMBERSHIP	SA	01	13.00	13.00	00.0	13.00	00.0	13.00	00.0	13.00	00.0	.00	00.0

```
EBSCO BUILDING
RED BANK, NJ 07701    /201/ 842-3600    /TELEX 132-404/
HISTORICAL PRICE ANALYSIS BY TITLE CODE                 03/10/86    PAGE 17

RB  81549-00
```

TITLE CODE	TITLE	FREQ	SUB	PRICE 1982 FEB	PRICE 1983 FEB	% INCR	PRICE 1984 FEB	% INCR	PRICE 1985 FEB	% INCR	PRICE 1986 FEB	% INCR	TOTAL INCREASE	%
949353007	WEST AFRICAN JOURNAL OF ARCHAEOLOGY	AN	01	22.95	21.67	05.6-	19.64	09.4-	17.19	12.5-	25.68	49.4	2.73	11.8
950921262	WESTERN CANADIAN ANTHROPOLOGIST /FORMERLY/ NAPAO	SA	01	3.44	5.96	73.3	5.74	03.7-	7.78	35.5	7.56	02.8-	4.12	119.7
957276009	WIENER VOLKERKUNDLICHE MITTEILUNGEN/RE REVIEW OF ETHNOLOGY/	AN	01	28.90	28.90	00.0	28.90	00.0	7.44	74.3-	9.74	30.9	19.16-	66.2-
959779000	WISCONSIN ARCHAEOLOGIST	QR	01	15.00	15.00	00.0	15.00	00.0	15.00	00.0	15.00	00.0	.00	00.0
964352009	WORLD ARCHAEOLOGY	TQ	01	35.82	31.13	13.1-	42.00	34.9	50.00	19.0	50.00	00.0	14.18	39.5
969744317	WYOMING ARCHAEOLOGICAL SOCIETY MEMBERSHIP	SA	01	15.00	15.00	00.0	15.00	00.0	15.00	00.0	15.00	00.0	.00	00.0

```
** 226 TITLES      ** CUSTOMER TOTAL ***   6,823.72**  7,182.52   7,716.43**  8,138.44**  8,751.85**  1928.13  28.3
                     AVERAGE PRICE            30.19       31.78      34.14       36.01       38.72      38.72
                                                         05.3        07.4        05.5        07.5

DEAR CUSTOMER:
BASED ON THE TOTALS THE AVG. YEARLY INCREASE IS EQUAL TO  07.0%
```

Fig. 12.4. EBSCO historical price analysis by title code. Reproduced by courtesy of EBSCO.

PLACE OF PUBLICATION	1984				1985				
	By Exchange or Gift	By Purchase		Total Book Receipts	By Exchange or Gift	By Purchase		Total Book Receipts	% Change
	Number	Number	Average Price		Number	Number	Average Price		
Afghanistan	2	20	$8.00	22	11	0	0	11	-50.0
Albania	0	103	6.52	103	0	116	$6.75	116	12.6
Algeria	20	106	9.69	126	16	184	11.09	200	58.7
Anguilla	0	8	12.31	8	0	5	8.70	5	-37.5
Antigua & Barbuda	6	15	5.86	21	0	4	7.93	4	-81.0
Argentina	581	1,290	8.75	1,871	285	1,295	12.33	1,580	-15.6
Australia	1,738	598	20.91	2,336	1,271	557	16.63	1,828	-21.7
Austria	623	913	19.25	1,536	3,120	814	18.06	3,934	156.1
Bahamas	0	1	59.75	1	2	22	12.92	24	2,300.0
Bahrain	17	15	16.93	32	39	34	13.19	73	128.1
Bangladesh	188	1,252	.91	1,440	75	307	2.29	382	-73.5
Barbados	7	115	7.76	122	6	39	13.23	45	-63.1
Belgium	656	486	18.89	1,142	289	381	18.80	670	-41.3
Belize	10	12	6.60	22	6	7	13.36	13	-40.9
Benin	3	23	7.12	26	0	10	15.34	10	-61.5
Bermuda	2	10	12.32	12	2	30	13.44	32	166.7
Bhutan	3	61	38.93	64	4	55	34.73	59	-7.8

FOOTNOTES

[1]Formerly Upper Volta. New name became effective on August 4, 1984.

[2]Includes: Guadeloupe, Martinique, Guyane (French Guiana), St. Martin and St. Barthélemy.

[3]Includes figures for Namibia.

[4]Includes: Great Britain (England, Scotland, and Wales), Northern Ireland and miscellaneous island possessions.

[5]The relatively small number of monographs acquired by exchange, gift or purchase is due to the majority of current U.S. imprints being selected for addition to the Library's permanent collections from copyright deposits and the CIP program.

Fig. 12.5. Acquisitions of monographs by the Library of Congress. From *Library of Congress Information Bulletin* 45, no. 16 (21 April 1986): 113-19.

Fig. 12.5.—*Continued*

PLACE OF PUBLICATION	1984 By Exchange or Gift Number	1984 By Purchase Number	1984 By Purchase Average Price	1984 Total Book Receipts	1985 By Exchange or Gift Number	1985 By Purchase Number	1985 By Purchase Average Price	1985 Total Book Receipts	% Change
Bolivia	53	256	$7.85	309	95	180	$8.24	275	-11.0
Botswana	54	0	0	54	22	0	0	22	-59.3
Brazil	3,750	1,548	3.73	5,298	2,564	2,370	4.52	4,934	-6.9
Brunei	7	0	0	7	2	12	4.56	14	100.0
Bulgaria	1,378	723	7.50	2,101	1,639	1,008	7.58	2,647	26.0
Burkina Faso [1]	0	0	0	0	3	3	7.01	6	0
Burma	190	38	1.42	228	301	12	1.67	313	37.3
Burundi	7	0	0	7	18	1	10.07	19	171.4
Cambodia	7	0	0	7	4	0	0	4	-42.9
Cameroon	2	90	9.91	92	4	119	8.49	123	33.7
Canada	4,148	1,520	14.85	5,668	5,160	1,524	15.09	6,684	17.9
Cape Verde	3	0	0	3	0	4	10.13	4	33.3
Cayman Islands	6	1	8.75	7	0	23	5.20	23	228.6
Central African Republic	0	3	7.13	3	0	6	7.25	6	100.0
Chad	0	0	0	0	0	3	6.50	3	0
Chile	277	308	16.01	585	818	578	9.76	1,396	138.6
China (People's Republic)	12,236	9,282	4.48	21,518	17,564	5,799	5.76	23,363	8.6
Colombia	305	767	15.76	1,072	614	513	15.25	1,127	5.1
Comoros	0	0	0	0	13	0	0	13	0
Congo	5	25	12.74	30	1	1	16.75	2	-93.3
Costa Rica	259	228	10.71	487	86	275	13.50	361	-25.9
Cuba	464	214	7.95	678	258	220	9.94	478	-29.5
Cyprus	84	43	9.35	127	285	56	16.27	341	168.5
Czechoslovakia	618	769	6.08	1,387	675	720	6.10	1,395	0.6
Denmark	2,105	741	12.68	2,846	2,184	568	15.17	2,752	-3.3
Djibouti	15	0	0	15	7	5	11.31	12	-20.0
Dominica	0	10	4.60	10	2	6	1.66	8	-20.0
Dominican Republic	177	241	10.46	418	122	299	11.72	421	0.7
Ecuador	72	249	7.62	321	114	477	9.36	591	84.1

PLACE OF PUBLICATION	1984				1985				
	By Exchange or Gift	By Purchase		Total Book Receipts	By Exchange or Gift	By Purchase		Total Book Receipts	% Change
	Number	Number	Average Price		Number	Number	Average Price		
Egypt	2,706	786	$4.41	3,492	2,454	750	$7.27	3,204	-8.2
El Salvador	4	108	9.88	112	23	169	12.59	192	71.4
Equatorial Guinea	9	12	11.79	21	0	0	0	0	-100.0
Ethiopia	1,222	0	0	1,222	1,032	12	3.68	1,044	-14.6
Fiji	25	1	6.50	26	22	0	0	22	-15.4
Finland	3,068	857	17.78	3,925	2,661	853	18.03	3,514	-10.5
France	3,320	4,567	14.78	7,887	2,425	4,990	14.95	7,415	-6.0
French Antilles [2]	3	86	15.47	89	11	149	15.54	160	79.8
Gabon	0	0	0	0	0	1	6.25	1	0
Gambia	16	3	4.92	19	0	10	8.66	10	-47.4
Germany (Federal Republic)	5,271	8,884	18.25	14,155	5,123	8,195	17.51	13,318	-5.9
Germany (Democratic Republic)	995	694	11.39	1,689	788	468	9.02	1,256	-25.6
Ghana	38	19	4.88	57	16	95	2.98	111	94.7
Greece	123	1,126	5.81	1,249	120	923	6.37	1,043	-16.5
Grenada	0	45	3.27	45	5	34	5.97	39	-13.3
Guatemala	18	78	15.53	96	66	71	17.95	137	42.7
Guinea	0	46	6.86	46	0	33	12.22	33	-28.3
Guinea-Bissau	0	7	9.39	7	18	0	0	18	157.1
Guyana	18	30	5.60	48	0	8	9.78	8	-83.3
Haiti	25	72	11.66	97	129	115	9.47	244	151.5
Honduras	4	169	5.88	173	8	168	5.78	176	1.7
Hong Kong	51	931	9.71	982	48	999	9.76	1,047	6.6
Hungary	648	957	7.75	1,605	592	1,736	8.12	2,328	45.0
Iceland	6	126	11.92	132	8	5	15.39	13	-90.2
India	3,021	6,479	11.22	9,500	2,475	5,677	8.99	8,152	-14.2
Indonesia	385	1,366	3.71	1,751	1,084	585	4.62	1,669	-4.7
Iran	117	1,262	9.23	1,379	214	1,304	13.32	1,518	10.1
Iraq	133	165	6.17	298	128	125	6.99	253	-15.1
Ireland	231	320	10.69	551	163	294	9.77	457	-17.1

Fig. 12.5. — *Continued*

PLACE OF PUBLICATION	1984 By Exchange or Gift Number	1984 By Purchase Number	1984 By Purchase Average Price	1984 Total Book Receipts	1985 By Exchange or Gift Number	1985 By Purchase Number	1985 By Purchase Average Price	1985 Total Book Receipts	% Change
Israel	749	1,668	$12.34	2,417	546	1,755	$12.74	2,301	-4.8
Italy	972	4,561	13.13	5,533	892	6,181	13.88	7,073	27.8
Ivory Coast	40	74 .	19.47	114	30	82	12.80	112	-1.8
Jamaica	18	153	9.13	171	21	141	7.35	162	-5.3
Japan	3,062	12,360	16.53	15,422	2,818	8,535	14.19	11,353	-26.4
Jordan	86	108	8.76	194	120	223	5.77	343	76.8
Kenya	434	63	8.67	497	340	96	10.25	436	-12.3
Korea (North)	40	879	13.46	919	63	263	5.86	326	-64.5
Korea (South)	385	2,271	14.14	2,656	285	3,807	13.47	4,092	54.1
Kuwait	152	99	11.31	251	84	30	9.08	114	-54.6
Laos	0	11	.81	11	2	0	0	2	-81.8
Lebanon	60	1,274	11.14	1,334	119	685	12.32	804	-39.7
Lesotho	5	0	0	5	2	0	0	2	-60.0
Liberia	14	3	12.53	17	1	9	7.73	10	-41.2
Libya	32	112	8.17	144	14	0	0	14	-90.3
Liechtenstein	1	0	0	1	1	6	38.66	7	600.0
Luxembourg	1,303	2	16.72	1,305	788	0	0	788	-39.6
Macao	0	0	0	0	8	0	0	8	0
Madagascar	9	27	2.95	36	6	40	11.90	46	27.8
Malawi	100	20	3.27	120	76	5	13.06	81	-32.5
Malaysia	80	395	6.89	475	40	204	7.03	244	-48.6
Maldives	24	12	.34	36	32	0	0	32	-11.1
Mali	2	1	6.50	3	1	7	5.57	8	166.7
Malta	6	0	0	6	29	0	0	29	383.3
Mauritania	0	0	0	0	1	0	0	1	0
Mauritius	73	19	5.46	92	95	3	10.95	98	6.5
Mexico	1,727	1,106	10.02	2,833	1,057	1,334	7.71	2,391	-15.6
Monaco	3	0	0	3	0	0	0	0	-100.0
Mongolia	22	0	0	22	14	1	15.00	15	-31.8
Montserrat	0	3	5.08	3	0	0	0	0	-100.0

PLACE OF PUBLICATION	1984 By Exchange or Gift Number	1984 By Purchase Number	1984 By Purchase Average Price	1984 Total Book Receipts	1985 By Exchange or Gift Number	1985 By Purchase Number	1985 By Purchase Average Price	1985 Total Book Receipts	% Change
Morocco	17	307	$7.67	324	38	331	$9.18	369	13.9
Mozambique	8	5	6.94	13	0	1	8.25	1	-92.3
Nepal	274	711	1.46	985	73	188	3.33	261	-73.5
Netherlands	1,013	1,545	15.01	2,558	947	1,318	13.70	2,265	-11.5
Netherlands Antilles	36	11	9.77	47	28	24	14.56	52	10.6
New Caledonia	0	1	29.00	1	0	0	0	0	-100.0
New Zealand	1,116	72	16.32	1,188	794	112	12.88	906	-23.7
Nicaragua	18	223	11.34	241	33	153	12.66	186	-22.8
Niger	20	12	18.86	32	19	4	6.75	23	-28.1
Nigeria	163	195	9.97	358	163	377	14.47	540	50.8
Norway	549	507	15.18	1,056	425	708	14.27	1,133	7.3
Oman	10	9	10.00	19	19	66	8.89	85	347.4
Pakistan	1,211	442	2.60	1,653	1,306	703	2.49	2,009	21.5
Panama	116	73	17.13	189	38	69	14.78	107	-43.4
Papua New Guinea	47	0	0	47	54	49	7.47	103	119.1
Paraguay	92	184	9.11	276	7	139	9.09	146	-47.1
Peru	317	468	9.17	785	134	471	8.96	605	-22.9
Philippines	404	385	18.07	789	435	493	12.61	928	17.6
Poland	1,455	846	9.36	2,301	1,077	737	10.43	1,814	-21.2
Portugal	677	793	6.16	1,470	552	889	4.75	1,441	-2.0
Puerto Rico	94	123	11.69	217	32	239	6.01	271	24.9
Qatar	32	3	.90	35	93	30	5.17	123	251.4
Reunion	8	16	42.76	24	9	10	23.42	19	-20.8
Romania	489	711	2.29	1,200	275	1,060	2.18	1,335	11.3
Rwanda	4	0	0	4	28	3	65.85	31	675.0
St. Christopher (Kitts)-Nevis	0	31	4.87	31	3	1	7.25	4	-87.1
St. Lucia	0	40	6.85	40	0	9	5.47	9	-77.5
St. Vincent	0	7	6.24	7	0	6	11.41	6	-14.3
Saudi Arabia	220	105	32.35	325	183	93	6.71	276	-15.1

Fig. 12.5.—*Continued*

PLACE OF PUBLICATION	1984 By Exchange or Gift Number	1984 By Purchase Number	1984 By Purchase Average Price	1984 Total Book Receipts	1985 By Exchange or Gift Number	1985 By Purchase Number	1985 By Purchase Average Price	1985 Total Book Receipts	% Change
Senegal	8	41	$14.58	49	42	66	$12.84	108	120.4
Seychelles	7	1	9.35	8	10	1	9.68	11	37.5
Sierra Leone	5	7	26.25	12	0	22	8.55	22	83.3
Singapore	46	228	12.22	274	24	142	13.61	166	-39.4
Somalia	111	0	0	0	100	1	47.46	101	-9.0
South Africa [3]	638	337	12.64	975	1,157	403	8.87	1,560	60.0
Spain	990	4,023	12.16	5,013	1,235	4,469	15.18	5,704	13.8
Sri Lanka	340	1,078	1.96	1,418	180	193	2.75	373	-73.7
Sudan	102	32	12.36	134	152	16	21.03	168	25.4
Surinam	7	44	7.75	51	3	30	12.15	33	-35.3
Swaziland	2	0	0	2	18	2	6.51	20	900.0
Sweden	2,226	752	15.48	2,978	838	1,091	16.45	1,929	-35.2
Switzerland	1,413	2,280	17.89	3,693	626	2,079	19.82	2,705	-26.8
Syria	25	26	11.37	51	24	301	8.73	325	537.3
Taiwan	1,026	4,282	13.21	5,308	1,299	4,907	13.62	6,206	16.9
Tanzania	158	4	51.78	162	94	10	54.90	104	-35.8
Thailand	1,235	507	4.01	1,742	1,021	569	3.71	1,590	-8.7
Togo	26	0	0	26	0	23	11.83	23	-11.5
Trinidad & Tobato	17	25	16.74	42	7	21	19.63	28	-33.3
Tunisia	73	119	9.74	192	114	185	12.31	299	55.7
Turkey	482	489	5.85	971	360	232	4.76	592	-39.0
Turks & Caicos Islands	0	14	.25	14	0	3	1.75	3	-78.6
Uganda	0	8	7.20	8	8	10	29.96	18	125.0
United Arab Emirates	15	0	0	15	11	13	7.56	24	60.0
United Kingdom [4]	1,749	4,916	21.20	6,665	1,666	3,578	17.91	5,244	-21.3
U.S.A. [5]	1,960	22,964	18.10	24,924	2,974	21,847	17.34	24,821	-0.4
U.S. Misc. Pacific Islands	0	0	0	0	0	1	6.00	1	0
U.S.S.R. [6]	8,702	7,914	4.35	16,616	8,298	11,533	3.47	19,831	19.3

PLACE OF PUBLICATION	1984				1985				
	By Exchange or Gift	By Purchase		Total Book	By Exchange or Gift	By Purchase		Total Book	
	Number	Number	Average Price	Receipts	Number	Number	Average Price	Receipts	% Change
Uruguay	26	291	$11.76	317	98	445	$11.75	543	71.3
Vatican City	1	0	0	1	0	3	94.53	3	200.0
Venezuela	465	747	11.16	1,212	421	981	12.76	1,402	1815.7
Vietnam	91	0	0	91	358	0	0	358	293.4
Virgin Islands (U.K.)	0	7	19.39	7	0	6	16.37	6	-14.3
Virgin Islands (U.S.)	8	61	8.20	69	4	28	10.53	32	-53.6
Yemen (Arab (Republic)	3	1	8.45	4	0	20	13.10	20	400.0
Yemen (Democratic Republic)	0	0	0	0	0	1	15.03	1	0
Yugoslavia	496	590	7.91	1,086	423	703	4.74	1,126	3.7
Zaire	7	66	10.60	73	5	132	8.28	137	87.7
Zambia	166	4	6.14	170	59	17	5.81	76	-55.3
Zimbabwe	82	98	6.73	180	16	75	12.63	91	-49.4
TOTAL	89,379	136,282	8.72	225,661	93,189	132,260	10.87	225,449	-0.1

Allocation of Monies

Normally the monies for collection development are provided as lump sums, at least for unrestricted accounts. Allocation systems are intended to match monies available with needs. The process provides guidelines for selection personnel because the allocation sets limits and expectations on purchases in a subject area or type of material. Ordinarily, the process would also reflect the collection development policy statement priorities. If the collection development officer has used one of the collecting intensity systems in the policy, it is reasonable to expect that those levels will be reflected in the allocations. How one goes about matching the needs and monies available is complicated. One must consider a number of factors such as past practices, differential publication and inflation rates, level of demand, and actual use. Implementing a formal system takes time and effort. There is some debate whether it is worthwhile allocating the monies. Opponents to allocation claim it is difficult to develop a "fair" allocation model and is time-consuming to calculate the amounts needed. They also claim that because the models are difficult to develop, they are left in place too long once they are established. Finally, they suggest that accounts may not be spent effectively because there is too much or too little money available and it is difficult to effect transfers from one account to another. Proponents claim allocations provide better control of collection development and are a more effective way to monitor expenditures.

The fact of the matter is that some allocation does take place, regardless of the presence or absence of a formal allocation process. When there is no formal system, the individuals responsible for spending the monies engage in an informal balancing of needs and the availability of funds for different activities for classes of material. It seems reasonable, if the process is going to take place one way or another, that the formal process has the best chance of achieving a fair balance. For example, the Cornell University libraries shifted from a system in which "the changes in expenditure levels among various fields were largely unplanned.... There is no question that allocation of resources for maintaining and building the collections must be systematized and the management information available for allocation decisions improved."[4] In a small library, a formal process may not be necessary, but the person(s) involved in spending monies on collection development should consider all the factors each year before making shifts in expenditures.

Formal allocation may only be dividing monies between monographic and serial purchase accounts. Even this "easy" division is no longer easy, since serial prices increase more rapidly than other materials costs. How long can one shift monies from other accounts to maintain serial subscription levels without damaging the overall strengths of the collection? Several different approaches have been used to allocate funds, such as format, subject, unit, users, language, and formula. Most libraries that use a format allocation system use several approaches. Many small libraries, including most school media centers, employ the format system: monographs, serials, and audiovisuals are the broad groupings; these funds may be subdivided by subject (language arts), grade level (5th grade) or user group (professional reading). Monographs are sometimes divided into current, retrospective, and replacement. Where approval, blanket order, and standing order plans are extensively used, monies will be set aside for these programs before other allocations are made. Public libraries and academic libraries may allocate by unit (branch) and the unit may in turn make further divisions, such as reference, general collections, special collections, children's, young adult, or undergraduate. Subject allocations are common in large libraries.

Formula allocations have come into use in large libraries, especially academic libraries. Several formulas have been proposed over the years, and no one formula has been generally accepted. Each library must decide which, if any, formula is most appropriate for its special circumstances. Only factors that can be quantified are taken into account by a formula. This does not mean there is no subjective judgment involved, just that the process depends on weightings, circulation data, production figures, inflation and exchange rates, number of users, and so forth. Figure 12.6 provides an example of an allocation formula, in this case a modified version of William McGrath's 1975 formula. Formulas can and do become complicated and, of course, address only those factors that one can quantify. If they take into account enough factors, they can provide an equitable method for allocating available monies.

1) Establish the subjects to be included.

2) Tabulate the total annual circulation for each selected subject field.

3) Determine the average cost of books published in each selected subject field.

4) Multiply the average cost of books by the annual circulation.

5) Total the cost-use column.

6) Divide the subject cost-use by the total cost-use to determine percentage cost-use.

7) Multiply percent cost-use by the total amount to be allocated for all subjects.

Fig. 12.6. Example of allocation computation.

When deciding how to set up an allocation system many factors need to be considered. One of the most comprehensive listings of these factors was prepared by Cornell University Library, and is given in figure 12.7 in a modified form, deleting specific Cornell material:

1. *Historical Factors*

   a. Recent past experience with the collection, based on informed views of librarian or bibliographer. Is the collection improving, deteriorating, or showing little change?

   b. Special features of the collection that have made it distinguished or particularly useful.

   c. Have there been noteworthy stages of development in the past?

2. *Evaluative Factors*

   a. Level of acquisitions as reported in annual reports. Include forecasts by librarian or bibliographer, library committee, or library liaison and identification of future needs.

   b. Faculty and graduate student evaluations.

3. *Environmental Factors*

   a. Ratings of academic programs served, by outside agencies and by internal agencies.

   b. Ratings of academic programs served, by faculty liaison groups. For example, views and opinions would be sought from faculty liaison group for social sciences as to where, and in what areas or subjects, emphasis or special resources might be needed.

Fig. 12.7.—*Continued*

    c.   Indicators of academic activity. For example, the number of full-time faculty; graduate enrollment for departments, schools, or colleges served; undergraduate enrollment, undergraduate courses, undergraduate majors.

    d.   Views and opinions of deans or academic programs served. Where do they rank in the college's or school's order of priorities?

    e.   Trends in publishing and research output. Develop means for estimating publishing and research output in specific academic fields.

4. *Growth Factors*

    a.   Tabulate rate of growth in items added (net) to the collection in comparison to total system rate of growth and possibly, in comparison to related (selected) collections or libraries.

    b.   Tabulate comparative percentage of growth in volumes as a share of total system growth.

    c.   Tabulate growth in monograph titles, using shelflist measurements.

    d.   Tabulate growth of microform units.

    e.   Tabulate number of serial titles and number of serial subscriptions by year.

    f.   Tabulate number of serial subscription cancellations.

    g.   Tabulate serial duplications.

    h.   Calculate volume equivalents for serials in specific subject groupings.

5. *Cost and Expenditure Factors*

    a.   Tabulate by year, book fund expenditures as percentage of total book expenditures for total system.

    b.   Tabulate total book fund expenditures for monographs, standing orders and monographic series, and serials.

    c.   Unit cost figures for monographs (volumes) by year.

    d.   Average subscription cost by year, without gifts or exchange subscriptions.

6. *Special Support Factors*

    a.   Endowment income.

    b.   Money gifts.

    c.   Other restricted fund support.

7. *Special Needs*

8. *Political Factors*

   (Collection Development and Management at Cornell, p. 71-73.)

Fig. 12.7. Factors in designing an allocation system. From *Collection Development and Management at Cornell* (Ithaca, N.Y.: Cornell University Libraries, 1981), 71-73. Reprinted by permission.

The resources section of the Resources and Technical Services Division of ALA has attempted to develop guidelines for allocation systems, including descriptions of their respective advantages and disadvantages.

Encumbering

One aspect of accounting and financial management in collection development that is a little different from typical accounting practice is the process of encumbering. This is a process that allows one to set aside monies to pay for ordered items. When the library waits 60, 90, or 120 days or more for orders, there is some chance that the monies available will be either over- or underspent if there is no system that allows for "setting aside" monies. Figure 12.8 provides a simple example of how the process works.

	Unexpended	Encumbered	Expended
Day 1	$1000.00	0	0
Day 2	Order a $24.95 list price item:		
	$975.05	$24.95	0
Day 62	Order received, invoice shows 15% discount and vendor paid postage:		
	$978.79	0	$21.21

Fig. 12.8. Encumbering process.

Needless to say, this system is more complex than the example suggests, since most libraries place multiple orders and receive items every day. With each transaction the amounts in each column change. One seldom knows precisely how much money is left. If the system takes back all unexpended funds at the end of the fiscal year, the collection development staff will want to know how well they are doing as they enter the final quarter of the year.

Several factors complicate the issue, even when monies are encumbered. One factor is delivery of the order(s). Vendors may assure their customers that they will deliver before the end of the year but fail to do so, and the encumbered money may be lost. Sometimes the order is never delivered and, again, the librarian loses. These are two reasons why a firm but reasonable date for automatic cancellation of unfilled orders is important. Another factor is pricing and discounts. Prices are subject to change without notice on most library materials, which means the price may be higher on delivery than when ordered. Discounts are also unpredictable and are subject to change. Because of the uncertainty, most libraries encumber the list price without any freight charges and hope that the amount will be adequate. Of course, exchange rates enter the picture for foreign acquisitions and the question of when the rate is "set" can be a critical issue. Certainly, the rate is not set when the item is ordered, but is it set by the date the invoice was prepared, the date the invoice and item(s) are received, or the date the check is made out to pay the invoice? With foreign orders one can expect anywhere from four months to a longer, indeterminate amount of time to elapse between order placement and delivery. (Tozzer has had orders arriving five years after the order was placed.) In periods of rapid rate changes, even a four-month difference can greatly affect the amount of money that is left to be spent.

Moving "monies" back and forth, especially in a manual system, can lead to errors, so the acquisitions department needs a good bookkeeper. Automated accounting systems speed up the recording activities as well as provide greater accuracy, as long as the inputting is correct. Despite the uncertainty that exists with the encumbering system, it is still better than just having unexpended and expended categories, since without it one would not know what amount was represented by items ordered but not received.

Special Problems

Over the past few years, as the U.S. Postal Service has reduced the difference between postal rates such as "library rate," the cost of shipping items has grown. For example, in 1970 it cost $0.18 to ship a two-pound book; in 1980 it cost $0.80. Some publishers and vendors are involved in what is called "freight pass-through" (FPT). Originally, in 1981, FPT was intended to create a two-tier pricing system so as to enable bookstores to pass on the freight charges to the customer. That is, the bookstore would be charged an "invoice" price and the dust jacket would carry the higher FPT price. Some publishers use a percentage of the invoice price (3 or 4 percent) while others use a flat fee ($0.50). The problem for libraries buying from jobbers is determining what price is used when calculating the library discount. Most contracts with jobbers call for discounts on "list" price— is the list price the invoice price or the FPT price printed on the dust jacket? Jobber practice has varied from one extreme to the other. While the percentages are small, as are the amounts of money for any one title, the accumulated effect on an acquisition budget can be great. This is just one more example of the need to be familiar with and follow the book trade, and to understand how publishers' and vendors' charges may affect our collections.

Another practice of publishers has had some negative impact on the collection budgets of U.S. libraries. Since late 1983, many British publishers have established higher prices for their journals when the subscriber is located in the United States. For example, in 1984, *Philosophy Magazine* was £197 in the

United Kingdom and elsewhere in the world, except in the United States, where it was $560.00 (approximately £300). The U.S. prices range from about 12 percent to 70 percent higher. The rationale for such differences is difficult to understand and accept. In fact, none of the British publishers' statements about why there should be such a dual system are convincing. At the present time, 1986, all one can say is that the publishers have stated they will hold the line at 1986 prices for some time. That "concession" was the result of the protest of the American Library Association concerning the matter. There is some evidence that the practice is spreading; for example, Harrassowitz now charges a higher price for German and Dutch journals, if the buyer is in the United States.

One must be constantly aware of changes in prices and in invoicing practices so as to gain the maximum number of additions to the collection. Watch for changes and demand explanations of freight and handling charges, inappropriate dual pricing systems, or other costs that may place additional strain on the budget. By understanding basic accounting principles and using the reports and records generated by the library's accounting system, one will be better able to monitor the use of available monies and use them effectively to meet the needs of the "public."

Selected Sources of Recently Published Library Materials Price Information

"Average Book Prices." *Library Association Record* 87 (April 1985): 154-55. Derived from UKMARC files of the British Library Bibliographic Services Division.

Blackwell North America, Inc. *Approval Program Coverage and Cost Study 1984-85*, n.d. Includes a new version by LC class.

Brown, Norman B., and Jane Phillips. "Preliminary Survey of 1984 Subscription Prices of the U.S. Periodicals." *RTSD Newsletter* 10, no. 2 (1985): 19-20.

Buch und Buchhandel in Zahlen. Frankfurt am Main: Buchhandler — Vereinigung GmbH., 1985.

Coutts Library Services, Inc. *Cumulative Blanket Order Statistics for February 1st, 1984-January 31, 1985*. 13 March 1985. Statistical breakdown by LC class.

De La Garza, Peter J. "Cost Statistics for Latin American Publications." *SALALM Newsletter* 12 (March 1985): 3.

Dessauer, John P. *Book Industry Trends 1985*. New York: Book Industry Study Group, Inc., 1985. Tables 4A and 5A are of particular interest.

"Données Statistiques sur L'Edition de Livres en France Année 1984." *Livres Hebdo* 48 (25 November 1985): 99-124.

Grannis, Chandler B. "U.S. Title Output, Average Prices: Final Figures for 1984." *Publishers Weekly* (23 August 1985): 41-44. Summary of earlier prices appears in *Bowker Annual.*

Hill, George R., and Joseph M. Boonin. "Music Price Indexes: 1984 Update." *Notes* 41 (March 1985): 492-97.

Horn, Judith G., and Rebecca T. Lenzini. "Price Indexes for 1985: U.S. Periodicals." *Library Journal* 110, no. 13 (August 1985): 53-58. Now produced by Faxon. U.S. Serials Services Price Index not included. Editor's note: Price indexes for 1986: U.S. periodicals published in *Library Journal* (15 April 1986).

Lenzini, Rebecca T. "Periodical Prices 1983-1985 Update." *Serials Librarian* 9 (Summer 1985): 119-30.

"Library of Congress Book Receipts, 1983 and 1984." *Library of Congress Information Bulletin* (14 October 1985): 289-91. Arranged by country of publication.

"North American Academic Book Price Index 1980/81-1984/85." A preliminary table presented to ALA/RTSD/RS/Library Materials Price Index Committee at its Midwinter Meeting, 20 January 1986.

Lynden, Frederick C. "Reporting Book Prices." *Book Research Quarterly* (Spring 1985): 107-10. A regular column.

Lynden, Frederick C. "Reporting Book Prices: Text Book Prices." *Book Research Quarterly* (Summer 1985): 87-89.

Lynden, Frederick C. "Reporting Book Prices: Foreign Book Prices." *Book Research Quarterly* (Fall 1985): 82-84.

"Periodical Prices." *Library Association Record* 87 (May 1985): 204-5. Compiled by Blackwell's Periodical Division.

"Price Index for Legal Publications Summary." *Association of American Law Libraries Newsletter* 17, no. 5 (December 1985): 97.

Research Associates of Washington. *Higher Education Prices and Price Indexes: 1985 Update.* Washington, D.C.: Research Associates of Washington, 1985.

Smith, Dennis E. "Prices of U.S. and Foreign Published Materials." In *Bowker Annual of Library & Book Trade Information, 1985*, 471-88. New York: R. R. Bowker, 1985.

Soupiset, Kathryn A. "College Book Price Information 1984." *Choice* (April 1985): 1107-11.

Williams, Sally F. "Reporting Book Prices." *Book Research Quarterly* 1, no. 4 (1986): 85-88.

Wood, Lawraine. *Average Prices of British Academic Books: January to June 1984.* Loughborough University of Technology, Centre for Library and

Information Management, report no. 37. Loughborough, England, 1984. This is the last report published using figures supplied by the BNB. A new index based on figures supplied by B. H. Blackwell was planned for publication in 1986.

Notes

[1]Joan Neuman, "Rising Prices of Books Stirs Library Alarm in N.Y.," *Library Journal* 111 (15 April 1986): 22.

[2]G. Stevenson Smith, *Accounting for Libraries and Other Not-for-Profit Managers* (Chicago: American Library Association, 1983).

[3]American National Standards Institute, Z39 Committee, *Criteria for Price Indexes for Library Materials* (New York: American National Standards Institute, 1974). ANSI Z39.20.

[4]*Collection Development and Management at Cornell* (Ithaca, N.Y.: Cornell University Libraries, 1981), 67.

Further Reading

General

Bonk, S. "Rethinking the Acquisitions Budget: Anticipating and Managing Change." *Library Acquisitions: Practice and Theory* 10, no. 2 (1986): 97-106.

Bowker Annual of Library & Book Trade Information. New York: R. R. Bowker, 1955- . (annual).

Mann, Peter. "Library Acquisitions: The Economic Constraints." *The Bookseller* (14 June 1986): 2338-44.

Schad, J. "Allocating Book Funds." *College & Research Libraries* 31 (May 1970): 155-59.

Schauer, B. *Economics of Managing Library Services.* Chicago: American Library Association, 1986.

Williams, S. F. "Reporting Book Prices." *Book Research Quarterly* 1, no. 4 (1986): 85-88.

Academic

Collection Development and Management at Cornell. Ithaca, N.Y.: Cornell University Libraries, 1981.

Enikhamenor, F. A. "Formula for Allocating Book Funds." *Libri* 33 (June 1983): 148-61.

Kohut, J. "Allocating the Book Budget: Equity and Economic Efficiency." *College & Research Libraries* 36 (September 1975): 403-10.

Lynden, F. C. "Library Materials Budgeting in the Private University Library." In *Advances in Librarianship*, by M. H. Harris. New York: Academic Press, 1980.

Magrath, W. E. "Allocation Formula Derived from a Factor Analysis of Academic Departments." *College & Research Libraries* 30 (January 1969): 51-62.

McPheron, W. "Quantifying the Allocation of Monograph Funds." *College & Research Libraries* 44 (March 1983): 116-27.

Soupiset, K. A. "College Book Price Information 1985." *Choice* 23 (March 1986): 999-1003.

Public

Bender, A. "Allocation of Funds in Support of Collection Development in Public Libraries." *Library Resources and Technical Services* 23 (Winter 1979): 45-51.

McGarth, S. "A Pragmatic Book Allocation Formula for Academic and Public Libraries." *Library Resources and Technical Services* 19 (Fall 1975): 356-69.

"Public and Academic Library Acquisition Expenditures." In *29th Bowker Annual of Library & Book Trade Information*. New York: R. R. Bowker, 1984.

School

"Book Buying Barely Up in School Libraries." *Publishers Weekly* 227 (17 May 1985): 32.

Halstead, K. "Price Indexes for School and Academic Library Acquisitions." In *29th Bowker Annual of Library & Book Trade Information*, 389-93. New York: R. R. Bowker, 1984.

Special

Norton, R., and D. Gautschi. "User-survey of an International Library's Resource Allocation." *Aslib Proceedings* 37 (September 1986): 371-80.

13

Acquisition— Automation

By now it should be clear that acquisition work involves many details and extensive record keeping. From a collection development point of view, having detailed and accurate records is essential for effective planning. Manual systems have worked well and continue to do so in many acquisitions departments. Computerized systems offer the potential for greater accuracy, more detail, high speed, and faster distribution of results. Figure 13.1 illustrates the acquisition process; each step has already been discussed. If one knows how computers operate, the potential for computer applications in all but two of the steps, numbers 1 and 10, should be clear. In fact, all but steps 1 and 10 have been computerized in one or more systems. Someday, when all library clients have their own personal computers and can access the library's computer system, the request process may also be automated.

Step 2, verification, was one of the last to be computerized. The key was to have access to large bibliographic databases that contained both current imprints (preferably all current imprints) and retrospective imprints. A second factor was the number of searching methods that could be used in all the databases that would be examined. Very often the person making a request fails, or is unable, to provide complete or correct information about the desired item. Lacking complete information, searchers often must employ a variety of search strategies before securing all the needed information. Most of the databases have provided author and title searching, but subject searches are also important in verification work as well as in obtaining series information. While more and more systems now allow some subject searching, they have not proven too satisfactory. With each passing year, the retrospective search capability improves, but most verification work for pre-1960 imprints is still manual searching. A computer system for the antiquarian and out-of-print book trade (Book-Ease) is available, but it is

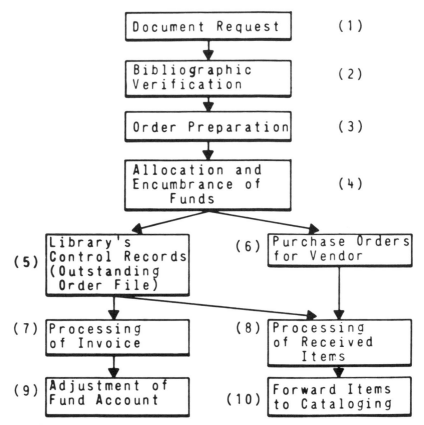

Fig. 13.1. Acquisition process. From Marty Bloomberg and G. Edward Evans, *Introduction to Technical Services for Library Technicians*, 5th ed. (Littleton, Colo.: Libraries Unlimited, 1985), 23.

basically a word processing or spreadsheet system for the individual store. If, and when, enough dealers have systems that contain catalogs and auction book prices, it may be possible to develop an o.p. database, but that will be a long time in coming.

Order preparation, encumbering, account reconciliation, and other accounting functions were among the first activities to be automated. Today most large and medium-sized acquisitions departments have all or most of their bookkeeping functions in some computerized system. Even one-person libraries can be automated if the library can acquire a personal computer. Software exists that would allow automation of the library's bookkeeping routines. Order preparation is generally available in commercial systems or through bibliographic utilities; most major jobbers offer some type of computer-aided order placement. We are getting closer to the day when orders can be accurately and quickly processed just using ISBNs or ISSNs and SANs (see chapter 10).

Receiving items is not yet fully automated. The possibility of books and journals having their ISBN or ISSN printed on them using a bar coding system does hold out the prospect of quick and accurate receipt work. It would then be possible for the computer to check the bar code number against an outstanding order file and indicate on a screen whether the item was ordered and in how many copies. Presently, only the bookkeeping aspects of receipt work are included in most automated acquisition systems.

What to Look for in Automated Acquisitions Systems

Richard Boss, in *Automating Library Acquisitions: Issues and Outlook* reported that the most important features of an automated acquisition system, as identified by librarians, were:

1. Database access

2. Name/address file

3. Purchase order writing

4. Online ordering

5. In-process file

6. Claiming

7. Receiving/paying

8. Funds accounting

9. Management information

10. Vendor monitoring[1]

In *Introduction to Technical Services for Library Technicians*, 5th ed., I also listed 10 functions that would be desirable in any good system. My list is at a more detailed level than the Boss listing, but there is some overlap:

1. Verify the bibliographic data for a requested item.

2. Verify that the item is not already on order or in process.

3. Verify price and availability. (This was a problem until vendors began to automate their operations.)

4. Prepare the purchase order.

5. Encumber the correct amount of money.

6. Produce claims for late or nondelivered orders.

7. Maintain and update the on-order/in-process file.

8. Record receipts of orders and check for completeness of the order.

9. Prepare payment authorization forms for orders.

10. Prepare the necessary financial and statistical reports for the department.[2]

As noted earlier, access to large bibliographic databases is essential for verification work. An ideal system would allow full access to bibliographic data on items in the collection. (This will never be possible unless libraries are able to convert their manual catalogs and other files; the cost of such conversion work is very high and many people question the cost benefit of such conversion activities.) Access to the various bibliographic utilities, to vendor systems (for checking availability and speed of delivery), and to an online items-in-print database would complete the desired system. Although this ideal does not yet exist, it is coming closer to reality. Bowker's *Books in Print* is available online, several vendor systems do allow for searching without order placement with that vendor, and bibliographic utilities are working out their interface problems so that it will be possible to search in more than one.

Libraries currently have a wide selection of systems to consider. Joseph R. Matthews's "Growth and Consolidation: The 1985 Automated Library System Marketplace" identifies 37 automated library systems and 25 companies offering acquisition software programs for microcomputers (personal computers).[3] In addition, he lists six library developed systems that are offered to other libraries. With so many systems to choose from, it would seem to be just a matter of which, not when.

While there is little doubt that automating library activities will continue, there is a need to be cautious and thoughtful in making a selection. One might expect that the greatest concern would be in regard to the new or smaller firms that are entering the marketplace, but an increasing problem is the question of how long there will be support for the system selected. The 1 February 1986 issue of *Library Journal* contained three articles about "vendor abandonment" of automated systems, and an April 1986 *Library Journal* issue carried a news item entitled "Librarians Attack OCLC for Abandoning Systems."[4]

A Total System

Although an automated acquisition system is a great help in collection development and management, it is not the complete answer. Ideally, a total system will be developed that will integrate all aspects of public and technical service. While librarians recognize, at least in theory, that the two services are interrelated and for administrative reasons exist as separate entities, barriers do arise. Manual systems developed and maintained in a department may be viewed as proprietary, and when work space is limited, access to the files by nondepartment members may be difficult. Automated systems tying together a number of terminals can ease problems of access.

Figure 13.2 is a simplified model of the technical services aspect of a hypothetical total library system. The figure helps demonstrate how a set of standard files can be maintained and updated for use by a variety of different functional areas. Libraries of the future will probably adhere to a total systems

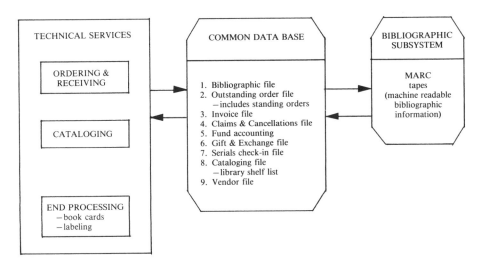

Fig. 13.2. A total technical services system. From Marty Bloomberg and G. Edward Evans, *Introduction to Technical Services for Library Technicians*, 5th ed. (Littleton, Colo.: Libraries Unlimited, 1985), 30.

design in planning automated activities. By adding such public service files as circulation and ILL, the collection development staff can see the total picture more quickly.

Although the total system is still some distance away, even for technical services, some online systems do exist that come close to a total system. Several library organizations exist whose primary purpose is to help achieve a total system. There are four general types of organizations offering packaged computer systems for library technical service processing. They are:

1. Library cooperatives and consortia, which provide for the sharing of materials and expertise. These include organizations like the Research Libraries Group (RLG), which organized its membership to provide the capacity to work together to meet mutual needs through interinstitutional planning and cooperation.

2. Nonprofit computerized bibliographic organizations, which provide their services on a fee basis to members. Examples are Online Computer Library Center, Inc. (OCLC) and Western Library Network (WLN).

3. Commercial vendors with "turnkey" (ready-to-operate) systems for cataloging, materials control, and acquisition. Biblio-Techniques, Carlyle Systems, Inc., and Library Systems Services are examples of commercial organizations selling systems that may be linked to look like an integrated library system.

4. Broker networks or library service centers that arrange for cooperating institutions to obtain automated services at discounted prices. AMIGOS Bibliographic Council (Dallas), SOLINET (Southeastern Library Network), and SUNY/OCLC (State University of New York and Online Computer Library Center) are examples of this group.

Due to their involvement in total systems and increasing networking responsibilities, many of these organizations can now be perceived of as fulfilling a wide variety of roles. Neither significant increases in library purchasing power nor reductions in demand for library services are probable in the near future. Automation is one way for libraries to help resolve these two problems.

Some of the most important developments in automated integrated systems in the last five years have been: (1) the growth in the number of organizations offering services, and (2) the number of subsystems available. A major problem is that almost every organization's system will operate with only one computer – for example, IBM or Apple – but not both. Thus, if the library already has or can gain access to a computer, the range of vendors one can select may not be as large as one might expect or wish. Another important fact is that by mid-1984, all of the major bibliographic utilities had decided to use IBM PCs as their terminals of choice.[5] This decision will mean that software vendors will develop strong lines for library applications on IBM PCs, since there will be many such terminals in place. What must be and is being developed is a system for linking different automated library systems. Currently, the Library of Congress, the RLG, and the WLN – with the assistance of the Council on Library Resources – are testing such a system. When the system is available, a major step toward the ideal integrated system will have been taken.

Before describing some of the large systems, a few words explaining some of the basic concepts are in order. For many years, before there was much work done with automated systems, technical service librarians talked about *centralized processing* and *cooperatives. Centralized processing* was and is viewed as serving the technical service needs of one library system – a school district, a city, a county, or even a state or nation. (For example, much of the technical service work for Veterans Administration libaries and U.S. military post libraries is handled by means of centralized processing.) *Cooperative processing* is usually taken to mean a formal agreement covering some or all technical services being performed for a group of independent library systems. Generally, what is exchanged is information – reducing duplicate work – and occasionally a service (such as card production or order placement). *Networks* and *consortia* are terms that tend to be used interchangeably. There are technical differences in their meanings, but they can be considered to be formal associations of independent libraries which are often used for aid in technical service activities.

Major Online Bibliographic Services

At this time there are three major noncommercial online bibliographic networks in the United States: Online Computer Library Center, Inc. (OCLC), Research Libraries Information Network (RLIN), and the Western Library Network (WLN). Each system started as an online cataloging project but over time has become increasingly technical service oriented, with acquisition and serial components. All three also provide an interlibrary loan component.

However, the cataloging aspect is still the most widely used part of the systems. The three networks were originally established to serve rather different types of libraries. OCLC (whose full name formerly was Ohio College Library Center) was established to serve the needs of colleges and universities in Ohio, RLIN was created to serve the needs of large research libraries, and WLN was primarily for public and private libraries in the state of Washington. Over the years these networks have expanded their membership, taking in or at least serving new members that do not fit the original group profile; however, each database still strongly reflects its initial orientation. There is also a Canadian network, UTLAS.

OCLC

OCLC offers computer support service for cataloging, acquisition, interlibrary loan, and serials control. The cataloging support system is the largest segment of these services and the one used by most libraries. According to the 1984/85 *Annual Report*, there were 6,082 member libraries, including the serials union list participants.[6] The database contains over 12 million records, including MARC records. (About 78 percent of the cataloging data are contributed by member libraries.) In 1984/85, approximately 28,000 bibliographic records were being added to the database each week. Fees for services are based on use of the database, original cataloging contributed to the database, and the number of cards ordered. OCLC also offers accession lists and magnetic tapes of each member library's holdings, as cataloged by OCLC.

Until recently, the primary function of OCLC was to provide online cataloging information. Now it also provides acquisition and serials services, as well as interlibrary loan work. Each library using OCLC constructs a profile of its cataloging needs, including the type of cataloging information required, the number of catalog cards needed for each item cataloged, and any special information required on the card. Searching of the bibliographic database is done by using a CRT terminal with a keyboard. The information displayed on the CRT can be modified to satisfy local needs or to reflect cataloging for different editions of a work. A typical modification is to change the call number to conform to local needs. When the cataloging information on the display meets the library's requirements, the user pushes a "produce" key on the keyboard, telling the computer to produce a set of cards for the library. The cards are produced, filed in alphabetical order, and mailed to the requesting library.

Over the years, library literature has been filled with articles on the various weaknesses of OCLC. OCLC, however, has stood the test of time and is one of the most successful applications of library computerization. Nonetheless, there are some valid criticisms that may affect daily work: (1) duplicate entries for the same item are in the database, sometimes with significantly different information; (2) the quality of some contributed cataloging is poor, causing some libraries to accept only cataloging contributed by the Library of Congress and major libraries known for quality cataloging; and (3) presently, there is no authority control for the form of a name or subject heading. These criticisms, however, are made primarily by large research libraries. The high "hit" rate (large number of items found) and overall quality of the database counterbalance any weaknesses for most libraries. Another problem is that the service center is located in the Eastern time zone, so hours of operation are in Eastern Standard

Time (Monday-Friday, 6:00 a.m. to 10:00 p.m., and Saturday, 8:00 a.m. to 8:00 p.m.).

OCLC's "Acquisitions Subsystem" provides access to the Online Union Catalog from which orders may be generated. There are an online in-process file, automatic transfer of constant data (bibliographic information) to other online files, fund accounting and report generation, as well as receipt and claiming. The multiple purpose "action form" is completed and mailed by OCLC to appropriate sources, vendors, and libraries. Like most systems, it allows one to verify bibliographic information, the library holdings, and the in-process file in one step.

There is no direct automatic transmission with the subsystem of orders to vendors. Like most library-based systems, verification of price and availability is sometimes difficult, since the information may not be in the database, and even if it is, it probably is not current. Overall, with the above limitations, the system covers the 10 features desirable in an automated system. Naturally, if the library is using other OCLC services, the advantage of having everything integrated may outweigh any inherent system limitations. At present (1986) the OCLC "Oxford Project" is underway, and when completed the database and the way libraries use the system will be very different.

RLIN

The second major national computer-based cataloging service, RLIN, is a service offered by the Research Libraries Group (RLG), members being major research libraries in the United States. RLIN was created in 1978 from the BALLOTS cataloging system originally developed to serve Stanford University. BALLOTS is an acronym for Bibliographic Automation of Large Library Operations using a time-sharing system. RLIN is much smaller than OCLC in the number of libraries served—in 1984, RLIN served about 400 libraries—however, it serves nine of the twelve largest research libraries in the United States. As of 1984, the RLIN database contained about 12 million items, including 10 million book records that include MARC cataloging from the Library of Congress. The records are divided into seven files: archival control, books, films, maps, recordings, scores, and serials.

Each library develops a profile of its cataloging needs and its requirements for catalog cards. Cataloging records are also available on magnetic tapes. Information is displayed on a CRT that has a keyboard for communicating with the computer in a manner similar to that used for OCLC.

Special features and services of RLIN differ from OCLC: (1) the database can be searched by subject heading and added entries, which is not yet possible on OCLC; (2) because each library has a separate file in RLIN, a library can compare cataloging information from several libraries; and (3) in addition to catalog cards and magnetic tapes, "catalog worksheets" that contain information found in searches are available. (The worksheets are used in-house to prepare cataloging for input into RLIN.) Many academic librarians believe the quality of cataloging information in RLIN is more reliable than in other major databases, as fewer libraries, and a high proportion of large university libraries, contribute data.

Verification is done online and allows the searcher access not only to the library's own holdings records, but also to the holdings of the Library of Congress and the member libraries. As with online systems based on library holdings and/or MARC tapes, the searcher must remember that failure to find an item does not necessarily mean that it does not exist, but merely that it is not in the database searched. (Similarly, failure to find an item in *BIP* does not mean that it is not in-print.) Clearly, failure to find an item in RLIN or OCLC will mean that verification will be something of a problem, and there is a strong possibility the information is incorrect. Also, remember that generally it is not possible to verify cost information or availability in either system.

One unusual feature of RLIN's system is that a library can maintain, in the acquisition system, not only a record of titles ordered, but also titles considered and rejected. In a large library where many persons are involved in collection development, readily available information about rejected titles can be a time saver. A searcher, by going back and forth between the cataloging and the acquisition databases, can verify very quickly the bibliographic information, the library's holdings, and whether or not the item is in-process.

Preparing the order is then done in the acquisition system. Orders are printed either in the library or at RLG. No matter which approach is used, however, the orders are still mailed to the appropriate vendor by the library—direct electronic order placement with a vendor or jobber is not possible at this time. When the order is prepared, claim periods, the number of claims to be made, and the cancellation notice preparation time lines are input. The system will automatically produce the claims and cancellation notices at the correct times, unless the field indicating that that item has been received is activated. The system, while not perfect, can be of great value in large libraries or research libraries.

WLN

The newest and smallest of the three bibliographic services is Western Library Network (WLN). WLN, like OCLC and RLIN, provides online cataloging information, catalog cards, computer output microfilm (COM), and book catalogs. Originally, membership was limited to the state of Washington, but over the years service has been extended to several Western states. WLN recently added members in Japan and Australia and changed its name to Western Library Network to reflect its expanded scope. In mid-1984, about 140 member libraries were using WLN services. WLN has no plans to expand into a national network. In mid-1984, the database included about three million records and was growing by about 300,000 items annually.

WLN has two major operational systems: the cataloging system and the acquisition system. The cataloging or bibliographic system is noted for its emphasis on authority control of names and subjects. Only Library of Congress (LC) MARC format is used, and WLN conforms to LC's policy in using AACR2 headings with indicated notes and *see* references. The authority control subsystem is interactive, and records can be "called up," edited, or input online.

Perhaps the most complete acquisition subsystem from a noncommercial source can be found in WLN. The system has ordering, claiming, receiving, and payment capabilities for all formats, not just books. Currently, serials are handled through this system, but a separate serials control subsystem is being developed (ordering, check-in, claiming, subscription placement, binding, fund accounting). A circulation control subsystem is being used in member libraries.

The WLN system may be widely used in the future since a company by the name of Biblio-Techniques began to market a turnkey system based on WLN software. The package being offered provides indexed access and maintenance for a full MARC database and authority, and for acquisition and accounting functions. Biblio-Techniques also offers a modified version of the WLN circulation system. The "Acquisition Subsystem" consists of four files: in-process, standing orders, name and address, and account status. These files, combined with cataloging files, allow the library to operate and maintain acquisition records for an item from selection to "on-the-shelf status." One special feature is that the system handles both individual and standing order transactions.

As might be expected, the in-process file is the heart of acquisition subsystems and is based on the MARC record. Online access to the file is provided by purchase order number, or indirectly through what is termed the "Bibliographic Subsystem" (the cataloging subsystem), using any of the full set of "Inquiry" facility access points (including LCCN, ISBN, ISSN, Title Keywords, author, subject, series, corporate heading [author, subject, or series], keywords). The in-process file records can handle all information used in the acquisition process, such as encumbering, claiming, receiving, as well as basic bibliographic data for all types of library materials. Information in this file can be updated online and is available immediately as the order cycle proceeds. The accounting functions of encumbering, invoicing, disencumbering, and disbursing are also provided. Upon completion of the order cycle, a "receiving report" can be produced which contains invoice information on materials received from the vendor and acts primarily as a voucher for payment. The actual creation of order records and the screen displays that are used are described later in this section.

The "Standing Orders File" contains information related to subscriptions or to any other orders that are renewed or reordered on a periodic basis. "Standing orders file" records are maintained in the same format as records in the "in-process file." At the time an order is to be renewed or reordered, a copy of the record in the "standing orders file" is transferred to the "in-process file" and then processed along with other orders. After the order is received and paid for, payment information is copied back to the "standing orders file" so that a payment history can be maintained. Online access to the "standing orders file" is provided directly by purchase order number. Indirect access through the "Bibliographic Subsystem" is available using any of the full set of "Inquiry" facility access points. Serials check-in on an issue by issue basis is not provided by the "Acquisition Subsystem."

The "name and address file" contains the names and addresses of vendors, main libraries, branch libraries, and other locations. "Order and accounting profile" information is also stored in this file. Online access to the names and addresses of libraries is available by library NUC symbol or identification number. Online access to vendor names and addresses is by vendor identification number or mnemonic device.

UTLAS

The University of Toronto Library has been instrumental in starting a Canadian bibliographic network, UTLAS (University of Toronto Library Automation Systems). The library has been involved in MARC work since 1965, and since 1970 it has sold cards produced from MARC tapes to libraries in Canada. The University of Toronto system is tied into a number of other

Canadian networks—for example, UNICAT/TELECAT (a consortium of Ontario and Quebec libraries) and TRIUL (Tri-University Libraries). As of early 1984, more than 600 libraries were using some or all of its processing services. It has a database in excess of 22 million records. The system allows for online editing and for producing printed cards, book catalogs, COM catalogs, acquisition lists, and selective book lists. The major criticism of the system is that until 1977, there was no standard for inputting records; however, since that time, UTLAS has implemented a standardization requirement. The system is beginning to attract American libraries but still is far behind the "Big Three," at least in the United States.

The UTLAS system (Online Acquisitions Control System) is similar to the other bibliographic utilities in that the basic functions are covered—verification to payment. What is special about this system and WLN is that, unlike OCLC and RLIN, it is possible to place many orders electronically: "speedier service through electronic communication with vendors holding UTLAS vendor accounts." Another special feature of UTLAS is its international scope; the bibliographic database for verification covers much more than American publishers' output and publications in the English language. It is true that RLIN, with its research library orientation, is somewhat international in scope, but it cannot compare to a system that includes—in addition to the Library of Congress, the National Library of Medicine, and the MARC tapes—the National Library of Canada, the British Library, four Japanese university libraries, and 600 other academic, public, special, and government libraries around the world. There are more than 15 million bibliographic and authority records in the UTLAS system.

Innovative Interfaces, Inc. (III), has a system (INNOVACQ) that operates on its own or can be fully integrated into the UTLAS system and other utilities, although they do not publicize that fact as openly as UTLAS does. Anyone who has seen a demonstration of INNOVACQ is impressed by the power of the system, including the graphics. Demonstrations of a serials module that they are developing are equally impressive. The major problem from the library's point of view is that the system must be operated on a computer system developed by III. For many libraries the cost is too great, despite the quality of the system.

Service Centers/Broker Systems

The systems just discussed are producers of bibliographic databases and other services. Another type of network exists, one in which the member libraries secure services from a third party. In some instances this is a banding together of many small libraries whose individual needs for such services are small, but when combined with a number of other libraries, are significant. Such a network then contracts for the needed services. For example, when the change to OCLC, Inc., took place, the original Ohio State members formed OHIONET, because only networks could have representation on the new governing board of OCLC. Some examples of networks that supply various technical service capabilities to member libraries, but do not generate services, are New England Library Information Network (NELINET), California Library Authority for Systems and Services (CLASS), Midwestern Library Network (MIDLNET), and Southeastern Library Network (SOLINET).

Variety in organization and function is the primary characteristic of such networks. Most of them were established in the very late 1960s or early 1970s, often for the purpose of providing member libraries with some type of cooperative technical service processing. Some attempted to develop their own automated system – just as OCLC, WLN, and to a lesser extent BALLOTS and UTLAS, have done. Soon it became apparent that it was not necessary to "reinvent the wheel," so some networks attempted to use existing databases, in particular OCLC, more or less to replicate that system, accompanied by whatever were felt to be necessary local modifications. Eventually, existing online services like OCLC allowed for sufficient local variation and it became simply more economical to use the services under contract negotiated by the network.

One important service program of these networks is the training of the technical service staffs of member libraries in the use of the online bibliographic database. This removes the burden of training from the local library and from the central staff of the online service. The networks put on workshops to update skills as well as train new staff, or they provide the material for training. Almost all of these systems provide many other cooperative activities.

Another feature, already alluded to, is that there has been a growing concern about the way major online systems are governed. While all of them started off as cooperative ventures with individual libraries as members, growth in membership created problems of representation. There was and is some concern that the systems would be dominated by the large libraries, who are the major users. The arrangement now in operation for OCLC representation on the governing board is through networks, not individual libraries.

Commercial Systems

As stated earlier, one major change has been in the number of organizations that offer software packages or turnkey systems to libraries. Some of these packages or systems were developed by libraries (for example, Biblio-Techniques and WLN, Midwest Library Service and the Tacoma Public Library's Uniface, and Hewlett-Packard and Virginia Tech's VTLS), while others were developed by companies for the library market (for example, Carlyle Systems, Advanced Library Concepts, and DataPhase). Other systems are library developed and are being marketed by the library (for example, the Pennsylvania State University Library system). Just a sampling of the variety of systems now available can be offered in this chapter.

Midwest Library Service has a system (MATSS) that was developed at the Tacoma Public Library. At present the system is compatible and can interface with OCLC and WLN. By means of the interface system, a library can verify, order, claim, and handle fund accounting. It can also produce catalog cards and spine labels. Since the system is available through Midwest Library Service systems, the IBM PC is the system of "preference," although other intelligent terminal systems can be employed.

DataPhase and CL Systems, Inc. (CLSI) are examples of independent systems. DataPhase's system operates as a complete package covering most library functions that can be automated economically at the present time: circulation, reserve book room, technical services (cataloging), acquisitions, bookings (audiovisual), and backup security. DataPhase provides for system interface with RLIN, OCLC, and others for bibliographic data.

A special feature of CLSI's system is its routing subsystem. It allows for the tracking of an item. This subsystem could be used to route periodicals and other materials to staff members, as well as to monitor the length of time the items are held. Very often a person receives an item, does not immediately have time to read it or examine it in detail, sets it aside for future use, and then forgets about it. The subsystem, with its time element, could alert the person responsible for routing items that an item has been "forgotten."

R. R. Bowker tried to market the Bowker Acquisition System (BAS) with access through BRS (Bibliographic Retrieval Services). The system was to allow ordering from "vendor of choice." Limited success in marketing the system caused Bowker to drop BAS. However, it is still possible to search BIP online through BRS.

Baker and Taylor (as one example of a vendor system) has several automated acquisition systems available: LIBRIS II™ is a system tied into the Baker and Taylor mainframe computer system, and several variations under Bata Systems™ are designed to allow libraries to use their computer systems.

LIBRIS II™ is a more fully developed version of the LIBRIS™ system. Searching is done in the approximately 350,000-title database created by Baker and Taylor. The database is updated weekly, much as the Bowker BBIP is, and reflects the most recent status of a title. Orders can be generated online and electronic order placement starts Baker and Taylor fulfillment procedures within 24 hours, thus saving significant time, especially on rush orders. The system allows for fund accounting and is capable of retaining both the current and previous years' budgets for reconciliation purposes. A warning system is incorporated into accounting systems to protect against overspending a fund. Posting a receipt and backorder information is automatically handled for Baker and Taylor orders. (Note: The system can be used to print orders for other vendors.)

Three services are available under the Bata SYSTEMS™ program: (1) Title Search and Order; (2) Full Acquisition System; and (3) Title Confirmation Service. Title Search and Order is an online service that allows the library to search Baker and Taylor's database, order electronically from Baker and Taylor, and print order slips using an asynchronous terminal, a 300- or 1200-baud modem, and a printer. The Full Acquisition System is a combination software package and online service that enables the library to control all ordering, fund accounting, and report functions by using a personal computer. Hardware requirements are a single disk drive computer with a 64-256K RAM and hard disk with a minimum storage capacity of 10 megabytes using either a MS/DOS or C/PM operating system (for example, IBM PC/XT, Texas Instrument's Professional, the Tandy 2000, or the Kaypro 10), a 1200-baud modem, and an 80-column printer. The Title Confirmation Service is a software package for personal computers that allows book orders to be keyed in by ISBN and sent on telephone lines toll free to Baker and Taylor. Bibliographic data are transmitted back to the library for onsite printing of slips and title confirmation. Unfortunately, at the present time this service will work only with IBM, Apple, or TRS-80 personal computers (single disk drive and 64K RAM). A library must also have a 1200-baud modem and an 80-column printer.

One other service from Baker and Taylor (that became available in 1984) is the Bata PHONE.™ This device is a hand-held data terminal which allows libraries that do not own IBM, Apple, or TRS-80 personal computers to place electronic orders with Baker and Taylor. It is a small battery powered device that attaches to a telephone using an acoustical coupler. Orders are placed using the ISBN and up to 340 titles per order are possible. Baker and Taylor mails a printed acknowledgment of the order within 24 hours of receipt of the order. It also offers, as an optional feature, to send an individual order slip for each title to the library.

Future Developments

What about the future of automated acquisition systems? One does not have to be much of a prophet to predict a trend toward greater and greater growth in the use of online systems. Furthermore, it seems likely that in our lifetime the technical service aspects of our hypothetical total library system will exist with a national online bibliographic database. Positive steps are already being taken in that direction, and even some toward an international system.

Undoubtedly hardware and software technology, especially in the area of the small, relatively inexpensive mini (home) computer systems, will make it increasingly possible for local variations to exist and yet allow the library to tie into regional and national systems. The idea that homes and offices of the future will all have CRTs that tie into the online catalog of a library is no longer just a daydream. In fact, OCLC experimented in 1980 with a local (Columbus, Ohio) cable television company (the system provides subscribers with access to the Columbus and Franklin County public libraries and information about their services and holdings), and libraries elsewhere are also exploring the idea of home access to bibliographic data.

With each new subsystem bringing the total integrated library system closer to reality, collection development can become more effective and efficient. But despite the marvels of technology, there will always have to be intelligent, widely read, humanistically and service-oriented information professionals making the decisions and planning the systems.

Notes

[1]Richard Boss, *Automating Library Acquisitions: Issues and Outlook* (White Plains, N.Y.: Knowledge Industry Publications, 1982), 21.

[2]Marty Bloomberg and G. Edward Evans, *Introduction to Technical Services for Library Technicians*, 5th ed. (Littleton, Colo.: Libraries Unlimited, 1985), 24.

[3]Joseph R. Matthews, "Growth and Consolidation: The 1985 Automated Library System Marketplace," *Library Journal* 111 (1 April 1986): 25-37.

[4]"Librarians Attack OCLC for Abandoning Systems," *Library Journal* 111 (1 April 1986): 21.

[5]Joseph R. Matthews, "Competition and Change," *Library Journal* 109 (1 May 1984): 853-60.

[6]Online Computer Library Center, Inc., *Annual Report 1984/85* (Dublin, Ohio: OCLC, 1985).

Further Reading

General

"Automated Acquisitions." In *Library Automation for Library Technicians*, by J. I. Tracy, 48-69. Metuchen, N.J.: Scarecrow Press, 1986.

Boss, R. *Automating Library Acquisitions: Issues and Outlook.* White Plains, N.Y.: Knowledge Industry Publications, 1982.

Bryant, B. "Automating Acquisitions: The Planning Process." *Library Resources and Technical Services* 28 (October 1984): 285-98.

Chamberlain, C. E. "Automating Acquisitions." *Library HiTech* 3, no. 3 (1985): 27-29.

Hay, V. "Microcomputer Use in a Mainframe Acquisition Environment." *Information Technology and Libraries* 5 (March 1986): 58-61.

Holmes, L. S. "Systems Acquisitions and Vendor Expectations." *Library HiTech* 2, no. 2 (1984): 110-12.

Matthews, J. R. "Growth and Consolidation: The 1985 Automated Library System Marketplace." *Library Journal* 111 (1 April 1986): 25-37. (For several years Matthews has written an annual review of development in library automation.)

Academic

Clark, C. D., and C. L. Feick. "Monographic Series and the RLN Acquisitions System." *Serials Review* 10 (Fall 1984): 68-72, 10 (Spring 1985): 69-75.

Ra, M. H. "OCLC Acquisitions Subsystem at the City College Library." *Library Acquisitions: Practice and Theory* 9, no. 1 (1985): 83-92.

Public

Bills, L. G. "Making Decisions about Automation for Small Libraries." *Library Resources and Technical Services* 29 (April 1985): 161-71.

Dowlin, K. W. "I Am Not Willing to Destroy My Library in Order to Change It." *Library Association Record* 85 (December 1983): 447-51.

Epstein, S. B. "Through the Cracks of Progress?" *Library Journal* 109 (1 May 1984): 872-73.

Heitshu, S. C. "Changing Acquisitions Systems." *Technicalities* 4 (April 1984): 3-7.

School

Bernhard, K. E. "Computer Applications in the Library Media Center." *School Library Media Quarterly* 12 (Spring 1984): 222-26.

Boehmer, M. C. "Computerizing the Small-School Library." *Catholic Library World* 54 (November 1982): 162-65.

D'Anci, M. "Acquisitions with an Apple." *Technicalities* 4 (August 1984): 9.

Earl, B. "An Apple in the Library." *School Librarian* 33 (March 1985): 12-17.

Frechette, J. "Library Acquisitions on a Micro Scale." *School Library Journal* 3 (November 1985): 142-43.

"Technology in School Library Media Centers." *Drexel Library Quarterly* 20 (Winter 1984): entire issue.

Special

Becker, J. "How to Integrate and Manage New Technology in the Library." *Special Libraries* 74 (January 1983): 1-6.

Broering, N. C. "Symposium on Integrated Library Systems." *Medical Library Association Bulletin* 71 (July 1983): 305-42.

McConnell, K. S. "Automation of Gulf States Utility Company Library." *Texas Library Journal* 60 (Summer 1984): 52-53.

Moskowitz, M., and C. W. Alcorn. "Collection Managers Micro." *Technicalities* 5 (March 1985): 11-14.

Veatch, J. R. "Automating Government Documents Orders with a Microcomputer." *Government Publications Review* 12 (March 1985): 137-41.

14

Weeding the Collection

Selection in reverse is one way that some persons like to think about weeding or collection control. Unfortunately, weeding is something most librarians think about but seldom do. Nevertheless, this process is as important as any other in the system of developing collections, for without an ongoing weeding program, a collection can quickly become obsolete. The major function of a library is to acquire, store, and make available knowledge resources; obviously, no library can acquire and store the world's total production of knowledge resources for any current year. Some of the world's largest libraries (the Library of Congress, the British Library, Bibliothèque Nationale, and others) do manage to acquire a major portion of the important items. Nevertheless, even these giants of the library world cannot do it alone. Eventually they are confronted, just as is the smallest library, with three alternatives as they reach their limits of growth: (1) acquire new physical facilities, (2) divide the collection (which also requires space), or (3) weed the collection (which may or may not require new space). Only if a library acquires a completely new and adequate building can a librarian avoid selecting items for relocation.

What Is Weeding?

Weeding (*stock relegation* in the United Kingdom or *deselection* more recently in the United States) has been defined by H. F. McGraw as "the practice of discarding or transferring to storage excess copies, rarely used books, and materials no longer of use."[1] He defined *purging* as "officially withdrawing a volume (all entries made for a particular book have been removed from library records) from a library collection because it is unfit for further use or is no longer needed."[2] The term *purging* applies more to the library's files than to items themselves. Most purged items are not destroyed, they are disposed of in some fashion—through gifts and exchange programs or Friends of the Library book sales, or through "sale" to an out-of-print dealer for credit against future purchases. The end result is that a patron who may later request a purged item will have to use interlibrary loan in order to secure a copy.

Storing, on the other hand, retains the item but in a "second level" of access. Second-level access is normally not open to the client and is frequently some distance from the library. Most second-level access storage systems house the materials as compactly as possible in order to handle the maximum number of items. Generally, a library staff member retrieves the desired item from storage. Depending upon the storage unit's location and the library's policy, the time between client request and receipt of the desired item ranges from a few minutes to as much as 48 hours. Nevertheless, this arrangement is usually faster than an interlibrary loan.

Before a weeding program is implemented, an evaluation of library policies and goals must take place. This evaluation should also include analysis of the present situation, consideration of possible alternatives, feasibility of a weeding program in terms of all library operations, faculty cooperation, types of libraries involved, types of materials collected, and (a very important factor), cost. Some of the data for the weeding program should have come from the collection evaluation activities that the selection officers and others have undertaken on a regular basis. An active (i.e., ongoing) weeding policy should be part of the library's collection development policy. Selection and weeding are similar activities: first, they are both necessary parts in an effective collection development program, and second, both require the same type of decision-making rules. The same factors that lead to the decision to add an item can also lead to a decision to remove the item sometime later. Book selection policy will determine weeding policy.

Selection policies, if properly prepared, will help reduce the weeding problem by controlling growth. Nevertheless, the time eventually will come when something will have to be done to control the growth of the collection. Either there will be no more space in the stacks or access to the material will have become so cumbersome that most clients fail to find what they need. When this happens some hard, costly decisions will have to be made: build a new building, split the collection, or weed it. These three major alternatives are time-consuming and expensive processes. A policy of continuous weeding will be much more effective in the long run. Lazy librarians, like lazy gardeners, will find that the weeding problem only gets larger if nothing is done.

One piece of library folklore helps slow down or stop many weeding programs. I have never met anyone who actually has had the following happen, but everyone agrees that it does happen:

1. No matter how strange an item may seem, at least one person in the world will find it valuable.

2. No matter how long a library keeps these strange items, 10 minutes after one of them has been discarded, the one possible user in the world will walk in and ask for that item.

The basic rule seems to be that one person's garbage is someone else's greatest treasure. This is the fundamental problem confronted by collection development staffs every day, and when the collection is based upon current user needs, weeding can be a major activity as those needs change. Some years ago Eugene Garfield discussed weeding in *Current Contents*, and noted that

> weeding a library is like examining an investment portfolio. Investment advisors know that people don't like to liquidate bad investments.... Just like frustrated tycoons, many librarians can't face the fact that some of their guesses go wrong. They continue to throw good money after bad, hoping like so many optimistic stockbrokers that their bad decisions will somehow be undone. After paying for a journal for ten years, they rationalize, *maybe* someone will finally use it in the eleventh or twelfth year.[3]

Type of Library Background

Because different types of libraries have significantly different clientele and goals, we will look at them from slightly different points of view. Although the basic problems, issues, and methods of weeding apply to all libraries, variations occur in what is done with the "weeds" after they have been pulled.

The Public Library

The purpose of the public library may be viewed as supplying those library materials that meet the current needs and interests of a very diverse community of users. In the public library, demand for materials should be an important factor influencing selection and weeding; therefore, materials no longer of interest or use to the public are the ones that should be considered for storage or discard. Storage is usually considered only for large municipal public libraries whose collections include research materials. As for discarding, it has been estimated that a complete turnover in public library collections should take place once every 10 years, although actual practice probably falls far short of that goal. If storage is contemplated, this usually means separating the little-used books from a working collection that will receive a high degree of use, and then discarding duplicates, worn out volumes, and obsolete material. It is said that if a collection contains many items of little interest, those that are useful will not be so readily visible or accessible. Costs involved in maintaining a large collection are also a consideration.

Two books are especially useful in planning public library weeding projects: Stanley J. Slote's *Weeding Library Collections—II*, second edition, and Joseph P. Segal's *Weeding Collections in Small and Medium-Sized Libraries: The CREW Method*.[4] Both draw upon circulation data, with Slote's system relying almost exclusively on circulation data to identify possible weeding candidates. Segal's system uses age of the publication, circulation data, and several subjective elements he labels MUSTY (M = misleading, U = ugly [worn out], S = superseded, T = trivial, and Y = your collection no longer needs the item). The CREW in Segal's title represents *C*ontinuous *R*eview *E*valuation and *W*eeding. Ideas and methods described in both books can be used in other small libraries, especially school media centers.

The Special Library

Special libraries have had to exercise the most stringent weeding policies because of strict collection size limitations, usually the result of a fixed amount of storage space. Paula M. Strain examined the problem of periodical storage and cost of industrial floor space and found that the cost is so high that libraries must make very efficient use of each square foot.[5] The library in such a situation is examined with the businessperson's eye toward economy and efficiency. Also, the collections of such libraries often comprise technical material, much of it in periodical format with a rapid and regular rate of obsolescence. The major concern of special libraries is meeting the current needs of their clientele. In such a situation, weeding materials is easier because of the comparatively straight-forward and predictable use patterns, the homogeneous nature of the clientele and its small size, and the relatively narrow goals of the special library. Weeding is done with little hesitation because costs and space are such prime considerations. Many of the bibliometric measures described in an earlier chapter can be valuable in setting up weeding programs in special libraries. A recent book addressing the special requirements of weeding in some types of special libraries is Ellis Mount's *Weeding of Collections in Sci-Tech Libraries*.[6]

The Academic Library

Traditionally, the purposes of the academic research library have been to select, acquire, organize, *preserve* (this has had special emphasis), and make available the full record of human knowledge. Demand for a book has not been considered a valid measure of its worth in these institutions, since many books are—or may be—of research value, even if little used. Why then are weeding programs being considered in the context of the academic library? The role of the college and university library is changing. Whenever change of role is discussed, the information explosion is cited as one cause. It is clear to most collection development staffs that it is futile to expect any one institution to locate and acquire all of the printed matter that is coming into existence. Nor can they organize it, house it, or make it readily accessible to their public. (No one person can manage to absorb all the relevant material that would supposedly be available, even if everything, in fact, were being collected and preserved.) Several of the articles that can be of assistance in developing a weeding program in an academic library are discussed later in this chapter.

School Media Centers

School libraries and media centers are more highly structured in their collection development practices than other types of libraries. In most schools and school districts, the library's funds are expended with the advice of a committee made up of teachers, administrators, and librarians. The need to coordinate collection growth with curriculum needs is imperative. Generally speaking, media centers have a very limited amount of space; thus, when there is a major shift in the curriculum (new areas added and old ones dropped), the library must remove (weed) most of the old material. To some degree, the school's problems in weeding are lessened by the fact that usually other community libraries or a larger school district library exist to serve as a major back-up resource.

In addition to the Slote and Segal books, two excellent and fairly recent articles about weeding school media collections should be consulted when planning a school media weeding project: Anita Gordon's "Weeding: Keeping Up with the Information Explosion," and the Calgary Board of Education, Educational Media Team's "Weeding the School Library Media Collection."[7] Gordon's article, although short, does provide a good illustration of how one may use some "standard" bibliographies (*Senior High Catalog*, for example) in a weeding program. The Canadian article provides a detailed, step-by-step method for weeding the school collection.

Why Weed?

Several important reasons are almost always cited for weeding:

- To save space

- To improve access

- To save money

- To make room for new materials

These are the theoretical reasons that one finds stated in the literature. If the volume of literature is any indication of the degree to which weeding is practiced, there would be no need for conferences and workshops on the subject. Unfortunately, librarians tend to write more about weeding (and cooperative networks) than they work at implementing the concept(s). In part, this is because theory and the real world do not exactly coincide. Often, from a realistic point of view, no other solution to space problems suggests itself except weeding. Existing space is filled, and there is no more space in the library, which means that something must go. If C. N. Parkinson had written about libraries, he probably would have proposed a collection development law—collections expand to fill the space available.

In 1944, Fremont Rider determined that between 1831 and 1938, American research libraries doubled the size of their collections every 16 years, an annual growth rate of 4.25 percent.[8] Since then, studies have shown a gradual decrease in the annual growth rate (to about 2.85 percent); nevertheless, libraries often reach their limits of growth. The implications of an annual growth rate are fairly obvious. In addition to the problem of limited shelf space, rapid growth of library collections leads to several other problems: (1) existing space is often not used efficiently, (2) obtaining additional space is expensive, and (3) servicing the use of collections becomes difficult because of undifferentiated access to materials of all ages, types, and subjects.

Do theory and practice concerning saving space coincide? Very definitely! Compact storage systems do, in fact, save space. The conventional rule-of-thumb allows for 15 volumes per square foot (500,000 volumes thus would require more than 33,000 square feet). A compact shelving system using a sliding shelf arrangement can handle 500,000 volumes in slightly more than 14,000 square feet—a savings of more than 50 percent (an average of about 35 volumes per square foot). Using a rail system of moving ranges, such as "Space Saver," savings of more than 80 percent can be achieved; less than 7,000 square feet can house one-half million volumes.

Obviously, a price must be paid for saving space: special shelving costs more than conventional systems. It is interesting to note, however, that Ralph Ellsworth, in *Economics of Book Storage in College and Research Libraries*, noted that conventional systems are also very expensive.[9] Although his 1969 cost figures have not been updated, the relationships still hold: conventional shelving, $1.31 per volume; sliding shelves, $1.24; moving range system $0.91. Thus, one aspect of cost can be lowered by using a compact storage system; however, the cost is only for the building and shelving. A number of other important cost factors must be considered.

One basic theme of this book is that libraries exist to provide service. Archival libraries provide service, so our discussion naturally includes them, since they, too, eventually run out of space. However, service and size frequently do not go together. Anyone who has used a major research library knows that it takes time and effort to locate desired items. Often, such a library will be the only location for certain materials, which is clearly an important service; however, very few clients claim that such libraries are easy or convenient to use. Generally speaking, people still like (or at least are made to think that they like) everything to be convenient and easy-to-use. Thus, it is possible that a smaller, well-weeded collection will be viewed as providing better service than a larger collection—so long as it has what patrons want.

Is there improved access? Here theory and practice start to diverge. Some staff members and patrons would give enthusiastically positive answers. Others would be equally definite in their negative response. For those who require quick, easy access to current materials, the thoughtfully weeded collection becomes ideal. Dated, seldom used materials are out of the way and, perhaps, the cards may even be out of the main public catalog. If the material one wants falls into the right category, it may take twice as long to determine whether or not the library owns the item in question. Furthermore, it may take several days to see the desired material if it must be retrieved from a remote storage area. Thus, the answer to the question of whether weeding improves access is sometimes yes, sometimes no.

Finally, does weeding save money? Here the answer is probably no. Theory and reality are far apart at this point. As indicated, the cost per volume stored is usually lower using a compact storage system. However, a number of other important costs should be examined. For instance, it is possible quickly to reduce the size of a collection by some arbitrary figure or percentage. One method of weeding in a public library would be to withdraw all books published before 1920 (or some other date) that have not circulated in the past five years. Unfortunately, just withdrawing the items from the shelves does not complete the process. All the public and internal records must be changed to reflect the new status of the withdrawn books. For each item removed from the active collection, all library records for the item either must be removed or have the new status recorded on them. Automated catalog formats do allow for more rapid record updating; however, there are still some labor costs to consider.

In addition to the cost of record modification, one must consider the cost of deciding which items to remove, the cost of collecting and transporting them to their new location, and, if they are stored, the cost of recovering them when required. Even if the system of storage is less expensive per volume than conventional stacks, these hidden costs can quickly mount well beyond the apparent savings. Another cost, too often overlooked, is the cost to patrons of having delayed access to desired materials and even the loss of good public relations. Despite the cost factors, however, every library will eventually be confronted by some type of weeding program. One detailed cost model for storage and weeding programs in academic libraries was developed by the University of California. The major features of the model are described in Gary S. Lawrence's "A Cost Model for Storage and Weeding Programs."[10] Anyone planning a large-scale weeding and storage project should read this article.

Almost every large library has some form of weeding program. It may not be called a weeding program, but the effect is the same. Yale University, for example, boxed certain classes of material after they were acquired and processed—they called it *book retirement*. The University of California, Los Angeles, library system has something called the TOE (temporary one entry) system. Here the order slip with an accession number is filed in the public catalog, and the book is shelved by accession number. Books in this system are not classified and are, therefore, separately housed. Other libraries use "brief listing" or some other labels and processes that, in effect, create storage collections of limited access. Most of these systems are not viewed as methods of controlling collection growth. If they were, perhaps librarians would be more receptive to the idea of weeding, and the items going into these collections would be reviewed more carefully.

Barriers to Weeding

Weeding is a process to which everyone gives lip service, but few librarians are able or willing to practice the art. A story of questionable veracity, but one to the point, concerns a teacher of book selection who insisted that there was only one possible test to determine a person's suitability to be a librarian. The test would be conducted in a doctor's office and the candidate librarian's blood pressure would be taken on arrival at the office. The person would then be given a new book and told to rip out one page and throw the book in a waste basket. If the candidate's blood pressure were to rise above the first reading, that individual could not be a librarian. True or not, the story does emphasize one of the most significant barriers to weeding—the psychological one.

Some of the most frequent excuses for not weeding are:

- lack of time

- putting it off

- fear of making a mistake

- fear of being called a "book burner"

These reasons are, to a greater or lesser extent, psychological. No matter how long the book about to be weeded has remained unused, a librarian's reaction may be that someone will need it tomorrow. Also, an unused book or audiovisual raises two important questions: why wasn't it being used? and why did the library buy it in the first place? Just like anyone else, librarians are reluctant to admit that a mistake has been made. The possibility of erroneously discarding some books will always exist. But to use this fear of making a mistake as the reason for not weeding a collection is inexcusable.

Another barrier, which is political as well as psychological, comes from patrons and governing boards. An academic library may feel that it needs to institute a weeding and storage program, but fail to do so because of faculty opposition. If past experience is any indication, one can count on everyone being in favor of weeding the collection; but they are reluctant to have their areas of interest extensively weeded. Sometimes librarians assume that there will be opposition and, therefore, never suggest such a program. There will naturally be opposition; however, if the issue is never raised, there is no chance of winning support. The possibility also exists that assumed strong opponents will not materialize and that persons one least expects will turn out to be strong advocates. Certainly, any weeding and storage problems will cause some inconvenience to some users. Fear of political consequences has kept many weeding programs from being proposed.

Related to the political barrier is the problem of size and prestige. Many librarians, library boards, and users rate libraries by size, the "bigger the better." This brings us back to the epigraph of this book: "No library of a million volumes can be all BAD!" Quantity does not ensure quality. Collecting everything and throwing nothing away is much easier than selecting and weeding a collection with care. We risk no political opposition, our prestige remains high, and only the taxpayers and patrons are hurt.

Practical barriers to weeding also exist. Time can be a practical as well as a psychological barrier to weeding. Even the processes of identifying the most suitable criteria to employ, and then developing and selling a useful weeding program, require significant amounts of time. Beyond this is the time required to train the staff to pull the "weeds," to change the records, and finally, to dispose of the "weeds." With a small library staff, it will be very hard to find the time to undertake a major weeding project. This is one excellent reason for having a continuous program—there will be no need for a *major* program. For any library to start a weeding program is, inevitably, a major project. After the first project is finished, an ongoing procedure can and should be implemented as part of the normal workload. The best way to approach a major project is to seek special funds and extra, temporary staff to support the work. In the section on criteria for weeding, we will discuss further the practical aspects of deciding which criteria to use in selling the project, and in training staff.

Occasionally, legal barriers to weeding are encountered. Although not a frequent problem, when it does arise, it is very difficult to handle. This is particularly true in public-supported libraries where regulations govern the disposal of anything purchased with public funds. In some cases, no disposal is allowed, whereas in other instances, the material must be sold (often by means of bids or auctions). Any means of disposal that gives even the impression of "government book burning" will cause public relations problems and should be avoided, even if legal.

Criteria for Weeding

Weeding is not an overnight process, and it is not a function that can be performed in isolation from other collection development activities. Several factors must be considered, including the library's goals, whether the funds for buying more satisfactory titles are available, the relationship of a particular book to others on that subject, the degree to which the library is to function as an archive, and the possible future usefulness of a book. Only when one considers all the factors can a successful weeding program be developed.

Once the need for a weeding policy is recognized, several lists of criteria can help in deciding which items to weed. The following fairly comprehensive list was compiled by H. F. McGraw:

- Duplicates

- Unsolicited and unwanted gifts

- Obsolete books, especially science

- Superseded editions

- Books that are infested, dirty, shabby, worn out, juvenile, etc.

- Books with small print, brittle paper, and missing pages

- Unused, unneeded volumes of sets

- Periodicals with no indexes[11]

Of course, the mere fact that a book is duplicated or worn out does not necessarily mean that it should be discarded. Past use of the item should be the final, deciding factor. Also, some consideration should be given to the question of whether it will be possible to find a replacement if that is what is required. The books and articles cited earlier provide additional criteria.

Three broad types of criteria can be discerned regarding the weeding of books: physical condition, qualitative worth, and quantitative worth. Physical condition, for most researchers, is not an effective criterion. In most cases, poor physical condition results from overuse rather than nonuse. Thus, books in poor condition are either replaced or repaired. (There is little indication in the literature on weeding that "poor condition" is intended to cover the brittle paper problem. As will be discussed in a later chapter on preservation, brittle paper is a major problem.) Consequently, if condition is used as a criterion, only a few items will probably be withdrawn unless brittle paper is included, in which case large numbers of books would be candidates.

Qualitative worth as a criterion for weeding collections has been employed, but because of the highly subjective nature of value judgments, this generally has not been effective. In essence, the same factors governing the selection of a title are in effect when weeding. Is it possible for the person who selected an item some years ago to say, now, "remove" it? The answer is yes, but all of the psychological barriers to weeding come into play. Probably the best way to employ this method is to use a group decision process, and in this case, patrons ought to be consulted, even if it is just a storage decision.

Any group assessment will be slow, however, and it has been demonstrated that past usage as a criterion has been as effective as a subject specialist in predicting future use. Also, it is faster and cheaper when the past use data are at hand. We shall explore this in depth later in the chapter, when we review some of the major studies that have been conducted on weeding.

C. A. Seymour summed up weeding problems in "Weeding the Collection" as follows:

> When the usefulness and/or popularity of a book has been questioned, the librarian, if the policy of the library permits discarding, must decide the following:
>
> a) if the financial and physical resources are present or available to provide continuing as well as immediate housing and maintenance of the book;
>
> b) if the book can be procured, within an acceptably short time, from another library at a cost similar to, or lower than, the cost of housing and maintenance within the library;
>
> c) if allowing the book to remain in the collection would produce a "negative value."[12]

The problems that plague monograph weeding also apply to serials. A major difference, however, is that journals are not homogeneous in content. Another difference is that the amount of space required to house serial publications is often greater than that required to house monographs. Thus the cost is often the determining factor in weeding (i.e., although there may be some requests for a particular serial, the amount of space that a publication uses may not be economical or warrant retaining the full set in the collection).

Of course, the poor library patrons must not be forgotten (although sometimes it seems that they are the last to be considered). Limited space is not the only reason that a library collection should be weeded. The pros and cons of patron benefit from an active weeding program are also vital considerations. Based upon personal research projects, I can say that the percentage of librarians who think that a patron should be able to make personal decisions concerning which materials to use (out of all possible materials available, i.e., no weeding) is much less than the percentage who strongly believe that a no-weeding policy is, in fact, detrimental to the patron.

Academic faculty members often lack complete familiarity even with materials in their own subject fields; faced with two to seven million volumes in a collection, how can a student be expected to choose the materials most helpful to his or her research?

Large libraries, particularly research libraries, weed to store rather than discard, and these are two somewhat different processes. Criteria useful in making discarding decisions often do not apply to storage decisions. It is important to recognize that the primary objective of these two different forms of treatment is not necessarily to reduce the total amount of money spent for library purposes. Instead, the primary objective is to maximize, by means of economical storage facilities, the amount of research material made available to the patron. Two fundamental considerations, then, are involved in a weeding for storage program: (1) how will books be selected for storage? and (2) how will they be physically stored?

In 1960, Yale University embarked upon its Selective Book Retirement Program, funded by the Council on Library Resources, to determine how best to cope with the problem of limited shelf space while continuing to build quality research collections and provide good service. The Council outlined the following objectives for Yale in *Yale's Selective Book Retirement Program*:

a) to expedite the Yale University Library's Selective Book Retirement Program (from 20,000 to 60,000 volumes per year) and to extend it to other libraries on the campus;

b) to study (in collaboration with the faculty) the bases of selection for retirement for various subjects and forms of material;

c) to study the effects of the Program on library use and research by faculty, graduate and undergraduate students;

d) to ascertain what arrangements may compensate for the loss of immediate access caused by the program;

e) to explore the possible effectiveness of the Program toward stabilizing the size of the immediate-access collection;

f) to publish for the use by other libraries of the policies, procedures, and results thus discovered.[13]

According to the report, all objectives but "d" were fulfilled.

The decision as to which books would actually be removed from the first level of access to storage was based on:

1. A study of books on the shelves.

2. Value of a title as subject matter.

3. A volume's importance historically in the field.

4. Availability of other editions.

5. Availability of other materials on the subject.

6. Use of a volume.

7. Physical condition.[14]

In other words, selection was based on the *subjective judgment* of individual librarians, some of whom were subject bibliography specialists. The librarians determined that general policies regarding weeding were easier to formulate than those that applied to specific fields, that it was easier to recommend weeding of

specific titles than groups or kinds of books in specific fields, and that unantici-
pated mechanical problems greatly affected weeding procedures. These last problems included:

1. Lack of regularity in weeding (i.e., finding an adequate number of
   faculty and staff members and the time to keep the process going
   satisfactorily).

2. Diminishing returns over a long period (i.e., the longer the program
   existed, the more difficult the weeding process became).

3. The "Ever-Normal-Granary" theory (one of the purposes of the selective
   retirement program was to discover whether a library can control the
   growth of its collection by annually removing from the stacks the same
   number of volumes as it adds); it was discovered that in order for the
   theory to be practical, either fragmentation into department libraries
   must occur, or the library administration must be willing to manage its
   collection and facilities solely on the principle of stabilization—neither
   of which Yale was willing to do.

4. Disagreement among weeders (i.e., the narrower viewpoint of faculty
   due to subject specialty versus the broader viewpoint of the librarian).[15]

Another unforeseen problem was a general feeling of discontent among
faculty members and students. Neither group really understood the storage
problem, and both objected to any type of change. Students particularly disliked
the fact that they could not browse through the storage area.

In their *Patterns in the Use of Books in Large Research Libraries*, revised
edition, Fussler and Simon reported some very interesting ideas and statistical
findings concerning the *usage factor* in selective weeding of books for storage.[16]
Although they recognized that frequency of circulation or use of books is not
always an accurate measure of the *importance* of books in large research
libraries, Fussler and Simon hoped to determine whether some statistical method
could be employed that would identify low-use books in research libraries. They
based their investigation on the assumption that such a system could be used to
identify low- or seldom-used books for storage; for frequently used books, the
concern is to provide good access at the first level. Use/circulation data can be
used for the "first cut," that is, to identify *potential* materials. The final judgment
of what to send to storage or discard must be made by the collection development
staff and other interested persons. Blindly following the usage data can create
more problems than it solves.

The authors concluded that past use of an item was the best predictor of
future use. Given the nature of a large research library, a 15- to 20-year study
period was thought to be best, but a five-year period provided sound data.

Fussler and Simon's study is considered valuable because of their outlining
of factors that affect the validity of comparing criteria (e.g., between two
research collections) for removing books for storage, and because of their
findings concerning the advantages of libraries devising "similar rules." These
factors will be helpful reminders to any library considering a selective weeding
program:

1. Differences between libraries in composition of the collection in specific subject areas.

2. Differences in size of collections.

3. Differences in size of university populations.

4. Differences in nature of university populations.

5. Differences in kind of record-of-past use.[17]

In addition to these factors that affect comparisons, Fussler and Simon's findings indicated that their methods would produce similar percentages of use in a variety of library settings—type, clientele, and collection size. They also concluded that scholars at different institutions have very similar reading interests. Finally, they identified three practical alternatives for selecting books for storage:

1. Judgment of one or a few expert selectors in a field.

2. An examination of past use of a book and/or its objective characteristics.

3. A combination of these two approaches.[18]

Of these alternatives, they concluded that an *objective system (i.e., statistical measure) ranks books more accurately in terms of probable value than does the subjective judgment of a single scholar in the field.* They did recommend, however, that subject specialist faculty review the books that had been selected for storage by these objective means before the books actually were stored.

Richard Trueswell quantitatively measured the relationship between the last circulation date of a book and user circulation requirements, and their effect in turn on weeding.[19] He hoped to determine a quantitative method of maintaining a library's holdings at a reasonable level, while at the same time providing satisfactory service to the user. (His method could also be used to determine multiple copy needs, thus increasing the probability of a user's finding the needed books.)

Trueswell's basic assumption was that the last circulation date of a book is an indication of the book's "value." In his analysis, he determined the cumulative distribution of the previous circulation data (which he assumed represented the typical circulation of a given library), and then determined the 99th percentile, which was used as the cutoff point for stack thinning. By multiplying the previous monthly circulation figures and the distribution for each month after the 99th percentile point was established, he was able to calculate the expected size of the main collection.

In applying this method to a sample from the Deering Library at Northwestern University, Trueswell predicted that 99 percent of circulation requirements could be satisfied by 40 percent of the library's present holdings (i.e., 60 percent of the holdings could be removed to storage without significantly affecting the users).[20] Trueswell did admit that many of his basic assumptions were questionable and that only through future research can more reliable information be obtained. Additional research has in fact been generally supportive of his results.

Another study of note is Aridamen Jain's 1968 investigation, *Report on a Statistical Study of Book Use*, another quantitative study of book use, but one based on very different assumptions than the two studies described above.[21] Although his statistical manipulations may completely baffle a nonstatistician, the theory behind his method of measuring book use is easily understood. The purpose of his study was to examine mathematical models and statistical techniques for determining the dependence of circulation rate on a book's age, as well as on certain other characteristics. He hoped to indicate that the *age* of a book is the most significant variable both in predicting rates of monograph usage and in deciding which books should be taken from the first level of access and transferred to storage. He reviewed other studies concerned with determining whether the frequency with which groups of books with defined characteristics are likely to be used in a research library can be predicted by statistical methods. He hoped to point out by comparison that the probability of a book's not being used is an efficient method of predicting use by taking into account the age of the book.

Jain's model seems to be particularly valuable in selective weeding for two reasons. One is that, contrary to the "total library collection" sampling method used by Fussler and Simon in their studies, Jain, like Trueswell, derived his data from all of the books checked out for a *specific time period* (i.e., without regard to the total library collection). Jain felt that this method was superior to that used by Fussler and Simon. Although their method ensures the gathering of information on the *same* books over a longer period of time, his method is much more conducive to a statistical design and data collection—missing data and lack of control are no longer problems. A second reason for this model's importance is that by using the specific time period sampling method, *relative use* of books within the library can be determined. Using the method of Fussler and Simon, this is not possible. Jain felt that the relative use concept was more efficient in studying the usage of books than the collection method.

Many other weeding studies have been conducted, and they all generally agree that weeding based on past use data provided the most satisfactory results. Although most of the studies were geared to academic libraries, Stanley Slote found that the method *also worked in public libraries*. It should be noted that a British study by J. A. Urquhart and N. C. Urquhart has taken exception to these findings, especially for serials.[22] As so many reports conclude, further research is needed; however, in this case, past usage is a reasonable criterion if one is weeding for storage. On the other hand, the questions raised by the Urquharts would seem to indicate that librarians should go slow in applying the past usage criterion when selecting items for purging.

Almost every conceivable combination of "objective" criteria has been investigated at one time or another in hope of finding the best one for weeding. Language; date of publication; subject matter; frequency of citation; and listing in bibliographies, indexes, and abstracting services have all been tried. Citation analysis and presence or absence of indexing or abstracting have usually been used with serials and periodicals.

The preponderance of evidence points to the past use criterion as the one most reliable for weeding for storage. If the library has a circulation system that leaves a physical record of use in each book or if it has a memory store (automated system) that can easily be used, there will be little difficulty.

Unfortunately, over the past 20 years, many libraries have switched to circulation systems that do not allow easy or economical access to usage data. An automated circulation system is capable of providing the needed information but few, if any, contain a deselection module.

Records Retention

Some information professionals in a special library or information center environment find themselves in charge of the organization's paper files (the organization's archive). Just as print and audiovisual collections eventually exceed the space available, so do company files. When this happens, the equivalent of the library environment weeding process takes place. In the business setting, and when dealing with the organization's records, the term used for the process is "retention." A retention program, developed by the person in charge of the files (information specialist, librarian, or records manager) is designed to meet several objectives:

1. Assure protection of the organization's vital records.

2. Retain records of value or historical interest.

3. Restrict storage equipment and floor space, in high-cost areas, to active records.

4. Store inactive records in low-cost storage facilities.

5. Release reusable materials—audiotapes, magnetic tapes, or floppy disks, for example—as quickly as possible.

6. Destroy records that have served their purpose.

With only slight rewording, these objectives could be applied to many library settings.

Documents are classified in several different ways: as record or nonrecord, as active or inactive, and by value or use. A record is an official document of the organization, while nonrecords are "convenience" copies. With a multiple-part order form, the "ribbon" copy of the order would be a record and all the other copies would be nonrecord. Photocopies, carbon copies, and microforms are almost always nonrecord items. Active records are those which are used in current operating activities and which are consulted on a regular basis. The cutoff between active and inactive is decided by the organization (perhaps one consultation in six months may make a record active); however, the decision is influenced by the amount and cost of available storage space. Normally inactive records are stored away from the main facilities of the organization, often in special warehouses designed to store the inactive records of many organizations. Value is determined by the way the record is or would be used. Typical categories of "value" are legal, operating, administrative, fiscal, research, and historical.

To some extent, the question of when a record has served its purpose and can be destroyed is determined by various national and local legislation. It is estimated that only about 10 to 20 percent of all records retained must be retained for legal reasons. Knowing what that 10 to 20 percent should be can prove to be a challenge. Several guides are available that assist in making retention decisions: *Code of Federal Regulations* (Government Printing Office), *Index to Federal Record-Keeping Requirements* (National Records Management Council), and *Retention and Preservation of Records with Destruction Schedules* (Records Controls, Inc.). The National Records Management Council also publishes *Time Capsule*, which assists in developing a proper historical records collection. Each type of record is listed on a "master retention schedule" which in turn lists the type of document, where it comes from, how long it is to be retained, where it is to be stored, in what form (according to law, some records must be retained in the original, while others may be microfilmed), and how it is to be destroyed.

While not all the issues are the same, there are some striking parallels between records retention and collection weeding.

Summary

One way to overcome some of the psychological barriers to weeding is to develop cooperative programs like that of the Center for Research Libraries (see chapter 16). As long as there is a continuing emphasis on independence and size, our patrons will be badly served. Too much material to buy, too little money to spend, too little space to service and store adequately what we do buy, too few staff members to help bewildered patrons find what they need, and too little time and money to weed collections to a human scale—these are but a few of the problems that librarians face. It is to be hoped that the need to plan *now* for solutions to these problems has been made clear. Clearly, any solution will directly involve the concept of cooperation—whether that occurs in centralized processing, cooperative selective weeding policies, or cooperative storage programs.

Notes

[1]H. F. McGraw, "Policies and Practices in Discarding," *Library Trends* 4 (January 1956): 270.

[2]Ibid.

[3]Eugene Garfield, "Weeding," *Current Contents* 15 (30 June 1975): 26.

[4]Stanley J. Slote, *Weeding Library Collections—II*, 2d rev. ed. (Littleton, Colo.: Libraries Unlimited, 1982); Joseph P. Segal, *Evaluating and Weeding Collections in Small and Medium-sized Public Libraries: The CREW Method* (Chicago: American Library Association, 1980).

[5]Paula M. Strain, "A Study of the Usage and Retention of Technical Periodicals," *Library Resources and Technical Services* 10 (Summer 1966): 295.

[6]Ellis Mount, ed., *Weeding of Collections in Sci-Tech Libraries* (New York: Haworth Press, 1986).

[7]Anita Gordon, "Weeding—Keeping Up with the Information Explosion," *School Library Journal* 30 (September 1983): 45-46; Calgary Board of Education, Educational Media Team, "Weeding the School Library Media Collection," *School Library Media Quarterly* 12 (Fall 1984): 419-24.

[8]Fremont Rider, *The Scholar and the Future of the Research Library* (New York: Handen Press, 1944), 17.

[9]Ralph Ellsworth, *Economics of Book Storage in College and Research Libraries* (Washington, D.C.: Association of Research Libraries, 1969).

[10]Gary S. Lawrence, "A Cost Model for Storage and Weeding Programs," *College & Research Libraries* 42 (March 1981): 139-41.

[11]McGraw, "Policies and Practices in Discarding," 269-82.

[12]C. A. Seymour, "Weeding the Collection," *Libri* 22 (1972): 189.

[13]L. Ash, *Yale's Selective Book Retirement Program* (Hamden, Conn.: Archon, 1963), ix.

[14]Ibid., 66.

[15]Ibid.

[16]H. H. Fussler and J. L. Simon, *Patterns in the Use of Books in Large Research Libraries*, rev. ed. (Chicago: University of Chicago Library, 1969), 4.

[17]Ibid., 125.

[18]Ibid., 208.

[19]Richard Trueswell, "Quantitative Measure of User Circulation Requirements and Its Effects on Possible Stack Thinning and Multiple Copy Determination," *American Documentation* 16 (January 1965): 20-25.

[20]Ibid., 20.

[21]Aridamen Jain, *Report on a Statistical Study of Book Use* (Lafayette, Ind.: Purdue University, 1968).

[22]J. A. Urquhart and N. C. Urquhart, *Relegation and Stock Control in Libraries* (London: Oriel Press, 1976).

Further Reading

General

Cooper, H. "Criteria for Weeding Collections." *Library Resources and Technical Services* 12 (Summer 1968): 339-51.

Evans, G. E. "Limits to Growth or the Need to Weed." *California Librarian* 38 (April 1977): 8-16.

Garfield, E. "Weeding." *Current Contents* 15 (30 June 1975): 26-27.

McGraw, H. F. "Policies and Practices in Discarding." *Library Trends* 4 (January 1956): 269-82.

Seymour, C. A. "Weeding the Collection." *Libri* 22 (1972): 137-48, 183-89.

Slote, S. *Weeding Library Collections—II*. 2d rev. ed. Littleton, Colo.: Libraries Unlimited, 1982.

Wezeman, F. "Psychological Barriers to Weeding." *ALA Bulletin* 52 (September 1958): 637-39.

Academic

Ash, L. *Yale's Selective Book Retirement Program*. Hamden, Conn.: Archon, 1963.

Ellsworth, R. *Economics of Book Storage in College and Research Libraries*. Washington, D.C.: Association of Research Libraries, 1969.

Fussler, H. H., and J. L. Simon. *Patterns in the Use of Books in Large Research Libraries*. rev. ed. Chicago: University of Chicago Library, 1969.

Jain, A. *Report on a Statistical Study of Book Use*. Lafayette, Ind.: Purdue University, 1968.

Lawrence, G. S. "A Cost Model for Storage and Weeding Programs." *College & Research Libraries* 42 (March 1981): 139-41.

Rider, F. *The Scholar and the Future of the Research Library*. New York: Handen Press, 1944.

Trueswell, R. D. "Quantitative Measure of User Circulation Requirements and Its Effects on Possible Stack Thinning and Multiple Copy Determination." *American Documentation* 16 (January 1965): 20-25.

Turner, S. J. "Trueswell's Weeding Technique: The Facts." *College & Research Libraries* 41 (March 1980): 134-38.

Urquhart, J. A., and N. C. Urquhart. *Relegation and Stock Control in Libraries*. London: Oriel Press, 1976.

Public

Mahoney, K. "Weeding the Small Library Collection." *Connecticut Libraries* 24 (Spring 1982): 45-47.

Segal, J. P. *Evaluating and Weeding Collections in Small and Medium-Sized Public Libraries: The CREW Method.* Chicago: American Library Association, 1980.

School

Gordon, A. "Weeding—Keeping Up with the Information Explosion." *School Library Journal* 30 (September 1983): 45-46.

"Weeding the School Library Media Collection." *School Library Media Quarterly* 12 (Fall 1984): 419-24.

Special

Bedsole, D. T. "Formulating a Weeding Policy for Books in a Special Library." *Special Libraries* 49 (May 1958): 205-9.

Fisher, W. "Weeding the Academic Business/Economics Collection." *Behavioral and Social Sciences Librarian* 4 (Spring 1985): 29-37.

Goldstein, C. H. "Study of Weeding Policies in Eleven TALON Resource Libraries." *Medical Library Association Bulletin* 69 (July 1981): 311-16.

Hulser, R. P. "Weeding in a Corporate Library as Part of a Collection Management Program." *Science and Technology Libraries* 6 (Spring 1986): 1-9.

Index to Federal Record-Keeping Requirements. New York: National Records Management Council, 1981.

Retention and Preservation of Records with Destruction Schedules. Chicago: Records Controls, Inc., 1984.

Strain, P. M. "A Study of the Usage and Retention of Technical Periodicals." *Library Resources and Technical Services* 10 (Summer 1966): 291-304.

Time Capsule. New York: National Records Management Council, 1981.

Weeding of Collections in Sci-Tech Libraries. Edited by Ellis Mount. New York: Haworth Press, 1986.

15
Evaluation

How useful is the collection? What are the strengths of the collection? How effectively have we spent our collection development monies? These are a few of the questions that may be answered by conducting a collection evaluation/ assessment project. Evaluation completes the collection development cycle and is closely tied to needs assessment activities. While the term *evaluation* has a number of definitions, there is a common element in all of them related to placing a value or worth on an object or activity. Collection evaluation involves both objects and activities as well as quantitative and qualitative values.

Dozens of people have written about collection evaluation—Stone, Clapp-Jordan, Evans, Bonn, Lancaster, Mosher, McGrath, and Broadus, to name a few (see "Further Reading"). While the basics have remained unchanged, the application of the basics has become more and more sophisticated. Computers have made it possible to handle more data, and in many instances, a wider variety of data in an evaluation project. Bibliographic databases and numeric databases can be used in some very interesting ways that would have been exceedingly difficult, if not impossible, just a few years ago (see, for example, Metz's *Landscape of Literatures*).[1] Despite the assistance of technology and increasingly sophisticated systems of evaluation, as Betty Rosenburg, one long-time teacher of collection development has repeatedly stated, the best tool for collection evaluation is an intelligent, cultured, experienced selection officer with a sense of humor, and a thick skin. Because there are so many subjective and qualitative elements in collection development, Betty Rosenburg's statement is easy to understand and appreciate. Unfortunately, this chapter will not be of help in developing any of the characteristics she identified as important. What it can and will do is to outline the basic methods that can be used in conducting an evaluation project and provide a few examples.

Background

Before undertaking any evaluation project, the purpose(s) and goal(s) should be carefully identified and clearly stated. One definition of evaluation is a judgment as to the value of X, based on a comparison, implicit or explicit, with some known value, Y. If the unknown and the (presumably) known values involve abstracts, or things that do not lend themselves directly to quantitative measurement, there can be differences of opinion regarding the "value." A book's value, or an entire collection's, may be determined on several bases: economic, moral, religious, aesthetic, intellectual, educational, political, social, and so on. The value of an item or a collection can go up or down, depending on which base is used. Combining several bases generates questions of the respective weight (or equality) of each. The point is that so many subjective factors come into play in the evaluation process that it is essential to work through the issues before starting. One important benefit of having the goals defined and the criteria for the values established ahead of time is that interpretation of the results is easier; it may also help minimize differences of opinion about the results.

Although libraries and information centers are interested in determining how they compare with similar organizations, one must beware of falling into an evaluation trap. Like all other aspects of evaluation, the use of comparative data presents a number of significant problems of definition and interpretation. What, for example, does library A stand to gain by comparing itself with library B, except perhaps an inferiority complex—or a delusion, as to its own status. No doubt some libraries are better than others, and comparisons may well be important in discovering why this is so. Yet comparison presupposes a close approximation of needs, as well as that norms developed for several organizations or municipalities approximate optimum conditions; neither assumption is likely to be well founded. While comparisons of libraries may be interesting and even helpful in some respects, a cautious approach should be taken to interpreting the significance of the findings.

Robert B. Downs, who had had many years of experience in surveying library resources, suggested the following in his article "Techniques of the Library Resources Survey":

> From the internal point of view, the survey, if properly done, gives one an opportunity to stand off and get an objective look at the library, to see its strengths, its weaknesses, the directions in which it has been developing, how it compares with other similar libraries, how well the collection is adapted to its clientele, and provides a basis for future planning.[2]

In addition, Downs believed that surveys can be preliminary steps to library cooperation in acquisitions and in sharing of resources. To date, there has been little success in cooperative collection development.

Evaluations may thus be conducted for several additional reasons, including the development of an intelligent, realistic acquisitions program based on a thorough knowledge of the existing collection; a justification for increased fund demands or for particular subject allocations; or the desire to increase the staff's familiarity with the collection. The major purposes of evaluation in education have also been applied to library collection evaluation. J. H. Russell, in his article "The Library Self-Survey," stated that a survey would provide a check of the effectiveness of the library; ... a kind of psychological security for the library staff and for the college faculty; ... a valuable instrument in public relations for the library; ... [and it would] force the library staff to formulate clearly the objectives of the library itself.[3]

By changing the environmental context, the statement could apply to any library.

Purposes of collection evaluation may be divided into two broad categories: internal reasons and external reasons. A number of these purposes are listed below.

Internal Reasons

1. Collection development needs

   • What is the true scope of the collection(s), (what subjects are covered)?

   • What is the depth of the collection(s) (amount and type of material)?

   • What use is made of the collection (circulated and within the library)?

   • What is the monetary value (insurance and capital assessment reasons)?

   • What are the strong areas of the collection (quantitative and qualitative)?

   • What are the weak areas of the collection (quantitative and qualitative)?

   • What problems, if any, exist in the collection policy and program?

   • What changes, if any, should be made in the existing program?

   • How well are collection development officers carrying out their duties?

   • Provide data for possible cooperative collection development programs.

   • Provide data for weeding/deselection projects.

   • Provide data to determine if full inventory of the collection is needed.

2. Budgetary needs

   • Assist in determining allocation(s) needed to strengthen weak areas.

   • Assist in determining allocation(s) needed to maintain areas of strength.

   • Assist in determining allocation(s) needed for retrospective collection development.

   • Assist in determining overall allocations.

External Reasons

1. Local institutional needs

   • Is the library performance marginal, adequate, or above average?

   • Is the budget request for materials reasonable?

   • Is the budget providing the appropriate level of support?

   • Is the library comparable to others serving a similar community?

   • Are there alternatives to space expansion (weeding or "something")?

   • Is the collection "too old?"

   • Is there sufficient coordination in the collection program (do we really need all those separate collections)?

   • Is the level of duplication appropriate?

   • Is the cost/benefit ratio reasonable?

2. Extra organizational needs

   • Provide data for accreditation groups.

   • Provide data for funding agency(ies).

   • Provide data for various networks, consortia, and other cooperative programs.

   • Provide data to donors.

Over the years I have been involved in a number of evaluation projects as a staff member or consultant, and have encountered all of the above reasons in one form or another. Not all the reasons apply to every type of information environment, but most have wide applicability.

Once the library purpose(s) is/are established, and the reasons for carrying out the evaluation are taken into account, decisions must be made about the most effective methods of evaluation. As indicated earlier, a number of techniques are available, and the choice depends in part upon the purpose and depth of the evaluation process. George Bonn's "Evaluation of the Collection" lists five general approaches to the problem of evaluation:

1. Compiling statistics on holdings.

2. Checking standard lists—catalogs and bibliographies.

3. Obtaining opinions from regular users.

4. Examining the collection directly.

5. Applying standards [which involves the use of various methods mentioned above], listing the library's document delivery capability, and noting the relative use of a particular group.[4]

Most of the new methods developed in the past 10 to 15 years have employed statistical procedures. Even the revised standards and guidelines of professional associations and accrediting agencies have employed statistical approaches and formulas in order to give evaluators some quantitative indicators of what is considered adequate. Standards, checklists, catalogs, and bibliographies are also tools of the evaluator. At the June 1986 ALA meetings in New York, there was a discussion of a draft of the *Guide to the Evaluation of Library Collections*, which divides the methods into "collection-centered measures" and "use-centered measures." Within each category a number of specific methods were identified.

In the early 1970s I was involved in a project that required a review of the literature on evaluation of library effectiveness (see "Further Reading"). We examined over 750 articles and reports and from that pool were able to establish six distinctive categories of measures employed to evaluate library effectiveness:

1. Accessibility

2. Cost

3. User satisfaction

4. Response time

5. Cost/benefit ratio

6. Use

Four surprising features emerged from the examination. First, almost none of the 750-plus studies provided a clearly stated purpose for the project. We also found some evidence of strong dissatisfaction with the outcome of some of the studies; in all cases of dissatisfaction a clear statement of purpose was lacking. Second, none of the methods then in use for evaluation was sufficiently sensitive to both quantitative and qualitative issues. No method was completely satisfactory from either the librarians' or nonlibrarians' point of view. (I have often wondered if part of the problem lies in the fact that there had been no agreement as to purpose(s) before the projects started.) Third, most methods placed a high value on circulation and accessibility. The high value was very often at the expense of quality and breadth. Finally, a most surprising finding was that none of the measures then in use, even in combination, took into account a total service program—and I believe that this is still true today. Of greatest importance, none of the measures did (or do, as far as I am aware) take conservation/preservation issues into account. (As is discussed in chapter 17, preservation is a major issue in collection management.)

Impressionistic Methods of Collection Evaluation

What impressionistic techniques for evaluation are employed? (Impressionistic measures would be included in ALA's collection-centered measures.) Some evaluators suggest examining a collection in terms of the library's policies and purposes, and preparing a distinctly subjective report based on impressions of the collection's worth and/or of its problems. The process might involve an overview of the entire collection; it might be confined to a single subject area; or, as is frequently the case, it may involve conducting shelf examinations of various subject areas. Normally, the concern is for estimating such qualities as the depth of the collection, its usefulness in relation to the curriculum and/or research, specifically known deficiencies, and strengths in special collections. Very rarely is the impressionistic technique used alone any more; that is, an evaluator walks into the stacks, looks around, and comes out with a "sense" of the value of the material (although there are stories of accreditation visiting teams doing little more). None of the surveyors who regularly use this technique limit it to "shelf reading." Rather, they prefer to collect the impressions of the library patrons who regularly use the collection, though these views may not be based on precise examinations. (This approach falls into my category of user satisfaction.) By collecting a variety of views one can draw more reliable, but still impressionistic, conclusions. We know that every patron makes such a judgment about the collection—often after only one brief visit. Therefore this approach is important, if for no other reason than that it assures some measure of patron input to the evaluation process.

Frequently this approach is used by an outside consultant, an experienced librarian, or an accrediting committee. The evaluation is based upon information drawn from various sources—personal examination of the shelves, quantitative measures, and the impressions of others more directly connected with the library in question. Subject specialists may be asked to give their impressions of the strengths and weaknesses of a collection in certain areas. This can be done by questionnaire and interview. Less frequently, specialists' impressions may constitute the entire evaluation. In addition, members of the library staff are often asked to give their impressions of the depth and usefulness of the collection in certain areas, and that information is sometimes compared to that given by the outside subject specialist(s).

Library self-studies have also made effective use of the impressions of subject specialists and librarians, again often in combination with list checking and other evaluative methods. One example of an impressionistic collection evaluation project carried out by librarians was done at the State University of New York at Buffalo (see "Further Reading"). The library's subject bibliographers were chosen to make the evaluation, and an impressive set of guidelines was developed. The bibliographers were to make a preliminary statement based on their own impressions of the state of the collection in their fields, and then to check the holdings against various appropriate bibliographies. They were to use their ingenuity in approaching the research collection, and they were to evaluate the book selection procedures, as well as faculty interest and aid. Once the actual data had been gathered, the original statement of impressions was to be re-evaluated. Since many large public libraries employ subject specialists, most special libraries have an in-depth subject specialty, and school libraries can draw on teachers for subject expertise, this method could be used in a variety of organizational environments.

The major weakness of the impressionistic technique is that it is so overwhelmingly subjective. The opinions of those who regularly use the collection as well as views of subject specialists obviously have importance. Impressions may be most useful as part of an evaluation when used in connection with other methods of examining a collection, but their value depends on the objectives of the individual evaluation project, and their significance depends on their interpretation.

Checklist Method of
Collection Evaluation

The checklist method of evaluation has been used by many different evaluators and with many different purposes in mind. It may be used alone, or in combination with other techniques—usually with the goal of coming up with some numerically based statement, such as "We (or they) have X percentage of the books on this list (or these lists)." Outside consultants frequently check holdings against standard bibliographies or suggest that the library do it and report the results. Checklists are a means of approaching the holdings for purposes of comparison. When I am asked to assess a collection in an educational institution, I use checklists as part of the process. Whenever possible, I ask a random sample of instructors to identify one or two bibliographies or "basic booklists" in their subject area that would be reasonable to use in evaluating the collection. The responses, or lack of responses, provides me with some information about each respondent's knowledge of his or her field's publications, and indicates the degree of interest in the library collection. When appropriate, I also use accreditation checklists, if there is a doubt about the collection's adequacy.

Accreditation committees frequently use checklists in evaluation, particularly for reference and periodical collections. The attitude of such committees is, of course, closely connected with the idea of "standards" for various kinds of libraries. The Committee on Standards for College Libraries made the following recommendation in "Standards for College Libraries":

Library holdings should be checked frequently against standard bibliographies, both general and subject, as a reliable measure of their quality. A high percentage of listed titles which are relevant to the program of the individual institution should be included in the library collections.[5]

As collections increase in size, there is less need to worry about formal checking or standard bibliographies. It does no harm, however, for the selectors to take a little time to review some of the "best of the year" lists put out by different associations. Selectors will be able quickly to identify items not selected and take whatever steps are deemed appropriate. Often such lists appear in selection aids and it takes little extra time to review the list and conduct a "mini-evaluation."

Self-surveys by the library staff also frequently make use of checklist methods. The first checklist self-survey was conducted by M. Llewellyn Raney in 1933 for the University of Chicago libraries. This survey used several hundred bibliographies to essentially check the entire collection for the purpose of determining future needs. There is little question that this was a good pioneering effort that demonstrated the value of using checklists in thoroughly examining the total book collection.

Obviously, a wide variety of checklists may be used in any situation. Libraries most often have standard lists of "basic" collections, but there has been a tendency to include more narrow subject bibliographies. Some surveyors have advocated increasing use of periodical and other indexes as additional checklists. Large research libraries (academic, public, or special) might consider using the basic lists to check basic collections, but they are more inclined to use standard subject bibliographies and specially compiled lists. One of the "checks" used in the RLG/ARL conspectus preparation (see chapter 3) employs the specially prepared checklist technique.

Actually, the specially prepared bibliography is probably the best way to go if the checklist method is to be most effective. A library may feel that compilation of a special list is impractical, and therefore may choose to make use of various standard lists. This is an acceptable procedure only if the lists are carefully chosen and used with the individual library's particular characteristics and needs in mind, and if the evaluator is careful in interpreting the results. It should be remembered that unless an examination of a collection is as thorough as, say, the University of Chicago survey, any checklist system is almost always only a sample. Thus the data are only as good as the sampling method employed.

The shortcomings of the checklist technique for evaluation are many, and seven criticisms appear repeatedly:

1. Titles are selected for a specific, not general use, and many more worthwhile titles are omitted.

2. Titles often have little relevance for a specific library's community.

3. Lists may be out-of-date.

4. Many titles that a library has on the same topic may be ignored by the checklist.

5. Interlibrary loan is not taken into account.

6. Checklists are always "approved" titles; there is no penalty for having poor titles also.

7. Checklists fail to take into account special materials which may be very important to a particular library.

A number of these criticisms would require the checklist to be all things to all libraries. All too often there seems to be little understanding that works are not of equal value and may not be equally useful for a specific library. While some older books continue to be well thought of for many years, an out-of-date checklist is of little utility in evaluating a current collection.

Obviously, the time involved in checking lists effectively is a concern when using this method. Spotty or limited checking does little good, but most libraries are unable, or unwilling, to check an entire list. It has been suggested that sampling techniques, in which lists might serve as "polls" or "strainers," might be an effective solution to the time problem. Normally, checklists are used to show the percentage of books from the list that is in the collection. This may sound fine, but there is no standard proportion of a list a library should have. Likewise, comparisons of one library's holdings with another's on the basis of percentages of listed titles is of little value, unless the two libraries have very similar service populations. In a sense the use of a checklist assumes some correlation between the percentage of listed books held by a library and the percentage of desirable books in the library's collection. This may or may not be a warranted assumption. Just as questionable is the assumption that listed books not held necessarily constitute desiderata, and that the proportion of items held to items needed (as represented on the list) constitutes an effective measure of a library's adequacy.

This lengthy discussion of the shortcomings of the checklist method should be considered more as a warning than a prohibition. There *are* benefits from using this method in evaluation. Many librarians feel that checking lists helps to reveal gaps and weaknesses in a collection, that the lists then provide handy selection guides if the library wishes to use them for this purpose, and that the revelation of gaps and weaknesses may lead to reconsideration of selection methods and policies. Often nonlibrary administrators respond more quickly and favorably to information about gaps in a collection when they are identified by using "standard" lists than when other means of identifying weaknesses are employed.

Statistical Methods of Collection Evaluation

Quantitative methods of evaluating a book collection are based on the assumption that a sufficient quantity of books is one valid indicator of quality. For example, this method compiles statistics concerning the number of volumes in the total collection and in its various parts, the expenditures for acquisitions, the relation of this amount to the size of the collection or to the total institutional budget, and other, similar data.

The standard checklists for opening-day collections operated on this premise. J. W. Pirie, when he compiled *Books for Junior Colleges*, stated that a junior college library needed 20,000 volumes to support a liberal arts curriculum.[6] *Books for College Libraries* assumed that a four-year college must have a minimum of 150,000 volumes, 20 percent of which should be bound periodical volumes and the other 80 percent monographic titles.[7] Similar assumptions are made in the ALA Public Library Association's "shorter list," *Books for Public Libraries: Nonfiction for Small Collections*.[8] One source of data (in the United States) for comparative purposes is the national shelflist count. A good review article describing the project and its utility is "The National Shelflist Count Project: Its History, Limitations, and Usefulness" by Joseph Branin, David Farrell, and Mariann Tiblin.[9]

The quantitative method has obvious limitations when it is applied to collections larger than a certain standard's minimum. While quality requires a certain minimum quantity, quantity alone does not guarantee quality. As Guy Lyle unequivocally stated: "The adequacy of the college library's book collection cannot be measured in quantitative terms. To judge a collection as superior or inferior on the basis of the volume of holding is as absurd as rating a college on the basis of its enrollment."[10] Librarians and information professionals in other environmental settings would agree with Lyle, even if their words might vary. The basic weakness in the quantitative method of evaluation lies in interpretation of the statistics when making value judgments about the collection. Often these data are used to compare one library with other libraries or with fixed, external standards. Both comparisons are of limited value.

Comparison with Other Institutions

Interinstitutional comparisons offer no objective criteria for evaluation, because institutions differ in their objectives, programs, and service population. For instance, a junior college with only a liberal arts program will require one type of library, whereas a community college with both a liberal arts curriculum and strong vocational programs will require a much larger collection. Comparing the first library to the second would be like comparing apples and oranges. There is simply no basis for comparison, and no point in it.

Comparisons of libraries are also made difficult, if not impossible, by the manner in which some libraries generate statistics about their collections. On paper, two libraries may appear very similar, yet in reality their book collections may differ widely. Eli Oboler documented this increasingly acute problem:

> One library, without any footnote explanation, suddenly increased from less than twenty-five thousand volumes added during 1961-62 to more than three times that number while the amount shown for books and other library materials only increased approximately 50 percent. Upon inquiry the librarian of this institution stated that, "from storage in one attic we removed forty thousand items, some of which have been catalogued, but in the main we are as yet unsure of the number which will be added. The addition of a large number of volumes also included about one-fourth public documents, state and federal, and almost fifty thousand volumes in microtext."[11]

One is reminded of the aphorism, "figures don't lie, but liars can figure."

It is generally agreed that the adequacy of a library's collection cannot be determined or measured solely in quantitative terms. Number of volumes is a poor measure of the growth of the library's collection in relation to the programs and services it provides. However, when standards are not developed in quantitative terms, budgeting and fiscal officers, who cannot avoid quantitative bases for their decisions, are compelled to adopt measures that seem to have the virtue of simplicity but may be essentially irrelevant to the library's function. It is therefore necessary to develop quantitative approaches for evaluating collections that can be used by officials in decision making, and which retain the virtue of simplicity while they are also relevant to the library's programs and services.

Formulas have also been employed as a way to assess the worth of library collections. Among the formulas receiving considerable attention are those of Clapp-Jordan, Washington State, California State, the ACRL formula for college libraries, and Beasley's formula for public libraries. Advantages associated with formulas include a greater potential for in-depth comparison between libraries and greater ease in preparation and interpretation. The disadvantage is an inability to assess qualitative factors that are important in the relationship between the library collection and patron needs. Furthermore, there is a lack of standard definitions of what is to be measured (e.g., no uniformity in use of the terms *titles* and *volumes*).

Clapp-Jordan Formula

Because there has been widespread disagreement with standards that have been devised, some librarians have developed additional criteria for determining the adequacy of a collection. One example of this type of formula is the Clapp-Jordan Formula, developed in order to have a firm argument for the planning, budgeting, and appropriating bodies with which the authors had to deal. Although formula approaches such as Clapp-Jordan have been accepted, there are always arguments as to whether these approaches best fit the library environment. An empirical study of the validity of the formula by R. M. McInnis (using linear regression analysis) concluded that (1) minimal level(s) of adequacy cannot be conclusively determined, (2) over-prediction or too high results are not produced, and (3) the Clapp-Jordan Formula can serve as a computed guide to minimum levels of library size.[12]

Washington State Formula

Through this formula, a modification of Clapp-Jordan, it is possible to establish baselines for both colleges and universities, since it takes into account both enrollment and program factors. Two Clapp-Jordan elements are not included in the Washington formula: an allowance of 335 volumes per undergraduate major and 12 volumes per honor student. Both elements are subject to wide variation of interpretation, which makes their interinstitutional comparability questionable. The formula used for determining quantitative adequacy of holdings in a unit* of library resources is presented in figure 15.1.

(1)	Units of Library Resources (2)
1. Basic or Opening Day Collection	85,000
2. Allowance per FTE Faculty	100
3. Allowance per FTE Student	15
4. Allowance per Masters Field When No Doctorate Offered in Field	6,100
5. Allowance per Masters Field When Doctorate Is Offered in Field	3,050
6. Allowance per Doctoral Field	24,500

Fig. 15.1. Washington State formula: determining quantitative adequacy of holdings in unit of library resources for colleges and universities. From Washington State Universities and Colleges, The Interinstitutional Committee of Business Officers, *A Model Budget Analysis System for Program 05 Libraries* (Olympia, Wash.: Evergreen State College, Office of Interinstitutional Business Studies, March 1970).

California State Formula

Based on the U.S. Office of Education standards, the California State formula takes into consideration opportunities for resource sharing by libraries in close proximity to one another. These goals are determined by specific, approved fields of graduate study and by the number of FTE (full-time equivalent) students, and are calculated as follows:

1. To a basic allowance of 75,000 volumes, for the opening day allowance of new college libraries and the first 600 FTE students.

2. *Add* 10,000 volumes for each additional 2,000 FTE students.

3. *Add* 3,000 volumes for each subject field of graduate study listed by the Office of Education in application for Title II funds.

*A "unit of library resources" is defined as follows: (1) One volume as defined by and reported to the U.S. Office of Education in the annual Higher Education General Information Survey, that is, "a volume is a physical unit of any printed, typewritten, handwritten, mimeographed, or processed work contained in one binding or portfolio, hardbound or paperbound, which has been classified, cataloged, or otherwise prepared for use. Includes government documents that have been classified and cataloged." (2) One reel of microfilm or eight microcards or microfiche as reported on the same survey.

4. *Add* 5,000 volumes for each approved joint doctoral program.

5. *Subtract* from the total computed 5 percent of such allowance when the college is closer than 25 miles from the nearest public institution of higher education, as determined by the chancellor.[13]

Formula A—ACRL Standards for College Libraries

An ad hoc ACRL committee on revision proposed the following standards:

The library's collection shall comprise all corpuses of recorded information owned by the college for educational, inspirational, and recreational purposes, including multidimensional, aural, pictorial, and print materials.

The library shall provide quickly a high percentage of such materials needed by its patrons.

The amount of print materials to be thus provided shall be determined by a formula (Formula A) which takes into account the nature and the extent of the academic program of the institution, its enrollment, and the size of its teaching faculty. (A volume is defined as a physical unit of any printed, typewritten, handwritten, mimeographed, or processed work contained in one binding or portfolio, hardbound or paperbound, which has been cataloged, classified, or otherwise prepared for use. For purpose of this calculation microform holdings should be included converting them to volume-equivalents. The number of volume equivalents held in microform should be determined either by actual count or by averaging formula which considers each reel or microform as one and five pieces of any other format as one volume-equivalent.)[14]

Formula A is also based on the Clapp-Jordan work and is similar to the Washington State formula. Again, an element used by Clapp-Jordan is not included in the formula, that is, the allowance of 12 volumes per honor student. It added one element that was not in either the Clapp-Jordan formula or the Washington State formula—6,000 volumes per "6th year specialist degree field."

The standards state that "libraries which can provide promptly 100 percent as many volumes or volume-equivalents as are called for in this formula shall, in the matter of quality, be graded 'A'. From 80-99 percent shall be graded 'B'; from 65-79 percent shall be graded 'C'; and from 50-64 percent shall be graded 'D'."[15]

As can be seen from the above examples, academic libraries have made extensive use of statistical tools for the purposes of evaluating collections. Perhaps the outstanding example of public library formulas is K. Beasley's *Theoretical Framework for Public Library Measurement*.[16] Beasley indicated that a statistical reporting system for libraries must have the following features:

1. The expressions should be stated in such a way that they themselves do not set values.

2. There should be a statistical or mathematical formula for each discrete element of a library program.

3. Enough variables must be used to delineate clearly the total pattern.

4. The statistics should state clearly the characteristics of the present — where we are now — and in such a manner as to facilitate forecasts of the future.[17]

Beasley's formula elements are familiar to most librarians, and are as follows:

$$\text{Potential Service } = \text{ B./P . C/P . S}$$

The elements or variables defined by Beasley are as follows:

B = all resource materials (perhaps) weighted

P = population served

C = circulation

S = study or research factor[18]

This formula makes no attempt to measure quality, and bases this on the assumption that quality is primarily a function of a type of personnel.

Usage Methods of Collection Evaluation

Over the past 20 years studying collection use patterns has increased in popularity as a means of evaluating collections. Two basic assumptions underlie this method: (1) the adequacy of the book collection is directly related to its use by students and faculty, and (2) circulation records provide a reasonably representative picture of the use made of the library. Such pragmatic evaluations of collection or "services" have proven distasteful to many professionals. As L. Carnovsky stated:

> In general surveys of college and university libraries, where surveyors have devoted attention to use, they have focused on rules and regulations, physical convenience of facilities, and stimulation of reading through publicity, browsing rooms, open stacks and similar matters. They have not been concerned with circulation statistics, and in fact, the statistics for college and university libraries issued by the Library Services Branch do not include them at all. This is tacit recognition of the fact that circulation is largely a function of curriculum and teaching methods, and perhaps also of the realization that the sheer number of books a library circulates is no measure at all of its true contribution to the educational process. In spite of the fact that Wilson and Tauber advocated the maintenance of circulation

records, Wilson and Swank, in their survey of Stanford University reported: "Because statistics of use are kept for only a few of the University libraries and those that are kept are not consolidated and consistently reported, it is impossible for the surveyors to present any meaningful discussion or evaluation of this significant aspect of the library program."[19]

Usage data, normally circulation figures, are objective and can be employed in making value judgments about individual collections. Moreover, the data are not affected by legitimate peculiarities in the objectives of the college that the library serves. Like the Clapp-Jordan formula, use studies can be tailor-made for any library, rather than forcing the library into a standard mold.

Use studies serve as a useful check on one or more of the other evaluation methods. They are also helpful in weeding the collection. An important factor is to have adequate amounts of data upon which to base the judgment. As computer-based circulation systems become more common, usage data should become relatively easy and inexpensive to gather. An example of a recently published study that made extensive use of circulation data is Paul Metz's *Landscape of Literatures: Use of Subject Collections in a University Library.*[20]

Certainly there are problems in interpreting circulation data in terms of the "value" of a collection. Circulation data cannot reflect use generated within the library, such as of reference collections and noncirculating journals. Even for circulated items, there is no way of knowing how the material was used; perhaps the volume was used to prop open a window or press flowers. Also, the "value" derived by a patron from a circulated item has not been studied enough to make possible an accurate assessment of the collection's worth. For some libraries and research or archival institutions, for example, usage factors are only a small part of the overall mission. The new guide for evaluating collections being prepared by ALA provides a good overview of the advantages and disadvantages of each method outlined above, along with a number of other techniques.

It is clear that much research must be done before collection evaluation can assume its more useful role in collection development. There is no disagreement that collection evaluation is a difficult task, and its results probably will always be relative. Thus, the evaluator must be willing to live with what are, at best, tentative results.

Although no one evaluation method is adequate by itself, a combined approach is most effective. Most evaluation projects now employ several different methods to take advantage of the strengths of each technique. Karen Kruger prepared a guide for the Illinois State Library that was intended to aid in cooperative collection development; it also provides an effective evaluation technique.[21] David V. Loertscher and Janet Stroud's *PSES: Purdue Self-Evaluation System for School Media Centers* offers a multiple approach for examining school media center collections.[22] A comprehensive plan is outlined in Blaine Hall's *Collection Assessment Manual.*[23] When I have served as a consultant on collection evaluation projects, I have found the following steps to be most effective. After goals and objectives are determined:

1. Develop an individual set of criteria for quality and value.

2. Draw a random sample from the collection and examine the use of the items (shelf list sample).

3. Collect data about titles wanted but not available (ILL requests).

4. Keep a record of titles picked up from tables and in stack areas (in-house use).

5. Keep a detailed record of interlibrary loan activities.

6. Find out how much obsolete material is in the collection (for example, science works over 15 years old and not considered classics).

7. If there are some checklists that have some relevance for the library, check them; *but* also do some research concerning the usefulness of these checklists.

8. Relate findings to the library's local goals and objectives.

Collection evaluation is time-consuming as an activity, but only after the task is finished will the staff *know* what strengths and weaknesses exist in the collection. Once this is known, the collection development staff can formulate a plan to build on the strengths and correct the weaknesses. This assumes that the assessment of strengths and weaknesses is done in terms of the library's goals, objectives, and community needs. After the first effort, if the process is retained as an ongoing one, the work will be less time-consuming, and with each assessment the judgment should come closer to the realities of the collection's value.

Notes

[1]P. Metz, *Landscape of Literatures: Use of Subject Collections in a University Library* (Chicago: American Library Association, 1983).

[2]Robert B. Downs, "Techniques of the Library Resources Survey," *Special Libraries* 23 (April 1941): 113-15.

[3]J. H. Russell, "The Library Self-Survey," *College & Research Libraries* 17 (March 1956): 127-31.

[4]George Bonn, "Evaluation of the Collection," *Library Trends* 22 (January 1974): 265-304.

[5]Committee on Standards for College Libraries, "Standards for College Libraries," *College & Research Libraries* 20 (July 1959): 277.

[6]J. W. Pirie, comp., *Books for Junior Colleges* (Chicago: American Library Association, 1969).

[7]H. Voigt and J. Treyz, *Books for College Libraries* (Chicago: American Library Association, 1967).

[8]*Books for Public Libraries*, 3d ed. Edited by C. Koehn (Chicago: American Library Association, 1981).

[9]Joseph Branin, David Farrell, and Mariann Tiblin, "The National Shelflist Count Project: Its History, Limitations, and Usefulness," *Library Resources and Technical Services* 29 (October 1985): 333-42.

[10]Guy Lyle, *Administration of the College Library*, 4th ed. (New York: H. W. Wilson, 1974), 399.

[11]Eli Oboler, "Accuracy of Federal Academic Library Statistics," *College & Research Libraries* 25 (September 1964): 494.

[12]R. M. McInnis, "Formula Approach to Size: An Empirical Study of Its Efficacy in Evaluating Research Libraries," *College & Research Libraries* 33 (May 1972): 191.

[13]California State Colleges, Office of the Chancellor, Division of Academic Planning, *Report on the Development of the California State Libraries: A Study of Book, Staffing and Budgeting Problems* (Los Angeles, November 1970).

[14]American Library Association, "Standards for College Libraries," *College & Research Libraries* 20 (July 1959): 277.

[15]Ibid.

[16]K. E. Beasley, "Theoretical Framework for Public Library Management Measurement," in *Research Methods in Librarianship*, ed. H. Goldhor (Urbana, Ill.: University of Illinois, Graduate School of Library Science, 1968).

[17]Ibid.

[18]Ibid.

[19]L. Carnovsky, "Survey of the Use of Library Resources and Facilities," in *Library Surveys*, ed. M. F. Tauber and I. R. Stephens (New York: Columbia University Press, 1967), 68.

[20]Metz, *Landscape of Literatures*.

[21]Karen Kruger, *Coordinated Cooperative Collection Development for Illinois Libraries* (Springfield, Ill.: Illinois State Library, 1982).

[22]David V. Loertscher and Janet Stroud, *PSES: Purdue Self-Evaluation System for School Media Centers* (Fayetteville, Ark.: Hi Willow Publishing, 1976).

[23]Blaine Hall, *Collection Assessment Manual for College and University Libraries* (Phoenix, Ariz.: Oryx Press, 1985).

Further Reading

General

Aguilar, W. "Application of Relative Use and Interlibrary Demand in Collection Development." *Collection Management* 8 (Spring 1986): 15-24.

Bonn, G. S. "Evaluation of the Collection." *Library Trends* 22 (January 1974): 265-304.

Clapp, V. W., and T. Jordan. "Quantitative Criteria for Adequacy of Academic Library Collections." *College & Research Libraries* 26 (September 1965): 371-80.

Carnovsky, L. "Survey of the Use of Library Resources and Facilities." In *Library Surveys*, edited by M. F. Tauber and I. R. Stephens. New York: Columbia University Press, 1967.

Downs, R. B. "Technique of the Library Resources Survey." *Special Libraries* 32 (April 1941): 113-15.

Evans, G. E. "Review of Criteria Used to Measure Library Effectiveness." In *Reader in Library Management*, edited by R. Shimmer. London: Clive Bingley, 1976.

Lancaster, F. W. *The Measurement and Evaluation of Library Services.* Washington, D.C.: Information Resources Press, 1977.

McGrath, W. E. "Collection Evaluation Theory and the Search for Structure." *Library Trends* 12 (Winter 1985): 241-66.

Mosher, P. H. "Quality and Library Collections: New Directions in Research and Practice in Collection Evaluation." *Advances in Librarianship* 13 (1984): 65-76.

Rossi, P. H., and H. E. Freeman. *Evaluation: A Systematic Approach.* Beverly Hills, Calif.: Sage Publications, 1985.

Russell, J. H. "The Library Self-Survey." *College & Research Libraries* 17 (March 1956): 127-31.

Wiemers, E., et al. "Collection Evaluation: A Practical Guide to the Literature." *Library Acquisitions: Practice and Theory* 8, no. 1 (1984): 65-76.

Academic

Borkowski, C., and M. J. MacLeod. "Implications of Some Recent Studies of Library Use." *Scholarly Publishing* 11 (October 1979): 3-24.

Branin, J., D. Farrell, and M. Tiblin. "National Shelflist Count Project: Its History, Limitations, and Usefulness." *Library Resources and Technical Services* 29 (October 1985): 333-42.

Broadus, R. N. "Use Studies of Library Collections." *Library Resources and Technical Services* 24 (Fall 1980): 317-24.

Cassatta, H. B., and G. L. Dewey. "Evaluation of the University Library Collection." *Library Resources and Technical Services* 13 (Winter 1969): 450-57.

Hall, B. H. *Collection Assessment Manual for College and University Libraries*. Phoenix, Ariz.: Oryx Press, 1985.

Kent, A., et al. *Use of Library Materials: The University of Pittsburgh Study*. New York: Marcel Dekker, 1979.

Lyle, G. *Administration of the College Library*, 4th ed. New York: H. W. Wilson, 1974.

McGrath, W. E. "Multidimensional Mapping of Book Circulation in a University Library." *College & Research Libraries* 44 (March 1983): 103-15.

McInnis, R. M. "Formula Approach to Size: An Empirical Study of Its Efficacy in Evaluating Research Libraries." *College & Research Libraries* 33 (May 1972): 190-98.

Metz, P. *Landscape of Literatures: Use of Subject Collections in a University Library*. Chicago: American Library Association, 1983.

Moran, M. "Concept of Adequacy in University Libraries." *College & Research Libraries* 39 (March 1978): 85-93.

Mosher, P. H. "Collection Evaluation in Research Libraries." *Library Resources and Technical Services* 23 (Winter 1979): 16-32.

Nisonger, T. E. "Annotated Bibliography of Items Relating to Collection Evaluation in Academic Libraries." *College & Research Libraries* 43 (July 1983): 300-11.

Oboler, E. H. "Accuracy of Federal Academic Library Statistics." *College & Research Libraries* 25 (September 1964): 494-96.

Pirie, J. W., comp. *Books for Junior Colleges*. Chicago: American Library Association, 1969.

"Pittsburgh University Studies of Collection Usage: A Symposium." *Journal of Academic Librarianship* 5 (May 1979): 60-70.

"Standards for College Libraries." *College & Research Libraries* 20 (July 1959): 274-80.

Stone, E. O. "Measuring the College Book Collection." *Library Journal* 66 (June 1941): 941-43.

Public

Beasley, K. E. "Theoretical Framework for Public Library Measurement." In *Research Methods in Librarianship*, edited by H. Goldhor. Urbana, Ill.: Graduate School of Library Science, University of Illinois, 1968.

Books for Public Libraries, 3d ed. Edited by C. Koehn. Chicago: American Library Association, 1981.

Goldhor, H. "Analysis of an Inductive Method of Evaluating the Book Collection of a Public Library." *Libri* 23, no. 1 (1973): 6-17.

_____. "A Report on an Application of the Inductive Method of Evaluation of Public Library Books." *Libri* 31 (August 1981): 121-29.

Kruger, K. *Coordinated Cooperative Collection Development for Illinois Libraries*. Springfield, Ill.: Illinois State Library, 1982.

Newhouse, J. P., and A. J. Alexander. *An Economic Analysis of Public Library Services*. Lexington, Mass.: Lexington Books, 1972.

Palmour, V. E., et al. *A Planning Process for Public Libraries*. Chicago: American Library Association, 1980.

Wiemers, G. *Materials Availability in Small Libraries*. Occasional Papers, 149. Urbana, Ill.: Graduate School of Library and Information Science, University of Illinois, 1981.

Zweizig, D., and B. Dervin. "Public Library Use, Users, Uses." In *Advances in Librarianship*, edited by M. J. Voigt and M. H. Harris, 231-55. New York: Academic Press, 1977.

School

Daniel, E. H. "Evaluation of School Library Media Centers." *Bookmark* 38 (Winter 1980): 287-91.

_____. "Performance Measures for School Librarians." In *Advances in Librarianship*, edited by M. J. Voigt and M. H. Harris, 1-51. New York: Academic Press, 1976.

Evaluating the School Library Media Program. Chicago: American Association of School Librarians, 1980.

Loertscher, D. V., and J. G. Stroud. *PSES: Pursue Self-Evaluation System for School Media Centers*. Fayetteville, Ark.: Hi Willow Publishing, 1976.

Thomason, N. W. "Evaluating a School Media Center Book Collection." *Catholic Library World* 53 (Spring 1981): 87-88.

Special

McClure, C. R., and B. Reifsnyder. "Performance Measures for Corporate Information Centers." *Special Libraries* 75 (July 1984): 193-204.

Norton, R., and D. Gautschi. "User Survey of an International Library: Expectations and Evaluations." *Aslib Proceedings* 37 (April 1985): 195-206.

Rice, B. A. "Science Periodicals Use Study." *Serials Librarian* 4 (Fall 1979): 35-47.

Strain, P. M. "Evaluation of a Special Library." *Special Libraries* 73 (July 1982): 165-72.

Wender, R. W. "Counting Journal Title Usage in Health Sciences." *Special Libraries* 70 (May/June 1979): 219-26.

16

Cooperative Collection Development and Resource Sharing

Some years ago, Richard Dougherty wrote an article entitled "Library Cooperation: A Case of Hanging Together or Hanging Separately."[1] The title reflects a widely held view on library cooperation. Since then dozens of articles have been published, almost all calling for some form of cooperative/coordinated collection building and/or resource sharing. There has been limited progress toward cooperative collection development and resource sharing but almost no progress in establishing a coordinated national program that will assure one copy of almost any research item with little or no unintentional duplication. There is a difference between a program that has a goal of little or no duplication in defined areas and a program that does not. *Webster's Third International Dictionary* defines *cooperative* in part as "given to or marked by working together or by joint effort toward a common end"; while *coordinate* is defined as "to bring into a common action, movement, or condition; regulate and combine in harmonious action."[2] Cooperative collection development programs are likely to grow, but the future of coordinated collection development appears dim.

The Nature of Cooperative Systems

In many ways, library cooperation is like the weather — we all talk about it, but none of us is able to control it. As with weather modification, many individuals work on the problem, but with little success. A primary reason is that we do not really understand what we are trying to accomplish. Figure 16.1 presents a very general overview of the possible combinations of cooperative collection development. This figure represents the hope we all have of reaching the librarian's millennium of total cooperation between libraries and access to all of the world's information resources (UNESCO's Universal Availability of Publications — UAP).

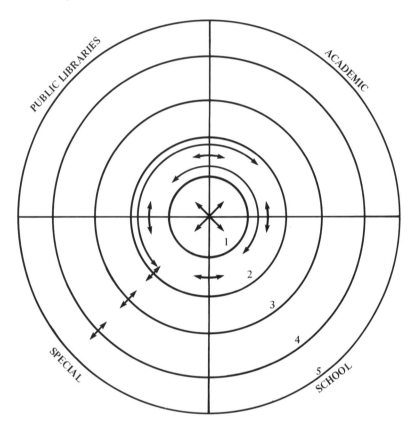

1 Community
2 Local Area
3 Region
4 National
5 International

Fig. 16.1. Ideal of interlibrary cooperation (networking). Adapted from Mary Dugan, "Library Network Analysis and Planning," *Journal of Library Automation* 2/3 (September 1969): 157-75.

This ideal is a long way off, even at the local level. Many classes of patrons still get different levels of service in different libraries in the same community. Even personality differences between chief librarians can create minor but real barriers to effective cooperation at any level. As one moves farther out in the circles of the figure, it is harder to work out major cooperative programs. No longer do just library and patron needs decide the issue of whether to cooperate or not. Legal, political, and economic issues tend to dominate the decision-making process.

Models of Cooperative Activity

Michael Sinclair, in "A Typology of Library Cooperatives," proposed four theoretical models of cooperative activity (see figure 16.2).[3] Although the concepts are Sinclair's, the following interpretation is mine. (Sinclair's article should be read in its entirety to gain a full understanding of his model.)

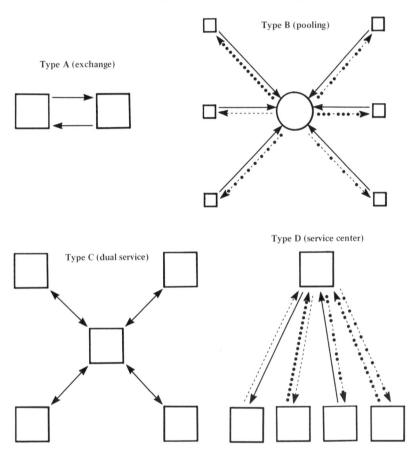

Fig. 16.2. Models of library cooperative activities. A graphic interpretation of M. P. Sinclair, "A Typology of Library Cooperatives," *Special Libraries* 64 (April 1973): 181-86.

Type A. This is a bilateral *exchange model,* in which materials are exchanged between *two* participating libraries. In practice, where such an exchange is found, the exchange rate is usually calculated upon a proportional basis, according to some agreed-upon value (e.g., one for one, two for one). Resource sharing, reciprocal borrowing, and interlibrary loans are based on the exchange model.

Type B. This is a multilateral development of Type A and can be called, for convenience, the *pooling model.* In this model, more than two libraries contribute to and draw from a common pool of materials. Many of the early library systems were of this type; in a sense OCLC started as a "pool."

Type C. This *dual-service model* is one in which two or more participating libraries take advantage of the facilities of one of the participants to produce a common output—for instance, a union list. The term *dual-service* is used to distinguish this model from the next and to emphasize the fact that *all* participants, including the facilitator, contribute to the common output. Many of the early library systems have evolved into this type and frequently refer to the "flagship" library. This is the model that would represent RLIN.

Type D. This model is one in which a number of libraries employ the services of a facilitating participant to input and process materials for individual purposes, rather than toward the end of a common output. Hence, it is called the service-center model. Today's bibliographic utilities, such as OCLC and WLN, are of this type.

These four types seem adequate to cover all existing systems; however, new systems now under consideration may not fit into this categorization.

The Something-for-Nothing Syndrome

Any library cooperative system is built on a series of assumptions that should be examined with considerable care. Perhaps the most important assumption, although the one least often stated, is that all of the participants in the system are or will be equally efficient in their operations involving the cooperative activities. No one assumes that every member will achieve the same benefits or contribute materials that are equally valuable; each is assumed to be somewhat unusual, if not unique. Why then assume that each is equally efficient? Given the slightest thought, it is clear that one cannot legitimately make such an assumption. However, if the assumption is not made, it is very difficult to believe that everyone will gain more, or at least get back the same value as was contributed. In a sense, librarians try to fool themselves that each will get something for nothing by joining a cooperative system. Each library hopes that it will be the one to get back more than it put into the system. During periods of low funding from outside sources libraries have a tendency not to cooperate. According to Boyd Rayward, "networks (cooperatives) are a phenomenon of relative affluence. They cannot be created unless each member at the local level has sufficient resources of time, staff, materials, and basic equipment and supplies to participate."[4]

If a library enters into a cooperative program with the "something for nothing" goal in mind, there is little hope of success. There are always many real costs, which any good accountant could determine. In addition, there are many costs of cooperation that no cost accounting system can identify, much less control. Two of the most important "uncontrolled costs" from a collection development point of view are ease of access and speed of delivery. Any cooperative system will place a higher cost on these two factors, if they are compared to local ownership; that is, it will always take as long, if not considerably longer, to gain access to a desired item, and it will entail more work for both the patron and the library. These costs are not often considered, as it is difficult if not impossible to translate them into monetary units. Often, then, this difficulty means ignoring costs and *assuming* that benefits will be high. (Later in this chapter some studies about these factors will be described.)

Patrons' costs are seldom considered in any manner; the assumption is that cooperation will only result in increased benefits for the users. Sometimes the extra work of filling out one more form or answering one extra question is considered from the library's point of view, but almost never from the standpoint of the patron. Small increases are usually thought to be insignificant, but, while a single increase may be very small, in time or in aggregate, such increase(s) may be very significant. Nevertheless, a true cooperative collection development program can provide patrons with a much broader range of materials than would be possible for one library working in isolation.

Two examples of these problems will illustrate this point. In the United States, the interlibrary loan (ILL) system is slowly ceasing to function effectively. The early assumption was that *everyone* would gain as a result of the free exchange of resources. Yes, an increase in work load was seen for some of the libraries with larger collections, but they would be doing some borrowing and the added volume of work was not expected to be great in any event. Today, we know that the work load in the larger institutions is tremendous—so great that a solution must be found. (Something always costs something.) Most of the net lending libraries now charge for ILL service. At Tozzer Library our lending-to-borrowing ratio is 34 to 1; one staff member devotes at least 30 percent of her time to filling incoming ILL requests. The British National Lending Division arose as a direct result of the same problem; unfortunately, such a system is much harder to establish in the United States.

The second example is from Denmark. Copenhagen's public library established a system for reciprocal borrowing rights with suburban public libraries. A high percentage of the persons living in the suburbs work in the central city. Danes are avid readers and are as inclined as anyone else to use the convenient rather than the inconvenient services. So it was not surprising to find them using the most convenient public library for their general library needs, and it seems that for a great many suburbanites, the most convenient location is the Copenhagen system, not their local library. The cost for providing this "free" service rose so much that several politicians suggested either dropping the arrangement or charging a nonresident fee. Certainly, the librarians did not like the idea of charging a fee. The point again is that the original planning projection was based on the idea that it would be possible to expand service without increasing costs (something for nothing).

What Can Be Gained through Cooperation

One can identify six general benefits that could arise from any library cooperative effort. One of the major advantages is certainly improved access—improved in the sense that there may be a greater range of materials and/or better depth in a subject area. Generally, this does not mean more copies of a particular title, at least not significantly more. It certainly does not mean faster service—normally, it will mean an increase in the average time it takes to secure an item. This is offset by the increase in the number of titles available in a system.

A second benefit is that it may be possible to stretch limited resources. One danger in suggesting that cooperation may benefit the public or even the professional staff is that the idea of getting something for nothing will be implanted. Too often, people view cooperation as a money-saving device.

Cooperation does *not* save money for a library. If two or more libraries combine their efforts, they are not going to spend any less money — an effective cooperative program will divide up work and share results.

Sharing work results leads to other benefits. If work is divided up, there can be greater staff specialization. One person can concentrate on one or two activities rather than on a great number, and the specialization should result in better overall performance. Naturally, better performance should provide the patron with better service, and thus, perhaps, greater satisfaction. Reducing unnecessary duplication is the second result of sharing work. The reduction may be in work performed or materials purchased, but just how much unnecessary duplication will be eliminated must be carefully studied *before* the cooperative agreement is signed. Vague discussions about reducing duplication, without an in-depth study of the situation, usually lead to high expectations and, all too often, to dashed hopes. Nevertheless, reduced duplication is a real potential benefit.

By actively advertising its presence and services, a cooperative program may reduce the number of places a patron will need to go for service. However, this benefit is more theoretical than real in most systems. A lack of union lists has generally negated this potential benefit, but the situation is improving as more libraries go online.

A final benefit, and one not too frequently discussed, is an improvement in the working relationships between cooperating libraries. This is particularly true when there are different types of libraries involved in one system. Persons can gain a better perspective on others' problems as a result of working together on mutual problems. Also, learning about the special problems that another type of library encounters helps one to know what its staff can or cannot do. At least some systems have found this to be so important that they have set up exchange internships for staff members — both professional and nonprofessional.

More specific examples of what might result from a cooperative arrangement include such things as better or additional public services. For example, it may be possible as a result of shifting work loads to extend the hours of reference service or to increase the number of children's programs. Another possibility is to expand the service area. Perhaps the combined resources of the system will allow for providing service to persons or areas that no one library could reach using only its own resources.

As for many other areas of collection development, the Resources and Technical Services Division of the ALA has generated guidelines for cooperative collection development. The "approved" document is discussed in an article by Paul H. Mosher and Marcia Pankake, "A Guide to Coordinated and Cooperative Collection Development."[5] The guidelines provide details on benefits, problems, and recommendations which fit easily into this chapter's more general concepts.

In terms of collection development, cooperative programs should force the library to have better knowledge of its collection. The library has to know both what it has and what the other members have. The RLG conspectus (discussed in chapter 3) and ARL's National Collection Inventory Project (NCIP), which uses the conspectus model, are intended to do just that: to identify who has what and in what strength. When most academic libraries have completed their conspectus it should mean that sharing problems of selection and collection development should be possible; however, this is still some distance in the future. If there is to be a division of collection responsibility by subject area, each library will have to have an in-depth knowledge of its own collection before reaching a meaningful cooperative agreement. Even if there is no final agreement, the process of examining the collection will be of great value in future work. Also, the opportunity to share with others the problems and solutions should improve each participant's capabilities.

Figure 16.3 is a small example of how a program, such as the conspectus, might draw together the data from a variety of libraries. How the data are used and interpreted is another matter, but using form standardized subject lists to identify collection strength is a first step toward possible cooperative/coordinated collection development. Cooperative/coordinated collection development is a goal we should all strive to accomplish.

Cooperative systems may also free time for such things as more in-service training, more and better public relations, or just more planning. All of these activities require a lot of time to be effective but, depending upon the nature of the cooperative, a considerable amount of time may be made available for such activities. Again, a little of the something-for-nothing syndrome comes out. What cooperative systems do *not* mean is that someone else is doing one's work for free, since if that were the case, the system would eventually fail. What they do mean is that a librarian will be doing something for other member libraries and they will be doing things for him or her.

Basically, a cooperative program, properly organized, will allow for more specialization, more service, and more time to do things effectively. Remember, there are trade-offs. One gets *nothing* for nothing! Good service costs time and money, and there are no magic formulas for gaining extra time or services. What is required is hard work on identifying areas where each potential member has something to gain and something to contribute. In the long run, these two elements must be equal for all members of a system or it will fail.

SUBJECT STRENGTH SURVEY SUMMARY

PAGE 2 OF 11   AUGUST 1981

SUBJECT AREA	SPECIFIC SUBJECT	COLLECTION SIZE BOOKS	COLLECTION SIZE OTHER	BUDGET	CIRCULATE YES	CIRCULATE NO	MACHINE READABLE YES	MACHINE READABLE NO	CATALOGED YES	CATALOGED NO	WILL PARTICIPATE YES	WILL PARTICIPATE NO	LIBRARY
Art	Fiber arts	700		n/a	x		x		x		x		JeffCo-Arvada
	Drawing and decorative	1040		Gen. b.	x		x		x		x		Arapahoe Reg.
	Geo. E. Burr		etching etc.	n/a		x		x		x			Denver Public
	Blunt Art Print		1250 prints	n/a				x		x	x		Canon City Pub.
	Fore-edge Pnt	55		Gen. b.		x							Univ. Col. -B
Asian Studies	Model coll.		275 misc.	LSCA		x	x		x		x		JeffCo-Villa
Bibles	Foreign lang.	246		Gen. b.		x							Univ. Col. -B
Blind/Deaf	Large print	430		Gen. b.	x		x		x		x		Canon City Pub.
	Hearing impaired	40		Gen. b.	x			x	x		x		Arapahoe Reg.
	Large print	1000		n/a	x		x		x		x		JeffCo-Arvada
	n/a	700		Endowed	x			x	x			x	Colo. School Deaf & Blind
Botanical	n/a	10760		Sales, etc.	x			x	x		x		Denver Bot. Garden
Business	n/a	4000		Gen. b.	x		x		x		x		JeffCo-Villa
	n/a - tax	456		Gen. b.	x		x		x		x		Weld Co.
	& career info	350		Gen. b.	x		x		x		x		Englewood

Fig. 16.3. Colorado State Library subject strength survey.

Barriers to Cooperation

A number of working cooperatives exist, but certainly not as many as the literature would lead one to expect. More time is spent talking about the benefits of cooperation than is spent building a cooperative system. Unfortunately, the list of barriers to cooperative activities among libraries is much longer than the list of benefits. This is not to say that all the items on the two lists are of equal importance; they are not. Many of the barriers are of a minor nature, from a theoretical point of view; however, there are still real, practical problems. The barriers can be divided into eight broad categories: (1) desire for local self-sufficiency; (2) size and status; (3) technological sufficiency; (4) psychological barriers; (5) experience barriers; (6) traditional/historical barriers; (7) physical and geographical barriers; and (8) legal, political, and administrative barriers.

Local Self-Sufficiency

Local self-sufficiency traditionally has been the goal of the majority of libraries. Yet almost all libraries now realize that the goal is unattainable, even for the great national libraries of the world. There are always some items that are not in their collections and never will be. Why be concerned with self-sufficiency? As discussed earlier, one of the main factors in collection development is meeting patron demand. Being able to deliver a "need" item from the local collection provides satisfaction for both the patron and the library staff. Furthermore, the speed of delivery is faster on the average than if the material must be secured through interlibrary loans.

Pressure for local self-sufficiency is probably greatest from patrons. Human nature seems to be such that when we want something, we want it now. Socialization slowly modifies an individual's desire for immediate need satisfaction but never completely eliminates this drive. (When we have our wants satisfied immediately, we are much happier than when we have to wait.) Admittedly, 99 percent of our information needs are not in a life-threatening category and thus we can afford to wait, but we still do not like it. Because librarianship is service oriented, it is not surprising to find the library staff trying to satisfy as many patron needs at once as they possibly can.

Patron pressure is particularly strong when there is a proposal to share collection development responsibilities among libraries. Any knowledgeable library user knows something about the speed of interlibrary loans. (Some countries, usually relatively small ones, have very efficient interlibrary loan systems and thus have been able to do more with cooperative collection development.) A natural reaction from such a patron upon hearing the proposal might be "What will happen to my area of interest? I do not want the library to stop buying my materials. I cannot afford to wait months for ILL!" If the library has carefully developed the collection in terms of patron needs, what can be given up? How does one respond to patron inquiries about the impact of the proposed cooperative? How can a library be an effective member without giving up some areas? Almost always, the library's level of funding will not be enough to buy as much as was purchased before and still take on new cooperative obligations. Therefore, some areas will have to be given up or sharply reduced.

How nice it would be if easy, quick answers existed to these and a number of related questions. If easy answers existed, everyone would be involved in collection cooperatives. In the absence of a speedy delivery system from other member libraries, librarians seeking cooperative arrangements will face strong patron opposition in many cases. An effective and truthful public relations program, one pointing out all the advantages to be gained by membership, will be the most important method of gaining support. Most of the answers to questions about cooperation will depend upon the local collection and those of the cooperating libraries.

Tom Ballard's provocative article, "Public Library Networking: Neat, Plausible, Wrong," raises a number of points regarding patrons.[6] He makes a strong case, with data to support his arguments, that for public libraries and others in a multiple system the idea of cooperative collection development with an eye toward resource sharing (ILL, generally) is fine but does not work. Drawing on data from a number of systems across the United States, he shows that interlibrary lending accounts for very little of the total circulation, almost always representing less than 2 percent of the total. He cites studies that indicate people tend to select from what is available on the shelf at the time they come in, even if it is a second or third choice, rather than seek out the desired material. (This is a clear example of the law of least effort.) Although he emphasizes, and gives examples concerning, the public library, his statements hold some truth for anyone who has worked in a school media center or an academic library serving undergraduates. Undoubtedly part of the explanation is that many people are not aware of the possibility of getting needed items somewhere else, so more active "marketing" may be necessary. Another part of the explanation is that many people wait until the last minute to seek out needed information and cannot wait a few days to get the precise information. Perhaps a third part of the explanation is that most people do not really need or want the material enough to pay the price we place on its delivery. If it is immediately available, fine, if not, forget it. It makes a strong case for local self-sufficiency.

Size and Status

Size and status are factors of less importance in cooperative collection building than in weeding. However, they do arise, as giving up some areas of collecting responsibility may have an impact on growth. Not all areas have the same number of items produced per year, and thus they do not increase in size at equal rates. If a library must give up a fast growth area and have only areas of low growth, its overall growth rate may drop. In addition to the growth rate within a subject area, there is the cost of materials to be considered. Many science and technology items cost 25 to 50 percent more than social sciences and humanities items, so that fewer titles can be acquired for the same amount of money. If size and status are important to the library and parent institution, it may be difficult if not impossible to find an agreeable breakdown of collecting responsibilities that does not have an adverse impact on the library's growth rate.

Technological Sufficiency

Surprisingly, the hope that new technological developments will vastly increase the storage capacity of a library is also a barrier. In some instances, pressure for cooperative collection development comes from a lack of physical space in which to store the collection. Eliminating unnecessary duplication of low-use items can result in more space for heavily used materials. However, if new technology will allow storage of the equivalent of the Library of Congress or British Museum Library collections in space no larger than an office desk or less, why worry about running out of space? In addition, the potential for local self-sufficiency may be raised again. If microfiche collections can be purchased for less than hard copy, the book budget can be used to acquire a great many more items. Increased acquisition rate naturally will increase the title count and thus raise the status of the library. An increased depth and scope in the collection plus almost immediate satisfaction of patron needs are what libraries are all about, right?

New technologies will solve our problems and almost do away with the need to do any selection work — at least that is what salespersons claim for their newest devices. Sometimes it seems as if the charlatans who once sold cure-all elixirs simply stopped peddling bottles of magic liquid because selling mysterious electronic black boxes to librarians is more profitable and easier. Many technological devices do work and work effectively for librarians, but to gain this result means a significant cost. In a sense, we still hope to get something for nothing. We hope that new developments will solve library problems at no increase in expenses. To date, there has been no such development. One cost is traded for another, and in some cases, what initially seems to be a reduction in cost later becomes a significant increase in long-term costs. Many systems are not compatible with any other system, and the librarian who selects such a system may well end up trapped. Also, the longer an existing, limited system is retained, the higher the cost will be to convert to a newer or more useful one.

Finally, new developments are continually being announced, making yesterday's latest "cure-all" obsolete overnight. Perhaps the hardest factor to handle is the announcement about what is under development and is being tested in a prototype system. Prototypes all too often fail to live up to expectations, but they do hold out a hope that will cause some librarians not to investigate joining cooperative efforts.

Psychological Barriers

Psychological barriers may exist for the staff members or patrons of the libraries attempting to establish a cooperative. Some arise from a preference for the known over the unknown. Change can be threatening, and a move to cooperative programs from a self-sufficient program can be viewed as a threat. Personal status or even job security may appear to be threatened. Feelings of this type usually develop because planners have not provided adequate information about the proposed system. Bits and pieces of information acquired through the grapevine usually provide more than enough fact and rumor to raise fears of things to come. Accurate information about the new system, communicated directly to all concerned, even if there is a potential threat to employment, is better than allowing rumor to circulate. Unfortunately, even if the information is accurate, staff members sometimes will believe that communiques are deliberately false. In the first case, a slight extra effort will eliminate the barrier. In the second case, the actual problem has nothing to do with the concept of library cooperation, and there will be little hope for a successful program until the credibility issue is resolved.

Loss of autonomy may be a real or imagined barrier to cooperation, and both patrons and the library staff may express this fear. ("Who will decide X?" "What voice will we have?" "Won't Y library dominate the system?" and so forth.) There should be concern about the issue raised in such questions, and any good cooperative agreement will directly address these issues. However, the worry will be expressed, or at least be present, long before any written agreement exists. Dealing with this problem early and directly should help to ensure the successful conclusion of the project.

Inertia, indifference, or unwillingness to change are psychological factors often encountered. ("Things are going okay." "Why make more work?") Sometimes passive resistance is more difficult to overcome than active opposition. Persons actively opposing cooperation present arguments which may be addressed and perhaps effectively countered. It is much harder to counter the unspoken attitude that "it is an outstanding idea but we need to work on the following local problem first." Even when the plan is implemented, too many indifferent persons in the system can reduce the chances of success. Again, an active public relations program and good in-service orientation about the new system are the best insurance against having inertia and indifference undermine the project.

In cooperative collection development, the problems of who is to make decisions and of specific local needs are frequently voiced. Also, because selection is a very subjective matter, it is hard to get agreement on policies and priorities. The more people are involved in decision making, the more difficult it becomes to achieve agreement. For a cooperative collection development program, agreement must be reached among the representatives of libraries in the proposed system regarding the system's priorities, a process that in itself may take a very long time. Even representatives who have been checking with their own libraries throughout the negotiations will want to examine the statement in terms of local priorities, after the system priorities are fully set forth. When conflicts arise between the two sets of priorities, and there usually are some, the resolution will have to come from individual libraries. If the library staff helped establish the local priorities, they should be involved in resolving the conflict between local and system needs.

Dislike of "standardization" and unwillingness to accept "outsider errors" are two related barriers that develop over a long period of time. Yet almost every cooperative project will result in more standardization of activities or at least in filling out more forms. Also, inevitably, there will be mistakes by "outsiders." The full impact of either factor cannot be fully known until the system is operative. Information on these factors from similar systems will help reduce such fears but will never completely overcome them.

Occasionally, personality differences can present significant problems in achieving a cooperative agreement. Strong or dominant personalities or a strong authority drive on the part of individual librarians are usually the source of these problems. If two or more such personalities become involved in the process of establishing or operating a cooperative system, there is little hope that the system will be able to operate effectively. Personal needs will almost inevitably take priority over system needs.

Past Experience

What was done in the past can present problems for a cooperative project. What we did for the patrons in the past is one area of concern. Do we have an adequate knowledge of what our patrons need and want? Furthermore, even if we know the current situation, the needs and wants can change very quickly. Certainly, selection officers deal with these two issues every day in developing the collection. Why is it an any greater problem for a cooperative? Lacking adequate knowledge of our local patron needs and future changes makes it very difficult to determine what we can give up or effectively contribute to the cooperative. Each potential member is confronted with the same problem, but the major difficulty lies in the speed with which adjustments may be made in a network of more than two members. It is much easier to make adjustments in the local library in response to new needs when one does not need to worry about the impact that the adjustments will have on other libraries. Of course, any proposed change may require modification of the original agreement. While most changes would be minor, each one should be discussed with other member libraries.

Perhaps the best-known American effort at cooperative collection development was the Farmington Plan (more about the plan at the end of this chapter). It no longer exists for several reasons. One important reason was the changing interests of the member institutions. An area once considered important by a member would become less and less important *to its local patrons*. When this happened, pressures to buy materials in a new area of local interest while maintaining the Farmington Plan responsibilities became great. Some institutions were able to trade responsibilities with one another, while others devoted less and less attention to their assigned areas; occasionally, an area was simply ignored. With this type of experience recorded in the literature and in the background of the many persons who attempted to make the Farmington program work, it will be difficult to convince libraries to try again.

Almost every program is modified in its first few years of operation, but again, these modifications are seldom described in the literature. Attempts to find out what has been accomplished by sending out a questionnaire are seldom very satisfactory, since response rates are low and a standard closed response form seldom produces enough useful information when surveying a wide range of activities. If such a form does cover enough topics, the length is usually so great that many persons refuse to answer it. On the other hand, respondents often think open response forms are too time-consuming to bother with.

The result is a general lack of knowledge about what has and has not succeeded in cooperative efforts. A directly related problem is a lack of data, adequate in depth and breadth, of what a system will cost. So many factors go into calculating the cost of a system that often the monetary figures from an existing system are of little value (not that many systems have made available detailed cost figures). Taking into account regional differences in salary, living conditions, and costs; computing direct and indirect cost factors; fixing methods of depreciating capital expense items; and deciding just what will or will not be included in overhead costs are just a few of the problems that make comparisons between cooperative systems unsatisfactory.

Traditional/Historical Barriers

Incompatibility of procedures is a fact that must be faced at some point by all cooperatives. "We have *always* used *this* procedure, and *it* works" is a statement heard over and over again in cooperative planning meetings. Some of these barriers are reasonably easy to overcome if everyone is really interested in forming a system. Not so easy to resolve are certain other operational problems, such as differences in classification systems being used. The decision to use LC in the RLG conspectus was not easily made, nor does it make it easy for non-LC libraries to complete the forms.

Examples of other types of historical and traditional barriers that must be overcome are institutional competition, special rules, funding problems, and inability to satisfy local needs. The last problem is and always will be with us. No matter how much money is available to develop local service, some imaginative patron or staff member can think of a new need or service that would use up all available money. A variation on both Maslow's "wants hierarchy" and one of Parkinson's laws is that organizations, like people, always have wants slightly in excess of their ability to satisfy those wants. If this local need combines with the desire for local self-sufficiency, librarians will never be able to agree to any cooperative effort.

Related to the inability to ever completely satisfy local needs with local resources are the institutional competition and funding problems. Often, at the local level, public, school, and community college libraries all compete for the same local tax money. Each type of library may have a certain legal minimum due it, but beyond the minimum, the situation is very competitive. In some manner, though, the community will establish a maximum total amount that it is willing to devote to library services. If allocations are not made by a formula or weighting system, the total will be determined through the politics of the budgetary process. Furthermore, each type of library will be counting as patrons a large number of persons who also use other types of libraries, a duplication of patron count. Collections, in fact, reflect the dual role of patrons. Educational libraries have "recreational" materials and recreational (public) libraries have "educational" materials. The "competition" for the same patron, causing a sizable duplication of materials in some cases, results in significant funding problems. Attempts to extract additional monies for cooperative activities from local funding authorities are not likely to be successful unless they see the request as a device for stabilizing, if not reducing, local funding.

Finally, there are problems of rules and regulations to be overcome—usually a matter of who may use a certain type of library. As long as the cooperative membership is composed of one type of library, there are few problems of this kind. When several different types of libraries join a system, there may be significant problems. Archival and special collection libraries may have a number of restrictions on who may use the material, just as some professional libraries (e.g., law and medicine) do. Normally, this is not a major barrier, although it is time-consuming to make certain that all the rules and regulations are taken into account and adjusted.

Physical and Geographical Barriers

Physical and geographical barriers are often such that they keep a cooperative from being formed or some libraries from joining a system. One problem is lack of physical space in a library. Local patrons use the collection and reader stations to the maximum, so acquiring additional patrons would result in long waits or no service. Small archival libraries (special libraries where the materials must be used in the library) are often faced with this problem. Even large facilities, especially academic libraries, are often confronted with this problem; however, the opportunity to borrow materials provides a viable alternative if the library wants to solve the problem of lack of reader stations. Insufficient storage space for materials unfortunately is not as easy to resolve. Cooperative collection development proposals *may* reduce the need for storage space in some subject areas in the future, but they will add demands in other areas. Normally, such proposals *do not* address the issue of older materials already in a collection. If there is to be a new central storage unit for low-use items (for example, the Center for Research Libraries), then some space may be gained, but this usually does not solve the long-term space problem.

Physical distance between member libraries may mean that the delay in service will be too great for patron acceptance. Use of telecommunications is making this less and less of a problem. Yet, as is so often the case, solving one problem creates a different one, and here the new problem is copyright. One of the major roadblocks to passage of the new U.S. Copyright Law was the new technology and efforts to establish resource-sharing networks. What impact would such networks have on the property rights of the copyright holder? This is uncertain. Until this aspect of copyright law is tested in the courts, all one can do is guess what, if any, influence it will have on cooperative collection building. In March 1986 *LJ Hotline* reported that the "Information Industry Association and the Association of American Publishers are talking about setting up a task force to 'respond to private sector interests in library networking.' Concern at the expansion of network activities into electronic services and network control over materials and technology buying decisions are cited."[7]

One way to get around the use of telecommunications is to give patrons reciprocal borrowing rights. That is, a person holding a valid borrower's card from any member library is allowed to use it in any other library in the system. As long as the distances between the member libraries are not too great, this is a viable solution, up to a point. Before this will work effectively, there must be some form of union catalog or access to member holdings files. One problem, even with online catalogs, is serials. Most libraries do not include information on the latest issue of a periodical received in the catalog. Furthermore, many do not include government documents in the catalog unless they are part of the general collection. Many libraries maintain separate catalogs of audiovisual materials. The list of exceptions is very long. The point is that in many libraries, a patron may have to consult several different catalogs in order to determine the total local resources on a single topic.

An alternative to a systemwide list is, of course, the telephone. However, if there is a high use of reciprocal borrowing privilege, the level of telephone "reference" service may reach rather alarming proportions. Will member libraries be able to afford a separate "do you have?" telephone line and the personnel to handle the calls? At first, this may seem like a small matter, a cost that the local library can absorb. Perhaps, but perhaps not; it appears to be more of the something-for-nothing concept. The Copenhagen public library is not the first, only, or last library to find that reciprocal borrowing may carry a high price tag over the long run.

Two other barriers are differences in collection size and patron population. Libraries with large collections legitimately become worried about creating too great a pressure on their collections and becoming a net lender instead of having a balance between lending and borrowing ("resource rape"). When this danger exists for a proposed system, planners must include a mechanism to balance the contributions for the members. Balance is always a problem, but for resource-sharing cooperatives, it is particularly hard to achieve. Size alone is not an adequate measure of a library's resources. Naturally, the size of the user population enters into consideration. Of greater importance, though, is the composition of the entire group and their needs. For example, a medium-sized public library may not place as much pressure on a large academic library as might a small academic library. Thus, collection size, patron needs, and patron population combine to create a complex situation for developing a system that will balance each library's contribution and use.

Legal, Political, and Administrative Barriers

Legal and administrative barriers can be both complex and unique. One set of legal barriers can be illustrated by referring back to figure 16.1 (page 332). Each circle represents a different level of government and political concern. To develop the library system combining all four major types that is least wasteful (in the sense of not duplicating resources and services unnecessarily), jurisdictional lines must be crossed, raising questions such as: Where do the funds come from for a multijurisdictional system? Who will control the funds? Will there be a lessening of local control? Is it legal to take money from one jurisdiction to be spent in another? What are the politics of securing enabling legislation for such a system? Attempts to start at the local level and work upward in the hierarchy of government sometimes succeed because the persons involved are more familiar with the way that local needs are related to the political system.

Starting at the national level usually reduces the number of jurisdictional questions and results in better funding. Although the national approach has some major advantages, it also has significant disadvantages. One of the most frequent responses to a national plan from the local authorities is "What do the bureaucrats in the capital know about our problems? No one on the planning committee ever asks us what we need, much less comes to see our program." Suspicion is the key word here, followed by possessiveness ("What is the real motive for this project, and why should we give up local control?"). These problems, of course, are not just library problems; they are part of the political process. Another problem is that the many national plans, in order to allow for local variation, are not developed in enough detail to make them functional. Unfortunately, reporting results to national authorities often consumes more administrative time than is saved by cooperative activities. Finally, regional jealousies and a desire for political gain may dominate the entire process, thus negating most of the advantages that might have been achieved for library patrons across the country. Other problems may be national and/or regional accreditation needs. Accreditation standards may present a few barriers for educational institutions, but by and large, these are minor and may pose no problem in the future as the economic necessity for cooperation is not only recognized but accepted.

Another problem is the need to maintain two systems for a period of time. Dual operations are always a part of the start-up procedure in any cooperative system, but generally, the two systems are simultaneously operative for only a short period of time. However, even two or three months of dual operation may create a real economic burden for some members with tight operating budgets. All that can be done is to keep the transition period as short as possible. Finally, complex systems require extensive training of staff, and thus some loss of normal productivity will occur while the staff is in training sessions. A complex system usually also means that more mistakes will be made, and longer transition periods will be observed.

Over the last few pages, we have looked at several kinds of barriers to establishing a cooperative system. By implication, the message has been that cooperatives are difficult to establish and cooperative collection development (resource sharing) systems are among the most difficult. Despite what may seem to be a litany of problems, *cooperatives can be established*, and are becoming more and more a matter of economic necessity.

What to Avoid

The following five points about what will cause a cooperative to fail are drawn from the literature on the topic. Avoid these pitfalls and a system will have a good chance of succeeding:

1. Do not think of the cooperative as supplementary and something it is possible to do without.

2. Planners should spend time working out operational details.

3. The system should cause major operational changes in the member libraries.

4. Do not think of the system as something-for-nothing for the library.

5. Do have the cooperative's funding and operation handled by an independent agency.

An indication of the difficulties associated with developing resource sharing is found in an article by Maryann Dugan, "Library Network Analysis and Planning."[8] A group of 109 head librarians was asked to indicate what type of cooperative activities would be appropriate to develop. Ten major activities were identified; the librarians then ranked these in terms of their desirability and the need to develop cooperatives. Their ranking is indicative of the attitudes we have been discussing:

1. Union list

2. Interlibrary loan

3. Facsimile transmission

4. Networking

5. Reference service

6. Regional centers

7. Central facility

8. Type of library centers

9. Central processing

10. Collection management

In one sense, resource sharing was both first and last; union lists, interlibrary loan, and facsimile transmission are forms of resource sharing. However, for these to be most useful, in terms of both being cost-effective and gaining access to the full universe of knowledge, collection management must also occur. Without cooperative collection management, the situation is the same as it has always been. Certainly, more union lists are needed, but if everyone is buying basically the same materials, what is really gained? We have used interlibrary loan for years as well as variations of facsimile transmission. The message seems to be cooperate, so long as doing so does not have a negative impact on local autonomy and self-sufficiency.

Seven "models" for cooperative collection development are identified in the ALA guidelines cited earlier (p. 332): the Farmington Plan, NPAC system, "Library of Congress," Center for Research Libraries, Mosaic overlay of collection development policies, status quo, and combined self-interest. The Farmington Plan was an attempt by major American research libraries to have one copy of any currently published research work available somewhere within the United States. After years of effort it was given up in the 1970s. Acquisition responsibility in the Farmington Plan was originally assigned on the basis of institutional interests. In 20 years, those interests changed, but the goal of "one copy" remained. Another problem was that some areas were not a major area of interest to any institution. Sufficient *national* interest existed to warrant coverage, but deciding which institution should have the responsibility for buying such materials was a constant problem. A careful study of why the Farmington Plan failed may provide invaluable data for future cooperative ventures. In the final analysis, it probably failed as a result of not avoiding the pitfalls listed earlier. The Scandia Plan (very similar in concept to the Farmington Plan) in the Nordic countries has experienced similar problems. This plan has never achieved the same level of activity as the Farmington Plan, primarily due to problems of changing needs and the assignment of responsibilities.

The National Program for Acquisition and Cataloging (NPAC) was another attempt at acquiring quantities of research materials from outside the United States and also assuring that the material would be cataloged. (Cataloging of the Farmington material was also a stumbling block.) The Library of Congress was the focal point in NPAC, but there was consultation with other research libraries in the United States about what subjects and areas would be included in the program. Public Law 480 (PL 480) was, and to a limited extent still is, a variation or element of NPAC. This program, which in 1986 operates only in India, used federal funds (but in local currency) to buy quantities of books in local languages in a number of countries. Again the Library of Congress was responsible for operating the program, including cataloging, and distributing the materials to participating academic libraries. As the "surplus" local currencies were expended, the program has been reduced and it is likely to cease to exist in a few years. PL 480 was not intended to be a cooperative collection development plan in the usual sense of the term. It might be best characterized as a centralized acquisition and cataloging program.

A somewhat related, joint acquisition program that has failed is the Latin American Cooperative Acquisition Plan (LACAP). LACAP was a commercial undertaking designed to share costs and problems of acquiring quantities of research material, on a regular basis, from Latin American countries. Although a number of research libraries in the United States still collect extensively in Latin America, they could not sustain the program. Three factors probably played an important role in the demise of LACAP. First of all, mostly low-use material was being acquired. In periods when funding is tight, hard choices have to be made and low-use items are always a prime area for cutting when cutting has to be done. Second, the plan started in a period when many institutions were developing "area study" programs and there was an expectation that this would be a growing field. Economic conditions changed and institutions stopped planning for new programs and often cut some of the most recently established programs. As a result, there were not as many institutions interested in participating in LACAP. Finally, and this is just a suspicion, the book trade in many Latin American countries has matured and it is no longer as difficult to locate reliable local dealers in various countries. If one can buy directly and reliably at a lower cost, because the middle level of expense is removed, it is reasonable to buy the most material possible with the funds available.

The "Library of Congress" system is described as "a variation of the Farmington Plan." In general terms, it might be thought of as a centralized (coordinated) system in which the national library and the research libraries in a country work together to ensure that at least one copy of all relevant research materials would be available. As described, the system would include libraries "divesting themselves of those subjects or areas in which its own interests were weak."

Two of the most successful "cooperative" programs are the Center for Research Libraries (CRL) in the United States, and the British National Lending Division (BLD). One reason for their success is that they operate as independent agencies. Their purpose is to serve a diverse group of member libraries; in essence, they have *no local constituency* to serve. Another major difference for CRL is that there is no attempt to acquire high-use items; in fact, just the reverse is true. With no local patron population to be served, the fiscal resources can be directed toward low-demand items of national interest.

CLR does face some major decisions regarding its collection policies. One issue is whether it should build a broad-based (many subjects/areas), selective collection or be comprehensive in a few areas? A second issue relates to the need for a single source for low-use periodicals (National Periodicals Center concept) and what role CRL should play. An interesting article by Sarah E. Thomas, "Collection Development at the Center for Research Libraries: Policy and Practice," suggests that the number of the Center's periodical holdings is not as unique as many members would like (only 20.66 percent of the Center's titles were unique).[9] Local needs of member libraries would account for some of the duplication. Also, the project looked at title holdings in the United States, not just at CLR member libraries, so some of the duplication undoubtedly occurred in nonmember libraries. What of the future? One would hope that the Center will continue to develop in the direction of being the holder of unique materials. With better delivery systems, perhaps libraries can supply low-use items quickly enough from CLR and let patrons know about the system which would allow for less duplication of low-use items.

"Mosaic overlay of collection development policies" is what the RLG conspectus and ARL National Collection Inventory Project (NCIP) are trying to accomplish. The purpose is to assure national coverage; to identify collection gaps nationally; to serve as a basis for libraries taking on collecting responsibilities (primary collecting responsibility, PCR); to assist in directing scholars to strong collections; to create a consistent basis for collection development policies; to function as a communication device signaling changes in collection activities; to serve as a link between collecting policies and processing and preservation policies; to serve as a possible fund-raising tool; and finally, to stimulate interest in and support for cooperative programs. Whether NCIP and RLG efforts will succeed in achieving that long list of purposes, only time will tell. (The basic format of the conspectus was outlined in chapter 3.) In essence the final product will be an assessment of what are now in 1986 close to 7,000 subject categories by the participating libraries, giving each appropriate subject category a value of 0 to 5. When that is done, we shall know which libraries think they have strong or weak collections in each area, but we will not know exactly what is in the collections. The assessment will identify gaps and will be useful for referral purposes and perhaps for ILL if the library is online and the library seeking the information has the capability of tapping that database. The thought of each of some 200 or so research libraries (a generous estimate of potential participants) accepting its share of the potential 5,000 PCRs, about 25 PCRs each, is grand. Will it happen? It would be wonderful if it did. However, as of 1986 only RLG members are involved in accepting PCRs.

The status quo approach, as the label implies, would keep things as they are. Such a model would assume that the sum total of current collecting activities, primarily the research libraries and archives, achieves the comprehensiveness needed. By sharing in-process and catalog files, online of course, adequate access could be achieved and individual purchase decisions could be made with the knowledge of who has or has not ordered an item. It is doubtful that many research librarians really believe that the current system is achieving the needed level of coverage. Perhaps the NCIP results will demonstrate that the present method is adequate, in which case the status quo can continue.

The combined self-interest plan is something of a multitype system, in that a "significant number of libraries would combine with one or more major libraries." In a sense, this is what the Collection Development Committee of the Colorado Council on Library Development has been attempting to create, with the Denver Public Library and University of Colorado Library System serving as the "major libraries." The committee goals and objectives, as outlined in "Developing Collections in Colorado," are:

GOALS:

1. To work toward coordinated collection development policies for all libraries in the state to give greater access to materials for all Colorado citizens.

2. To assess budgetary constraints affecting local and statewide collection development and to work for increased funding and resources to overcome restraints.

OBJECTIVES:

1. To have individual libraries recognize their role in collection development and to prepare their own collection development policy in terms of its own clientele and role within the state.

   A. Each library should define whom they serve as their primary client.

   B. Each library should determine and define the needs of that client.

   C. Each library should have a mission statement or goal.

   D. Each library should establish written priorities for allocation of resources.

2. To raise the awareness of individual librarians about collection development including an understanding of what collection development is and the training needed for it.

3. To determine what materials the state does not have and to make recommendations for providing those needed resources within Colorado.

4. To encourage preparation of regional and statewide collection development plans.

   A. Identifying local and state responsibilities.

   B. Assisting libraries to delineate responsibilities for materials.

5. To coordinate current collection development activities within the state and provide a clearinghouse for collection development information.[10]

Again, the RLG conspectus and the ALA policy guideline concepts have been combined to develop policy statements. With all types of libraries involved, problems developed and remain in some cases unresolved, and not everyone has viewed the concept with enthusiasm. Progress is being made, and it appears that multitype library cooperative collection building will work, to some extent, in Colorado. (See figure 16.3, page 338, for an example of what this group has done.)

At the international level there is the ambitious UNESCO program, Universal Availability of Publications (UAP). Although it is not actually a cooperative collection development plan, it must be mentioned. In concept UAP is grand. It proposes that all published knowledge, in whatever form it is produced, should be available to anyone whenever he or she wants it. Every information professional knows there is a long way to go in achieving that goal, even in countries with strong library systems and economies, let alone in developing countries. As Maurice Line has stated, "One of the main reasons why the situation with regard to UAP is so unsatisfactory is that availability has been approached piecemeal; particular aspects such as acquisitions and interlending have been tackled by individual libraries or groups of libraries, but uncoordinated piecemeal approaches can actually make things worse.... UAP must ultimately depend on action with individual countries."[11] If the concept is to succeed, it will be necessary to develop coordinated collection development plans in all countries and develop effective delivery systems because everyone cannot buy, process, and store everything everywhere.

Cooperative collection development is difficult. Local needs often seem to be at odds with broader needs of the area or nation. However, problems of funding and local practices can be overcome. As new delivery systems become available, we may be able to break down the need for local self-sufficiency. It will be a long, slow process, but it is necessary to keep striving for the UAP goal.

Notes

[1]Richard Dougherty, "Library Cooperation: A Case of Hanging Together or Hanging Separately," *Catholic Library World* 46 (March 1975): 324-27.

[2]*Webster's Third New International Dictionary* (Springfield, Mass.: G & C Merriam, 1976).

[3]Michael P. Sinclair, "A Typology of Library Cooperatives," *Special Libraries* 64 (April 1973): 181-86.

[4]Boyd Rayward, "Local Node," in *Multiple Library Cooperation*, ed. B. Hamilton and W. B. Ernst (New York: R. R. Bowker, 1977), 66.

[5]Paul H. Mosher and Marcia Pankake, "A Guide to Coordinated and Cooperative Collection Development," *Library Resources and Technical Services* (October/December 1983): 417-31.

[6]Tom Ballard, "Public Library Networking: Neat, Plausible, Wrong," *Library Journal* 107 (1 April 1982): 679-83.

[7]*LJ Hotline* 15, no. 11 (17 March 1986): 4.

[8]Maryann Dugan, "Library Network Analysis and Planning," *Journal of Library Automation* 2 (1969): 157-75.

[9]Sarah E. Thomas, "Collection Development at the Center for Research Libraries: Policy and Practice," *College & Research Libraries* 46 (May 1985): 230-35.

[10]"Developing Collections in Colorado," *Colorado Libraries* 8 (December 1982): 78.

[11]Maurice Line, "Universal Availability of Publications: An Introduction," *Scandinavian Public Library Quarterly* 15 (1982): 48.

Further Reading

General

Coordinating Cooperative Collection Development: A National Perspective. Edited by W. Luquire. New York: Haworth Press, 1986.

"Developing Collections in Colorado." *Colorado Libraries* 8 (December 1982): 78.

Dougherty, R. "Library Cooperation: A Case of Hanging Together or Hanging Separately." *Catholic Library World* 46 (March 1975): 324-27.

Dugan, M. "Library Network Analysis and Planning." *Journal of Library Automation* 2 (September 1969): 157-75.

Line, M. "Universal Availability of Publications: An Introduction." *Scandinavian Public Library Quarterly* 15 (1982): 48-49.

Metz, P. "Duplication in Library Collections: What We Know and What We Need to Know." *Collection Building* 2, no. 3 (1980): 27-33.

Mosher, P. H. "A National Scheme for Collaboration in Collection Development." In *Coordinating Cooperative Collection Development*, edited by W. Luquire. New York: Haworth Press, 1986.

Mosher, P. H., and M. Pankake. "A Guide to Coordinated and Cooperative Collection Development." *Library Resources and Technical Services* 27 (October/December 1983): 417-31.

Networks for Networkers: Critical Issues in Cooperative Library Development. New York: Neal-Schuman, 1980.

O'Connell, J. B. "Collection Evaluation in a Developing Country." *Libri* 34 (March 1984): 44-64.

Sinclair, M. "A Typology of Library Cooperatives." *Special Libraries* 64 (April 1973): 181-86.

Sohn, J. "Cooperative Collection Development: A Brief Overview." *Collection Management* 8 (Summer 1986): 1-10.

Academic

Edelman, F. "Death of the Farmington Plan." *Library Journal* 98 (15 April 1973): 1251-53.

Glicksman, M. "Some Thoughts on the Future of the Center for Research Libraries." *Journal of Academic Librarianship* 10 (July 1984): 148-50.

Holickey, B. H. "Collection Development vs. Resource Sharing." *Journal of Academic Librarianship* 10 (July 1984): 146-47.

International Conference on Research Library Cooperation. Edited by John Heager. New York: Haworth Press, 1986.

Munn, R. F. "Cooperation Will Not Save Us." *Journal of Academic Librarianship* 12 (July 1986): 166-67.

Rutsein, J. "Cooperative Collection Development among Research Libraries: The Colorado Experience." In *Coordinating Cooperative Collection Development*, edited by W. Luquire. New York: Haworth Press, 1986.

Thomas, S. E. "Collection Development at the Center for Research Libraries." *College & Research Libraries* 46 (May 1985): 230-35.

Public

Abbott, P., and R. Kavanagh. "Electronic Resource Sharing Changes Interloan Patterns." *Library Journal* 111 (1 October 1986): 56-58.

Ballard, T. H. *Failure of Resource Sharing in Public Libraries and Alternative Strategies for Service.* Chicago: American Library Association, 1986.

_____. "Public Library Networking: Neat, Plausible, Wrong." *Library Journal* 107 (1 April 1982): 679-83.

Fiels, K. M. "Coordinated Collection Development in a Multitype Environment." *Collection Building* 7 (Summer 1985): 26-31.

Public Library in the Bibliographic Network. Edited by Betty S. Turock. New York: Haworth Press, 1986.

Rayward, B. "Local Node." In *Multiple Library Cooperation*, edited by B. Hamilton and W. B. Ernst. New York: R. R. Bowker, 1977.

Yelland, M. *Local Library Co-operation.* London: British Library, 1980.

School

Doan, J. K. "School Library Media Centers in Networks." *School Library Media Quarterly* 13 (Summer 1985): 191-99.

Dyer, Ester R. *Cooperation in Library Service to Children.* Metuchen, N.J.: Scarecrow Press, 1978.

Rogers, J. V. "Networking and School Media Centers." In *Advances in Librarianship*, edited by M. H. Harris. New York: Academic Press, 1981.

Special

Jennings, D. M. "Computer Networking for Scientists." *Science* (28 February 1986): 943-80.

17
Preservation

A major premise of this book is that collection development is the central function of collection management. However, collection management also entails a number of other functions, including the preservation and conservation of the collection. Because there should be a concern for preservation and conservation throughout the collection development process, it seems appropriate to place responsibility for preservation with the collection managers. Preservation is an issue, starting with the purchase decision, which ought to include consideration of how well the material will "stand up" to the expected use, and ending with the question of what to do about worn, damaged materials and items identified in the weeding process. *Preservation* and *conservation* are terms used to identify the subject of this chapter and they are often used interchangeably. Their dictionary meanings are similar, but there is a slight difference. To *conserve*, as defined in *Webster's Third New International Dictionary*, means "to keep in a safe or sound state as by deliberate, planned or intelligent care." To *preserve* is defined as "to keep safe from injury, harm or destruction; to keep or save from decomposition."[1] Library and information center interest in this subject has two major elements: one is the general handling of materials in the collection and the other is what to do about materials that are decomposing. In this chapter I use the term *conservation* in reference to the handling and storage issues and *preservation* in reference to the problems of longevity, while recognizing that the two are interrelated.

Conservation Factors

If the collection is properly stored and handled in a controlled climate, and if some disaster preparedness plans are in place, the useful life of materials will be lengthened and preservation problems reduced. Books and other items will wear out more quickly than they should if good conservation methods are not employed.

Environmental Control

Climate control in the library is essential to conservation. Few libraries will be able to follow the Newberry Library's example of creating a stack area, 10 stories high, double shelled, windowless, and monitored by a computerized environmental system. Something less complex, however imperfect, will help extend the useful life of most materials. The major concerns for environmental control are humidity, temperature, and light. These factors are taken into account when a library building is being designed. Unfortunately, it is often the case that there are conflicting "ideal" environmental requirements in a library: human needs and material needs. Newberry Library's new stacks are maintained at 60 degrees +/- 5 degrees Fahrenheit; people are not too happy to engage in sedentary work all day at that temperature. Most libraries were designed with human environmental requirements first and the material's needs second. Thus, building design characteristics represent one problem for good conservation practice. Another problem has been the recent emphasis on energy conservation, which led to cooler temperatures in the winter and higher temperatures in the summer. Cooler winter temperatures are better for the materials, but the temperature is still higher than 60 degrees. Where the greatest damage has occurred is in the summer and where reduction in fuel consumption has been the first priority. Air conditioning is reduced and this frequently means less control over the relative humidity.

The Library of Congress Preservation Leaflet no. 2 recommends a temperature of 55 degrees Fahrenheit in storage areas and not more than 75 degrees Fahrenheit in reading areas (below 70 degrees if possible), all with a 50 percent relative humidity. Paul Banks, a well-known preservation specialist who set the standards for the Newberry storage area, also recommended 50 percent relative humidity. For most libraries constructed after World War II, there is little chance of having temperature differentials in storage and reading areas because the design concept called for integrating readers and materials. Also, in most libraries the temperature and humidity range is much greater than +/- 5 degrees.

Why be concerned with humidity? Because changes in humidity can physically weaken materials in the collection, which in turn can create added costs for repair or replacement. Books (including bound periodicals) are made up of a number of different materials—paper, cloth, cardboard, thread, man-made fabrics, adhesives, and sometimes metal (staples). Often, a single book will have several different types from each category; for example, heavy endpapers, a moderate weight paper for the text, and coated paper for illustrations. Each component will absorb and lose water vapor (humidity) at a different rate. As the amount of water vapor goes up or down, there is constant shrinking and swelling of the materials. When water is absorbed the material expands, and it shrinks as it dries out. With each expansion and contraction, the material weakens slightly.

The differences in these rates for the different components in the book also weaken the bond between them, making the book more likely to "fall apart." Holding the humidity constant stabilizes the materials. How much water vapor is normally present is important; paper fibers are subject to cracking or breaking when humidity is below 40 percent. At 65 percent or higher, the chances of mildew and mold formation increase. The "musty" smell of the antiquarian bookshop may contain more than a hint of mildew or mold, something one does not want in the library. Other materials (microfilms, videotapes, photographs, and so forth) are also adversely affected by humidity changes. Microforms should be stored in humidity levels below those for paper-based materials.

Recalling some basic chemistry, we know that increasing the temperature also increases chemical activity. Roughly, chemical reactions double with each 10-degree increase in temperature. Freezing books would be the best way to preserve them; however, it is not likely that readers would be willing to sit about in earmuffs, overcoats, and mittens. There is no way of foretelling what the staff might do under these circumstances. One would be fortunate to achieve a controlled temperature below 70 degrees Fahrenheit in areas where people work for extended periods. One reason for wanting the lower temperatures is to slow down the chemical decomposition of wood pulp paper, which the majority of the books and journals contain. However, lower temperatures only slow down the process, they do not stop it. A second reason is that temperature changes cause fluctuations in the humidity. All formats are sensitive to temperature variations and are best stored in an environment with minimal changes. In fact, *constant* high temperatures and humidity are less damaging than cycles of highs and lows.

Lighting influences conservation in two ways. First, it is a contributor to the heat buildup in a building. Naturally, it is taken into account when a heating, ventilating, and air conditioning system is designed. Fluorescent lighting is not a major heat contributor, but in older libraries where incandescent fixtures are employed heat can be a problem. If the light fixtures are close to the materials, there can be significant temperature differentials from the bottom to the top shelf in a storage unit. Windows and sunlight combine to generate heat as well, and create "mini"-climates. The Newberry Library windowless storage unit eliminates the sunlight problem. Many libraries were designed with numerous windows to provide natural lighting and satisfy people's desire to see outside. The cost of these designs has been high, both in terms of money spent to reduce the sunlight problem after a few years and in damaged materials.

The second concern is the ultraviolet radiation which occurs in sunlight, and fluorescent and tungsten lights. Ultraviolet light is the most damaging form of light because it quickly causes materials to fade, turn yellow, and become brittle. Windows and fluorescent light fixtures should be equipped with ultraviolet screens and/or filters. Tungsten lighting has the lowest levels of ultraviolet radiation, but these lights also should be filtered. The longer materials are exposed to light, the more quickly damage will occur. Nonprint materials are even more light-sensitive and require greater protective measures.

Air filters that reduce the gases in the air inside the library are useful, though expensive. In large urban areas, a variety of harmful gases are added to the air during the day. Few buildings have airlocks and ventilating systems that remove all harmful gases. Whenever it is economical, the ventilation system should remove the most harmful substances, even though some will enter the building as people come and go. Sulfur dioxide is a major pollutant that should be filtered out, because it combines with water vapor to form sulfurous acid. Hydrogen sulfide, another common pollutant, also forms an acid that is harmful to both organic and inorganic materials. Filters can also reduce the amount of solid particles that are present in the air. Solid particles act as abrasives, and as such they contribute to the wearing out and wearing down of materials. Dusty, "gritty" shelves wear away the edges of bindings, and all too often dusting book shelves is not in anyone's job description.

Finally, insects contribute to the destruction of books and other items in the collection. Silverfish enjoy nothing more than a feast of wood pulp paper, flour paste, and glue. Cockroaches seem to eat anything but have a taste for book glue. Termites prefer straight wood but wood pulp paper is a good second choice. Larder beetle larvae (book worms), while lacking intellectual curiosity, can devour *War and Peace* in a short time. Finally, book lice enjoy the starch and gelatin sizing on paper. There are other less destructive insects that can infest collections in the temperate zones; in a tropical setting the numbers and varieties increase dramatically. Control of insects presents a few challenges, since the pesticides also create pollution problems. Naturally, the best control is to keep the insects out. Gifts to the library should be examined carefully before being housed in an area where insects could get into the general collection. Shipments that arrive by sea mail also need careful examination. As the concern for the environment increases, many of the in-library fumigation units have had to be closed or extensively (and expensively) modified. This may mean using commercial systems with additional costs and delays in getting and keeping material on the shelf.

Proper Handling

Storage and handling is the second element in a good conservation program. An obvious question: are the storage units appropriate for the materials? Too narrow and/or shallow a shelf will result in items being knocked off and damaged. Filling shelves and drawers too tightly is poor conservation. Anyone with extensive experience in shelving books (except perhaps a preservation specialist) has probably found a way to squeeze in "just one more book" onto a shelf when some shifting would be in order. Cracked and damaged book spines are the result of such practices, as well as torn head bands resulting from people trying to pull out a book from a fully packed shelf. Books should be vertical or horizontal on the shelf, not leaning this way and that. Fore-edge or spine shelving is equally bad; the textblock is attached to the case with the expectation that the book will be shelved with the spine vertical to the shelf. Proper supports and bookends aid in keeping materials in good order. Poorly constructed or finished supports can be more damaging to the materials than having none at all.

Teaching people how to handle the material properly is important, and this includes patrons as well as staff. Some librarians regard the "housekeeping" concerns as bad for the "image." I suppose it can be, but if it is made clear that monies spent on the repair and replacement of materials ultimately means less money to buy new material, people see there is a point. With bindery fees going up all the time, it does not take more than two or three items sent to be rebound to equal the cost of a new book.

Fire and water damage are disasters that can and should be prepared for to minimize losses should a disaster strike. Even with a fire, water damage will probably be more of a problem. Rainstorms, broken pipes, and defective air conditioning systems are the most common sources of library water problems. By having a plan ready and people who know how to implement the plan, losses can be kept to a minimum.

Locating water, gas, and electrical system shut-offs is a good starting point in developing a preparedness plan. Check on fire extinguisher locations, and be certain they are tested on a regular basis and that all staff members know how to use them. There are three types of fire extinguishers ("A" for wood and paper type fires, "B" for oil and electrical, and "C" for either); match type to location and anticipated problem. Prepare floor plans, clearly identifying locations to shut-offs and extinguishers. Color coding the stack areas, thus indicating priorities, can save valuable time during salvage operations. Assign specific duties to staff members and conduct drills. Organize an emergency telephone "tree" for contacting staff and others, for both working and nonworking hours. Although it is not always possible to change storage locations, attempt to house the irreplaceable and most valuable materials in the best (safest) location. Best or safest is usually *not* the basement or the top level of the building.

Salvage operations require careful planning, and adequate personnel and materials. It is a good idea to develop a list of potential volunteers if the situation is too large for the staff to handle within a reasonable time frame. What types of supplies are required? The best way to handle large quantities of water-soaked paper is to freeze them and then process the material as time and money allow. One should identify companies with large freezer facilities and discuss with them the possibilities of using or renting their freezers in case of an emergency. Often they are willing to be involved at no cost because of the positive publicity they can gain from such an agreement. Large grocery store chains and major meat packing plants are possible participants in the plan. Refrigerated trucks can be most useful in the summer months when there is a major water damage problem. Getting wet materials to the freezing units is a problem; milk crates, open plastic boxes, or clothes baskets are very good, as they allow water to drip out. Cardboard boxes cause problems because they absorb water. Plastic interlocking milk crates are best, because they are about the right size for a person to handle when they are three-fourths filled with wet material. Sometimes local dairies are willing to assist by supplying free crates for the duration of the emergency. Freezer paper is needed for wrapping up the materials—never use newsprint because it tends to stick and the ink comes off. Thymol crystals are important in defumigation and help to keep mold under control. Major chemical suppliers should be able to secure them in a short time if they are not in stock. Finally, find some drying facilities; vacuum drying is generally the best way to handle the wet items. Often such facilities are difficult to locate and usually can handle only a small volume of material, so materials may be in the freezer for a long time while a small quantity is done whenever the source and funding permit.

Two other very important steps should be taken. One is to identify the nearest conservation specialist(s). Most are willing to serve at least as a telephone resource and often they will come to the scene. A second important step is to arrange for special purchasing power. Although some groups, organizations, and companies may be willing to assist free of charge, often many will not be, and there may be a need to make a commitment quickly to a specific expense. Having to wait even a few hours for approval may cause some irreversible damage. Read about the methods of handling different formats in different disaster situations and develop a plan. A few suggested readings are included at the end of this chapter.

Although most "disasters" are minor—a few hundred water damaged items—a major disaster is always possible. One example is the 29 April 1986 fire that struck the Los Angeles Public Library. For more than 10 years there was concern about the fire danger, but the hope that a new building would be constructed forestalled major modifications in the existing building. According to *Library Hotline*, it took 1,700 volunteers working around the clock to shrink wrap and freeze the 400,000 water soaked books (about 20 percent of Central Library's collection).[2] In addition, the city is to pay a salvage contractor $500,000 for his firm's services. One can only speculate what the costs and problems might have been with no disaster preparedness plan.

Preservation Factors

Without question, the major source of conservation and preservation problems is acidic wood pulp paper. William J. Barrow is the person most often associated with identifying acid as the cause for the deterioration of wood pulp paper. The problem is not new, but people are now seeing the full implications of Barrow's, and other researchers', findings. In 1957 the Council on Library Resources funded a study on durability of paper. Estimates vary as to just how big the problem is. A project I was involved in estimated that over 600,000 out of two million books in the UCLA library system in 1979 were brittle or moderately brittle (a corner would break off with two or fewer folds). This was based on a random sample of books in the collection. An estimated one million volumes in Widener Library (Harvard University) are in a similar condition,[3] while a six-million-volume estimate has been made for the Library of Congress.[4]

Acidic residues left over from the wood pulp paper manufacturing process are the culprits. As the care and expense in the paper manufacturing process rise, the amount of residue drops. Newspapers are printed on high-acid paper, while some books are printed on acid-free wood pulp paper. The Council on Library Resources has tried to establish some guidelines for publishers, manufacturers, and librarians for the use of acid-free paper in book production. The CLR report states that "acid-free paper *need not be more expensive* than acidic paper of the quality normally used in hardbound books."[5] The guidelines provide standards for both performance (acid content) and durability (folding and bending), as well as long-term book binding for the initial commercial binding.

While the guidelines may help reduce the future problems, they cannot help the present situation. Each year the number of brittle items will increase until the guidelines are followed by the majority of publishers. What can be done about materials that are self-destructing in the stacks? By maintaining the environmental factors (temperature, humidity, light) at the recommended levels the process will be slowed and thus this is a first step to take. For the brittle materials in the collection, the two concerns are permanence (shelf life) and durability (use). Permanence is the first issue, and there are several ways to stop the acidic activity. Once permanence is assured, several options exist to enhance durability.

As of mid-1986 there is one mass deacidification system in general use (Wei T'o) and another system that is being carefully re-examined (the Library of Congress DEZ process). After several problems, including an explosion at the test site, the LC system is being studied in terms of its safety. Considerable debate has taken place over the relative merits and costs of the two systems. With the explosion at the LC site, the issue will not be resolved until a safe handling process can be established.

Both systems are designed for "mass" deacidification, that is, to treat large quantities of books at the same time, rather than handling individual books a page at a time. According to the developer of Wei T'o (Richard D. Smith), it is a wide-ranging preservation process: it deacidifies, prevents oxidation, prevents biological attack (insects and fungus), prevents photochemical attacks (light, particularly ultraviolet), and helps increase longevity by helping control "wear and tear."[6] LC's system is designed to deacidify. Both require special facilities designed to handle large quantities of books and other materials using acidic paper. *Library Hotline* has reported that "the $11 million being spent by LC would build a number of smaller Wei T'o systems which would have had the capacity (together) of processing a great many more books than the LC facility will handle."[7] Both systems employ a pressure technique to force the chemical agents into the paper and bindings. Cost estimates for the mass processes, not including physical facilities and equipment, range from under $2.00 to over $7.00 per item. (Not a small cost when considering the hundreds of thousands of items needing treatment, and one wonders where the money will come from and if it will decrease the amount available for collection development.) The Wei T'o system also has a method of strengthening paper by the addition of acrylic resin in a process similar to its deacidification method. George Cunha, an internationally known preservation specialist, is preparing (1986) a factual comparison of LC and Wei T'o systems, which is to be published in a Library Technology Program Report and issued by the American Library Association.

Once the material is acid-free it must be strengthened if it is to be handled on a regular basis. There are two widely used systems to strengthen the material, in addition to the Wei T'o. One is polyester encapsulation and the other is lamination. Both use chemically inert transparent material to cover the brittle, but deacidified paper. Encapsulation uses plastic films and results in a somewhat stiff page that is rather like the identification card or badge containing a person's photograph and signature. Lamination employs linen and results in a more flexible page, but it takes more time and labor to produce. Because of the high cost lamination is very rarely used today.

Options for Handling the Brittle Materials

Given the magnitude of the acid paper problem, almost every library will be faced with a variety of decisions regarding what to do. Here, if nowhere else, collection development staff must enter the preservation picture. When an item in the collection is found to have deteriorated to the point that it cannot be rebound, what should be done? Ten options exist:

1. Ignore the problem and return the item to storage.

2. Withdraw the item from the collection and do not replace.

3. Seek a reprint edition, on acid-free paper.

4. Have the material microfilmed and decide what to do with the original.

5. Have the material converted to an optical disk system.

6. Have the material photocopied, on acid-free paper, and decide what to do with the original.

7. Seek a replacement copy in the out-of-print trade.

8. Have an acid-free protective enclosure made for the item and return to the collection.

9. Have the item withdrawn from the main collection and place in a secondary storage facility.

10. Have the item restored (deacidified and strengthened).

Ignoring the problem for some materials is the most reasonable alternative when one is confident that long-term retention is unnecessary or undesirable, and only a limited amount of use is probable. If there is little or no probability of use in the near future, then withdrawing the item is probably the most effective option.

Seeking a reprint edition printed on acid-free paper is probably the least expensive option for materials that are deemed to be worth long-term storage and where moderate to heavy use is expected. Reprints are not going to be found for all the items that are self-destructing on the shelves—only the more popular titles are reprinted. Several companies are set up to serve the reprint market, including AMS, Scholarly Reprints, Kraus, Harvester Press Microform Publications, and Research Publications. *Guide to Reprints, Books on Demand*, and *Guide to Microforms in Print* are three sources of information about a broad range of titles. *Note*: Just because the item is available as a reprint does not necessarily mean that it is printed on acid-free paper. It is important to specify that a copy on acid-free paper is desired.

Microformat and optical disk storage of the brittle material are also options. Until recently (1983), microfilming was the most common way of storing the content of brittle materials in a secondary form. The cost of making the "master" negative is high but once that has been done duplicate copies are relatively inexpensive to make. Thus, if the primary collection development issue is with preserving the intellectual content of the brittle material and not with the item as an "artifact," a microformat may be the best solution. It may be possible to locate a master copy of an item, thereby reducing costs. Two places to check are the *National Register of Microforms Masters* and *Guide to Microforms in Print*. The *Register* covers more than 3,000 library and publisher holdings worldwide and is produced by the Library of Congress. *Guide to Microforms in Print* (Meckler Publishing) is similar to *BIP* since it lists titles from commercial publishers (worldwide). *The Directory of Library Reprographic Services* (Meckler Publishing) can be of assistance in identifying libraries with the capability of making a master if that is what needs to be done. So far only the Library of Congress has experimented with analog videodisk technology. The advantages are high-density storage (54,000 graphic images, for example, can be stored on one disk) and random access. Optical disks on the other hand are used to store print material. A disk can hold about 3,000 pages of text or 200,000 catalog cards. Both technologies have potential for assisting in solving our preservation problems. As might be expected, there is a relatively high cost associated with these systems, but as more organizations use optical or analog disk technology, it is reasonable to expect the cost to decline. Some publishers and even the Copyright Office have raised questions regarding the legality of converting copyrighted material to a disk format. How this differs in principal from microfilming, which no one seems to have questioned, I do not know.

Under U.S. Copyright Law it is possible for a library to make a single complete copy of an out-of-print item (see Sec. 108 [e]) after a reasonable search has been made. A photocopy of the original may be the best option where moderate use is expected and no reprint can be located, since many people dislike using microformat readers. This is an especially good alternative when it is not necessary to preserve the original item and moderate use is expected. Photocopying and microfilming cause physical wear on bound materials, and for a rebound item to be properly duplicated it should be taken apart. Generally, in the photocopy process there is also some loss in image quality; obviously, it is not recommended for items with photographs and illustrations. Several paper manufacturers offer "buffered" (acid-free) paper for photocopy machine use (for example Hollinger, Process Materials, and Xerox). When the photocopies are bound, it is necessary to specify that buffered materials be employed. *Note*: If acid-free paper or deacidified paper comes into contact with acidic material the acid will "migrate" into the acid-free paper and the process starts all over.

Going into the out-of-print market for a replacement copy should be considered carefully before starting a search. Although a replacement copy may be available at the lowest price of any of the options, what will be gained? Unless the replacement copy has been stored under much better conditions than the original copy, both will be in about the same state of deterioration. It is probable that the replacement copy will be less worn (as long as it is not an ex-library copy), but there will be little difference in the acidic state. Frequently the replacement copy will have been housed in an even more uncontrolled environment than the library and thus be in greater need of preservation than the original copy. Locating a replacement copy in the o.p. market can be a long-term affair lasting months and often years. Given the time factor, it will still be necessary to decide what to do with the item in hand. If it is brittle, should a patron be allowed to use it while the library is waiting for a replacement copy that may or may not be found? Additional use may make it difficult, or perhaps impossible, to exercise other options if a replacement is not found. Although the o.p. is a frequent first choice, it is probably the least suitable if long-term preservation is needed.

Protective enclosures or containers are in many ways a "stopgap" treatment. The brittle item is enclosed in an acid-free container (paper, plastic, cardboard) which protects it from unnecessary handling; this is often used for secondary storage of the original (hopefully deacidified) when a surrogate copy has been placed in the general collection. The most common method is to use acid-free cardboard to prepare a "phase" box made to the size of the item to be stored. Bindery supply firms as well as commercial binderies offer a wide range of prefabricated "standard size" phase boxes, as well as the materials to allow construction of custom-made boxes. They also supply laminating and encapsulating materials, as well as the supplies needed to deacidify books, using a book by book (manual) approach. Unfortunately, the materials, including acid-free mending tapes and adhesives, tend to be expensive, and sometimes libraries decide not to use the proper materials in order to save a small amount of money.

Certainly there is no need to use expensive mending materials on an item that one knows will be thrown away in time, but all too often we do not know which items will be kept and which will go.

Secondary storage is also a stopgap measure in most cases. It may become the most common first option when the quantity of brittle materials escalates beyond our ability to handle the daily amount. A controlled environment with limited handling would slow down the destructive process and buy us some additional time to determine which of the more permanent solutions should be implemented. The essential element is the controlled environment; just placing the materials in a remote storage area with the same or worse climate control accomplishes little or even causes further deterioration. One danger of the storage area solution is that all too often, the old adage "out of sight out of mind" applies. Without a preservation officer or someone on the staff charged with supervising preservation activities, the storage area can become a dumping ground for materials that no one wants to think about "today." Even in the controlled environment, the disintegration continues day and night until we do something to stop it.

Restoration is very expensive, and not all or even most of the brittle items should be restored. As noted earlier, the deacidification process is expensive, and added to that are costs of restoring strength to the individual pages and binding. Several years ago I worked with Daniela Moneta, who has written a specialization paper on the costs of alternative treatments of brittle material. Figure 17.1 contains data from her paper—naturally the costs would be different (higher) today. However, the relationship of the costs to one another should be approximately the same. (Her study assumed that the item in need of preservation or conservation was a 250-page quarto size book.)

Although this chapter has emphasized books and paper, other library materials are also in need of care, and some action is being taken. For example, CLR, the Mellon Foundation, and the National Endowment for the Humanities (NEH) are working with the American Film Foundation on producing a documentary film on the subject of preservation of library materials. This is particularly appropriate because motion picture film is another major preservation problem. All photographic products (microfilm, photographs, motion picture films) are also self-destructing on the shelves of libraries and archives. There is some hope that video disks will provide a more stable storage medium for older materials, but little testing has been done on the longevity of such systems. The Library of Congress is using analog videodisks to store images from old glass lantern slides, photographs, motion picture publicity stills, and architectural drawings.

LEVEL ONE—Rare material in brittle condition

Treatment A: Preservation of the material as an artifact with a surrogate copy to protect the original from excessive handling.

Deacidification, aqueous if possible.
Mending and tissue lamination of pages.
Return to original binding or case, or rebind and preserve original binding in book box as an artifact.
Construct custom-made box.
Microfilm and produce paper copy (Copyflo) to protect the original from excessive handling, or contract to have the material reprinted, or photocopy material.

Cost:

Deacidification, tissue lamination ($1 a page)		$250
Restoration of binding		50
Custom-made box		45
One of the following:		
Microfilm (silver)	$25	
Film, Copyflo, bind	45	
Photocopy & bind	25	
Reprint	25	
Average cost		30
Total		$375

Treatment B: Polyester book.
Preservation of the material as an artifact.
No surrogate copy is necessary since the polyester book can withstand a certain amount of handling.

Deacidification, aqueous if possible.
Mending and encapsulation of pages.

Cost:

Deacidification, mending, encapsulation and
    post binder.

                                    Total $250

LEVEL TWO—Semi-rare material in brittle condition

Preserve as an artifact for artistic or bibliographical reasons, because of the binding, graphics, illustrations, or typographical importance.

Do not restore.
Vapor deacidify.
Construct custom box, phase box, or protective wrapper.
Produce surrogate to protect original from excessive handling, i.e., microfilm or reprint. To photocopy would be too damaging.

Cost:

Vapor deacidify.		$ 5
One of the following:		
Custom-made box	$40	
Phase box	5	
Protective wrapper	3	
Average cost		16
One of the following:		
Microfilm, special handling for bound material in fragile condition	$50	
Film, Copyflo, bind.	70	
Reprint	25	
Average cost		48
Total		$69

LEVEL THREE—Research material in brittle condition

Treatment A: Preservation of the informational content of the book, discard artifact.*

Demand for information to circulate in hard copy; microfilm and Copyflo, photocopy or reprint.

Cost:

One of the following:		
Film, Copyflo, bind	$45	
Photocopy & bind	25	
Reprint	25	
Average cost		$32
Total		$32

Treatment B: Preserve information and discard artifact.*

Low demand, microfilm and have paper copy available only from reader/printer.

Cost:

Microfilm		$25
Total		$25

LEVEL FOUR—Expendable material

Discard artifact.*
Do not preserve information.

Cost:	Total	$0

---

*No figures given for cost to discard.

Fig. 17.1. "Options for Handling Brittle Books." Reprinted with permission of Daniela Moneta.

Cooperation and the Future

Because of the magnitude of the problems confronting libraries and scholars, it seems clear that cooperative preservation needs to take place. The Council on Library Resources has been supportive of the development of a national preservation plan. ARL and RLG have been collecting statistics on research library preservation activities and developing guidelines. The National Endowment for the Humanities has provided funding for microfilming projects. A program for educating preservation librarians was established at the Columbia University Library School, and many large libraries are hiring full-time preservation specialists. The Library of Congress publishes a newsletter, *National Preservation News*, and the American Institute for Conservation of Historic and Artistic Works (AIC) provides a forum for concerned individuals to discuss preservation and conservation issues. Naturally, the American Library Association and many of its divisions have an active interest in this area, as do most other library associations around the world. Much remains to be done, but with several groups actively working on the problems, the future looks much brighter than it did even five years ago.

Notes

[1] *Webster's Third New International Dictionary* (Springfield, Mass.: G & C Merriam, 1976).

[2] *Library Hotline* (12 May 1986), 2.

[3] *Harvard Crimson*, 23 October 1986, 1.

[4] *Book Longevity* (Washington, D.C.: Council on Library Resources, 1982).

[5] Ibid., 9.

[6] Richard D. Smith, "Mass Deacidification: The Wei T'o Way," *College & Research Libraries News* (December 1984): 588-93.

[7] *Library Hotline* (11 February 1983), 1.

Further Reading

General

Bohem, H. *Disaster Prevention and Disaster Preparedness*. Berkeley, Calif.: Office of the Assistant Vice-President, Library Plans and Policies, University of California, 1978.

Book Longevity. Washington, D.C.: Council on Library Resources, 1982.

Brittle Books: Reports of the Committee on Preservation and Access. Washington, D.C.: Council on Library Resources, 1986.

Cunha, G., and D. Cunha. *Library and Archives Conservation: 1980s and Beyond.* 2 vol. Metuchen, N.J.: Scarecrow Press, 1983.

Greenfield, J. *Books, Their Care and Repair.* New York: H. W. Wilson, 1983.

Jackson-Beck, L. "Problems of Preservation." *Collection Building* 7 (Summer 1985): 21-25.

Morris, J. *Library Disaster Preparedness Handbook.* Chicago: American Library Association, 1986.

Morrow, C. C., and C. Dyal. *Conservation Treatment Procedures.* 2d ed. Littleton, Colo.: Libraries Unlimited, 1986.

Morrow, C. C., and G. Walker. *Preservation Challenge.* White Plains, N.Y.: Knowledge Industry Publications, 1983.

Nyren, K. "DEZ Process and the Library of Congress." *Library Journal* 111 (15 September 1986): 33-35.

_____. "LC Reports Flaws in DEZ Process Will Contract with Chemical Firm." *Library Journal* 111 (August 1986): 22.

Ratcliffe, F. W. *Preservation Policies and Conservation in British Libraries.* London: British Library, 1984.

Smith, R. D. "Mass Deacidification: The Wei T'o Understanding." *College & Research Libraries News* 48 (January 1987): 2-10.

_____. "Mass Deacidification: The Wei T'o Way." *College & Research Libraries News* (December 1984): 588-93.

Thomson, G. *Museum Environment.* 2d ed. Stoneham, Mass.: Butterworths, 1986.

"Wei T'o vs DEZ Debate." *Library Hotline* 16 (11 February 1985): 1.

18
Legal Issues

Collection development activities are influenced by many laws and regulations. Two of the topics discussed here are a concern only for U.S. libraries. However, the majority of the chapter addresses two concepts, copyright and lending rights, that are of worldwide interest. The two minor legal issues relate to the U.S. Internal Revenue Service (IRS) regulations.

One of the IRS regulations has to do with gifts and donations to a library or not-for-profit information center. Any gift "in kind" (books, journals, manuscripts, and so forth) that has an appraised value of more than $5,000 must be reported to the IRS by the receiving library. A second regulation now forbids the receiving party, in this case a library, to estimate a value for the gift-in-kind. The valuation must be made by a third disinterested party or organization. Normally an appraiser charges a fee for this service, and the donor pays the fee. Most often the appraisers are antiquarian dealers, and they usually charge a flat fee for the service unless the collection is very large or complex. In appraising such a collection, they frequently charge by the hour. Typically with small gifts the library writes a letter of acknowledgment that indicates the number and type of items received. Donors then can set a value on the gift for tax purposes. According to an article by Norman Tanis and C. Ventuleth, there have been increased problems in securing gifts.[1] Just what impact the U.S. 1986 Tax Reform Act will have is impossible to foretell, but with major restrictions being imposed on "charitable" deductions it seems likely to magnify prior problems.

Another IRS regulation or ruling (the Thor Power Tool decision) also has had some influence on acquisition practices in the 1980s. The ruling held that a practice common to business, including publishing, of "writing-down" the value of inventories to a low level each year was illegal. The practice had resulted in a "paper" loss that was deducted from the income, thus reducing tax liability. The

U.S. Supreme Court decided that to do this was to take a current deduction for an estimated future loss and said that this could not be allowed. Only if the inventory is defective or if there is "objective evidence" that the inventory was offered for sale below cost can the write-down be employed.

What does the Thor decision have to do with collection development? The answer is that publishers have followed this practice of writing-down inventories and many claim that it was the only way they could afford to publish small press runs of books expected to be slow sellers (taking four to five years to sell out the first printing). Publishers talked about destroying some of their stock and some did so. In 1981 and 1982 jobbers indicated that they had received increased o.p. and o.s. reports from publishers. Blackwell North America stated in one of its promotional flyers (in mid-1981), "we are receiving more o.p., o.s. and generally non-reports, than ever before. In fact, our reports to libraries on unavailable titles have increased 47 percent over a year ago." There has been some hope that the U.S. Congress might pass some legislation exempting publishers, but as of 1986 nothing had happened. Concern has decreased but publishers tend to declare items out-of-print more quickly now than before the Thor decision. No one is certain whether there has been a decline in short run titles published, or whether such a decline, if it exists, is directly linked to the Thor decision or is merely due to a changing economy. What the decision does mean is that librarians should not count on finding this year's imprints available in a year or two. In the past a library might well have decided not to buy some current items, thinking that they could be ordered in a year or two, when funding would be better. Today it is probably best to buy it now rather than to wait.

Copyright

Is copyright an issue in collection development? The answer is yes. Cooperative collection development efforts are dependent upon sharing resources through interlibrary loan or some reciprocal borrowing agreement. How will the new copyright law affect these programs? As noted in chapter 16, the Information Industry Association has formed a task force to look at the issue of library resource sharing. Only time will provide the definitive answer to the question of what changes will be necessary to comply with the present law. What is clear is that libraries have modified their copying policies as well as interlibrary loan practices. For example, under the new law, a library in a not-for-profit setting may "borrow" not more than five articles per year from any given journal. Should it borrow more than five, it is assumed that the borrowing was in lieu of placing a subscription and is a violation of the law. If libraries may not freely exchange books, periodicals, or photocopies of copyrighted items, it will be difficult to develop effective cooperative systems.

Copyright is granted to the creators of works to protect their interest in the work. Originally, copyright was intended to protect against unauthorized printing, publishing, importing, or selling of multiple copies of a work: in essence, it was protection from the unauthorized mass production and sale of a work. Libraries, on the other hand, are established to disseminate information on a mass, normally free-of-charge basis. With the development of fast and cheap photocopying, a new problem arose. There might be only single copies made for a patron; however, the aggregate number of copies has been high. The volume of copying became so great that copyright holders felt that their rights were being violated, and some probably were correct.

In the past, copying printed matter for personal use was limited. Word-for-word hand copying of extensive sections of books or complete magazine articles was very uncommon — people took notes. Today, quick, relatively inexpensive copy services exist everywhere. All of us have made photocopies of complete journal articles rather than take notes, and many of the articles were from current issues of periodicals that we could have purchased for not much more than the cost of the copied item. We have all done it and, if we thought about it at all, felt that "just one copy isn't going to hurt anyone." Unfortunately, as the number of such copies mounts, so does the problem.

With audiovisual materials, the problem is acute (in video- and audiotapes, for instance). Institutions and individuals who own the hardware to play these materials also have copying capabilities. Control of audiovisual copying is even more difficult to achieve for audiovisual materials than for books or journals. Preview copies help control the institutional buying situation, as they tend to show wear to such an extent that many persons would not want to reproduce a copy. If the preview copy is too worn, however, the buyer may decide that the item lacks technical quality and therefore not buy it.

Library patrons and society in general, however, have certain rights to gain access to and use of copyrighted material. Where to draw the line between creators' and users' rights is a very complicated problem. An editorial by J. Berry in *Library Journal* summed up the complex issues involved in library copying:

> Here at *LJ* we are often asked why the magazine has not come out strongly on one side or the other of the copyright issue. We are after all a library magazine.... In the case of copyright, however, our library-mindedness is somewhat blunted by the facts of our existence as a publication which is in copyright and is published by an independent, commercial publisher. Not only is copyright protection fundamental to our continued fiscal health, [but] we believe that authors and publishers deserve compensation for their creative work and for the risks taken to package and deliver that creative effort to users of it.
>
> Like any magazine publisher we have winced when it was obvious our rights in our published material have been violated.... Yet there is the other side, the flattery in the notion that people want to read what we print, and the gratification that so many share our view of its importance.
>
> So the issue of copyright, particularly of library copying, is deeply complicated for us.... We don't believe that "fair use" should be eliminated, but we can't subscribe to the view that wholesale copying should be allowed for "educational purposes."
>
> The answer has to be compromise.[2]

Several points need to be emphasized about copyright. First, the problem of how to handle the rights of creators and users is worldwide — worldwide in several senses. First, each country has to deal with its local copyright problem, and it must also be concerned about international copyright. Second, much of the controversy centers on educational and library copying. Third, copyright has divided authors, publishers, and producers from libraries, schools, and patrons, with the result that once very friendly working relationships have almost been destroyed. The problem has not yet reached the point of hostility, but unless true compromises are developed, that hostility may develop. Finally, there is concern over what new technological developments may bring—online systems are viewed as both threat and promise by all of the parties to the copyright controversy.

Most librarians agree that creators' rights should be protected, and even that some rights have been violated in and by libraries. Recognition of those facts is tempered by direct daily contact with users and their needs. Often it is a matter of an item not being easily available, or it involves articles reporting the results of work carried out using government funds. Since government documents are not copyrighted, many persons feel that reports of work carried out using government funds should be public property (even if published by private enterprise).

Historical Background

Producers must be encouraged to risk creating something new and make it available to society. This is true whether we are concerned with a capitalist or socialist economic system; without adequate incentives, the producer will not produce. For publishers and media producers, copyright is one of the main incentives. In essence, copyright states: "Person(s) X owns this creation; if you are not person(s) X, before you make copies of this creation for more than your own personal use, you must get written permission from person(s) X."

England was the first country to legalize creative ownership; in 1710, the English Parliament passed the Statute of Anne, the first copyright bill. This law did two things: (1) it gave Parliamentary recognition to a royal decree of 1556, and (2) it gave legal recognition to a work's author as the ultimate holder of copyright. While contemporary copyright laws exist to encourage the creation of new, original works and encourage their wide public distribution, the 1556 decree had a rather less noble purpose: repression of the freedom of religion, in this case, the Protestant Reformation. Censorship rather than free public dissemination of information and thought was the goal. By investing all publishing rights with the Stationers' Company, which represented all major English publishers, the Star Chamber (which controlled the Stationers' Company), hoped to control the flow of information to the English people.

Certainly the Statute of Anne was a notable piece of legislation and did more than merely give legal sanction to censorship. In the two centuries preceding the Statute, many changes had taken place in English society. Although by 1710 authors and publishers were allied in the fight to retain or gain more control over the use of their creations, it was an uneasy alliance, since the authors were (and are) the true creators of the copyrighted works. As the creators, authors felt that they should have a greater share and say in the way in which their works were distributed and the profits divided. Prior to 1710, all rights resided with the publisher. With the enactment of the Statute, authors were granted a 14-year monopoly on the publication of their works. An additional 14 years would be granted at the end of the first period, if the author was still living. Thus, for 28 years the creator of a work could benefit from the publication of that work.

The American colonies developed a copyright concept similar to the English model. Indeed, the concept was so ingrained in American legal thought that it was incorporated into the Constitution, wherein the U.S. Congress has been delegated the power "to promote the Progress of Science and Useful Arts, by securing for limited Times to Authors and Inventors the exclusive Right to their Respective Writings and Discoveries." Starting in 1790 and ending in 1891, the U.S. Congress passed legislation granting exclusive rights to American authors and their representatives, but it refused to grant copyright to nonresident foreign authors. Only books, maps, and charts were covered by the original act. (Even in 1790, the act covered nonbook formats.)

In 1831, Congress passed an act extending the copyright term—the new first term was for 28 years, while the second remained at 14 years. Extension of the exclusive rights has been of concern in all countries since the start of the nineteenth century. Today, it is still the heart of the matter: how far and for how long should the copyright owner control the use of the item? By 1870, copyright had been extended to cover art prints, musical compositions, photographs, "works of fine arts," translation rights, and the right to dramatize nondramatic works; performance rights were included for plays and musical compositions by 1897. The Chace Act of 1891 finally granted copyright to nonresident foreign authors, *if* their work, published in English, was *printed* in the United States. In 1909, a totally new copyright act was passed.

The 1909 Act was in force until 1 January 1978. While the 1909 Act passed through Congress more quickly than the current law, it was a matter of extended debate from 1905 to 1909. As with the 1978 law, several important issues had to be resolved in 1909—the libraries' rights to import books printed in foreign countries and the use of copyrighted music on "mechanical instruments"—phonograph records and piano rolls. After considerable debate, both rights were granted in the 1909 Act. Libraries could import a limited number of copies of a foreign work, and copyright owners were to be compensated for the use of their music in mechanical devices. (The later development of jukeboxes, which was not covered in the 1909 law, has caused a problem. The "problem" was that a new "technology"—the jukebox—was not identified in the law and there was no mechanism for paying copyright owners for the repeated use of their works in a jukebox, which was designed to make a profit for the machine's owner.) Composers were concerned with technological developments in 1909; authors and publishers were concerned with technological developments in 1978. The entire issue of new technologies has made copyright ever more complex.

Other provisions of the 1909 law (as passed and amended over the years) include coverage of motion pictures; the owner of a nondramatic literary work controlling public "renditions" of the work *for profit* and the making of transcriptions or sound recordings of the work; foreign authors being given full copyright protection so that the United States could join the Universal Copyright Convention (in 1954); coverage of all sound recordings; two copyright terms of 28 years each, with a renewal requirement for the second term; and all works being required to carry a notice of copyright. Several of these provisions have created barriers for American and foreign producers, and they have also made it difficult for the United States to be an effective member of a worldwide copyright program. The three major stumbling blocks have been term of protection, the renewal requirements, and the manufacturing clause.

At the international level, there have been two important copyright conventions, the Berne (1886) and the Universal (1952). Until the Berne Convention was signed in 1886, international copyright was in a chaotic state, with reciprocity only on the basis of bilateral treaties. Some countries, like the United States, made no such agreements; and during the nineteenth century, a new form of piracy appeared—literary piracy. Some countries signed the Berne Convention, notable exceptions being the United States and Russia. Basically, the signatories agreed to give one another the same copyright protection that their own citizens received. A 1908 revision required that this coverage be given automatically—no forms had to be filed by the individual copyright owner. As the convention now stands, the minimum term of copyright is the lifetime of the creator plus 50 years; this term of copyright protection holds for translations as well as the original work.

There are several reasons why the United States is not a party to the Berne Convention. Automatic coverage of a work (with no need for forms) means that the U.S. requirement that copyright notice appear on or in the work could not apply. Surprisingly, one of the most vocal and effective groups requesting retention of the notice requirement was librarians, who claimed that it would create problems and a hardship if the notice were not there. (Somehow this has not been a significant problem for libraries or librarians in the signatory countries.) Another problem was their term of coverage: the United States granted a total of only 56 years, while the convention's term is life plus 50 years. The manufacturing clause was also a problem because English-language books and periodicals written by foreign authors had to be manufactured in the United States to gain American copyright. Two other issues also played a role in keeping the United States from signing the Convention: one was the need to give retroactive coverage to foreign works that the United States now considers to be in the public domain; the other was the "moral" protection right for the copyright owner. The "moral rights" are concerned with protecting the copyright owner from misuse of the work and prevent "any action in relation to said work which would be prejudicial to the author's honor or reputation."

The United States did sign the Universal Copyright Convention (UCC) in 1954. How is it that the United States is able to sign one convention but not the other? There are two important differences between them. First, UCC does not provide automatic copyright without formalities. The formalities, however, are that a work carry the letter "c" in a circle, the name of the owner, and the date of first publication. This satisfies the U.S. notice requirement and presumably makes life easier for American librarians. The second difference is that the term of copyright may be whatever term the country granted its citizens at the time of signing; the only minimum is 25 years for all works other than photographs and applied arts. (These last two categories must have at least 10 years' protection.) There are penalty provisions for a Berne Convention signer's withdrawing from the Berne Convention in order to belong to the UCC. (There is no penalty for being a member of both conventions.) To date, 40 of the Berne members have also joined the UCC.

In 1971, both the Berne Convention and UCC were modified to ensure that certain licensing rights would be granted to developing countries. The revisions provide a mechanism for forcing a copyright owner to grant the use rights to developing countries under certain conditions, in effect, compulsory licensing. Most of the signatories of the two conventions have approved the revisions at this time. Certainly the revisions have helped control what was becoming the second age of international piracy of literary and creative works. Nevertheless, some countries are not party to any copyright agreement, nor do the publishers in those countries bother to seek a license; so piracy is still alive in the 1980s.

PL94-553

On 1 January 1978, Public Law 94-553 went into effect. The new American copyright law had been passed on 19 October 1976, after more than 15 years of debate. After years of waiting and arguing, producers and users have a new set of regulations. Unfortunately, the issues that had caused the most disagreement are not fully resolved by the law. The three major issues, as far as libraries are concerned, were and still are:

1. What is "fair use?"

2. What types of service may a library offer and not infringe on copyright?

3. What, if any, compensation should be granted the copyright owner for use of the material, and how can it be paid?

The following highlights of the new copyright law are extensively adapted from the American Library Association's *Washington Newsletter*, a noncopyright item. They provide an accurate summary of the major points in the law as they *may* affect libraries. Many sections of the law are ambiguous: producers read the law one way, but users (including librarians) read it another. Librarians are particularly concerned about the impact on their situation of being in the middle between the producers and the ultimate users; interlibrary loan practices; and cooperative acquisition and collection development programs, especially the way intrasystem loans may be affected. At this time, no one is certain how the issues will be resolved. Everyone seems to agree, however, that in the last analysis, the issues will be resolved in the courts. Certainly there have been more vigorous and successful efforts by copyright holders to enforce their rights.

Highlights of the New Copyright Law[3]

Copyright protection is for the life of the author plus 50 years. The Register of Copyright is to maintain current records of the death dates of authors of copyrighted works. Effective 1 January 1978, existing copyrights under the old system were extended to span a total of 75 years, automatically in the case of copyrights already renewed for a second term, but only if renewed in the case of first-term copyrights (Sec. 302).

The "fair use" doctrine is given statutory recognition for the first time. Traditionally, fair use has been a judicially created limitation on the exclusive rights of the copyright owner, developed by the courts because the 1909 copyright law made no provision for any copying. In the new law, fair use allows copying of a limited amount of material without permission from, or payment to, the copyright owner, when the use is reasonable and not harmful to the rights of the copyright owner (Sec. 107).

The new law also extends copyright protection to unpublished works. Instead of the old dual system of protecting works under common law before they are published and under federal law after publication, the new law establishes a single system of statutory protection for all works, whether published or unpublished (Sec. 301).

The manufacturing clause is eventually to be repealed. The clause, which grants U.S. copyright to English-language books and periodicals by American authors only if printed in the United States, was to be repealed on 1 July 1982, *but the manufacturing clause is still a problem in 1986.* Canada was exempted from the manufacturing clause as of 1 January 1978 (Sec. 601).

Copyright liability is extended to two previously exempted groups—cable television systems and the operators of jukeboxes. Both will be entitled to compulsory licenses (Sec. 111, 116).

A five-member Copyright Royalty Tribunal has been established to review royalty rates and to settle disputes among parties entitled to several specified types of statutory royalties in areas not directly affecting libraries (Sec. 801).

Library Approaches to PL94-553

Every librarian should have some knowledge of all of the following sections of the law. The sections of the law and the content of handbooks on the law can be helpful in developing a collection; however, when questions arise, the best source of information is an attorney who handles copyright cases. What follows is *not* intended to be nor should it be interpreted as legal advice.

(Sec. 102-105) defines works protected by copyright.

(Sec. 106) defines the exclusive rights of the copyright owner.

(Sec. 107) provides the basis of the right of fair use.

(Sec. 108) authorizes certain types of library copying.

(Sec. 108 [g]) identifies library copying not authorized by the new law.

(Sec. 602 [a] [3]) relates to the importation of copies by libraries.

Works Protected by Copyright

Copyright protection extends to *literary* works; *dramatic* works; *pantomimes* and *choreographic* works; *pictorial, graphic,* and *sculptural* works; *motion pictures* and *other audiovisual* works; and *sound recordings* (Sec. 102).

Unpublished works by U.S. and foreign authors are protected by the new copyright statute, as are published works by U.S. authors. The *published* works of foreign authors are subject to copyright under certain conditions, including coverage under national treaties such as the Universal Copyright Convention (Sec. 104).

United States government works are excluded. The new law did not change the basic premise that works produced for the U.S. government by its officers and employees are not subject to copyright (Sec. 105).

There is *no outright prohibition against copyright in works prepared under government contract or grant.* The *Conference Report on General Revision of the Copyright Law 94-553* stated:

There may well be cases where it would be in the public interest to deny copyright in the writings generated by Government research contracts and the like; it can be assumed that, where a Government agency commissions a work for its own use merely as an alternative to having one of its own employees prepare the work, the right to secure a private copyright would be withheld. However, there are almost certainly many other cases where the denial of copyright protection would be unfair or would hamper the production and publication of important works. Where, under the particular circumstances, Congress or the agency involved finds that the need to have a work freely available outweighs the need of the private author to secure copyright, the problem can be dealt with by specific legislation, agency regulations, or contractual restrictions.[4]

Exclusive Rights of Copyright Owners

Section 106 states the exclusive rights of copyright owners.

Subject to sections 107 through 118, the owner of copyright under this title has the exclusive rights to do and to authorize any of the following:

1. to reproduce the copyrighted work in copies or phonorecords;

2. to prepare derivative works based upon the copyrighted work;

3. to distribute copies or phonorecords of the copyrighted work to the public by sale or other transfer of ownership, or by rental, lease, or lending;

4. in the case of literary, music, dramatic, and choreographic works, pantomimes, and motion pictures and other audiovisual works to perform the copyrighted work publicly;

5. in the case of literary, musical, dramatic, and choreographic works, pantomimes, and pictorial, graphic, or sculptural works, including the individual images of a motion picture or other audiovisual work, to display the copyrighted work publicly.

It is important to understand the significant *limitations* to the exclusive rights stated in Section 106, which are stated in Sections 107 through 118.

Fair Use

It was generally agreed that at least some kinds of copying were fair and should be permitted. The problem lies in defining what constitutes fair use. The law codifies the fair use doctrine in general terms. The statute refers to such purposes as criticism, comment, news reporting, teaching, scholarship, or research; and it specifies four criteria to be considered in determining whether a particular instance of copying or other reproduction is fair. The statutory criteria (Sec. 107) are:

1) the purpose and character of the use, including whether such use is of a commercial nature or is for nonprofit educational purposes;

2) the nature of the copyrighted work;

3) the amount and substantiality of the portion used in relation to the copyrighted work as a whole; and

4) the effect of the use upon the potential market for or value of the copyrighted work.

Depending upon the circumstances, fair use might cover making a single copy or multiple copies. For example, the statute specifically states that multiple copying for classroom use may fall within the category of fair use copying. In deciding whether any particular instance of copying is fair use, one must always consider the statutory fair use criteria.

Guidelines for Copying

Guidelines developed by educators, publishers, and authors provide some indication of what various parties believe(d) reasonable for fair use. The guidelines were not part of the statute, but they were included in the House Judiciary Committee's report on the copyright bill. They are *Guidelines for Classroom Copying in Not-for-Profit Educational Institutions* and *Guidelines for Educational Uses of Music.*

Library Copying Authorized by Section 108

In addition to copying that would fall within the fair use section of the statute, certain types of library copying that may not be considered fair use are authorized by Sec. 108. Sec. 108 in no way limits the library's fair use right (Sec. 108 [f] [4]).

Section 108 (a) contains general conditions and limitations that apply to the authorized copying outlined in the rest of the section. These general conditions apply:

1. The copy is made without any purpose of direct or indirect commercial advantage.

2. The collections of the library are open to the public or available not only to researchers affiliated with the library but also to other persons doing research in a specialized field.

3. The copy includes a notice of copyright.

The status of special libraries in profit-making institutions with respect to the criterion "without direct or indirect commercial advantage" (Sec. 108 [a] [1]) is clarified in the House Judiciary Committee's report and in the conference report:

it is the library or archives within the institution that must meet the criteria, not the institution itself.

In addition to the general conditions of Section 108 (a), it is possible for contractual obligations between a publisher or distributor and a library to limit copying that would otherwise be permitted by Section 108. It is also true that the limited types of copying authorized by Section 108 can be augmented by written agreement at the time of purchase (Sec. 108 [f] [4]).

Possible Contractual Limitations on Section 108

Section 108 (f) (4) states that the rights of reproduction granted libraries do not override any contractual obligations assumed by the library at the time that it obtained a work for its collection. In view of this provision, librarians must be especially sensitive to the conditions under which they purchase materials, and before executing an agreement that would limit their rights under the copyright law, they should consult with legal counsel.

Single Copy of Single Article or Small Excerpt

The library's own collection: Section 108 (d) authorizes making a single copy of a single article or a copy of a small part of a copyrighted work in the library's collections, provided that (a) the copy becomes the property of the user; (b) the library has no notice that the copy would be used for any purpose other than private study, scholarship, or research; and (c) the library both displays prominently at the place where copying requests are accepted, and includes on its order form, a warning of copyright in accordance with those requirements that the Register of Copyrights has prescribed by regulation.

On 16 November 1977, the *Federal Register* published the new regulation and provided the form for the warning signs that need to be posted near library copy machines (see figure 18.1).

Interlibrary loan copying: Section 108 (d) authorizes making a single copy of a single article or a copy of a small part of a copyrighted work for purposes of interlibrary loan, provided that all of the above conditions regarding a single copy of a single article from the library's own collections are met, and further provided (Sec. 108 [g] [2]) that requests for interlibrary loan photocopies are not in such aggregate quantities as to substitute for purchases or subscriptions. The wording of the statute places responsibility for compliance on the library requesting the photocopy, not the library fulfilling the request. The National Commission on New Technological Uses of Copyrighted Works (CONTU), in consultation with authors, publishers, and librarians, has developed guidelines to assist libraries in complying with this provision. A library or archive may receive no more than five photocopies per year of articles published in the restricted issues of a periodical. (They may be five copies of one article or single copies of five different articles.) The restriction applies only to issues published within the last five years. Duplication of older issues is limited only by the broad provisions of Section 108 (g) (2) that prohibit copying which by its nature would substitute for a subscription.

NOTICE WARNING CONCERNING COPYRIGHT RESTRICTIONS

The Copyright law of the United States (Title 17, United States Code) governs the making of photocopies or other reproductions of copyrighted material.

Under certain conditions specified in the law, libraries and archives are authorized to furnish a photocopy or other reproduction. One of these specified conditions is that the photocopy or reproduction is not to be "used for any purpose other than private study, scholarship, or research." If a user makes a request for, or later uses, a photocopy or reproduction for purposes in excess of "fair use," that user may be liable for copyright infringement.

This institution reserves the right to refuse to accept a copying order if, in its judgment, fulfillment of the order would involve violation of copyright law.

Fig. 18.1. Text, official copyright warning sign. From *Federal Register* (16 November 1977).

Coin-Operated Copying Machines

Section 108 (f) (1) and (2) make clear that *neither libraries nor library employees* are liable for the unsupervised use of reproducing equipment located on library premises, provided that the machine displays the notice quoted above to the effect that the making of a copy may be subject to the copyright law. The library patron making the copy is not excused from liability for copyright infringement, however, if his or her copying exceeds fair use, as provided by Section 107.

Library Copying Not Authorized by Section 108

With the exception of audiovisual news programs, Section 108 does not authorize a library to make multiple copies. Two general types of library copying that are not clearly defined in the statute are specifically not authorized by Section 108. Stated only in the most general terms, the definitions of these types of library copying are susceptible to many interpretations.

The first is called "related or concerted reproduction or distribution of multiple copies." This related or concerted copying by libraries is not authorized, whether the copies are all made on one occasion or over a period of time, and whether intended for aggregate use by one individual or for separate use by individual members of a group (Sec. 108 [g] [1]).

The second type of library copying not authorized by Section 108 is called "systematic reproduction or distribution of single or multiple copies." Because many librarians feared that this term might be interpreted to preclude a wide range of interlibrary lending systems, this section of the bill was amended to make clear that whatever may be meant by the term *systematic*, copying for purposes of interlibrary loan as specifically authorized by Section 108 (d), discussed above, would not be prohibited by Section 108 (g) (2), so long as it does not substitute for purchases or subscriptions. The wording of the statute places responsibility on the library requesting the photocopy from another library for the use of a patron, not on the library filling the request (Sec. 108 [g] [2]).

Agencies such as the National Commission on New Technological Uses of Copyrighted Works (CONTU) are now studying the types of library copying not authorized by Section 108. The National Commission on Libraries and Information Science (NCLIS) funded a study to analyze library photocopying and to conduct a feasibility test of a possible royalty payment mechanism. It is important to remember that the new copyright law does not set up any licensing or royalty payment schemes for library copying. It focuses primarily on the kinds of copying that libraries can do without such schemes. It merely states in Section 108 (g) the two types of library copying that are not authorized by Section 108.

Importation of Copies by Libraries

In general, the new law prohibits the importation of copies of works without the permission of the copyright holder. There are, however, certain exceptions to this general prohibition, one of which is directly related to libraries. Section 602 (a) (3) states that a nonprofit scholarly, educational, or religious organization may import no more than one copy of an audiovisual work for archival purposes only, and no more than five copies of any other work "for its library lending or archival purposes, unless the importation of such copies or phonorecords is part of an activity consisting of systematic reproduction or distribution, engaged in by such organization in violation of the provisions of Section 108 (g) (2)."

Guidelines in Relation to the Statute

Libraries should consult the statute in order to exercise fully what rights they have under the new copyright law. Look first in the statute and the accompanying congressional reports to determine whether the copy can be made by a library or archives in a given situation:

audiovisual	108 (f) (3)
audiovisual work other than news	107, 108 (h)
book	107, 108
graphic work	107, 108 (h)
importing copies from abroad	602 (a) (3)
instructional transmission	107, 110
motion picture	107, 108 (h)
musical work	107, 108 (h)
periodical article	107, 108
pictorial work	107, 108 (h)
public broadcasting program	107, 108 (d) (3)
sound recording	107, 108, 114

Many organizations, especially educational institutions, issued their own guidelines based on the House Judiciary Committee's report. A sample guideline is reproduced in figure 18.2. Because there has been so much uncertainty about just what would or would not be allowed, a number of books have been prepared on the subject. Jerome K. Miller has become very involved in efforts to interpret the law; two of his books that are most useful to any information professional are *Applying the New Copyright Law: A Guide for Educators and Libraries* and *The Copyright Directory.*[5] (Note: The following guidelines were intended to "guide" teachers; when in doubt consult legal counsel. Also, as various infringement suits are filed and settled the guidelines are refined.)

Books and Periodicals

The following guidelines for the copying of books and periodicals under the Copyright Law Revision Act were established by agreement between national educational and authors' and publishers' groups for the purposes of setting minimum standards of educational fair use.

I. *Single Copying for Teachers*

A single copy may be made of any of the following by or for a teacher at his or her individual request for his or her scholarly research or use in teaching or preparation to teach a class:

A.   A chapter from a book;

B.   An article from a periodical or newspaper;

C.   A short story, short essay or short poem, whether or not from a collective work;

D.   A chart, graph, diagram, cartoon or picture from a book, periodical, or newspaper.

II. *Multiple Copies for Classroom Use*

Multiple copies (not to exceed in any event more than one copy per pupil in a course) may be made by or for the teacher giving the course for classroom use or discussions, provided that:

A.   The copying meets the tests of brevity and spontaneity as defined below; and

B.   Meets the cumulative effect test as defined below; and

C.   Each copy includes a notice of copyright.

Definitions

Brevity

(i)   Poetry: (a) A complete poem if less than 250 words and if printed on not more than two pages or, (b) from a longer poem, an excerpt of not more than 250 words.

    (ii)   Prose: (a) Either a complete article, story or essay of less than 2,500 words, or (b) an excerpt from any prose work of not more than 1,000 words or 10% of the work, whichever is less, but in any event a minimum of 500 words.

(Each of the numerical limits stated in "i" and "ii" above may be expanded to permit the completion of an unfinished line of a poem or of an unfinished prose paragraph.)

    (iii)   Illustration: One chart, graph, diagram, drawing, cartoon or picture per book or per periodical issue.

    (iv)   "Special" works: Certain works in poetry, prose or in "poetic prose" which often combine language with illustrations and which are intended sometimes for children and at other times for a more general audience, and fall short of 2,500 words in their entirety. Paragraph "ii" above notwithstanding, such "special works" may not be reproduced in their *entirety*; however, an excerpt comprising not more than two of the published pages of such special work and containing not more than 10 percent of the words found in the text thereof, may be reproduced.

Spontaneity

    (i)   The copying is at the instance and inspiration of the individual teacher, and

    (ii)   The inspiration and decision to use the work and the moment of its use for maximum teaching effectiveness are so close in time that it would be unreasonable to expect a timely reply to a request for permission.

Cumulative Effect

    (i)   The copying of the material is for only one course in the school in which the copies are made.

    (ii)   Not more than one short poem, article, story, essay or two excerpts may be copied from the same author, nor more than three from the same collective work or periodical volume during one class term.

    (iii)   There shall not be more than nine instances of such multiple copying for one course during one class term.

(The limitations stated in "ii" and "iii" above shall not apply to current news periodicals and newspapers and current news sections of other periodicals.)

III. *Prohibitions as to I and II Above*

Notwithstanding any of the above, the following shall be prohibited:

A.   Copying shall not be used to create or to replace or substitute for anthologies, compilations, or collective works. Such replacement or substitution may occur whether copies of various works or excerpts therefrom are accumulated or reproduced and used separately.

B. There shall be no copying of or from works intended to be "consumable" in the course of study or of teaching. These include workbooks, exercises, standardized tests and test booklets and answer sheets and like consumable material.

C. Copying shall not:

a. substitute for the purchase of books, publishers' reprints or periodicals;

b. be directed by higher authority;

c. be repeated with respect to the same item by the same teacher from term to term.

D. No charge shall be made to the student beyond the actual cost of the photocopying.

Fig. 18.2. Guidelines for copying.

Infringement

One who violates the rights of the copyright owner is a *copyright infringer.* Remedies available to the copyright holder for infringement include damages (actual or statutory, the latter set by statute at from $100 to $50,000), injunction, and recovery of court costs and attorney's fees. There is also criminal infringement (done willfully for commercial advantage or private financial gain), which is subject to a $10,000 fine and/or one year imprisonment.

Statutory damages are to be waived entirely for a library or nonprofit educational institution when the institution or one of its employees acting within the scope of his or her employment "believed or had reasonable grounds for believing that his or her use of the copyrighted work was a fair use under Sec. 107" (Sec. 504 [c] [2]).

Librarians and media specialists have a professional responsibility to learn about the basic library-related provisions of the new copyright law, and to review current practices in the light of such provisions. If current practices seem likely to constitute infringement under the law, the librarian should plan *now* for needed changes and be sure that the reason for such changes is well understood by library users. Above all, it is important to take the time and trouble to master the basic provisions of the statute so that the library will be exercising fully the rights it has under the new copyright law. Anything short of this would be a disservice to library users everywhere.

Mandated Five-Year Reviews

Although the library community as a whole worked hard to get a flexible copyright law that would neither harm publishers and authors nor curtail the public's access to information, there was no assurance the new law would achieve such a balance. The law requires a review of the library copying provisions every five years by the Register of Copyrights in consultation with librarians and representatives of authors and publishers. If a five-year review determines that the balance between the rights of copyright owners and the rights of the public is tilting too far in one direction, the Register is directed to make recommendations for legislative or other changes to correct the situation (Sec. 108 [i]).

Without documentation from libraries of all types in all parts of the country as to how the copyright law is affecting library service, the library community as a whole will be ill-equipped to press for changes in the law. We are assured by the statute of a review every five years, but to make such reviews beneficial to library users, librarians everywhere must prepare for each review.

As might have been expected, the 1982 review generated controversy with producers on one side and users on the other. In the end the Copyright Office asked Congress to pass additional legislation to achieve a better balance between the rights of creators and the needs of users of copyrighted works in libraries and archives. The view was that the creators were not being adequately protected. Four main areas were identified as needing legislative action: reproduction of out-of-print musical works (libraries currently are not allowed to do this), an "umbrella" statute (the proposed statute for forced licensing), copyright notice (this would require libraries to use the statutory notice on all photocopies they provide, as part of the conditions of copying), and unpublished works (to "make it clear" that unpublished works are not covered by Section 108). The Office also wished additional voluntary guidelines would be established and that all parties would participate in licensing agreements. Areas suggested for additional study were a copyright-compensation scheme based upon a surcharge on photocopying equipment, copyright compensation based on a percentage of the photocopying impressions made using sampling techniques, and issues relating to the impact of new technological developments on library use of copyrighted works. One set of guidelines has appeared since the Copyright Office Report. The *American Libraries* February 1986 issue carried the full text of "Library and Classroom Use of Copyrighted Videotapes and Computer Software." Certainly it is required reading for most public service personnel.

Copyright holders were quick to enforce their rights. One of the more notable suits was filed on 5 February 1980 by a group of book publishers for alleged copyright infringement against the Gnomon Corporation. Gnomon operates a number of photocopy stores in the eastern United States, many located near academic institutions. The publishers claimed the company encouraged copyright violations by promoting its "Micro-Publishing" service with university and college teachers. By mid-May 1980, publishers had their first favorable ruling and announced that their next target would be large for-profit corporations with libraries that did not use the Copyright Clearance Center. (More is said about CCC later in this chapter.) Although the publishers won their case against Gnomon, many photocopy service firms still promote similar services. As a university professor I have received a number of promotional pieces from such firms, indicating that collections of articles for classes do not violate copyright. What they do now is to enclose material (brief, certainly, and lacking many details) about Section 107 and to leave the interpretation to the reader. However, they take care to emphasize that multiple-copy classroom use is permitted.

In 1982, various publications carried an announcement that the Association of American Publishers (AAP) had followed up the announcement about corporate libraries and use of CCC. They had agreed to an out-of-court settlement after filing suit against E. R. Squibb and Sons Corporation, a large pharmaceutical company. Squibb agreed to pay royalty fees when articles were copied from technical journals, including the ones the corporation library subscribed to. Before the Squibb suit the publishers had also been successful in a suit against the American Cyanamid Company.

After their success against for-profit organizations AAP turned toward the not-for-profit sector. On 5 January 1983 the *Chronicle of Higher Education* carried a story that the AAP had filed suit in the New York district court against New York University, nine of its faculty members, and a photocopy shop near the university. New York University settled out-of-court and agreed that it would follow the 1976 guidelines and that faculty members who did not do so would not receive legal assistance from the institution if they were named in a future copyright infringement suit. At about the same time a Los Angeles secondary school teacher lost an infringement suit on the same grounds, failure to follow the 1976 guidelines. In 1984, the National Music Publishers Association got the University of Texas at Austin to stop alleged illegal photocopying of music by its Music Department.

When will the suits stop? Probably not until copyright holders believe, or know, that libraries, teachers, and other end users are following the guidelines. It would not be surprising to see suits against some large school districts and one or two large public libraries. While it is true that copyright holders do have rights, the law clearly states that libraries and other users do too. The suggestions given above about how to defend those rights and prepare for the next five-year review are important. If the first five-year review suggested to the Copyright Office that the copyright holders still had legitimate complaints, what will the next review conclude if we are not prepared to defend what little we have left?

Contractual Compliance

Following the various guidelines is one obvious way to achieve compliance. For some libraries the guidelines are too narrow and the cost of acquiring, processing, and housing the needed copyrighted material is high. Are these libraries and information centers cut off from needed information? No, not if they have enough money.

The Copyright Clearance Center (CCC) is a not-for-profit service designed to serve libraries and other users of copyrighted material by providing a central source to which to submit their copying fees. It is in a sense a licensing system, as CCC does not copy documents but functions as a clearinghouse. Several thousand organizations are "members"; many, if not most of these are libraries and information services. CCC handles both U.S. and foreign publications (over 4,000 titles). Figure 18.3 illustrates the format used in their *Publisher's Photo-Copy Fee Catalog*. The fees can be substantial when one realizes that the charge is for one article; however, the cost of having a law suit filed against an organization would be higher, and if that organization lost, it could cost as much as $50,000 plus other costs and fees. Another such service is the Television Licensing Center, which is set up to assist in legal off-the-air videotaping, an area of concern for school media centers as well as other educational institutions.

Where next with copyright? It is difficult to predict, but what is certain is that the copyright holders are not satisfied with the *status quo*. A new group, the American Copyright Council, was formed in mid-1985; its purpose is to lobby in Congress against things it believes would undermine the copyright law. "Copyright is more and more at risk these days, under challenge, attack, and erosion. 'It is becoming an endangered species,' said Stanley M. Gortikov, president of the Recording Industry Association of America and chairman of the

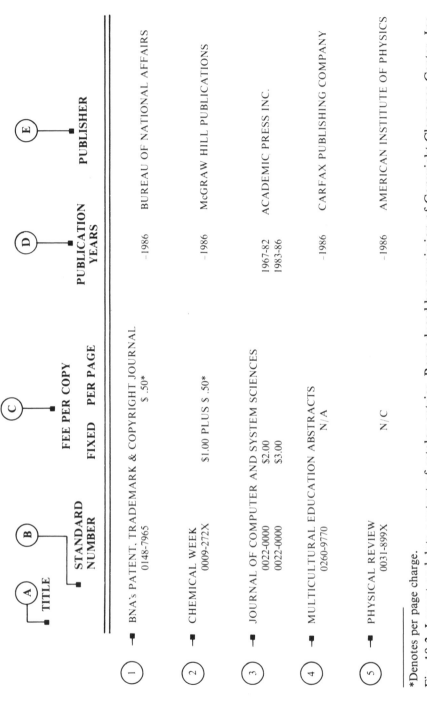

Fig. 18.3. Layout and data content of catalog entries. Reproduced by permission of Copyright Clearance Center, Inc. 27 Congress Street, Salem, MA 01970.

*Denotes per page charge.

new council."[6] Some of the 18 members of the Council are the American Federation of Musicians, AFL-CIO; the American Society of Composers, Authors, and Publishers; the Association of American Publishers; the Authors Guild, Inc.; Computer and Business Equipment Manufacturers Association; the Motion Picture Association of America; Time, Inc.; and Warner Communications, Inc. ALA and other groups representing the interests of the end user will have their hands full; it seems likely that fair use rather than copyright is the "endangered species."

Finally, there is also some pressure from not-for-profit organizations over their copyrights. Of greatest concern to libraries, archives, and information centers around the world is the question of who does "own" the data in various cooperative bibliographic utilities. Late in 1982 OCLC claimed copyright of its database, which was built up by the MARC database from LC and records contributed from member libraries. Member libraries quickly began to claim copyright to their contributed copy. An IFLA study in 1982 of 35 national libraries or national bibliographic agencies around the world noted that 9 of the organizations claimed copyright for their machine-readable records.[7] If additional royalty charges are made for the use of such records it will become ever more costly to attempt reasonable cooperative collection development programs.

Public Lending Right

Public lending right (PLR) is a system that allows an author to be compensated for the circulated use of his or her copyrighted work from libraries. Many Americans, including librarians, are not fully aware of this right. Elsewhere in the world it is better known and in most countries where it exists it is operating successfully.

Authors are compensated in some manner for the circulated use or presence of their works in a library. Where does the money come from? There are only three logical sources: the user, the library, or the funding authority. In most countries the money comes from a separate fund established for that purpose by the national government. Does the presence of a lending right program have any negative impact on library budgets? No one really knows, but it seems likely that there is some spillover which ultimately reduces library funding. A 1986 report from England indicated no adverse effects on library budgets as a result of PLR. Collections built using the demand principal will increase the pressure on the PLR fund, and a self-feeding cycle may begin which makes less money available to buy "marginal" (low-use) titles.

PLR started in the Nordic countries after World War II. Initially it was thought of as a way to encourage writers to write in languages that had only a small number of native speakers, for example, Danish, Finnish, Icelandic, Norwegian, and Swedish. For more than 20 years the concept did not spread beyond the Nordic area. Starting in the early 1970s the idea began spreading to the Netherlands (1972), the Federal Republic of Germany (1972), New Zealand (1973), Australia (1974), the United Kingdom (1983), and Canada (1986). Although some legislation contains the provision that all libraries are to be included, in most countries only public libraries are involved in data collecting. Details of the systems vary, but some form of sampling is used to collect the data unless there is a single source from which the public libraries buy their books. A good but somewhat dated source of detailed information on PLR is a 1981 issue of *Library Trends.*[8]

Canada joined the movement on 1 April 1986, although they call their system Payment for Public Use (PPU). It was decided that a $2.5 million fund was to be established by the national government to compensate authors for the circulation of their books by Canadian public libraries. In 1985 the Council of Writers Organizations was able to get U.S. Senator Charles Matthias of Maryland to submit PLR-enabling legislation. Will such legislation have much chance of passage? Probably not as long as the U.S. federal deficit is so high and budget cutting is the main concern of Congress, assuming that funding would follow other countries' practice of a national fund. Such an assumption may not be valid for several reasons: first, two other sources of funding are possible, the end user and the library; second, there is the worrisome Section 106 of the copyright law, which lists as an exclusive right "(3) to distribute copies or phono-records of copyrighted works to the public by sale or other transfer of ownership, or by rental, lease or *lending*" [emphasis added]; third, the attitude exemplified by a statement in *Publishers Weekly* in 1983: "The fate of a book after it is sold is an important one for the book industry, reflecting as it does the possibility of lost sales; pass-along readership of a book, unlike that of a magazine, does not translate into potential revenue."[9] Should publishers and authors, as well as others such as music producers (audio collections) and motion picture producers (video collections), join forces, we might well see another cost being imposed on libraries and their users. As a good friend from Norway is fond of saying, "that *is* something to ponder."

Summary

Copyright assures the right to seek tangible rewards for persons or organizations from the production of creative or informative works. Without users of copyrighted materials, the producers would realize little or nothing from their efforts. The two groups need to work together or everyone will lose. It would be desirable if once again we became partners in the dissemination of information and knowledge, rather than antagonists. Whatever does develop will not change the fact that it will not be possible to develop a library collection without considering the impact of copyright laws. The librarian should work to maintain a fair balance, but work for the users; they have few spokespersons.

Notes

[1]Norman Tanis and C. Ventuleth, "Decline in Donations? Effects of the Tax Reform Act of 1969," *Library Journal* 111 (1 June 1986): 41-44.

[2]J. Berry, "Copyright: From Debate to Solution," *Library Journal* 100 (1 September 1975): 1459.

[3]American Library Association, *Washington Newsletter* (15 November 1976).

4U.S. House of Representatives, *Conference Report on General Revision of the Copyright Law 94-553* (29 September 1976), 55.

5Jerome K. Miller, *Applying the New Copyright Law: A Guide for Educators and Libraries* (Chicago: American Library Association, 1979); *The Copyright Directory* (Friday Harbor, Wash.: Copyright Information Services, 1985).

6"Copyright Holders Unite in Face of Growing 'Risk'," *Rocky Mountain News*, 6 June 1985, 85.

7D. D. McDonald, et al., *International Study of Copyright of Bibliographic Records in Machine-Readable Form* (Munich: K. G. Saur, 1983).

8"Public Lending Right," *Library Trends* 29 (Spring 1981): 565-719.

9"The Pass-Along Market for Books: Something to Ponder for Publishers," *Publishers Weekly* 224 (15 July 1983): 20.

Further Reading

General

Berry, J. "Copyright: From Debate to Solution." *Library Journal* 100 (1 September 1975): 1459.

"Britain's Public Lending Right Is Manna to Authors: Gets No Library Complaints." *American Libraries* 17 (May 1986): 862.

Clark, C. "100 Years of Berne." *The Bookseller* 4209 (23 August 1986): 788-92.

"Copyright Holders Unite in Face of Growing 'Risk'." *Rocky Mountain News*, 6 June 1985, 85.

"Copyright Reform in Limbo." *The Bookseller* 4222 (21 November 1986): 2051.

Cornish, G. P. "Copyright Law and Document Supply 1983-1986. A Review of International Developments." *Interlending and Documents Supply* 14 (1986): 47-49.

Flaherty, D. H. *Privacy and Data Protection.* White Plains, N.Y.: Knowledge Industry Publications, 1984.

Johnston, D. *Copyright Handbook.* 2d ed. New York: R. R. Bowker, 1982.

_____. *A Copyright Guide.* 2d ed. New York: R. R. Bowker, 1982.

"Librarian's Guide to the New Copyright Law." *Washington Newsletter* (American Library Association) 28 (15 November 1976).

Loe, M. K. H. "Thor Tax Ruling after 5 Years." *Library Acquisitions: Practice and Theory* 10, no. 3 (1986): 203-18.

McDonald, D. D., E. J. Rodger, and J. L. Squires. *International Study of Copyright of Bibliographic Records in Machine-Readable Form.* Munich: K. G. Saur, 1983.

Milevski, S. N. "Information Technology Reflected in Public Laws of the Past Decade." *Library HiTech* 4 (Summer 1986): 23-27.

Miller, J. K. *The Copyright Directory.* Friday Harbor, Wash.: Copyright Information Services, 1985.

"Public Lending Right." Edited by Perry D. Morrison and Dennis Hyatt. *Library Trends* 29 (Spring 1981): 565-719.

Schrift, L. "After Thor, What's Next?" *Library Acquisitions: Practice and Theory* 9, no. 1 (1985): 61-63.

Sprehe, J. T. "Developing Federal Information Resources Management Policy." *Information Management Review* 2 (Winter 1987): 33-42.

Tanis, N. E., and C. Ventuleth. "Decline in Donations? Effects of the Tax Reform Act of 1969." *Library Journal* 111 (1 June 1986): 41-44.

U.S. House of Representatives. *Conference Report on General Revision of the Copyright Law 94-553.* Washington, D.C.: Government Printing Office, 1976.

"White Paper on Copyright Backs Licensing, Retains Fair Dealing." *The Bookseller* (9 April 1986): 1553, 1565-66.

"White Paper Opens Way to Accord on Copyright." *The Bookseller* (21 June 1986): 2411-12.

Wood, L. A. "Pass-Along Market for Books: Something to Ponder for Publishers." *Publishers Weekly* 224 (15 July 1983): 20.

Academic

Association of Research Libraries. Office of Management Studies. *Copyright Policies of ARL Libraries.* Washington, D.C.: Association of Research Libraries, 1984.

Butler, M. A. "Copyright and Academic Library Photocopying." *College & Research Libraries News* 4 (April 1982): 123-25.

Public

Right to Information: Legal Questions and Policy Issues. Edited by Varlejo Jana. Jefferson, N.C.: McFarland, 1984.

School

"Library and Classroom Use of Copyrighted Videotapes and Computer Software." *American Libraries* 17 (February 1986): 120-21.

Miller, J. K. *Applying the New Copyright Law: A Guide for Educators and Libraries.* Chicago: American Library Association, 1979.

Special

Calhoun, A. D., and L. Bendekgey. "International Software Licensing: Basic Legal and Business Issues." *Information Management Review* 2 (Winter 1987): 55-62.

Crawford, M. J. "Copyright, Unpublished Manuscript Records and the Archivist." *American Archivist* 46 (Spring 1983): 135-47.

Gasaway, L. N. "Audiovisual Material and Copyright in Special Libraries." *Special Libraries* 74 (July 1983): 222-39.

_____. "Nonprint Works and Copyright in Special Libraries." *Special Libraries* 74 (April 1983): 156-70.

"Gordon & Breach Sets 'Photocopy License' Requirement." *Library Journal* 111 (1 November 1986): 20.

"Impact of Copyright White Paper on BLDSC." *The Bookseller* 4208 (16 August 1986): 627.

Mount, E., and W. B. Newman. *Top Secret/Trade Secret.* New York: Neal-Schuman, 1985.

19

Censorship, Intellectual Freedom, and Collection Development

All of the topics discussed thus far are complex, and some touch upon a wide variety of social issues and concerns. None, however, is more complex than censorship and intellectual freedom. Intellectual freedom, free speech, freedom to read, and open access to information are possible alternative titles for this chapter. One examination question frequently used in library school courses in collection development has been some variation of "Is book selection actually book censorship? Please discuss."

Intellectual freedom and free speech will not be explored directly in this chapter. Although these are interesting and important concepts for anyone involved in collection development, their complexity is so great that each one has been the subject of numerous books and articles. (The further readings at the end of this chapter will provide a starting point for further reading on these topics.) It is important for all librarians to gain an understanding of these areas; but it is essential that all selection personnel understand the issues relating to censorship.

Many library associations have issued statements and taken public positions on questions of free speech and intellectual freedom. The American Library Association's *Freedom to Read* statement is a classic example. Most of the statements are filled with fine-sounding phrases, and the document(s) look useful when one is in the classroom or in a meeting discussing the theory or philosophy of intellectual freedom. On a day-to-day basis, these statements provide little assistance in collection development and are of limited value in fighting off the censor.

Intellectual freedom and free speech controversies usually revolve around interpretations of points of law and possible violations of existing law. Therefore, the fight is usually resolved by attorneys and judges rather than in the library by the librarians and the community. We hear about the cases that reach the courts but seldom about day-to-day, local problems. Naturally, each of the major cases started off as a local problem between the library and some of the community, but only a few reach the courtroom. Most often, the problem starts because someone objects to an item already in the collection. Depending upon the nature of the material, the level of emotional involvement, and the prior administrative actions (policies), the issue may be quickly resolved; or it can escalate until it reaches the courtroom.

If a controversy is resolved without the aid of attorneys, it will be a result of (a) staff with an excellent background in interpersonal relations; (b) a plan of action for handling complaints; (c) a lack of strong feelings on the part of the person making the complaint; (d) lack of concerted pressure from special interest groups; or (e) backup material from library associations. If the individual(s) making a complaint believes very strongly about the matter, very likely the library's attorney will become involved. From that point on, depending on the emotional involvement and financial resources, the issue may go from the lowest court to the highest court in the country before it is resolved.

The local issue usually is, and should be, defined as censorship. Charles Busha has provided a satisfactory definition of censorship as it concerns the library: "The rejection by a library authority of a book (or other material) which the librarian, the library board or some person (or persons) bringing pressure on them holds to be obscene, dangerously radical, subversive, or too critical of the existing mores."[1] The entire Busha article from which the quotation is taken is well worth reading. Actually, censorship has been a problem for libraries for just about as long as there have been libraries. Generally speaking, librarians attempt to resist censorship moves ("generally," because we don't know how many times complaints about an item are accepted and acted upon by removing the offensive item due to the fact that the librarian personally agrees with the person making the complaint). As is discussed later in this chapter, evidence suggests that there is a difference between librarians' attitudes toward the concept of censorship and their behavior in handling censorship problems. Librarians' success in fending off the censors' efforts is varied—there are both notable successes and spectacular failures. Unfortunately, no rules or guidelines will ensure success. It is possible to forestall many complaints and quickly resolve those that are made; however, there is always a chance that these procedures will fail and a legal battle will ensue.

Causes of Censorship

What are the causes or motivations that underlie the actions of a censor? As with all human behavior, the answer is involved and never simple. In every case, psychological elements relate to the need that some persons have to restrain others from expressing ideas or creating works that the would-be censor will find offensive. Political motivation underlies the actions of governments when they attempt to maintain control over the communication systems that may threaten that government or its policies. Frequently, the censor (government, groups, or an individual) claims to be motivated by protective reasons. Clearly, censorship is a paternalistic act toward both adults and children in that it limits their experiences and environment to influences acceptable to the censor. Social factors, which are difficult to differentiate from paternal factors, result from a desire to preserve a wholesome social setting and/or to reduce crime, both of which the censor may see as related to the presence of objectionable material in the library.

Freedom and censorship represent an opposition between the need to exercise some restraint so that social institutions intelligently protect citizens' rights and the need to ensure individuals' right to free choice. Some persons believe there should be no controls and would eradicate all laws, rules, and regulations. On the other hand, there are those who think that everyone but themselves must be protected and controlled. Somewhere between these extremes lies the necessary balance between freedom and restraint. Librarians, like everyone else, are involved in a day-to-day process attempting to achieve an appropriate balance.

The American Library Association (ALA) adopted a *Library Bill of Rights* (*LBR*) in 1948. ALA's Office for Intellectual Freedom (more about OIF later) vigorously promotes and publicizes the concepts contained in that statement. Unfortunately, the *Library Bill of Rights* is not part of our system of laws, and therefore provides no legal protection for libraries or librarians. What legal protection exists is contained in the freedom-of-speech provisions of the U.S. Constitution. Every U.S. citizen has the right to express opinions freely in speaking, writing, or with graphics; to distribute them; and to seek information from public sources without unnecessary restraint. The *Library Bill of Rights* outlines the basic freedom-of-access concepts that ALA hopes will guide library public services. It states that persons should be able to read what they wish without intervention from groups or individuals—including librarians. Since its adoption in 1948, the provisions of the *Library Bill of Rights* have helped librarians recommit themselves to a philosophy of service based on the premise that users of libraries should have access to information on all sides of all issues. The text of the document, as amended 2 February 1961, 27 June 1967 and 23 January 1980 by the ALA Council, is presented in figure 19.1.

The *Library Bill of Rights* is an important guide to professional conduct in terms of intellectual freedom. It is a standard by which day-to-day practices can be gauged against desired professional behavior in the realms of freedom of access to information, of communications, and intellectual activity.

Despite *LBR*, there is and always will be pressure to limit the type of material put into the library's collection. Occasionally, someone tries to solve the problem by labeling material in the same manner as the U.S. Surgeon General ordered labels for cigarette packages. To date, the efforts to label library materials have been about as effective in stopping persons from reading those materials as labeling cigarettes has been in stopping smoking. The practice usually takes the form of the placing of special marks or designations (stars, letters, and so forth) on certain classes of materials. Yet, the practice of labeling is prejudicial and creates bias.

Labeling practices are generally a defensive method that indicates, in effect, that "these books, films, magazines, records, or whatever format, may not meet with full community approval; therefore, if you wish to use them, be warned." Generally, labeling is considered to be contrary to principles of intellectual freedom, since librarians are not expected to establish and designate prohibited materials. Nor is it the librarian's duty to warn readers against such things as obscene language; descriptions of explicit sexual acts; or unorthodox political, religious, moral, and economic theories. If we are preservers and providers rather than censors, we need to bear in mind that most intellectual advances, in all fields, frequently involve controversy. A librarian's primary responsibility is to provide access to information for the patron, not to restrict it. Thus, the formal position of the ALA has been critical of labeling, and in 1951 the Association adopted an antilabeling statement, which was last amended on 15 June 1971 (see figure 19.2, page 398).

The American Library Association affirms that all libraries are forums for information and ideas, and that the following basic policies should guide their services.

I. Books and other library resources should be chosen for values of interest, information and enlightenment of all people of the community. In no case should library material be excluded because of the race or nationality or the social, political, or religious views of the authors.

II. Libraries should provide books and other materials presenting all points of view concerning the problems and issues of our times; no library materials should be proscribed or removed from libraries because of partisan or doctrinal disapproval.

III. Censorship should be challenged by libraries in the maintenance of their responsibility to provide public information and enlightenment.

IV. Libraries should cooperate with all persons and groups concerned with resisting abridgment of free expression and free access to ideas.

V. The rights of an individual to the use of the library should not be denied or abridged because of his age, race, religion, national origins or social or political views.

VI. As an institution of education for democratic living, the library should welcome the use of its meeting rooms for socially useful and cultural activities and discussion of current public questions. Such meeting places should be available on equal terms to all groups in the community regardless of the beliefs and affiliations of their members, provided that the meeting be open to the public.

Fig. 19.1. *Library Bill of Rights.* Adopted June 18, 1948; Amended February 2, 1961; June 27, 1967; and January 23, 1980 by the ALA Council. Reprinted by permission of the American Library Association.

Because labeling violates the spirit of the *Library Bill of Rights* the American Library Association opposes the technique of labeling as a means of predisposing readers against library materials for the following reasons:

1. Labeling is an attempt to prejudice the reader, and as such it is a censor's tool.

2. Although some find it easy and even proper, according to their ethics, to establish criteria for judging publications as objectionable, injustice and ignorance rather than justice and enlightenment result from such practices, and the American Library Association must oppose the establishment of such criteria.

3. Libraries do not advocate the ideas found in their collections. The presence of a magazine or book in a library does not indicate an endorsement of its contents by the library.

4. No one person should take the responsibility of labeling publications. No sizable group of persons would be likely to agree either on the types of material which should be labeled or the sources of information which should be regarded with suspicion. As a practical consideration, a librarian who labels a book or magazine might be sued for libel.

5. If materials are labeled to pacify one group, there is no excuse for refusing to label any item in the library's collection. Because authoritarians tend to suppress ideas and attempt to coerce individuals to conform to a specific ideology, the American Library Association opposes such efforts which aim at closing any path to knowledge.

Fig. 19.2. "Statement on Labeling: An Interpretation of the *Library Bill of Rights.*" Reprinted by permission of the American Library Association.

All of the ALA statements provide a philosophical base for resisting censorship. However, in the long run, success or failure will depend upon the individual librarian's personal beliefs and attitudes.

Forms of Censorship

A librarian will encounter three types of censorship: (1) legal or governmental, (2) individual or group pressure, and (3) self-censorship. As strange as it might at first appear, types 1 and 2 are easier to deal with than type 3. For type 1, there are two basic choices—comply or fight. Fighting to change a law or interpretation of a law is usually time-consuming and expensive. Because of the time and cost, this is seldom a matter of a single librarian or library fighting to bring about a change. Even in a matter involving a local ordinance, if there is to be a modification, there must be communitywide support. The library staff working alone has little chance of success.

Literary censorship has existed for a long time. The United States has seen an interesting mixture of individual and governmental censorship. Anthony Comstock was a person of strong beliefs and personality, whose efforts to control the reading materials of Americans were so vigorous and successful that a word was added to the English language—Comstockery. Indeed, Comstock was so vigorous in his efforts that, in 1873, Congress passed a law that attempted to outline a structure of national morality. For almost 75 years, this law went unchallenged, with the U.S. Postal Service designated as the government agency primarily responsible for enforcement at the national level. At the local level, several elements were at work. State and local governments passed similar regulations, and thus local police departments became involved in the control of "vice." Law enforcement agencies also had a lot of help from two citizen groups—Society for the Suppression of Vice and the Watch and Ward Society. The Society for the Suppression of Vice was the vehicle that Comstock used to gain support, and to show the depth of that support for his views. A primary activity of the society was to check on printed material available to local citizens, whatever the source (bookstores, newsstands, libraries—both public and private). Occasionally, if the society felt that local law enforcement officials were not moving fast enough, it would take matters into its own hands. Book burnings did take place, and great pressure was applied to anyone who was involved in buying or selling printed material to stock only items deemed "moral" by the censors. The phrase "banned in Boston" got its start as a result of the society's activity.

From 1873 until well into the twentieth century, the United States experienced a mixture of all three types of censorship: official censorship because of the 1873 law; group pressure from organized societies concerned with moral standards of their communities; and self-censorship on the part of publishers, booksellers, and librarians. A public or even a private stance by librarians against such censorship was almost unheard of, and workshops and seminars were held to assist librarians to identify "improper" books. Most of the notable librarians of the past are on record somewhere (ALA proceedings, speeches, or writings), as being in favor of this type of collection "development." As E. Geller noted, Arthur Bostwick suggested that it was reasonable that books such as *Man and Superman* should be purchased for the New York Library's reference collection (noncirculating), but not be purchased for branch library use.[2]

An interesting situation arose with foreign-language titles. Many authors were available in their own languages but not in English. Apparently, if one could read French, German, Spanish, Russian, or any other language, one was reading a moral book, but reading that same work in an English translation was immoral. To some extent the censorship atmosphere caused a few American authors to live abroad and occasionally have a larger foreign readership than in English-speaking countries (for example, Henry Miller). Librarians were no more vocal in protesting this situation than anyone else in the country at the time.

The period between 1873 and the mid-1950s exhibited all of the censorship problems one can encounter. From the 1930s to the mid-1950s, the 1873 law was slowly modified through various federal court decisions, including several by the U.S. Supreme Court. Today, we are still operating with that law as part of the U.S. code, but it is now so modified as to be a completely different law. Most court cases were between the government and publishers or booksellers, while librarians and their associations occasionally entered the suits as *amici curiae* ("friends" of the court) but very seldom as defendants or plaintiffs.

Major changes in the interpretation of the law began with the 1957 U.S. Supreme Court Roth decision. This decision established a three-part test for obscenity. First, the dominant theme of the work as a whole had to appeal to prurient interest in sex. Second, it had to be patently offensive because it affronted contemporary community standards in its representation of sex. Third, the work had to be utterly without redeeming social value. With that interpretation, more sexually explicit material became available in the open market. Not everyone was pleased with the new openness, and in 1973 the Supreme Court, in deciding the Miller case, modified the three-part test. The changes were: first, would an average person applying contemporary community standards find that the work, as a whole, appealed to prurient interest in sex?; second, does the work depict or describe in a patently offensive way sexual conduct specially prohibited in a state's law?; and third, does the work, as a whole, lack serious literary, artistic, political or scientific value? The effect of the decision was to reduce the national aspect by employing the test which emphasized local standards. This is the test that is still in place today.

Does the shift in emphasis matter? Very much so, especially in terms of production and distribution of materials. An example of what the effect can be occurred in 1982. *Show Me*, a children's book about sex, was taken out of distribution by its American publisher/distributor, St. Martin's Press. They stopped distribution because the U.S. Supreme Court upheld a New York state child pornography law. The book contains photographs of naked children. The New York law contains a strict provision barring the use of children in all sexually explicit films and photographs, obscene or not. St. Martin's had already successfully defended *Show Me* in Massachusetts, New Hampshire, and Oklahoma. However, the publisher decided that determining which of the 50 states it could legally ship the book to, as well as keeping track of individual orders, was much too difficult and thus stopped all distribution. Perhaps the most interesting aspect of this incident is that the book was written by a Swiss child psychologist (Helga Fleischhauer-Hardt) and the photographs were done by an American photographer (Will McBride). They prepared the book for a Lutheran church-sponsored children's book company in West Germany in 1974. The English-language edition was published in 1975, and St. Martin's stated that they had sold almost 150,000 copies in hard and paperback up to the time they ceased distribution.[3]

Some distributors and book clubs have started using labeling systems in an attempt to protect themselves from law suits. For example, one book club uses labels such as "Warning: explicit violence" or "Warning: explicit sex and violence." A few people have wondered if the labeling systems were thought to increase sales. Perhaps it serves a dual purpose. For a time one of the library distributors that serves many school media centers included warnings with "problem" books they shipped. Such labeling goes against the ALA statement on labeling but does reflect a growing concern with social values and with pressures to influence those values.

Today, just as during the period from 1873 to 1950, the most problems will be encountered with individual and group censorship. While no active Society for the Suppression of Vice exists today, librarians have increasingly been faced with organized pressure groups. What may at first seem to be a simple matter of a person's objecting to one book can become a major confrontation between a library and an organized pressure group. Much depends upon the energy and time that the would-be censor is willing to devote to the issue. Influential persons may be able to organize a group to generate even greater pressure than one person could. A librarian may encounter organized pressure groups based upon local interests and views (often religious or politically oriented), but seldom from a local group with broad national support. If such a group already exists, it will be extremely difficult to avoid at least an occasional debate (if not all-out battle) over some materials in the collection. Policy statements about controversial materials, ALA "Freedom to Read" documents, and other support materials will help to slow the process, but they will not stop it. Local groups are particularly hard to resist, as they can have a fairly broad base of community support and their mere existence indicates some active interest in certain problems.

A few examples will illustrate the problems facing many librarians in the United States during the 1980s. A 1983-1984 survey of Nassau County (New York) school districts reported that 23 percent of school media centers had been involved in one or more censorship incidents in the previous five years.[4] In almost every instance, the problem was resolved without removing the item(s) under question. The Minot, North Dakota School Board banned *Newsweek* magazine for a few months and a number of textbooks and library materials supporting a course on family living. *Newsweek* was banned because it was "too liberal."[5] Since 1981, Widefield, Colorado, has had a running battle labeled a "fight to save the sanctity of traditional American values: family, church and respect for authority."[6] Although it started as the result of one person's objections, this "campaign" soon involved much of the community, including the police, because of alleged vandalism and physical violence. Things have been calm since early 1984, but the tension is there, and the Widefield School District now has a four-page policy outlining the handling of questions regarding classroom and media center materials.

Much of the censorship pressure arises from a concern about children and is very broad based; it is not just about sex. Some parents do not believe that they are able to judge the materials that their children are exposed to in school or the library, and as a result, several organizations have been created to "review" materials for the worried parent (for example, Educational Research Analysts, Inc.; Mr. and Mrs. Gabler; America's Future, New Rochelle, N.Y.; the John Birch Society; and PONYU, Parents of New York United). An October issue of *Library Hotline* carried a news item about charges that American libraries fail to have enough, or often any, books on creation science.[7] Supporters of biblical creationism have suggested that libraries are censoring Christian materials and especially creationism literature (or science, as they label the concept). Anyone thinking about going into school media center work needs to be fully aware of what is taking place and to beware of the dangers and pitfalls that exist. The Island Trees Union Free School District decision of the U.S. Supreme Court in 1982 has *not* solved all the problems.

Not all the censors are concerned about children. Racism and sexism also come up fairly often. One of the more unusual cases was the Stack o' Wheat photograph incident in 1980.[8] "The Incredible Case of the Stack o' Wheat Murders" photographs also illustrates that it is not just public and school librarians who have all the fun of fighting off the censors. This problem occurred at the University of California, Santa Cruz library, and in the special collections room, at that. The 10 photographs, "The Incredible Case of the Stack o' Wheat Murders," taken by photographer Les Krims (4-by-5-inch photographs) were supposed to be a parody of theme murders and were used in a promotional effort. Each photograph shows a nude "gruesomely" murdered woman dripping blood, with a stack of wheat pancakes next to her. The dripping blood, however, was chocolate syrup and was to represent the "epitome of the series humor" (according to the accompanying text with the photographs). A young woman who learned of the photographs and who viewed them demanded their removal from the library's collection on the grounds they represented the sexploitation of women. When no action was taken, she went to the special collections room, ripped up the photographs and accompanying material, and poured chocolate syrup over the debris. The case quickly escalated into a significant problem for the campus and became involved with the many complex issues of freedom of expression, censorship, status of women, vandalism, and social justice.

When local pressure groups exist, the librarian may ask himself or herself "How will they react if I buy this item?" Thinking along these lines at least allows one to deal with one's worries. The *real* danger in the situation is when that thought is not at the conscious level. At that point, the pressure group will have almost accomplished its purpose—control over the type of material being selected. And they will have accomplished it through the librarian's self-censorship.

Self-censorship is our greatest problem. We all feel that "I" would never let "that" happen to me, but it is very hard not to have it happen. A few librarians would agree with Walter Brahm's philosophy—retreat and fight another day.[9] He reasons that censorship falls victim to the times; public opinion can only dampen censorship; society's mores cannot be led or changed willfully, and certainly not by libraries and librarians; and libraries are generally not the main battleground of intellectual freedom. Most librarians would take a public stance against this position, *if* it were stated in a theoretical sense and did not directly affect them. When it becomes a real issue and they are personally involved, though, it becomes another matter.

Examples of Censorship

Ramparts and *Evergreen Review*

A few additional examples of cases and surveys will illustrate the problem. In the late 1960s, two periodicals, *Ramparts* and *Evergreen Review* (*ER*) caused libraries and librarians to confront the censorship issue head-on. In Los Angeles, the public library had to fight a city councilman's efforts to have *ER* removed from the library.[10] The councilman was ultimately unsuccessful, but for a while the current *ER* issues were removed from public areas while the problem was being debated. The journal went back on the open shelves after the final decision was reached—a short-term victory for censorship, but in the end, a final victory for free access.

Not all librarians were so lucky. Richard Rosichan was dismissed as director of the Kingston Area (New York) Public Library because he fought to keep *ER*, despite both library board and John Birch Society pressure to drop it.[11] At the same time, the American Legion was demanding that he remove *Ramparts* because of its "un-Americanism." Groton (Connecticut) Public Library managed to retain its staff, but not its subscription to *ER*, after a four-month fight in the community, when the library's board of trustees finally ordered that all issues be removed from the library and the subscription canceled. This was done under the threat of fines and jail sentences for both the library board and staff. Head librarian John Carey issued a statement to the effect that this decision would affect the general acquisition policy.[12] One can only hope that he was wrong.

In between keeping an item on the shelves and its total disappearance is the "compromise" position to which librarians sometimes resort—restricted availability. The Philadelphia Free Library used this approach for *ER* when pressure began to be applied to have the title removed. The library renewed the subscription for the main building and one regional branch, but the issues were to be kept in closed stack areas and no one under 18 could examine the title.[13] Emerson Greenaway, director of libraries, said this was done because *ER* was "important sociologically." Who was the winner here, the censor or the librarian?

The above are only a small sample of the problems that arose with *Evergreen Review* and *Ramparts*, and they are only two of hundreds of periodicals that have been attacked over the years. In fact, *Newsweek* and *Time* are frequently questioned. The list of books that have caused trouble is immense, and the short list at the end of this section illustrates the range of titles—and indicates that one can never really tell what will cause trouble.

Some topics are more sensitive than others, and one might expect difficulty but not encounter any. However, sex, religion, and politics are always potential problems. If the librarian would buy or recommend the use of Jerry Rubin's *Do It!*; *Portnoy's Complaint*; *Jesus Christ, Superstar*; *The Joy of Sex*; *The Last Temptation of Christ*; *Dungeons and Dragons Players' Books* or the ALA film, *The Speaker*, he or she would be safe in some communities, and in others, unemployed.

Do It!

Rubin's book got a nontenured teacher fired, a tenured teacher reprimanded, and a department chairperson demoted—all in the same New Jersey county school system.[14] Although in this case it was the teachers who paid the price, the school libraries also lost their copies of the book. On the other hand, Mary Cuarato of Philadelphia tried, unsuccessfully, to force the Free Library to remove *Do It!* from its collection.[15]

Portnoy's Complaint

Portnoy's Complaint (or librarians' lament) was and is almost as great a problem. Jamestown Public Library (New York) more or less succeeded in resisting the attempts of the New York State Committee for Responsible Patriotism to have all of the "smut" removed—particularly *PC*. (It was placed on closed stack status but stayed in the collection.)[16] Librarians in Memphis, Tennessee, were less successful in their fight. After several months of attempting to counter charges of wasting tax money on "trash"—these charges were made by the mayor as well as by other community spokespersons—the library placed restrictions on the use of *Portnoy's Complaint*.[17] No one under 18 years of age could read the book. Not too much later, the city passed an ordinance defining obscenity for minors that contained clauses relating to library materials.

Jesus Christ, Superstar

Rockford High School, Michigan, was the location of a disagreement over music and texts. Materials relating to both the music and scripts for *Jesus Christ, Superstar* were removed entirely from the school system—both the library and the music department—because the musical was "sacrilegious."[18] Generally, there are fewer problems with music than with other formats in the collection. However, at times there has been concern about the lyrics of rock music, especially when a song is about sex and/or drugs. Generally, though, these items come and go so rapidly in popularity that pressure groups seldom have an opportunity to develop before the song has fallen from favor. So far (1986), despite strong efforts, a national labeling system for audiotapes and records, similar to that for the motion picture system, has not been implemented.

The Joy of Sex

Joy of Sex (*JOS*) is a type of book librarians would expect to receive complaints about. The textual material in itself could and does cause some persons discomfort, although the vocal expression of concern will be about the "bad" influence that this book (or ones similar) will have on children. Since in addition to the text there are some rather explicit drawings, this title is almost guaranteed to cause some librarians trouble somewhere. Indeed, it did just that: Naomi Piccolo, the director of the Mount Laurel Public Library, New Jersey, lost her job as a result of a dispute with the library board over the circulation of *JOS*. Two board members had read the book and found it very objectionable. Although Piccolo was not fired, she was asked to submit her resignation.[19]

Spencer Public Library (Iowa) also had a problem with *Joy of Sex*. In this instance, the city attorney notified the library board of a number of citizen complaints that had been received about *JOS* and were concerned with the fact that no restrictions were placed upon its circulation. Is restricted circulation a form of censorship? As far as Spencer, Iowa, was concerned, there was a new obscenity law aimed at regulating the availability of "obscene" materials to persons under 18, although the law did have a clause exempting educational materials in libraries. A nice touch, but is *Joy of Sex* educational? As far as *JOS* was concerned, the answer was no. What is obscene? Again, we are back to individual values and feelings. Each of us has developed these values over many years, and to some degree, each of us holds a unique world view that results in differences in opinion about such things as obscenity, quality, freedom of expression, and so forth.

The Last Temptation of Christ

A different type of book, Nikos Kazantzakis's *The Last Temptation of Christ*, drew criticism in many communities. Citizen groups were formed—"Citizens Committee for Clean Books"—in the hope that they could force the removal of all copies of the book. Generally libraries were able to resist the pressure.[20] In many respects, this book generated almost as many incidents as *Ramparts* and *Evergreen Review*. This perhaps reflects society's changing values, because to the best of this author's knowledge, no librarian lost a job because of *LTOC*, and most of the libraries received sufficient support from trustees and city councils to keep the book on the shelf.

The Last Temptation of Christ illustrates another phenomenon with which the librarian will have to deal—delayed but mass reaction. Kazantzakis's book was published in 1960, but many libraries had the title in circulation for three or four years before there was a problem. Once a title receives publicity—pro or con—interest in the item will increase. Thus, when a librarian hears about a title causing problems in another library, it should be no surprise if he or she receives complaints as well.

Dungeons and Dragons

Aurora Public Library (Colorado) had to deal with controversy over having *Dungeons and Dragons* (*D&D*) players' books (a popular game with many people; an estimated three million players, mostly young people) in its collection. A woman presented an official complaint and a petition with 150 signatures supporting the complaint. She claimed the game promotes "violence, Satanism and blasphemy of Christian terms." The complaint was withdrawn a short time later because the woman said she feared reprisals against herself and her widowed mother. However, the publicity then sparked a rash of complaints about other items in the library and a local evangelist began checking area public library collections for *D&D* players' books. He also tried to pursue the Aurora complaint, but as he did not live in the community he could not officially file a complaint. At about the same time, in Hanover, Virginia, a public school system was sued by the parents of a 16-year-old who committed suicide. The parents alleged the suicide was a direct result of his playing *D&D* in a school building. Wrongful death lawsuits related to games, movies, and television have been on the rise. So far as I know, none has involved libraries, but there is no reason to suppose libraries will be immune from a suit. Many libraries have materials on suicide. A 1983 issue (November) of *American Libraries* published some responses to the ALA Ethics Committee question, should you give a student a copy of *Suicide Mode D'Emploi?* The book is supposed to be linked to at least 10 suicides. If one believes in freedom to read, what should one do?

The Speaker

Up to this point, we have been concerned with pressure from outside the library. Unfortunately, librarians also have a tendency to be self-censors, and not too long ago we put on what can only be termed an amazing performance. The situation surrounding the film *The Speaker* provides just about every element one is likely to encounter in any censorship case. In order to fully understand all of the paradoxes that this event represents, one must read about the situation and view the film.

A few years ago, ALA's Committee on Intellectual Freedom was given funds to have a film produced on the problems of censorship and intellectual freedom. At the June 1977 annual convention, the film was shown to the membership, which generated one of the bigger, longer debates in ALA history. Seldom has there been as long or as bitter a debate within ALA over an issue that is presumably an article of faith in the profession. Many of the Black members of the Association labeled the film racist. Many other members agreed that the film was a problem for that or other reasons. An attempt to have ALA's name disassociated from the film failed, but not by much. Is that a move to censor? How does that differ from the definition given at the beginning of this chapter? Does that really differ from a publisher's deciding not to release a title because the work is found not to be in the best interest of the owner of the company?

As with every other problem of this type, we have no objective data on which to base a judgment. Not all Blacks or minority persons who view the film see it as racist. Just because one (even if large) group claims that an item is this or that, does the claim make it so? Is this really different from the Citizen's Committee for Clean Books saying that *The Last Temptation of Christ* is sacrilegious or the John Birch Society claiming that *Ramparts* and the *Evergreen Review* are anti-American? One hopes that most librarians will agree with Dorothy Broderick regarding *The Speaker*: "Let librarians across the country decide for themselves: if they find the film boring, let them not buy it. If they feel that using it will stir up trouble in their community—as if they had invited 'The Speaker'—let them ignore its existence. If the film is as bad as its opponents claim, it will die the natural death of an inadequate work in the marketplace."[21] If ALA's name had been removed, many persons would have felt that the first step in the suppression of the film would have occurred.

Librarians and Censorship

Realistically, all the situations discussed so far are of the type that one can easily identify and choose to fight or not. Given the foregoing sample of the problems that may be encountered, it should not be surprising to find librarians acting in a self-protective manner. How great a problem is this? Several studies have been done on this problem, but we will only explore the findings of two of the more widely known—Fiske's and Busha's.

Marjorie Fiske shook the library profession some years ago when she reported that a high percentage of librarians decided not to buy an item because it might cause a problem.[22] Some titles are very likely to cause trouble—for example, *Joy of Sex*—and are easy to identify. However, an examination of the sample list of titles that have caused trouble, makes it evident that some items are *not* easy to identify. Once the process of not selecting a title that has the potential for controversy is begun, it will be difficult to break the habit. Unfortunately, as with so many other habits, it is easy to slip into a behavior pattern and not even recognize what we have done.

Reasons such as "lack of funds," "no demand," or "poor quality" may be true, or they may be just a rationalization for not selecting an item that might make life troublesome. Other excuses, such as "I will buy it when someone asks for it" or "I don't like that author or producer; he or she never has anything worthwhile to say," are even clearer danger signs. Just because a librarian does not like an author or a subject does not mean that he or she has the right to keep others from having access. This may not be self-protective in the sense of job security, but it may be in terms of one's own psyche. In any case, the result is the same—censorship.

One way to raise the level of self-awareness is to periodically check one's holdings against various lists of "problem" items. How many does the library have? Less than 50 percent should cause one to question what is happening in the selection process. There may be perfectly good reasons why there are so few of these items, but until the librarian can give better reasons than the above, he or she cannot be complacent and say "I am not a censor."

Charles Busha's study examined librarians' attitudes toward censorship and intellectual freedom, and he compared his findings to scores on a standardized test that is an indirect measure of antidemocratic trends. His concluding sentence is probably a reasonable picture of all librarianship in the United States: "It is evident, as a result of opinion research, that midwestern public librarians did not hesitate to express agreement with cliches of intellectual freedom but that many of them apparently did not feel strong enough as professionals to assert these principles in the face of real or anticipated censorship pressures."[23]

A Sampling of "Problem" Books

The following list comprises 30 books that have been attacked for a host of reasons. Some may be surprising, others may not:

Allen, ed., *New American Story*	Reage, *The Story of O*
Baum, *Wizard of Oz*	Rechy, *City of Night*
Burroughs, *The Ticket That Exploded*	Richler, *Cocksure*
Catling, *The Experiment*	Rimmer, *The Harrad Experiment*
Cremer, *I, Jan Cremer*	Robbins, *The Adventurers*
De Berg, *The Image*	Selby, *Last Exit to Brooklyn*
Dixon, *Hardy Boys*	Sterling, *The President's Plane Is*
Durrell, *Tunc*	*Missing*
Friedman, *Totempole*	Susann, *Valley of the Dolls*
Genet, *Miracle of the Rose*	Sutton, *The Exhibitionist*
Himes, *Pinktoes*	Twain, *Tom Sawyer*
Jones, *Go to the Widowmaker*	Updike, *Couples*
Keene, *Nancy Drew*	Vidal, *Myra Breckinridge*
Killens, *Sippi*	Williams, *Rabbit Wedding*
Kyle, *Venus Examined*	Yafa, *Paxton Quigley's Had the Course*
McMurtry, *The Last Picture Show*	

What to Do before and after the Censor Arrives

The first step is to plan on having to face a censor, sometime. Prepare a policy statement on how complaints will be handled, and have it approved by all the appropriate authorities. There is nothing worse than facing an angry person complaining about some library materials and not having any idea of what to do. More than once, even with policies and procedures, the situation escalates into physical violence, and without any procedures, the chances of violence occurring go up. A typical procedure is to have the individual(s) file a formal complaint or fill out a form that specifies what is at issue. (Figure 19.3 illustrates one such form.) Several organizations have recommended forms, ALA and the National Council of Teachers of English for example, and they are all about equal in effectiveness. Once the policies and procedures are developed and approved, everyone working in public services needs to understand the system and receive training in implementing the system. (Sometimes role-playing is helpful in reinforcing the training.) ALA's Office of Intellectual Freedom has an excellent manual that provides details on what to do before the censors turn up. Another good source is Frances Jones's *Defusing Censorship: The Librarian's Guide to Handling Censorship Conflicts.*[24]

Since people differ, citizens may register their complaints by filling out the following form:

Author:

Title:

Publisher (if known):

Request initiated by _____

                    Name   Telephone No.

                 _____

                 Address

Complainant represents: Himself/Herself _____ Organization _____
If organization, give name:_____

1. Specify what you object to in the book (cite pages)_____
   _____

2. For what age group would you recommend this book?_____

3. What do you think might be the effects of reading this book?_____
   _____
   _____

4. What do you think is good about this book?_____
   _____

5. Did you read the whole book or just parts of it?_____

6. Do you know the literary critics' view of this book?_____

7. What is the theme of the book?_____

8. What action would you like the library to take about this book?
      Withdraw it from the shelves?_____
      Do not permit it in the children's room?_____
      Do not permit my child to sign it out?_____

9. What book would you recommend in its place?_____
   _____

                     _____

                     Signature of Complainant

                     _____

                     Date

Fig. 19.3. Patron's request for reconsideration of a book.

ALA's organizational structure for dealing with intellectual freedom (IF) concerns is somewhat confusing. The Intellectual Freedom (IF) Committee is responsible for making recommendations to the Association regarding IF matters. The Office for Intellectual Freedom has a full-time staff and is charged to educate librarians and others about IF and censorship matters. It also is the support service for the IF Committee and is expected to implement the Association's IF policies. As part of the educational function, OIF produces several publications: *Newsletter of Intellectual Freedom* (news and current developments in IF), *OIF Memorandum* (addressed to local library association IF committees), and the *Intellectual Freedom Manual.* They also coproduced a videotape that I have found to be very valuable in stimulating IF discussions with library school students, librarians, and especially with the general public, *Censorship or Selection: Choosing Books for Public Schools.* (OIF also funded the production of the film *The Speaker.*)

Although OIF does *not* provide legal assistance when a library faces a complaint, it does provide telephone consultation (occasionally with the addition of written statements or names of persons who might be able to testify for IF) and, but very rarely, comes to the library to provide moral and professional support. Often librarians are surprised to learn that OIF does not provide legal aid. Legal assistance *might* be available from the Freedom to Read Foundation (FRF). FRF is not part of ALA (a separate legal entity), although it is so closely affiliated that many people have difficulty seeing the difference. The Executive Director of FRF is also the Director of OIF, and with such a pattern it is not surprising that people think it is part of ALA. Be aware that there is no assurance of receiving financial or legal aid; there are too many cases and insufficient funds to assist everyone.

Anyone interested in becoming involved in IF activities should consider joining the Intellectual Freedom Round Table, which is the general membership unit of ALA related to IF. While ALA offers a variety of support services for handling censors' complaints, the best support is being prepared before the need arises.

Bibliotherapy

A common statement used when defending a book or other library material is that there is no definitive cause and effect relationship between reading or viewing and behavior. In support of this, we have ALA's *Freedom to Read* and the Educational Film Library Association's *Freedom to View* statements. However, there is a small body of literature on the use of reading in the treatment of illness. There are medical professionals who do believe that there is a cause and effect relationship. To date, no conclusive data exist to answer the question one way or another. I do know from my own experience — as a library intern in a Veterans Administration Hospital while in library school — that some doctors think the relationship exists. I was responsible for taking books and magazines to the locked psychiatric ward for the patients to read. Before I could take the loaded book truck to the patients, a doctor would examine every item and often remove items which I took back to the library after finishing my "rounds." Was I giving in to censorship? Was I violating the *Freedom to Read Statement*? There is much we do not know about reading or viewing and behavior. Perhaps when we know more, our freedom statements may need revision.

Summary

The problem of censorship is complex, and it is necessary to do a lot of reading and thinking about this topic. A final example may help to illustrate just how complex the issue is. Assume that a librarian is responsible for selecting materials for a small public library. Naturally, he or she needs this job to cover living expenses. A small group of persons in the community wants the librarian to buy certain items for the library collection; but he or she also knows of a large group of vocal and influential persons who would be very upset, and might even demand that he or she be fired, if the items were purchased. Should the librarian buy the item and risk his or her family's welfare and own career over this? If he or she does not buy the item, what can be said to the people who asked for its purchase? Does telling them they can get it somewhere else, or get it through interlibrary loan, really address that librarian's problem?

Finally, an article in *American Libraries* raised the question: "Is it censorship to remove all copies of *The Joy of Gay Sex* because it advocates sex practices that are now felt to be dangerous in light of the AIDS epidemic?"[25] Several librarians responded to the question, and there is some difference of opinion. One wonders how the respondents would have answered had the question been: "Is it censorship not to buy copy(ies) of *The Joy of Sex*?" As with all real problems, there is no simple, completely satisfactory answer.

Notes

[1]Charles Busha, "Intellectual Freedom and Censorship," *Library Quarterly* 42 (July 1972): 283-84.

[2]E. Geller, "The Librarian as Censor," *Library Journal* 101 (1 June 1976): 125.

[3]"Children's Sex Book Removed from Sale," *Rocky Mountain News*, 21 September 1982, 49.

[4]*Library Hotline* (12 March 1984), 1.

[5]*Bismarck Tribune*, 6 July 1984, 4.

[6]"Widefield Censor Schism Runs Deep," *Rocky Mountain News*, 25 June 1982, 10.

[7]*Library Hotline* (1 October 1984), 2.

[8]"Stack o' Wheat Photos Uproar," *Los Angeles Times*, 25 May 1980, pt. 8, 1, 22-24.

[9]"Knights and Windmills," *Library Journal* 96 (1 October 1971): 3096-98.

[10]*Wilson Library Bulletin* 48 (September 1969): 18.

[11]Ibid., 18.

[12]*Wilson Library Bulletin* 50 (April 1971): 717.

[13]*Intellectual Freedom Newsletter* 18 (January 1969): 5.

[14]*Intellectual Freedom Newsletter* 19 (September 1970): 17.

[15]*Intellectual Freedom Newsletter* 20 (January 1971): 2.

[16]*Library Journal* 94 (August 1969): 2722.

[17]*Intellectual Freedom Newsletter* 18 (November 1969): 98.

[18]*Intellectual Freedom Newsletter* 23 (May 1974): 54.

[19]*Intellectual Freedom Newsletter* 23 (September 1974): 111.

[20]*Intellectual Freedom Newsletter* 12 (July 1963): 34, 48.

[21]D. Broderick, "Son of Speaker," *American Libraries* 8 (October 1977): 503.

[22]M. Fiske, *Book Selection and Censorship* (Berkeley, Calif.: University of California, 1958).

[23]Charles Busha, "Intellectual Freedom and Censorship," 300.

[24]Frances Jones, *Defusing Censorship: The Librarian's Guide to Handling Censorship Conflicts* (Phoenix, Ariz.: Oryx Press, 1983).

[25]"Censorship in the Name of Public Health," *American Libraries* (May 1986): 306.

Further Reading

General

Ashaim, L. E. "Selection and Censorship: A Reappraisal." *Wilson Library Bulletin* 58 (November 1983): 180-84.

Brahm, W. "Knights and Windmills." *Library Journal* 96 (1 October 1971): 3096-98.

Broderick, D. "Son of Speaker." *American Libraries* 8 (October 1977): 503.

Busha, C. H. "Intellectual Freedom and Censorship." *Library Quarterly* 42 (July 1972): 283-84.

"Censorship in the Eighties." *Drexel Library Quarterly* 18, no. 1 (1982): entire issue.

"Censorship in the Name of Public Health." *American Libraries* (May 1986): 306.

"Children's Sex Book Removed from Sale." *Rocky Mountain News*, 21 September 1982, 49.

de Grazia, E., and R. K. Newman. *Banned Films.* New York: R. R. Bowker, 1982.

The First Freedom Today. Edited by R. B. Downs and R. McCoy. Chicago: American Library Association, 1984.

Geller, E. "Librarian as Censor." *Library Journal* 101 (1 June 1976): 1252.

Haight, A. L. *Banned Books.* 4th ed. New York: R. R. Bowker, 1978.

Hynes, A. M., and M. Hynes-Berry. *Bibliotherapy—Interactive Process.* Boulder, Colo.: Westview Press, 1986.

Jones, F. *Defusing Censorship: The Librarian's Guide to Handling Censorship Conflicts.* Phoenix, Ariz.: Oryx Press, 1983.

Lack, C. R. "Can Bibliotherapy Go Public?" *Collection Building* 7 (Spring 1985): 27-32.

Poppel, N., and E. M. Ashley. "Toward Understanding the Censor." *Library Journal* 111 (July 1986): 39-43.

Robotham, J., and G. Shields. *Freedom of Access to Library Materials.* New York: Neal-Schuman, 1982.

West, C. "Secret Garden of Censorship: Ourselves." *Library Journal* 108 (1 September 1983): 1651-53.

Academic

"Stack o' Wheat Photos Uproar, Pictures Spark Feminist Debate." *Los Angeles Times*, 25 May 1980, pt. 8, 1, 22-24.

Public

Allen, B., and L. O'Dell. *Bibliotherapy and the Public Library.* San Rafael, Calif.: San Rafael Public Library Bibliotherapy Project, 1981.

School

Arbetman, L. "Reviewing the Books School Children Read: Censorship or Selection?" *Georgia Social Science Journal* 14 (Spring 1983): 1-4.

Bosmajian, H. *Censorship, Libraries and the Law.* New York: Neal-Schuman, 1983.

Censorship Litigation and the Schools. Prepared by the Office for Intellectual Freedom. Chicago: American Library Association, 1983.

Mosley, M. "The School Library in Court." *School Library Journal* 27 (October 1981): 96-99.

Serebnick, J. "Book Reviews and the Selection of Potentially Controversial Books in Public Libraries." *Library Quarterly* 51 (October 1981): 390-409.

"Sex in Our Schools? Maybe Not in Minot." *Bismarck Tribune*, 6 July 1984, 4.

Sorenson, G. P. "Removal of Books from School Libraries 1972-1982." *Journal of Law and Education* 12 (July 1983): 417-41.

"Widefield Censor Schism Runs Deep." *Rocky Mountain News*, 25 June 1982, 10.

Woods, L. B., and L. Salvatore. "Self-Censorship in Collection Development of High School Library Media Specialists." *School Media Quarterly* 9 (Winter 1981): 102-5.

20

Collection Development and the Future

Looking toward the future is not as risky as predicting the future. These remarks are not intended to be predictions; rather, they are statements about possible developments.

Perhaps someday in the future, the book as we know it will be gone except as a museum piece or a collector's curiosity. Certainly video formats seem to be making tremendous strides and may in time be the sole format. We may, in our lifetime, see the end of the library as a facility to which patrons come to use materials. No matter what happens — changes in formats, services, or physical location — it seems likely that there will always be some system for disseminating information to the general population. It also seems probable that the world's output of information and recreational materials will continue to increase. Should all of these events come to pass, there will be just as much need for selectors who are capable of building appropriate collections as there is today.

There has been debate over "public" versus commercial firms operating traditional library and information center functions. Some evidence of the inroads commercial organizations have made into traditional library functions can be seen in the increase in the number of U.S. government libraries that are operated under contract with profit-oriented corporations. Information brokers are an increasing group of entrepreneurs who offer services that have traditionally been free library services. I hope the individuals who wrote the following are correct, though only time will tell:

Society's need to collect, preserve, and maintain the integrity and availability of records in all media is permanent, which is why it makes perfect sense for a public institution to be given the responsibility. Business can go bankrupt, merge, and be swayed by social and economic factors. And a business, no matter what it does, must ultimately be profitable. When the profit margin for a product or service declines, either a solution is found to stabilize or reverse the trend or the product is withdrawn. Even the most idealistic publishers do not reprint books that have stopped selling. Consider then, that since records of information and knowledge never cease to grow, average use per record must steadily decline. In the long run, profit cannot be made from permanently storing records. Some records must be purged. Any permanent collection/archive/database of records can only exist in the not-for-profit sector.[1]

Given the economic picture and inevitable growth in the output of information materials, the management aspect of selecting information will become more, not less, important in the future. As the volume of information and the forms in which it is available increase, libraries must be more selective. Emphasis is likely to shift to an evaluation of the cost or value of the information as opposed to the cost of the package. In the immediate future, the push/pull between buying serials or monographs will continue and perhaps increase in intensity. Over the longer run, it seems likely that the integration of information technologies will make the distinctions between different formats and print/nonprint increasingly blurred. We now see that it is impossible on economic grounds alone for any library to be comprehensive in its collection. Yet research and academic libraries for the past 30 years have been attempting to accomplish this impossible task.

Legal aspects of collection development will probably increase in importance. Copyright holders' efforts to enforce their rights will continue. Costs to libraries for compliance activities will increase, and the cost will have to be met in one of two ways. Additional funds must be set aside to purchase low- or moderate-use items (since ILL activity must decrease), or alternatively, more funds must be allocated to pay copyright holder use fees. As information formats become integrated there will be increased use of contracts or leases for materials the library acquires. Negotiating the terms of these contracts may become an important duty of the collection development officer(s). Public lending right legislation will probably be adopted sometime in the distant future in the United States. If and when it is implemented, it will probably not be financed by government-supplied funds but will have to be paid for by the patron and/or the library's budget. For a while American libraries debated who should pay for ILL and online search charges, and in the end the patron was and is asked to pay the costs. I see little likelihood that public lending rights will end up differently.

Early efforts at cooperative acquisitions failed for many reasons. One reason was that a period of large book budgets occurred, and vendors offered "pie in the sky" approval/blanket order plans that allowed rapid collection growth. Collection growth, though, is not the same thing as collection development. Selection personnel (subject bibliographers and specialists) were hired, but somehow real collection development seemed to be the exception rather than the rule. I know from personal research and consulting work that many of these persons spent the vast majority of their time writing reports, preparing statements of needs (mostly for more money to get more material), teaching courses, and working with the public. There is nothing wrong with these activities, but they are not selection activities. What developed were acquisition programs—i.e., acquire as much as possible—not collection development programs.

Today, economic realities have changed the picture. Approval/blanket order plans are very expensive, so libraries are more carefully defining their profiles for such plans. This means a move back to real selection. A question that no one has answered is whether the users of the libraries (where acquisition plans existed) are—or were—satisfied with the resulting collections. We can only speculate as to what the answer would be. Users of academic libraries that began to "develop" an engineering collection when no engineering program existed (nor would it exist 10 years later) felt that more selectivity was in order.

In the future, even if vast sums of money are available, the volume of information will have continued to increase and will still be beyond the control of any one library. Without question, there will be more need for in-depth subject knowledge in the library. Collection development personnel will need to have in-depth knowledge and will work in only one or two very narrow fields in order to select the most useful items for library patrons. Gone will be the day of the social science bibliographer, if in fact that day ever really existed. Perhaps it will not even be possible to be the anthropology bibliographer; it may be necessary to have even finer divisions. Cooperative acquisitions will be a normal part of a library program, as there will be no other choice.

Internationally, the concept of Universal Availability of Publications (UAP) will continue to be discussed, and in time steps will be taken to assure some degree of implementation. Ultimately the program will improve cooperation as countries improve distribution channels, have a better picture of demand, and thus produce the needed number of publications. Steps will be taken to properly preserve and conserve existing resources, and interlibrary lending will be recognized as a central function of adequate information access. A sense of what is hoped for in the future is seen in the proposed requirements for a national UAP system:

A national system should ensure:

1. Provision of all national imprints.

2. Provision of additional material to meet at least 70 percent of national needs.

3. Supply to remote users within three weeks.

4. Retention of material to meet future needs.

5. Access to international resources.

6. Minimum cost for levels of efficiency set.

7. Simplicity and convenience in use.

8. Regular monitoring of performance.[2]

While Western European and North American countries already come close to these standards, every country has some work to do to reach all of the above levels.

Whatever the future holds, one thing that is not likely to change is the intellectual challenge of creating the most appropriate resource collection for a community. Individuals with a great curiosity about what is happening in the world, an in-depth knowledge of information resources and their producers, and a knowledge of the problems and issues in building a library collection in their community will also find a rewarding and exciting career in librarianship.

Notes

[1] C. P. Briscoe, et al., "Ashurbanipal's Enduring Archetype," *College & Research Libraries* 47 (March 1986): 123.

[2] *UAP Newsletter* no. 7 (January 1986): 1.

Further Reading

General

Briscoe, C. P., et al. "Ashurbanipal's Enduring Archetype: Thoughts on the Library's Role in the Future." *College & Research Libraries* 47 (March 1986): 121-26.

De Sola Pool, I. *Technologies of Freedom.* Cambridge, Mass.: Harvard University Press, 1983.

Horowitz, I. L. "Expropriating Ideas: The Politics of Global Publishing." *The Bookseller* 4206 (2 August 1986): 528-32.

Line, M., and S. Vickers. *Universal Availability of Publications.* Munich: K. G. Saur, 1983.

Neff, R. K. "Merging Libraries and Computer Centers: Manifest Destiny or Manifestly Deranged?" *EDUCOM Bulletin* (Winter 1985): 8-16.

Oakeshott, P., and B. White. *Impact of New Technology on the Availability of Publications.* London: British Library, 1984.

Stam, D. H. "Think Globally—Collection Development." *Collection Building* 5 (Spring 1983): 18-21.

Author/Title Index

Subject Index